Lecture Notes in Computer Science 9248

Commenced Publication in 1973
Founding and Former Series Editors:
Gerhard Goos, Juris Hartmanis, and Jan van Leeuwen

Efthimios Tambouris · Marijn Janssen
Hans Jochen Scholl · Maria A. Wimmer
Konstantinos Tarabanis · Mila Gascó
Bram Klievink · Ida Lindgren
Peter Parycek (Eds.)

Electronic Government

14th IFIP WG 8.5 International Conference, EGOV 2015
Thessaloniki, Greece, August 30 – September 2, 2015
Proceedings

 Springer

Editors
Efthimios Tambouris
University of Macedonia
Thessaloniki
Greece

Mila Gascó
ESADE
Barcelona
Spain

Marijn Janssen
Delft University of Technology
Delft
The Netherlands

Bram Klievink
Delft University of Technology
Delft
The Netherlands

Hans Jochen Scholl
University of Washington
Seattle, WA
USA

Ida Lindgren
Linköping University
Linköping
Sweden

Maria A. Wimmer
Universität Koblenz-Landau
Koblenz
Germany

Peter Parycek
Donau-Universität Krems
Krems
Austria

Konstantinos Tarabanis
University of Macedonia
Thessaloniki
Greece

ISSN 0302-9743   ISSN 1611-3349   (electronic)
Lecture Notes in Computer Science
ISBN 978-3-319-22478-7   ISBN 978-3-319-22479-4   (eBook)
DOI 10.1007/978-3-319-22479-4

Library of Congress Control Number: 2015945145

LNCS Sublibrary: SL3 – Information Systems and Applications, incl. Internet/Web, and HCI

Springer Cham Heidelberg New York Dordrecht London
© IFIP International Federation for Information Processing 2015

Printed on acid-free paper

Springer International Publishing AG Switzerland is part of Springer Science+Business Media
(www.springer.com)

Preface

The 14th annual International IFIP Electronic Government Conference (IFIP EGOV 2015) was organized by the International Federation for Information Processing Working Group 8.5 (Information Systems in Public Administration), or IFIP WG 8.5 for short.

IFIP EGOV is a core scientific conference in the domain of ICT and public administration. This is reflected in the high quality of the papers presented each year from distinguished researchers, academics, and practitioners from around the world. Traditionally, the conference provides an environment that is suitable for presenting and discussing academically rigorous research in a friendly and inspiring manner.

As in previous years, IFIP EGOV 2015 was co-located with IFIP ePart, the 7th International Conference on eParticipation (IFIP ePart 2015), which aims at presenting current research on foundations, theories, methods, tools, and innovative applications of electronic participation.

IFIP EGOV and ePart have established a reputation of high-quality, successful conference organizations. At the same time, they continue innovating in an attempt to increase the value they provide to their attendees. In this respect, this year, for the first time, the dual conferences were organized around five tracks:

- The General E-Government Track
- The General eParticipation Track
- The Open Government and Open and Big Data Track
- The Policy Modelling and Policy Informatics Track
- The Smart Governance, Smart Government, and Smart Cities Track

The introduction of tracks aims to highlight important areas that are relevant to the core topics of research of the two conferences. The overall objective of the two conferences remains to attract scholars coming from different academic disciplines to present and discuss their latest research shedding light on different, sometimes even diverse, perspectives. With the introduction of a new organizational model of the dual conference, we were also happy to have as co-chairs a number of distinguished scholars who provide fresh insights into the conferences and who attract new relevant communities.

These proceedings cover completed research accepted for the General E-Government Track, the Open Government and Open and Big Data Track, and the Smart Governance, Smart Government, and Smart Cities Track. The completed research papers accepted in the General eParticipation Track and the Policy Modelling and Policy Informatics Track are published in the LNCS proceedings of IFIP ePart. Like last year, accepted contributions of ongoing research, innovative projects, and PhD papers as well as abstracts of posters and workshops of the dual IFIP EGOV and ePart conference are published in a complimentary joint proceedings volume by IOS Press.

The call for papers of the three tracks covered in this volume attracted a wide range of topics with 68 submissions, which included 25 accepted completed research papers (published in these proceedings) and 22 accepted ongoing research papers (published in the joint IFIP EGOV and ePart proceedings of ongoing research).

This volume includes completed research organized in four topical threads as follows:

- Foundations
- Open and Smart Government
- Services, Processes, and Infrastructure
- Application Areas and Evaluation

The Paper Awards Committee was again led by committee chair Olivier Glassey of IDHEAP, Lausanne/Switzerland. The Organizing Committee carefully reviewed the accepted papers and granted outstanding paper awards in various areas. The winners were awarded in the ceremony during the conference dinner, which is a highlight of each IFIP EGOV conference. The names of the award winners of IFIP EGOV can be found on the conference website: http://www.egov-conference.org/egov-conf-history/egov-2015/.

As in every proceedings volume we feel the need to thank the members of the IFIP EGOV 2015 Program Committee for their efforts in reviewing the submitted papers. The quality of the conference is directly related to the quality of peer reviews and we would like to once again acknowledge the work that the Program Committee members did.

This year, EGOV and ePart were organized in Thessaloniki, Greece, under the aegis of the University of Macedonia. The University of Macedonia has long been active in research in the areas of eGovernment and eParticipation. However, the success of a conference takes much more. We would therefore like to thank the team of the University of Macedonia and particularly Eleni Panopoulou but also Maria Zotou, Elina Nanopoulou, and Eleni Kamateri for their efforts in the excellent organization of the dual conference.

The University of Macedonia is a relatively new and small university. Its departments of Applied Informatics and Business Administration have worked together for these conferences. The University of Macedonia is located in Thessaloniki, Greece; a city with 2,500 years of history and at the same time a lively, artistic city and one of the largest student centers in South-Eastern Europe. The conference dinner was held at the Byzantine Museum and was preceded by an exclusive museum tour especially organized for conference participants. It could not have been more appropriate!

It was a real pleasure to have the conferences in such a suitable location and we are looking forward to IFIP EGOV 2016.

August/September 2015

Efthimios Tambouris
Marijn Janssen
Hans Jochen Scholl
Maria A. Wimmer
Konstantinos Tarabanis
Mila Gascó
Bram Klievink
Ida Lindgren
Peter Parycek

Organization

Conference Chairs

Efthimios Tambouris	University of Macedonia, Greece
Hans Jochen Scholl	University of Washington, USA
Marijn Janssen	Delft University of Technology, The Netherlands
Maria A. Wimmer	University of Koblenz-Landau, Germany
Konstantinos Tarabanis	University of Macedonia, Greece

General E-Government Track Chairs

Hans Jochen Scholl	University of Washington, USA
Marijn Janssen	Delft University of Technology, The Netherlands
Maria A. Wimmer	University of Koblenz-Landau, Germany

Open Government and Open and Big Data Track Chairs

Marijn Janssen	Delft University of Technology, The Netherlands
Bram Klievink	Delft University of Technology, The Netherlands
Ida Lindgren	Linköping University, Sweden

Smart Governance, Government, and Cities Track Chairs

Hans Jochen Scholl	University of Washington, USA
Mila Gascó	Escuela Superior de Administración y Dirección de Empresas (ESADE), Spain
Peter Parycek	Danube University Krems, Austria

Program Committee and Reviewers

Suha Alawadhi	Kuwait University, Kuwait
Vincenzo Ambriola	University of Pisa, Italy
Kim Normann Andersen	CBS, Denmark
Renata Araujo	UNIRIO, Brazil
Karin Axelsson	Linköping University, Sweden
Paul Brous	Delft University of Technology, The Netherlands
Wojciech Cellary	Poznan University of Economics, Poland
Bojan Cestnik	Temida d.o.o., Jožef Stefan Institute, Slovenia
Yannis Charalabidis	National Technical University Athens, Greece

Wichian Chutimaskul	King Mongkut's University of Technology Thonburi, Thailand
Flavio Corradini	University of Camerino, Italy
Ahmed Darwish	Ministry of State of Administrative Development, Egypt
Anna De Liddo	The Open University, UK
Yogesh Dwivedi	Swansea University, UK
Elsa Estevez	United Nations University, Macao, SAR China
Enrico Ferro	Istituto Superiore Mario Boella, Italy
Sabrina Franceschini	Regione Emilia-Romagna, Italy
Ivan Futo	National Tax and Customs Administration, Hungary
Andras Gabor	Corvinno Technology Transfer Center Nonprofit Public Ltd., Hungary
Rimantas Gatautis	Kaunas University of Technology, Lithuania
Christos Georgiadis	University of Macedonia, Greece
J. Ramon Gil-Garcia	Centro de Investigación y Docencia Económicas, Mexico
Olivier Glassey	Lausanne University, Switzerland
Johann Höchtl	Danube University Krems, Austria
Helle Zinner Henriksen	Copenhagen Business School, Denmark
Tomasz Janowski	UNU Operating Unit on Policy-Driven Electronic Governance, Portugal
Arild Jansen	University of Oslo, Norway
Luiz Joia	FGV, Brazil
Nikos Karacapilidis	University of Patras, Greece
Ralf Klischewski	German University in Cairo, Egypt
Katarina Lindblad-Gidlund	Mid Sweden University, Sweden
Euripidis Loukis	University of the Aegean, Greece
Luis Luna-Reyes	University at Albany, SUNY, USA
Gregoris Mentzas	National Technical University of Athens, Greece
Michela Milano	DEIS Università di Bologna, Italy
Carl Erik Moe	Agder University, Norway
Adegboyega Ojo	United Nations University - International Institute for Software Technology, Macao, SAR China
Eleni Panopoulou	University of Macedonia, Greece
Theresa A. Pardo	Center for Technology in Government, University at Albany, SUNY, USA
Vassilios Peristeras	European Commission, DG DIGIT, Interoperability Solutions for European Public Administration (ISA), Belgium
Rimantas Petrauskas	Mykolas Romeris University, Lithuania
Michael Räckers	European Research Center for Information Systems (ERCIS), Germany
Barbara Re	University of Camerino, Italy
Nicolau Reinhard	University of São Paulo, Brazil

Contents

Foundations

Channel Choice: A Literature Review 3
  Christian Ø. Madsen and Pernille Kræmmergaard

Conceptualising the Digital Public in Government Crowdsourcing:
Social Media and the Imagined Audience......................... 19
  Panos Panagiotopoulos and Frances Bowen

Steering the Digital Agenda at Arm's Length. All Wobble, No Spin:
The Contextual Lens... 31
  Maddalena Sorrentino, Marco De Marco, and Paolo Depaoli

E-Government Systems Design and Implementation in Developed
and Developing Countries: Results from a Qualitative Analysis 44
  Catherine G. Mkude and Maria A. Wimmer

Theoretical Support for Social Media Research. A Scientometric Analysis . . . 59
  Laura Alcaide Muñoz and Manuel Pedro Rodríguez Bolívar

Open and Smart Government

Big and Open Linked Data (BOLD) to Create Smart Cities and Citizens:
Insights from Smart Energy and Mobility Cases 79
  Marijn Janssen, Ricardo Matheus, and Anneke Zuiderwijk

Open Innovation Contests for Improving Healthcare – An Explorative Case
Study Focusing on Challenges in a Testbed Initiative 91
  Siri Wassrin, Ida Lindgren, and Ulf Melin

Public Accountability ICT Support: A Detailed Account of Public
Accountability Process and Tasks 105
  Rui Pedro Lourenço, Suzanne Piotrowski, and Alex Ingrams

Mediating Citizen-Sourcing of Open Government Applications – A Design
Science Approach... 118
  Mai Abu-El Seoud and Ralf Klischewski

Processing Linked Open Data Cubes............................. 130
  Efthimios Tambouris, Evangelos Kalampokis,
  and Konstantinos Tarabanis

Scrutinizing Open Government Data to Understand Patterns
in eGovernment Uptake   144
  Helle Zinner Henriksen

Advancing e-Government Using the Internet of Things: A Systematic
Review of Benefits   156
  Paul Brous and Marijn Janssen

Understanding Public-Private Collaboration Configurations
for International Information Infrastructures   170
  Bram Klievink

Services, Processes and Infrastructure

Inter-organizational Public e-Service Development: Emerging Lessons
from an Inside-Out Perspective   183
  Marie-Therese Christiansson, Karin Axelsson, and Ulf Melin

What Is This Thing Called e-Service? Interoperability Challenges
in e-Service Modelling.   197
  Svein Ølnes and Arild Jansen

Removing the Blinkers: What a Process View Learns About G2G
Information Systems in Flanders   209
  Lies Van Cauter, Monique Snoeck, and Joep Crompvoets

Makers and Shapers or Users and Choosers Participatory Practices
in Digitalization of Public Sector   222
  Katarina L. Gidlund

Why Realization Mismatches Expectations of e-Government Project
Benefits? Towards Benefit Realization Planning   233
  Dian Balta, Vanessa Greger, Petra Wolf, and Helmut Krcmar

Electronic Data Safes as an Infrastructure for Transformational
Government? A Case Study   246
  Joachim Pfister and Gerhard Schwabe

An Ontology of eGovernment.   258
  Arkalgud Ramaprasad, Aurora Sánchez-Ortiz, and Thant Syn

Application Areas and Evaluation

Privacy in Digital Identity Systems: Models, Assessment, and User
Adoption   273
  Armen Khatchatourov, Maryline Laurent, and Claire Levallois-Barth

Comparing Local e-Government Websites in Canada and the UK   291
    Laurence Brooks and Alexander Persaud

Evaluating a Passive Social Media Citizensourcing Innovation   305
    Euripidis Loukis, Yannis Charalabidis, and Aggeliki Androutsopoulou

Three Positives Make One Negative: Public Sector IS Procurement   321
    Aki Alanne, Pasi Hellsten, Samuli Pekkola, and Iiris Saarenpää

Proactivity Postponed? 'Capturing' Records Created in the Context
of E-government – A Literary Warrant Analysis of the Plans for a National
e-archive Service in Sweden   334
    Ann-Sofie Klareld

Author Index   349

Foundations

Channel Choice:
A Literature Review

Christian Ø. Madsen[✉] and Pernille Kræmmergaard

The IT University of Copenhagen, Copenhagen, Denmark
{chrm, pkrm}@itu.dk

Abstract. The channel choice branch of e-government studies citizens' and businesses' choice of channels for interacting with government, and how government organizations can integrate channels and migrate users towards the most cost-efficient channels. In spite of the valuable contributions offered no systematic overview exist of channel choice. We present a literature review of channel choice studies in government to citizen context identifying authors, countries, methods, concepts, units of analysis, and theories, and offer suggestions for future studies.

Keywords: Channel choice · E-government · Integrated service delivery · Literature review · Multichannel · Multi-channel

1 Introduction

Although the digitization of the public sector has taken place for decades [1] there is still a gap between the availability and uptake of online public services [2]. Even in the countries which are front runners in terms of citizens' adoption of electronic public services citizens keep using traditional channels in addition to online channels either as a supplement or as primary channels [3, 4]. The continued use of traditional channels where the interaction takes place between individual citizens and government employees is costly compared to interaction through a website or other forms of self-service applications.

Several literature reviews within e-government have presented and synthesized the findings of studies of citizens' adoption of online services [5–7]. However, these studies tend to focus on citizens' intention to adopt an individual e-government service in isolation [7]. The channel choice (CC) literature studies citizens' choice of channels, and the interplay that takes place between citizens' use of channels for interacting with public authorities [8]. In spite of the valuable contributions the CC literature offers, no systematic review of the CC literature exists.

To cover this gap we present a literature review of the CC field in e-government. Our review analyzes 36 papers which study government to citizen interaction (G2C) through more than one type of channel. We combine and expand Webster & Watson's [9] and Schlichter and Kræmmergaard's [10] methods for finding, classifying and analyzing papers.

© IFIP International Federation for Information Processing 2015
E. Tambouris et al. (Eds.): EGOV 2015, LNCS 9248, pp. 3–18, 2015.
DOI: 10.1007/978-3-319-22479-4_1

1.1 Scope of Review

Webster and Watson [9, p. xv] recommend that only one level of analysis is included in a literature review unless there is a strong rationale to include several levels. However, the studies within the CC field take place at several levels; insights from the analysis of how citizens choose channels for interaction with public authorities are used to make recommendations to these organizations on how to manage their channels. Due to this connection in the literature we include both levels in our review.

In the CC literature the terms channel or service channel are used to describe the various forms of communication available to citizens to interact with public authorities [11]. Reddick and Anthopolous [4, pp. 400–401] divide these channels into three types: traditional channels (face-to- face, telephone conversations and physical letters), e-government channels (web and e-mail) and new digital media (text messaging, social media and mobile apps). To focus our review, we only include papers which study at least two of these channel types. Further, only papers which study CC in a government to citizen context (G2C) are included. Results from studies of employees' CC may not be transferrable to citizens, as businesses' policies, structures and means of communication can affect employees' behavior. We want to study the managerial aspects of CC in e-government [1], and papers focusing on CC in relation to e-democracy or e-participation are omitted. Finally, due to the rapid technological development of online services, only papers published within the last decade (2005–2014) are included.

The papers are classified according to authors, country and methods based on a framework by Schlichter and Kræmmergaard [10]. Previous literature reviews of the e-government field have criticized scholars for not leaving their offices to collect data, for conducting cross-sectional rather than longitudinal studies, and for not studying what happens inside government organizations [12–14]. To find out if this criticism is applicable to the CC literature we expand the method classification to include researchers' involvement in the data collection process, the use of longitudinal studies, and practioners' involvement in the studies. As our topic is CC we also examine if the papers include data on channel traffic. For analyzing the papers we apply Webster and Watson's [9] conceptual analysis matrix identifying objects and level of analysis, conceptual models, and the theoretical frameworks used.

The next section present the methods used to find and analyze the papers in our review. In the third section we present a classification of the papers found, while section four presents the analysis of the papers. In section five we discuss the results with the aim of identifying gaps in the CC literature for future studies. Section six contains concluding remarks and limitations.

2 Method

The method section is divided into three parts. First we present the search for papers. We then present Schlichter and Kræmmergaard's [10] framework for the classification and Webster and Watson's [9] method for the concept-centric analysis.

2.1   The Search for Papers

The papers were found in a three step process following Webster and Watson [9].

1. Search for papers in selected journals and conference proceedings
2. Database search
3. Backwards and forwards searches

We began our search for papers in selected journals recognized as core e-government journals by scholars [15] and in the proceedings of EGOV. The first round of searches was conducted in January 2015 using keywords found through an iterative process. An initial series of keywords were supplemented as papers with new keywords were found. Further, inspired by Hofmann et al. [7] we contacted eight experts within the CC field for additional keywords, of which five replied. 13 keywords were used; *CRM, channel behavior, channel choice, channel ict architecture, channel integration, channel management, channel marketing, channel strategy, customer relationship management, integrated service delivery, multichannel, multi-channel and orchestrating service delivery.*

The keyword search included titles, abstracts, and keywords. After removing duplicates we ended with 239 papers. Papers were included if they focused on CC in a G2C context, included at least two types of channels, were published no later than 2005, and written in English. After reading the abstracts 212 papers were omitted as they only studied one type of channel or were outside the G2C domain. This left 27 papers of which two were omitted as they were inaccessible from the university libraries we had access to. After reading the remaining 25 papers 17 were included in the review.

Webster & Watson recommend that a database search is conducted as the second step to find additional papers. Following the recommendation of an expert in the field, we used the E-government Reference Library (EGRL). We downloaded EGRL version 10.0 (July 2014) to Mendeley Reference Manager for Windows (version 1.13.3) and conducted keyword searches in titles, abstracts and keywords using the 13 keywords. 56 papers were found of which 31 had been found in step 1, two were inaccessible, and one was written in Dutch. This excluded 34, leaving us with 22 papers. After reading these four papers were added to the pool bringing the total to 21.

The third step consisted of using Google Scholar to find papers that either referenced or were referenced to by the 21 papers. 68 papers were found which initially seemed relevant according to our selection criteria. We omitted four conference papers which were earlier editions of journal papers already found. Four papers were unavailable. After reading either the abstracts or the whole papers we were left with 15 relevant papers. These 15 papers were added to the final pool, bringing the total to 36. Appendix A presents an overview of the 36 papers.

2.2   Classification of Papers

For the analysis and coding we created a one page template for each paper which contained bibliographical information, abstracts, coding results and notes. This data was

Table 1. Classification of methods

Category	Description
Case study	Papers reporting on studies involved with a single site or a few sites over a certain period of time
Combined	Papers which do not rely on one primary method
Descriptive	Papers solely describing or arguing for a phenomenon and often very practically oriented
Design science	Papers that construct systems and/or tools
Field experiment	Papers which conduct field experiments
Theoretical	Papers analyzing existing theory, typically with the aim of developing new theory
Survey	Papers that gather data by means of questionnaires

Table 2. Types of data

Category	Description
Primary	Data generated by the researcher
Secondary	Data generated by another researcher
Tertiary	Data analyzed by another researcher

entered into a spreadsheet (MS Excel) and analyzed at an aggregated level. The classification of methods follow the framework by Schlichter and Kræmmergaard which they developed for a literature review of the enterprise resource planning field [10]. We removed one method category, archival, as it overlapped with other categories in the papers found. Table 1 presents the classification.

Researchers' involvement in data collection (Table 2) was coded following Blaikie [16, p. 161]. Longitudinal studies followed Blaikie's definition 'a study extended in time' [16, p. 201]. Practioners' involvement was coded if the authors had direct contact with government organizations' employees through workshops, interviews, surveys etc. Channel traffic was coded if it was presented in numerical form.

2.3   Concept-Centric Analysis of the Papers

To synthesize the CC literature we conducted a concept-centric analysis following Webster and Watson [9]. As we read the papers we created a template with the primary concepts covered, and the units of analysis. A pattern quickly emerged; part of the papers studies factors impacting CC at the individual level, while another part studies processes related to multichannel management (MCM) at the organizational level. Webster and Watson state that the conceptual analysis should be supplemented with information on the variables examined, and a conceptual and theoretical analysis of how and why the variables are related [9]. We therefore coded factors, processes and theories applied as well.

3 Classification of the CC Literature

In this section we present the classification of the papers according to authors, countries and methods applied. We also discuss practioners' involvement and the use of channel traffic in the papers.

3.1 Authors and Country

Table 3 presents an overview of the most prolific authors, while Table 4 presents the papers according to first author's country.

Table 3. Most productive authors within CC literature

Author	Papers
Pieterson, W.	11
Reddick, C.G.	6
Janssen, M.	4
Teerling, M.L. (with Pieterson)	4
Ebbers, W.E. (with Pieterson)	3
Kernaghan, K	3
Klievink, B. (with Janssen)	3

Table 4. First author's country

Country	Papers in pool
The Netherlands	14
US	10
Canada	5
Germany	2
Belgium	1
India	1
Italy	1
South Korea	1
UK	1
Total	36

The majority of the papers were written by a small group of authors from only a few countries. Three scholars have authored or co-authored 21 of the 36 papers.

The papers in the pool are written by first authors from nine different countries. Authors from The Netherlands have published 40 percent of the papers and authors from the Netherlands, US and Canada have published 29 of the 36 papers.

3.2   Methodology

Table 5 presents the papers according to the primary method applied. Four papers are labeled as 'combined' as they rely on several methods.

Table 5. Papers classified according to primary method

Category	Number of papers	Papers
Case study	12	[17–28]
Combined	4	[29–32]
Descriptive	2	[33, 34]
Design	1	[35]
Field experiment	2	[36, 37]
Theoretical	4	[3, 11, 38, 39]
Survey	11	[4, 8, 40–48]

Case studies and surveys are the most frequently applied methods. Eighteen papers include results from surveys, but only eleven use surveys as a primary method; ten study the factors that influence citizens' choice of channels and one studies the adoption of multiple channels in organizations. Twelve paper present individual or multiple case studies, based on documentary material and interviews, workshops or other forms of collaborations with practitioners. Four papers develop theory, and focus mainly on exploring and explaining government organizations' strategies for multi-channel management through various theoretical lenses. One paper presents a role-playing game as a method for involving case-workers multichannel management, and the results from applying this method in practice. None of the 16 of the papers which apply qualitative methods relies on one method. Rather, interviews or focus groups discussions are combined or conducted preliminary to a survey.

Table 6 presents the highest level of data in the papers according to researchers' involvement. Primary data has been collected for 22 of the 36 papers. Secondary data is used in seven papers which use survey results on individuals' CC and channel satisfaction for statistical modeling. Six papers present only tertiary data, while one paper does not present any data. Times series are used frequently, but only one paper presents a longitudinal study, with six months between data collection points.

There is a high level of practitioner involvement in the papers, largely due to the many case studies based on interviews with employees. Of the 36 papers, 21 include involvement or collaboration with practitioners. The authors' biographies reveal that four

Table 6. Level of data

Level of data	Number of papers	Paper
Primary	22	[17, 19–30, 32, 35–37, 40, 42, 46, 48]
Secondary	7	[4, 8, 41, 43–45, 47]
Tertiary	6	[11, 18, 33, 34, 38, 39]
No data	1	[3]

authors behind three of the papers [18, 19, 34] have worked in government organizations, in three cases at the top level.

Seven papers presents channel traffic, of which three presents the same data [11, 38, 40]. Three papers contain a single table or paragraph with channel traffic [8, 19, 23]. Finally one paper analyzes channel data as a part of a field experiment conducted in 2008 [37]. This data only concerns transactions; however, information inquiries related to the transactions are not presented. Further, except for the field experiment, the latest data on channel traffic is from 2006.

4 Concept-Centric Analysis of the CC Literature

This section present the concept-centric analysis of the pool of papers following Webster and Watson [9]. During coding we focused on the two overall concepts in the papers; CC which focuses on the factors that influence citizens' choice of channel and MCM which focuses on the processes and issues related government organizations management of multiple channels. Table 7 presents the result of this analysis.

Of the 36 papers 14 study CC at the individual level, while 15 study MCM at the organizational level. There are five papers which overlap these levels, of which two presents the results of field experiments and three are theoretical. One paper, presenting the results of a MCM design study takes place at the group level. One paper [11] does not fit into either level, but focuses on the channels and services delivered, and the development of channel traffic over time. None of the papers study CC at the group level, although a few briefly mention that citizens can also influence each other, or ask each other for help in dealings with public authorities.

4.1 Studies at the Individual Level

Of the 19 papers which study citizens' CC for interaction with public authorities three are theoretical and 11 use survey data either for descriptive analysis and/or to test the factors that influence this choice. Four papers explore the factors through qualitative methods, two of which also use surveys. Three papers study the effects of organizations' instruments for channel integration and migration, and how these instruments are

Table 7. Concept-centric analysis of papers

Papers	Concepts					
	Channel choice			Multichannel management		
	Unit of analysis			Unit of analysis		
	O	G	I	O	G	I
[4, 8, 17, 29, 31, 32, 40–42, 44–48]			●			
[18–25, 27, 28, 33, 34, 39, 43]				●		
[3, 26, 30, 36, 38]			●	●		
[35]					●	
[11]*						

Legend: O = organization, G = group, I = individual, * = service channel perceived by citizens. These studies are noteworthy as they cross the boundaries between the individual and organizational unit of analysis.

Most of the studies at the individual level apply variance models to test the impact of independent variables on citizen channel and/or source choice. Nine study citizens' satisfaction with a channel and/or interaction. Satisfaction is both studied as a dependent variable, based on channel chosen, and as an independent variable, where satisfaction with a previous encounter influence future interactions. The factors influencing channel choice have been found through qualitative studies, informed by previous studies, adoptions studies such as TAM [49], marketing theory, and theoretical frameworks from media and communication theory especially Media Richness Theory (MRT) [50], Channel Expansion Theory [51] and Uses and Gratifications research [52]. The papers test a number of different factors. To provide a simple overview we clustered the independent variables into four groups during coding. Note that satisfaction was studied both as an independent and dependent variable. Table 8 presents the factors studied, and the papers which study them.

An alternative to the variance models is presented by Teerling and Pieterson [30] who use a process model to illustrate how governments' marketing efforts and a person's previous experiences also influence channel choice. This model is interesting as it acknowledges that channel choice is not just a psychological process taking place within citizens, but also a social process where citizens can be influenced by external factors. This is important as government organizations can then impact citizens' CC before an interaction takes place.

4.2   Studies at the Organizational Level

The 21 papers which take place at the organizational level are much more diverse in terms of topics studied than those at the individual level. Table 9 presents an overview of these topics. Channel integration and migration are the most frequently studied topics, followed by inter- and cross organizational cooperation related to MCM. Due to the limits of this review we only briefly cover the topics here.

Pieterson's studies of government organizations' channel positioning strategies stand out as they are presented in four papers [3, 36, 38, 39]. He uses a process model to illustrate how public authorities can migrate citizens towards the most efficient channels to reduce administrative costs and increase citizen satisfaction. The studies are informed through theories from media science such as MRT, Bordewijk and van Kaam's [53] classification of tele-information services, a historical analysis of government organizations' channel strategies, and through a series of field experiments from the Dutch Channels in Balance project [24, 30, 36].

Kernaghan discusses the different types of MCM collaboration between government organizations and presents two models to visualize these variations. The first describes inter- and cross organizational partnerships, in terms of actors, services and channels involved [21]. The second model describes the degree to which organizations involved in MCM can be integrated, from informal cooperation, where they share information, to full consolidation, where they give up individual goals and policies and

Table 8. Factors related to citizens' channel choice

Variable	Examples of indicators	Theory	Papers
Channel characteristics	Multiple cues Level of interactivity Perceived ease of use Perceived usefulness	Media richness theory, marketing theory, technology adoption models	[3, 17, 26, 30, 32, 36, 38, 42, 45, 48]
Task characteristics	Type of task at hand Complexity of problem Ambiguity of information	Media richness theory, uses and gratifications research	[3, 4, 8, 17, 26, 29, 32, 38, 40–42, 44, 45, 48]
Personal characteristics	Socio-demographics (age, gender, race, education, income) Experience with channel, habits Trust in public authorities	Digital divide literature, technology adoption models, channel expansion theory,	[3, 4, 8, 29, 31, 32, 38, 40–42, 44–48]
Situational constraints	Availability of channels Price Distance to channels	Marketing theory,	[3, 26, 29, 32, 38, 40, 41, 47, 48]
Satisfaction	Satisfaction with channel Satisfaction with service encounter Satisfaction with previous encounters	Channel expansion theory, marketing theory,	[4, 8, 29–31, 36, 37, 41, 45]

Table 9. Concepts analyzed at the organizational level

Concept	Theory	Papers
Channel strategies	Media theory, technology adoption models	[3, 11, 38, 39]
Channel integration and/or migration	Media theory, technology adoption models	[24, 26, 27, 33, 34, 36, 37]
Inter- and cross-organizational cooperation, integrated service delivery	References e-government and e-commerce literature and institutional theory but no explicit theoretical framework	[18, 21, 23, 25, 28, 35]
Intermediaries	Intermediation theory, marketing theory, transaction cost theory,	[19, 20]
Other (various)	Technology adoption models	[22, 43]

become fully harmonized [33]. This is reminiscent of the vertical and horizontal integration of government organizations which is frequently studied in e-government literature, such as Layne and Lee's [54] often cited e-government web-stage model. Kernaghan differs from Layne and Lee, however, in that he does not present consolidation as an inevitable last stage, but rather as one of several strategic options to consider depending on one's needs and resources. In this way Kernaghan avoids the technologic determinism which the web-stage models have been criticized for. Kernaghan's studies are mostly informed through case studies, especially from Service Canada, rather than any explicit theoretical framework.

Klievink and Janssen [25] categorize challenges related to MCM coordination based on a literature review from several fields including e-commerce and e-government. They identify three layers which cover the political, organizational, and information and technological aspects to MCM coordination and present these in an analytical framework. Kernaghan and Flumian discuss similar barriers [18, 21] with a stronger emphasis on problems caused by changing political climates and power struggles.

In another study Klievink and Janssen focus on public and private intermediaries [20]. Based on case studies and transaction cost theory they discuss the positive roles intermediaries play in facilitating government to citizen interaction, and the strategies government organizations can employ in relation to them in the shape of a process model. Another perspective on intermediaries comes from Frey and Holden [19] who study the channel conflicts that can arise when private companies appear as intermediaries. The authors apply the theoretical concept of distribution channel management from marketing literature and two case studies to illustrate how government organizations can handle these conflicts. Like Janssen and Klievink they acknowledge the positive role intermediaries can play in MCM. However, Frey and Holden note the importance of protecting the interests of the private companies in addition to those of the government and citizens, while Janssen and Klievink are more concerned with ensuring that citizens have equal access to government services.

5   Discussion

In this section we discuss the results of our literature review with the aim of identifying methodological and knowledge gaps in the CC literature. Table 10 presents six areas for future CC studies, which could bring the field further forwards.

The CC literature is dominated by a few authors and countries. Many of the papers study actual use and involve practitioners. This limits the places where the studies could have been carried out, as well as their generalizability. Studies from other countries and of specific services could offer valuable contributions to the literature.

Many methods are used to collect and analyze data, but two types of studies stand out; statistical analysis of survey data of citizens' CC, and case studies of MCM at the organizational level. The studies of CC appear more harmonized and coherent than those of MCM. Part of this may be because they are carried out by a small group of

Table 10. Suggestions for future CC studies

Suggestion	Purpose
Studies from new countries and services	Increase analytical generalizability
More use of primary data and qualitative data	Improve statistical analysis of CC, and in-depth examination of specific areas
Direct observation and analysis of channel traffic	Supplement and update existing studies
Longitudinal studies	Analyze long-term effects of MCM instruments
Studies of CC at group level	Extend existing process models to include the effects of citizen-to-citizen interaction on CC
Field experiments	Bridge gaps between CC at individual level and MCM at organizational level

authors who cross-reference each other. However, these studies also revolve around one topic – individual's CC – use similar variance models and explicitly refer to the same theoretical frameworks to inform their analyses. There is a strong sense of progress and building on each other's work, and both empirical and theoretical contributions are offered. However, they are largely based on survey data from secondary data sets which the researcher cannot influence. Although a few studies use qualitative studies to inform the survey creation, CC scholars repeatedly state a need for supplementing surveys through qualitative methods [3, 4, 8, 40, 41, 47].

Methods of direct observation are time consuming to conduct, but they provide valuable contextual information [16] and could inform areas which have only been slightly touched upon; situational constraints, habits and how the service in question and its importance to the citizens influence CC. Observations could study an entire service encounter from the citizens' point of view and the interplay that takes place between channels during such an encounter. This would enable CC scholars to explore citizen initiated requests and explain why these requests occur and gain insight into channel switching and supplementing behavior.

Data on channel traffic could update and supplement the existing knowledge on MCM. Longitudinal studies of channel traffic could be used to evaluate the effects of MCM instruments on citizens' channel behavior. Most of the existing analyses of channel traffic are based on data which is a decade old, and it is unknown if the conclusions based on this data still hold up today.

Future CC studies could examine how citizens influence and help each other when interacting with government organizations. It is striking that the papers in this review focus at only the individual or organization level. There are no studies of CC at the group level, although both private and public intermediaries are mentioned at organizational level, and several studies mention that friends and family members can be intermediaries [25, 32, 44]. Teerling and Pieterson's process model seems suitable for this task as it illustrates external parties' influence on citizens' CC [30].

A series of conceptual models have been presented to illustrate channel integration and migration, inter-and cross organizational collaboration and barriers to MCM. However, most of the authors seem to either build new models or improve their own. Having presented some of the overlaps in the MCM studies at organizational level here, we would suggest that the existing conceptual models are criticized, tested or synthesized before new models are created. This could lead to a more mature and coherent field. We also recommend that theoretical frameworks are used to inform these models to a higher extent.

Finally we recommend that new field experiments are conducted to study the effects of MCM instruments. The existing studies have been valuable to bridge the individual and organizational levels, but they have been carried out in one country by a small group of scholars. New experiments could contribute by including new service areas, target groups, and MCM instruments. Further they could examine the effects of MCM on all available channels, rather than a few isolated channels. Field experiments could also to examine the effects of MCM instruments on new digital media, which previous experiments have not covered.

6 Conclusion

This paper has presented an overview of 36 papers from the CC literature found and analyzed following Webster and Watson [9]. The classification of the papers expanded a framework by Schlichter and Kræmmergaard [10]. The importance of supplementing the search for papers with forwards and backwards searches has been demonstrated as new papers were added in each step. Hofmann's method of contacting authors to inquire about keywords proved fruitful [7]. Our analysis has revealed multiple gaps in the CC literature. We have suggested six areas which future studies could address to contribute to the theoretical and empirical development of the CC field.

There are several limitations to our study. Many of the papers were found due to authors citing themselves. This self-citing means the pool of papers revolve around a few authors and countries. The effect may have been strengthened by the sources searched, keywords used, and the fact that papers from certain publishers were inaccessible. It is possible that we may have missed papers for these reasons. Our conceptual analysis is limited to two main areas due to author resources and spatial limitations. A synthesis of results, recommendations for practioners, and a more in-depth discussion of suggestion for future studies were omitted for similar reasons.

Future literature studies could address these limitations by expanding the search, classification and analysis conducted here. An analysis of author keywords, citations, sources and disciplines could illuminate the relationships between the papers and to other fields. Future studies could synthesize and discuss results, suggestions for future studies and recommendations for practioners. We welcome input from scholars on these issues and will gladly share our data for further analysis upon request.

Appendix A: Pool of Papers in the Review

ID	Author(s) and year	Source	Country
19	Frey, K. N., & Holden, S. H. (2005)	GIQ	US
21	Kernaghan, K. (2005)	IRAS	Canada
41	Reddick, C. G. (2005)	JEG	US
39	Pieterson, W., & Dijk, J. (2006)	IFIP EGOV Conference	Netherlands
11	van Deursen, A., & Pieterson, W. (2006)	ICA Conference	Netherlands
18	Flumian, M., Coe, A., & Kernaghan, K. (2007)	IRAS	Canada
32	Pieterson, W., & van Dijk, J. (2007)	Dg.o. Conference	Netherlands
38	Ebbers, W. E., Pieterson, W. J., & Noordman, H. N. (2008)	GIQ	Netherlands
40	Pieterson, W., & Ebbers, W. (2008)	IRAS	Netherlands
42	Pieterson, W., Teerling, M., & Ebbers, W. (2008)	IFIP EGOV Conference	Netherlands
34	Singh, A. K., & Sahu, R. (2008)	GIQ	India
29	Verdegem, P., & Hauttekeete, L. (2008)	IJEG	Belgium
20	Janssen, M., & Klievink, B. (2009)	IJEGR	Netherlands
36	Pieterson, W., & Teerling, M. (2009)	IFIP EGOV Conference	Netherlands
43	Reddick, C. G. (2009)	GIQ	US
23	Roy, J. (2009)	IJEG	Canada
35	Bharosa, N., Janssen, M., Klievink, B., van Veenstra, A., & Overbeek, S. (2010).	EJEG	Netherlands
28	Gagnon, Y. C., Posada, E., Bourgault, M., & Naud, A. (2010)	IJPA	Canada
25	Klievink, B., & Janssen, M. (2010)	Dg.o. Conference	Netherlands
26	Mundy, D., Umer, Q., & Foster, A. (2011)	EJEG	UK
3	Pieterson, W. (2010)	IJEGR	US
44	Reddick, C. G. (2010)	IJEGR	US
37	Teerling, M. L., & Pieterson, W. (2010)	GIQ	Netherlands
17	Barth, M., & Veit, D. (2011)	HICSS Conference	Germany
30	Teerling, M. L., & Pieterson, W. (2011)	IP	Netherlands
24	Van De Wijngaert, L., Pieterson, W., & Teerling, M. L. (2011)	IJIM	Netherlands
27	van Veenstra, A. F., & Janssen, M. (2010)	EJEG	Netherlands
48	Lee, J., & Rao, H. R. (2012)	ISJ	US
47	Reddick, C. G., Abdelsalam, H. M., & Elkadi, H. A. (2012)	ITD	US

(*Continued*)

(Continued)

ID	Author(s) and year	Source	Country
8	Reddick, C. G., & Turner, M. (2012)	GIQ	US
33	Kernaghan, K. (2013)	CPA	Canada
45	Pang, M. S., Mithas, S., & Lucas, H. (2013)	ICIS Conference	US
46	Plattfaut, R., Kohlborn, T., Hofmann, S., Beverungen, D., Niehaves, B., Rackers, M., & Becker, J. (2013)	HICSS Conference	Germany
31	Lamberti, L., Benedetti, M., & Chen, S. (2014)	GIQ	Italy
22	Nam, T., & Pardo, T. A. (2014)	GIQ	South Korea
4	Reddick, C., & Anthopoulos, L. (2014)	TGPPP	US

References

1. Chadwick, A., May, C.: Interaction between states and citizens in the age of the internet: 'e-government' in the United States, Britain, and the European Union. Governance-an Int. J. Policy Adm. **16**(2), 271–300 (2003)
2. European Commission: Public Services Online: Assessing User Centric eGovernment performance in Europe – eGovernment Benchmark 2012 (2013)
3. Pieterson, W.: Citizens and service channels: channel choice and channel management implications. Int. J. Electron. Gov. Res. **6**(2), 37–53 (2010)
4. Reddick, C., Anthopoulos, L.: Interactions with e-government, new digital media and traditional channel choices: citizen-initiated factors. Transform. Gov. People, Process Policy **8**(3), 398–419 (2014)
5. van de Wijngaert, L., Bouwman, H., Contractor, N.: A network approach toward literature review. Qual. Quant. **48**(2), 623–643 (2012)
6. Rana, N.P., Williams, M.D., Dwivedi, Y.K.: E-government adoption research: a meta-analysis of findings. In: 20th European Conference on Information Systems (ECIS 2012), pp. 1–10 (2012)
7. Hofmann, S., Räckers, M., Becker, J.: Identifying factors of e-government acceptance – a literature review. In: 33rd International Conference on Information Systems (ICIS 2012), pp. 1–10 (2012)
8. Reddick, C., Turner, M.: Channel choice and public service delivery in Canada: comparing e-government to traditional service delivery. Gov. Inf. Q. **29**(1), 1–11 (2012)
9. Webster, J., Watson, R.: Analyzing the past to prepare for the future: writing a literature review. MIS Q. **26**(2), 3 (2002)
10. Schlichter, B., Kraemmergaard, P.: A comprehensive literature review of the ERP research field over a decade. J. Enterp. Inf. Manag. **23**(4), 486–520 (2010)
11. Van Deursen, A., Pieterson, W.: The internet as a service channel in the public sector. In: International Communication Association Conference (ICA) (2006)
12. Heeks, R., Bailur, S.: Analyzing e-government research: perspectives, philosophies, theories, methods, and practice. Gov. Inf. Q. **24**(2), 243–265 (2007)

13. Madsen, C.Ø., Berger, J.B., Phythian, M.: The development in leading e-government articles 2001–2010: definitions, perspectives, scope, research philosophies, methods and recommendations: an update of Heeks and Bailur. In: Janssen, M., Scholl, H.J., Wimmer, M.A., Bannister, F. (eds.) EGOV 2014. LNCS, vol. 8653, pp. 17–34. Springer, Heidelberg (2014)
14. Yildiz, M.: E-government research: reviewing the literature, limitations, and ways forward. Gov. Inf. Q. 24(3), 646–665 (2007)
15. Scholl, H.J.: E-Government Reference Library v.10.0. http://faculty.washington.edu/jscholl/egrl/. Accessed 03 Jan 2015
16. Blaikie, N.: Designing Social Research. Polity, Cambridge (2012)
17. Barth, M., Veit, D.: Electronic service delivery in the public sector: understanding the variance of citizens' resistance. In: Proceedings of 44th Hawaii International Conference in System Sciences, pp. 1–11 (2011)
18. Flumian, M., Coe, A., Kernaghan, K.: Transforming service to Canadians: the service Canada model. Int. Rev. Adm. Sci. 73(4), 557–568 (2007)
19. Frey, K.N., Holden, S.H.: Distribution channel management in e-government: addressing federal information policy issues. Gov. Inf. Q. 22(4), 685–701 (2005)
20. Janssen, M., Klievink, B.: The role of intermediaries in multi-channel service delivery strategies. Int. J. Electron. Gov. Res. 5(3), 36–46 (2009)
21. Kernaghan, K.: Moving towards the virtual state: integrating services and service channels for citizen-centred delivery. Int. Rev. Adm. Sci. 71(1), 119–131 (2005)
22. Nam, T., Pardo, T.A.: The changing face of a city government: a case study of Philly311. Gov. Inf. Q. 31(S1), S1–S9 (2014)
23. Pietrabissa, A., Priscoli, F.D.: Admission control in variable capacity communication networks. In: Chiuso, A., Fortuna, L., Frasca, M., Rizzo, A., Schenato, L., Zampieri, S. (eds.) Modelling, Estimation and Control of Networked Complex Systems. UCS, vol. 2, pp. 223–238. Springer, Heidelberg (2009)
24. van de Wijngaert, L., Pieterson, W., Teerling, M.: Influencing citizen behavior: experiences from multichannel marketing pilot projects. Int. J. Inf. Manag. 31(5), 415–419 (2011)
25. Klievink, B., Janssen, M.: Coordinating e-government service delivery. In: 11th Annual International Conference on Digital Government Research (dg.o 2010). Digital Government Society of North America, Puebla, Mexico, pp. 209–216 (2010)
26. Mundy, D., Umer, Q., Foster, A.: Examining the potential for channel shift in the UK through multiple lenses. Electron. J. e-Gov. 9(2), 203–213 (2011)
27. Van Veenstra, A.F., Janssen, M.: Migration strategies for multi-channel service provisioning in public agencies. Electron. J. e-Gov. 8(2), 409–416 (2010)
28. Gagnon, Y.C., Posada, E., Bourgault, M., Naud, A.: Multichannel delivery of public services: a new and complex management challenge. Int. J. Public Adm. 33, 213–222 (2010)
29. Verdegem, P., Hauttekeete, L.: The user at the centre of the development of one-stop government. Int. J. Electron. Gov. 1(3), 258–274 (2008)
30. Teerling, M., Pieterson, W.: How to improve e-government use: an empirical examination of multichannel marketing instruments. Inf. Polity 16(2), 171–187 (2011)
31. Lamberti, L., Benedetti, M., Chen, S.: Benefits sought by citizens and channel attitudes for multichannel payment services: evidence from Italy. Gov. Inf. Q. 31(4), 596–609 (2014)
32. Pieterson, W., van Dijk, J.: Channel choice determinants; an exploration of the factors that determine the choice of a service channel in citizen initiated contacts. In: 8th Annual International Conference on Digital Government Research (dg.o 2007), vol. 228, pp. 173–182 (2007)
33. Kernaghan, K.: Changing channels: managing channel integration and migration in public organizations. Can. Public Adm. 56(1), 121–141 (2013)

34. Singh, A.K., Sahu, R.: Integrating Internet, telephones, and call centers for delivering better quality e-governance to all citizens. Gov. Inf. Q. **25**(3), 477–490 (2008)
35. Bharosa, N., Janssen, M., Klievink, B., Van Veenstra, A.: Guiding integrated service delivery : synthesizing and embedding principles using role-playing games. Electron. J. e-Gov. **8**(2), 83–92 (2010)
36. Pieterson, W., Teerling, M.: Channel integration in governmental service delivery: the effects on citizen behavior and perceptions. In: Wimmer, M.A., Scholl, H.J., Janssen, M., Traunmüller, R. (eds.) EGOV 2009. LNCS, vol. 5693, pp. 222–233. Springer, Heidelberg (2009)
37. Teerling, M., Pieterson, W.: Multichannel marketing: an experiment on guiding citizens to the electronic channels. Gov. Inf. Q. **27**(1), 98–107 (2010)
38. Ebbers, W., Pieterson, W., Noordman, H.: Electronic government: rethinking channel management strategies. Gov. Inf. Q. **25**(2), 181–201 (2008)
39. Pieterson, W., Van Dijk, J.: Governmental service channel positioning: history and strategies for the future. In: Communication Proceedings of the Fifth International EGOV Proceedings, pp. 53–60 (2006)
40. Pieterson, W., Ebbers, W.: The use of service channels by citizens in the Netherlands: implications for multi-channel management. Int. Rev. Adm. Sci. **74**(1), 95–110 (2008)
41. Reddick, C.: Citizen-initiated contacts with government: comparing phones and websites. J. E-Government **2**(1), 27–53 (2005)
42. Pieterson, W., Teerling, M., Ebbers, W.: Channel perceptions and usage: beyond media richness factors. In: Wimmer, M.A., Scholl, H.J., Ferro, E. (eds.) EGOV 2008. LNCS, vol. 5184, pp. 219–230. Springer, Heidelberg (2008)
43. Reddick, C.: The adoption of centralized customer service systems: a survey of local governments. Gov. Inf. Q. **26**(1), 219–226 (2009)
44. Reddick, C.: Comparing citizens' use of e-government to alternative service channels. Int. J. Electron. Gov. Res. **6**(June), 54–67 (2010)
45. Pang, M., Mithas, S., Lucas, H.: How channel choice and service failure influence customer satisfaction: the case of public services. In: Thirty Fourth International Conference on Information Systems, Milan (2013)
46. Plattfaut, R., Kohlborn, T., Hofmann, S., Beverungen, D., Niehaves, B., Rackers, M., Becker, J.: Unravelling (E-)government channel selection: a quantitative analysis of individual customer preferences in Germany and Australia. In: 46th Hawaii International Conference on System Science (HICSS 2013) (2013)
47. Reddick, C., Abdelsalam, H.M.E., Elkadi, H.A.: Channel choice and the digital divide in e-government: the case of Egypt. Inf. Technol. Dev. **18**(3), 226–246 (2012)
48. Lee, J., Rao, H.R.: Service source and channel choice in G2C service environments: a model comparison in the anti/counter-terrorism domain. Inf. Syst. J. **22**(4), 313–341 (2012)
49. Davis, F.D.: Perceived ease of use, and user acceptance of information technology. MIS Q. **13**(3), 319–340 (1989)
50. Daft, R.L., Lengel, R.H.: Organizational information requirements, media richness and structural design. Manage. Sci. **32**(5), 554–571 (1986)
51. Carlson, J.R., Zmud, R.W.: Channel expansion theory and the experiential nature of media richness perceptions. Acad. Manag. J. **42**, 153–170 (1999)
52. Katz, E., Blumler, J.G., Gurevitch, M.: Uses and gratifications research. Public Opin. Q. **37**(4), 509–523 (1973)
53. Bordewijk, J., van Kaam, B.: Towards a new classification of tele-information services. In: McQuail's Reader in Mass Communication Theory, SAGE Publications, London, pp. 575–586 (2002)
54. Layne, K., Lee, J.: Developing fully functional E-government: a four stage model. Gov. Inf. Q. **18**(2), 122–136 (2001)

Conceptualising the Digital Public in Government Crowdsourcing: Social Media and the Imagined Audience

Panos Panagiotopoulos[✉] and Frances Bowen

School of Business and Management, Queen Mary University of London,
Mile End, London E1 4NS, UK
{P.Panagiotopoulos,F.Bowen}@qmul.ac.uk

Abstract. Public sector organisations seem to be embracing social media for information dissemination and engagement, but less is know about their value as information sources. This paper draws from the notion of the imagined audience to examine how policy teams in the UK Department of Environment, Food and Rural Affairs (DEFRA) conceptualise the value of social media input. Findings from a series of interviews and workshops suggest that policy makers are broadly positive about sourcing useful input from social media in topics like farming and environmental policies, however audience awareness emerges as an important limitation. As different groups of the public use social media for professional activities, policy makers attempt to develop their own capacities to navigate through audiences and understand whom they are listening to. The paper makes suggestions about the technical, methodological and policy challenges of over-coming audience limitations on social media.

Keywords: Social media · Policy crowdsourcing · Digital engagement · UK government · Environment and farming · Case study

1 Introduction

Crowdsourcing is a broad term that describes activities where a large number of contributions from individuals are used to co-create value [1]. Crowdsourcing may or may not directly entail a problem-solving component, but there are many different ways in which it can be valuable for decision support in organisations (e.g. content production, task competition, voting, crowdfunding) [2]. The importance of crowdsourcing has been evident in public management with popular platforms that invite contributions from the public like Challenge.gov and the Open Government Public Engagement Platform in the USA [3, 4] or the UK government's Red Tape Challenge that collects feedback on regulations [5].

In parallel to government websites, the principles of crowdsourcing have wider implications for citizen-government relationships e.g. [4, 6]. Less institutionalised forms of crowdsourcing are becoming more widespread in the form of monitoring and aggregating content from open information sources and, more specifically, social media [e.g. 7–9]. It is common that social media users might provide direct feedback on policy topics, broadcast their own information or engage in discussions that can be informative

© IFIP International Federation for Information Processing 2015
E. Tambouris et al. (Eds.): EGOV 2015, LNCS 9248, pp. 19–30, 2015.
DOI: 10.1007/978-3-319-22479-4_2

for the work of government. There are increasing signals that social media can be useful as information sources in policy making [e.g. 7, 10], however our knowledge remains much less developed compared to crowdsourcing websites. Studies of social media in the public sector focus on strategic and operational benefits [11] or models of interactions with the public [10]. Understanding the value of social media as information sources can extend our knowledge and inform current practice as social media monitoring tools are being adopted by government organisations [12–14].

This paper explores the value of social media for government crowdsourcing through a series of interviews and workshops with policy teams in the UK Department of Environment, Food and Rural Affairs (DEFRA). As an explanatory lens of how policy makers frame social media input and information flows with the public, we draw from the notion of the imagined audience. This concept has roots in conceptualisations of the public and engagement around science and technology [15–18]. In digitally-mediated environments, the imagined audience indicates how social media users frame communication contexts and navigate through the multiple audiences that they perceive they are engaging with [19, 20].

Following an elaboration of the theoretical background in the next section, the paper describes the study methodology and findings. Policy makers were largely supportive of opportunities to source useful social media content in appropriately summarised forms, but representation of social media users and audience awareness were recognised as major limitations. The paper discusses the implications of these findings with a focus on overcoming audience limitations.

2   Social Media and the Imagined Audience

Social media include online networking (e.g. Facebook, LinkedIn), content sharing (e.g. YouTube, Pinterest) and blogging/micro-blogging platforms (e.g. WordPress, Twitter). The different functionalities of social media allow organisations and individual users to develop their presence, connect with others and share content according to their diverse aims (e.g. both social and professional) [21].

The pluralism of social media inevitably leads to audience fragmentation and distribution of activities across channels. On some occasions, social media users might have obvious motivations to engage on certain platforms (e.g. LinkedIn for professional networking), but on others these boundaries might be blurred both in terms of content (e.g. Twitter updates) and composition of networks (e.g. Facebook friends). It is furthermore common to observe dynamic audiences on social media that form temporarily around events or users' interests like TV shows [22]. As a result, the relationship between traditional and social media audiences can be challenging for organisations that are seeking to engage with new groups of the public or offer value to those who already engage e.g. [23, 24].

The imagined audience is a concept that refers to how social media users conceptualise the people with whom they are communicating [19, 20, 25]. As Marwick and Boyd emphasise [19], on most social media channels, users experience a collapse of multiple audiences into a single context; audiences that might have otherwise been distinct in the offline world like family, personal and professional contacts. Each social media platform has its own audience-feedback features (e.g. "likes", "shares" or "followers") [20], but in many situations it remains unclear how to select audiences or even how many users read each update. Particularly through Twitter's conversational features (mentions, retweets, hashtags), posted messages can travel through unknown and potentially infinite audiences that are difficult to measure [19]. As social media users make assumptions about their imagined audience, it is not only a case of elevated expectations; in fact, a large study with Facebook users shows that they commonly underestimate how many people view their content [26].

Beyond social media research, the concept of the imagined audience has been relevant to stakeholder engagement studies in science and technology. It originates from observations that discourses within industries, policy-making communities and generally amongst "experts" might rely on assumptions about the "public" or "imagined lay persons" who lack expert knowledge of a topic but have legitimate concerns or expectations (e.g. about chemicals or infrastructure planning) [15, 16, 18]. Whether seen as "stakeholders", "consumers" or "citizens", the public is generally perceived as a resource that needs to be managed even if not completely understood. Processes of conceptualising the public by experts usually have high influence on engagement practices and, subsequently, drive reactions from the public about technology trajectories (e.g. investments in renewable energy sources) [17, 18].

The concept of the imagined audience can illustrate important issues about the potential of social media as information sources in government. Related work mainly refers to public input and collaborative actions during emergency events e.g. [14, 27]. A study by Bekkers et al. [7] further suggests that in the Netherlands, organisations with established surveillance mechanisms like the police are more willing to consider social media as sources of information in comparison to policy teams in other departments that prefer the monitoring of closed information spaces (e.g. forums). In the UK government, there is some evidence of crowdsourcing exercises taking place to proactively identify conversations of interest, for example, in incidents of public health or campaigns about food safety and hygiene [12]. More technical approaches to social media crowdsourcing by Charalabidis et al. [8, 9] place emphasis on design and content aggregation elements so that policy makers are able to overview a large amount of information; the authors distinguish this approach as "passive" or "non-moderated" crowdsourcing.

As policy makers are considering the role of social media input, they inevitably have to make assumptions about the imagined audience. In practice, they need to "imagine" who are the people they are listening to or engaging with. At the next level, they need to make assessments about the usefulness of the collective input produced by social media audiences and the extent to which it can influence decisions. Many of these assessments about information flows with the public in policy making are not new, e.g. [28], but the volume, complexity and diversity of social media sources points to the need for a more detailed examination. Starting from the concept of the imagined audience, there is broader scope to examine the different crowdsourcing contexts in which policy makers turn to consider social media input.

3   Study Methodology

The research was organised in the form of a case study [29] and carried out as part of a wider project with the UK Department of Environment, Food and Rural Affairs DEFRA in which the researchers were involved. The selection of DEFRA as the case organisation for this study represents the typical but also the influential case [30], since DEFRA's work draws heavily on engagement with the public and the use of external stakeholder input in policy decisions. Furthermore, DEFRA hosts a large number of policy teams in different topics where crowdsourcing practices are potentially relevant but the size and composition of involved audiences differs; for example, activities range from farming reform and flood protection to specialised environmental issues like forestry, chemicals and pesticides.

Data collection for the scope of this study took place between November 2014 and February 2015 and involved three sources:

- Seven semi-structured interviews that lasted for one hour on average and were taped and transcribed following permission from participants. Further to the input from the interviews, the research team had opportunities to follow up with participants or their colleagues on topics of interest.
- Two workshops with five and six participants respectively. The workshops involved a demonstration of social media monitoring and visualisation tools relevant to a pilot analysis of farming networks on Twitter. Participants were asked to provide feedback on the value of the tools and brainstorm about future requirements. The workshops were not recorded but extensive notes were taken. Although providing full details about this exercise is not possible within the scope of this paper, the case findings include examples relevant to conceptualisations of the audience.
- A wide range of documentary evidence from a selection of policy topics, including consultations, response to consultations, social media posts and evaluation reports.

Selected participants for the seven interviews came from different levels of the civil service and policy areas mainly related to communications and regulations about the environment, farming and local growth. They are also involved in all the different stages of DEFRA's policy-making lifecycle (see Fig. 1 in the next section). Participants were first asked about their role within the organisation. Interview discussions then evolved around the following main questions:

- Generally, what type of input from external stakeholders does your role require? What kind of information flows support this input (e.g. consultations, surveys, other stakeholder engagement activities)?
- What are the different groups within the public that you would like to reach?
- How could information from social media change the ways in which you understand the needs of external stakeholders and the public?
- How do you think input from social media could support the work of your policy team and DEFRA in general?

Data analysis was carried out thematically based on the methodology described by Braun and Clarke [31]. This approach to data analysis is suitable for exploratory research

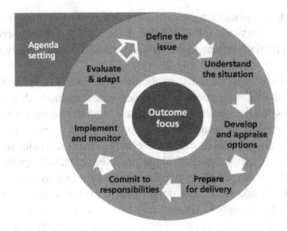

Fig. 1. DEFRA policy cycle

as it allows the flexible documentation of main themes from interview data. The focus of the analysis was on the identification of themes related to audience perceptions and information flows with the public. In most interviews, participants drew their narratives around social media audiences using examples from their own knowledge domain or experiences (e.g. following a Twitter hashtag or reading reports from social media analytics tools). The next section provides some more background about DEFRA's work and presents an overview of the findings.

4   Case Background and Findings

DEFRA is one of the largest government departments in the UK with remit in policy and regulation related to environmental protection, food production and standards, agriculture, fisheries and rural communities. DEFRA's objectives and priorities include the improvement of technical infrastructure in rural areas, increasing exports and competitiveness in the food chain, simplifying farming regulation and improving water quality [32]. The department employs over 10,000 staff working across 36 agencies and public bodies in England with devolved administrations in Wales, Scotland and Northern Ireland. There is also extensive cooperation with European Union authorities for environmental policies, including the high profile Common Agricultural Policy that involves a system of agricultural subsidies and programmes for farming and rural development.

4.1   Policy Making at DEFRA and the Role of Social Media

DEFRA's approach is explicitly focused on: (1) developing capabilities for evidence-based policy making (collecting evidence from as many sources as possible) and (2) implementing initiatives that aim at positive behavioural change (e.g. sustainable consumption, energy labelling, reducing food waste) [32, 33]. This approach to policy making is summarised in the form of the Policy Cycle shown in Fig. 1. Compared to more general models, it places emphasis on issue definition and situation understanding. This is necessary for the work of DEFRA due to the high complexity, economic impact and technical nature of environmental issues as well as the wide variety of stakeholders usually involved.

Engagement with the public is also explicitly one of DEFRA's priorities. The organisation has an overall commitment to evidence-based methods that meet criteria of rigorousness. This involves policy consultations, social science research and public understanding studies (e.g. geographical mapping, experiments, surveys and focus groups). There are also extensive stakeholder management activities involving professional associations, academic research teams and other external experts.

An important hub of DEFRA's public engagement and dissemination activities are the social media accounts. The department's presence has been organised on Facebook, LinkedIn, Google+, Storify and Flickr as well as 12 different Twitter accounts, which support diverse policy areas and communication needs (e.g. advice lines for farmers and fisheries, rural news, official statistics, Smarter Guidance and Data, air or water quality feeds). The main Twitter account @DefraGovUK has over 70 K followers and the more specialised accounts might have from fewer than 1 K followers to over 5 K. Some of these feeds are automated while most are managed individually by policy teams following internal guidance and training. Most of the department's 36 agencies and public bodies also manage their own social media presence on a selection of channels. Some of these accounts are clearly defined as informational in their purpose (news feeds) – others experience varying levels of interaction with the public.

4.2 Sources and Forms of Social Media Input

As many of DEFRA's traditional stakeholders have developed a digital networking presence, the potential value of social media input in policy decisions per se was rather uncontested by interview participants. There were however diverse opinions about the value of different sources and forms of social media input. Useful sources identified during interviews included a range of blogs, communities of practice, LinkedIn groups and Twitter hashtags/lists; content sharing websites and comments below popular news articles were generally considered as less important. Policy makers were developing their own assessments about the value of online sources based on accumulated experiences.

In terms of using social media input, there was wide agreement that for input to be considered as useful in any form it had to be relevant and appropriately summarised. An important example of this was #AgriChatUK, a national Twitter conversation that takes places weekly to discuss topics around farming. At least on two occasions, summaries from discussions were used as input to the appropriate policy teams – even as official consultation response. #AgriChatUK discussions were useful due to their clear focus, regularity and availability of weekly summaries. For less clearly relevant or more dynamic conversations, the sourcing of potentially useful content was more difficult due to technical and time constraints. Interview participants generally understood that open information channels like Twitter host a large amount of frequent, immediate and potentially relevant content, however the high "noise to signal" ratio made the value of this content not so obvious.

The use of commercial social media management and monitoring tools partially addressed this challenge. The organisation had experience with such tools at the central level in the context of monitoring popular trends and collecting updates for national campaigns or high-profile conversations. For example, a lot content was captured to oversee the reactions of Internet users against DEFRA's decision to implement a badger cull in 2012 (including content about a popular petition). Monitoring tools either managed internally or with the support of media companies would filter a large incoming flow of content and then produce ad hoc or periodic reports of trending content and influential contributors. This approach focused on popularity measures to select topics and filter content (e.g. retweets).

While this type of central monitoring extended traditional media briefings, some of the department's agencies had adopted monitoring software for more specialised needs. The most important crowdsourcing context was emergency events where DEFRA and its affiliated agencies need to facilitate timely communication of risks to the public and guide to appropriate actions. For example, the Environment Agency is the body responsible for handling emergencies related to natural disasters. Its main Twitter account has over 250 K followers and is part of Twitter Alerts, the network's official warning system. Monitoring related to emergencies like floods provided a clearly defined set of keywords and timeframes for sourcing and interpreting content. This was achieved through a combination of flood-related hashtags, direct mentions from the public and scanning content from open sources.

4.3   Conceptualisations of the Social Media Audience

Aligned with DEFRA's commitment to evidence-based policy making, all participants had a good understanding of traditional stakeholders, important influencers and the value of different public engagement activities. Subjective evaluations of the social media audience proved a quite challenging task that was evidenced in a set of common themes during the interviews and workshops.

Policy makers usually had to identify or make assumptions about how specific groups of professionals have a presence on social media, how they connect to each other, how they create content and whom they represent. Answers to these questions could be more straightforward for social networking groups (e.g. on LinkedIn) but less obvious on channels that support open information flows and dynamic conversations like Twitter, Facebook and blogs. For example, the popular discussions on #AgriChatUK suggested that many farmers and agricultural businesses have a presence on Twitter; however, mapping those networks and absorbing useful content outside specific conversations was challenging. Twitter lists or keyword searches could act as a first step of filtering but still resulted in a large amount of unstructured content that did not include information about the audience.

It is important to emphasise that audience limitations were not simply a matter of lacking demographic information about users but mainly about issues of sampling and representation. Ad hoc feedback suggested that social media users include a variety of domain experts as well as many users who are not experts but have a primary stake in policy topics. Furthermore, it was understood that social media users themselves collapse audiences into a single channel, hence posting content at diverse frequencies and with different intentions about whom they are talking to. As a result, monitoring social media content around keywords only captures the perspective of those users who decide to make a contribution within a specific timeframe, which inevitably leads to a "self-inclusion" perspective.

For policy makers with training in social science and economics research, exploratory analytics methods from large datasets of unstructured content could not be used as "evidence" the same way as traditional methods unless sampling and representation issues could be addressed. For example, our study identified an estimated network of 10 K or more Twitter users from the UK that tweet about issues relevant to farming. Analysis of a sample of large datasets over a period of six months revealed that these users post: (1) information about practical aspects of farming and rural life (including sharing photos), (2) comments and contributions to campaigns about topics like the price of dairy products and (3) to a lesser extent, opinions about the general state of the farming profession with reference to government decisions. Representation issues here were not per se related to the fact that a potential audience of 10 K Twitter users is only a small proportion of an estimated total of 250 K farmers and agricultural businesses in the UK [34]. The issue was that, apart from a general awareness of their professional identity, there was no systematic information in tweets or account metadata about who these users might be and what motivates them to contribute to specific discussions.

Despite limitations of audience awareness, study participants were confident to identify a positive aspect of crowdsourcing from large but unknown audiences. Compared to traditional methods and closed systems approaches to crowdsourcing, social media included more opportunities to source opinions from "real" people or groups of the public that extend beyond stakeholders who make regular contributions to policy consultations. An interviewee with experiences in assessing input from the Red Tape Challenge, the UK government's crowdsourcing system, highlighted the benefits of reaching more "real" people. Therefore, even if crowdsourced contributions could not be used as hard evidence, they could be valuable to broaden the perspective as information sources complementary to consultations.

5   Discussion and Conclusion

DEFRA provided a stimulating case to look at the value of social media as information sources due to the organisation's broad remit in environmental policies and commitment to evidence-based policy making. The concept of the imagined audience [19, 20, 25] framed our understanding of how policy makers conceptualise input from social media. It is important to understand how these subjective evaluations emerge because they can highly affect the extent to which contributions from the public are seen as a useful resource in policy decisions [15, 17, 18].

Indeed, our study found that there are important audience awareness issues when considering content from open forms of crowdsourcing on social media. Simply, policy makers find it difficult to understand or even make solid assumptions about whom they are listening to. Broadening the perspective of the audience was nevertheless recognised as an important prospect with opportunities to source opinions from groups that might not otherwise engage. The study also found that social media monitoring tools are used more widely to source contributions in clearly defined contexts like trending discussions, high-profile campaigns or emergency events. While in emergencies there is clear scope and timely monitoring is critical, the attention to popular discussions and campaigns rather follows Mergel's thoughts on using descriptive insights from popularity content [13].

It is interesting to compare those findings with analyses of policy crowdsourcing websites and particularly the UK government's Red Tape Challenge. Lodge and Wegrich [5] report that audience awareness was also an issue due to the anonymity of submissions, but the main shortcoming was that there were no explicit intentions or mechanisms to integrate input from the system in decisions. Content from social media sources gives access to a much larger pool of spontaneous, mostly not anonymous, but also less structured contributions. Policy makers were more confident that this type of content can provide useful insights if it is appropriately summarised as long as comes with contextual information that facilitates assumptions about the audience.

After identifying the importance of audience limitations, we need to consider how they can be overcome. A systematic way can involve the concept of an audience or crowd capability that is constructed and managed by an organisation [35]. Findings from our study suggest that developing such a capability could involve several levels of thinking including the following:

- The need to focus less on content itself and more on the composition of information networks or understanding how different groups of the public interact and engage in discussions (e.g. contributors of #AgricChatUK). This transition can have technical implications for the selection or development of social media monitoring tools that need to enable network-feedback features.
- Groups of the public can respectively be encouraged to organise and connect on social media so that their contributions can be sourced. This can be a task supported by intermediary organisations like professional associations, trade unions or other representation bodies that could facilitate professional networking and raise the profile of input from their own audiences.
- From the government perspective, the sourcing of contributions from open information sources can become more explicit to the public. Bekkers et al. [7] place this suggestion mostly in the context of surveillance; we position it as an opportunity to reiterate commitment to listening.
- Policy processes have to consider subjectivities of the audience as inevitable and understand their methodological implications. Earlier stages of the policy making lifecycle might seem more suitable for exploring social media input but our study indicated high interest for commitment, implementation and evaluation activities as well (Fig. 1).

These suggestions should be taken into account with considerations to the contextual limitations of this research. DEFRA's Policy Cycle and commitment to evidence-based policy might not be the most fruitful ground for experimental approaches to new data sources like social media. Furthermore, the identification of certain themes about social media and the audience by study participants cannot be seen as a complete overview of perceptions within the organisation or across the UK government. Finally, we need to consider that environmental and agricultural policies tend to attract a large number of views from diverse publics. In other policy topics, there might not be that much potential insight or the audience is more uniform, hence making assumptions about its composition less challenging.

Since the value of crowdsourcing and social media input might differ across policy topics, it would be important to examine activities or stages of the policy making process during which the social media audience is seen as a useful resource. Suggestions from reviews of crowdsourcing studies can provide several starting points and analytical models to be further developed and elaborated on in a public sector context [1, 2, 35]. Research in the area can also involve further case studies and exploratory analyses so that we can learn more about social media audiences and how to facilitate assumptions about their composition.

Acknowledgments. The authors gratefully acknowledge interview and workshops participants from DEFRA as well as Dr Chris Taylor for his involvement in data collection as part of the project team. The research was supported by the NEMODE network, Research Councils UK (New Economic Models in the Digital Economy).

References

1. Estelles-Arolas, E., Gonzalez-Ladron-de-Guevara, F.: Towards an integrated crowdsourcing definition. J. Inf. Sci. **38**, 189–200 (2012)
2. Chiu, C.-M., Liang, T.-P., Turban, E.: What can crowdsourcing do for decision support? Decis. Support Syst. **65**, 40–49 (2014)
3. Mergel, I., Desouza, K.C.: Implementing Open Innovation in the Public Sector: The Case of Challenge. gov. Public Adm. Rev. **73**, 882–890 (2013)
4. Linders, D.: From e-government to we-government: defining a typology for citizen coproduction in the age of social media. Gov. Inf. Q. **29**, 446–454 (2012)
5. Lodge, M., Wegrich, K.: Crowdsourcing and regulatory reviews: a new way of challenging red tape in British government? Regulation & Governance (advanced online publication) (2014)
6. Nam, T.: Suggesting frameworks of citizen-sourcing via Government 2.0. Gov. Inf. Q. **29**, 12–20 (2012)
7. Bekkers, V., Edwards, A., de Kool, D.: Social media monitoring: responsive governance in the shadow of surveillance? Gov. Inf. Q. **30**, 335–342 (2013)
8. Charalabidis, Y., Triantafillou, A., Karkaletsis, V., Loukis, E.: Public policy formulation through non moderated crowdsourcing in social media. In: Tambouris, E., Macintosh, A., Sæbø, Ø. (eds.) ePart 2012. LNCS, vol. 7444, pp. 156–169. Springer, Heidelberg (2012)
9. Charalabidis, Y., Loukis, E.N., Androutsopoulou, A., Karkaletsis, V., Triantafillou, A.: Passive crowdsourcing in government using social media. Transforming Gov. People, Process Policy **8**, 283–308 (2014)
10. Mergel, I.: A framework for interpreting social media interactions in the public sector. Gov. Inf. Q. **30**, 327–334 (2013)
11. Criado, J.I., Sandoval-Almazan, R., Gil-Garcia, J.R.: Government innovation through social media. Gov. Inf. Q. **30**, 319–326 (2013)

12. Panagiotopoulos, P., Barnett, J., Brooks, L.: Social media and government responsiveness: the case of the uk food standards agency. In: Wimmer, M.A., Janssen, M., Scholl, H.J. (eds.) EGOV 2013. LNCS, vol. 8074, pp. 310–321. Springer, Heidelberg (2013)
13. Mergel, I.: The social media innovation challenge in the public sector. Inf. Polity **17**, 281–292 (2012)
14. Kavanaugh, A.L., Fox, E.A., Sheetz, S.D., Yang, S., Li, L.T., Shoemaker, D.J., Natsev, A., Xie, L.: Social media use by government: from the routine to the critical. Gov. Inf. Q. **29**, 480–491 (2012)
15. Barnett, J., Burningham, K., Walker, G., Cass, N.: Imagined publics and engagement around renewable energy technologies in the UK. Public Underst. Sci. **21**, 36–50 (2012)
16. Maranta, A., Guggenheim, M., Gisler, P., Pohl, C.: The reality of experts and the imagined lay person. Acta Sociol. **46**, 150–165 (2003)
17. Walker, G., Cass, N., Burningham, K., Barnett, J.: Renewable energy and sociotechnical change: imagined subjectivities of "the public" and their implications. Environ. Plann. A **42**, 931–947 (2010)
18. Cotton, M., Devine-Wright, P.: Making electricity networks "visible": industry actor representations of "publics" and public engagement in infrastructure planning. Public Underst. Sci. **21**, 17–35 (2010)
19. Marwick, A.E., Boyd, D.: I tweet honestly, I tweet passionately: twitter users, context collapse, and the imagined audience. New Media Soc. **13**, 114–133 (2011)
20. Litt, E.: Knock, Knock. Who's There? The Imagined Audience. J. Broadcast. Electron. Media **56**, 330–345 (2012)
21. Kietzmann, J.H., Hermkens, K., McCarthy, I.P., Silvestre, B.S.: Social media? Get serious! Understanding the functional building blocks of social media. Bus. Horiz. **54**, 241–251 (2011)
22. Highfield, T., Harrington, S., Bruns, A.: Twitter as a technology for audiencing and fandom. Inf. Commun. Soc. **16**, 315–339 (2013)
23. Panagiotopoulos, P.: Towards unions 2.0: rethinking the audience of social media engagement. New Technol. Work Employ. **27**, 178–192 (2012)
24. Kidd, J.: Enacting engagement online: framing social media use for the museum. Inf. Technoly People **24**, 64–77 (2011)
25. Brake, D.R.: Who do they think they're talking to? Framings of the audience by social media users. Int. J. Commun. **6**, 1056–1076 (2012)
26. Bernstein, M.S., Bakshy, E., Burke, M., Karrer, B.: Quantifying the invisible audience in social networks. In: Proceedings of the SIGCHI Conference on Human Factors in Computing Systems - CHI 2013, p. 21. ACM Press, New York, USA (2013)
27. Panagiotopoulos, P., Bigdeli, A.Z., Sams, S.: Citizen–government collaboration on social media: the case of twitter in the 2011 riots in England. Gov. Inf. Q. **31**, 349–357 (2014)
28. Steward, J.: Public policy as information. Prometheus **31**, 3–19 (2013)
29. Yin, R.K.: Case Study Research: Design and Methods. SAGE Publications, Thousand Oaks (2014)
30. Seawright, J., Gerring, J.: Case selection techniques in case study research: a menu of qualitative and quantitative options. Polit. Res. Q. **61**, 294–308 (2008)
31. Braun, V., Clarke, V.: Using thematic analysis in psychology. Qual. Res. Psychol. **3**, 77–101 (2006)
32. DEFRA: DEFRA Business Plan. http://transparency.number10.gov.uk/business-plan/10. Accessed 22 Feb 2015

33. Collier, A., Cotterill, A., Everett, T., Muckle, R., Pike, T., Vanstone, E.: Understanding and influencing behaviours: a review of social research, economics and policy making in DEFRA (2010)
34. DEFRA Statistics: Agriculture in the United Kingdom. https://www.gov.uk/government/collections/agriculture-in-the-united-kingdom. Accessed 22 Feb 2015
35. Prpić, J., Shukla, P.P., Kietzmann, J.H., McCarthy, I.P.: How to work a crowd: developing crowd capital through crowdsourcing. Bus. Horiz. **58**, 77–85 (2015)

Steering the Digital Agenda at Arm's Length. All Wobble, No Spin: The Contextual Lens

Maddalena Sorrentino[1(✉)], Marco De Marco[2], and Paolo Depaoli[3]

[1] Università degli Studi di Milano, Milan, Italy
maddalena.sorrentino@unimi.it
[2] Uninettuno, Rome, Italy
marco.demarco@uninettunouniversity.net
[3] LUISS Guido Carli University - CeRSI, Rome, Italy
pdepaoli@luiss.it

Abstract. The paper uses a longitudinal case study of Italy's digital agency to investigate eGovernment and a subject that hovers at the far edge of the academic radar: *agencification*, or the setting up of semi-autonomous organisations that operate at arm's length from the relative ministry. The aim is to make a threefold contribution of international scope and significance to the eGovernment debate by mapping Italy's chosen path to public-sector innovation. Framing the country's digital agenda within the larger picture of ongoing New Public Management-driven administrative reforms, the authors assess whether mandating an arm's length body to steer the eGovernment strategies at public-sector macro level has been successful. The structural-instrumental, cultural and environmental lens used to analyse the key contextual factors shows how the continuity and discontinuity that has shadowed Italy's ICT policies can be blamed on shifts in leadership and diverse ideas of modernization; on the digital agency's multiple, even conflicting mandates; and on the misalignment of the 'original agency model' with the public machinery's embedded culture.

Keywords: Agencification · Egovernment · Digital agenda · ICT policy · Italy · New public management

1 Introduction

"Context is messy. Dealing with context in order to explain the outcome of a political or administrative process means taking into account the decisions and actions by individual politicians or bureaucrats, the media's attention (or not) of (alleged or real) administrative malfeasance, ad hoc informal linkages between domestic and transnational institutions, and so on". Taken from a recent study by Jon Pierre [1: 42–43], this quotation forms the point of departure for this research thread.

The specific focus of the qualitative paper converges on two topics of considerable interest: eGovernment and agencification. In this work, the term eGovernment is meant as an instrument of public action for its potential to address public problems and affect a wide range of organizations and society at large, in terms of impact on the relationship

© IFIP International Federation for Information Processing 2015
E. Tambouris et al. (Eds.): EGOV 2015, LNCS 9248, pp. 31–43, 2015.
DOI: 10.1007/978-3-319-22479-4_3

between citizens and institutions and the internal working of the public sector [2]. Agencification is interpreted as the disaggregation of government departments into single-purpose agencies [3, 4] that operate at arm's length. This design choice means that the ministries are responsible exclusively for developing the policies and that the agencies, while accountable to the ministry of reference, must operate under their own steam according to precise performance standards.

The article critically analyzes the uptake of eGovernment in Italy [5], using a longitudinal case study to respond to two research questions (RQ):

- *What institutional responses has Italy's government come up with to ensure the governance of its public-sector ICT policies?*
- *What explains the continuity and discontinuity of those responses?*

The first, descriptive RQ comes from the accepted knowledge that showing what happened on the ground is an ineluctable step of any rigorous research approach, not least because 'theory building and theory testing ... are themselves in part dependent on the availability of good descriptions' [6: 207]. The second, explanatory RQ refers to the 'long wave of Government innovation programs' [7: 254] and the agencification processes that have significantly shaped Italy's ICT policies and their outcomes since the 1990s.

Drawing on extant academic literature, official documents and the personal knowledge base of the research team of organizational scholars, the paper reconstructs the journey of a governmental agency created in 1993 to bring Italy's central administrations into the digital era, which, despite its short lifespan, has had to change both its name and position in the government machinery a good four times.

The 'structural-instrumental, cultural and environmental' are the three perspectives [8, 9] that enable the article to make an original, tri-directional contribution to the eGovernment research. Above all, it highlights how eGovernment and agencification are enmeshed in a Napoleonic administrative landscape, a context that has been relatively underexplored by the international literature [10, 11]. Second, it slots Italy's digital agenda into the larger scenario of political instability and NPM-driven reform waves [7]. In particular, the leadership shifts that have seen each new government impose their own modernization ideas on the country, the multiple, at times conflicting mandates given to the digital agenda agency, and the poor alignment of the 'agency model' with the culture embedded in the public machinery are the prime factors responsible for the continuity and discontinuity that shadows Italy's ICT policies. The article closes with an assessment of the national eGovernment strategies.

The article is organized as follows. Section 2 explains why the contextual lens was adopted to analyze agencification. Section 3 is dedicated to the methodological approach, while Sect. 4 frames the contextual backdrop of Italy's digital agency, charting its timeline, environment and effective level of success. The discussion presented in Sect. 5 reflects on the study's findings, which indicate that the myth perspective has ultimately succeeded over the government's arm's length, technocratic stance in giving momentum to Italy's eGovernment endeavour. Section 6 presents our final remarks, underscoring how the paper's two original features contribute to the current eGovernment debate.

2   Contextualizing Agencification

The intrinsic features of ICT-related policies (including the strategic role of the State, the ongoing internal debate for development resources, the inherent multilevel-structure of administrative systems, the involvement of the citizenry, and the role of the private sector) are of considerable interest to both eGovernment scientists and policy scholars. Adopting a contextual approach to the analysis of the 'course and outcome' [8] of the processes of agencification in digital government generally means acknowledging the constraints and influences exerted by the political mindset, the institutional background and the environmental forces, three aspects that need to be analyzed using, respectively, a *structural-instrumental, cultural* and *environmental* lens [9].

On the whole, reforms can be perceived from a *structural-instrumental* standpoint as conscious organizational design or reengineering, given that the structure is used by the decision makers as an instrument to achieve objectives. But this requires preconditions that give the leaders a solid grip on the reform processes and that enable them to 'score high on rational calculation or means-end thinking' (see Dahl and Lindblom [12] cited in [9]).

The emphasis on values and models borrowed from private firms has been the 'guiding light' of Italy's public sector organizational reforms for the past 25 years, as evidenced by the creation of arm's length bodies, or agencification [3: 1] [8]. In theory, agencification is supposed to improve organizational capability by giving managers more freedom to manage. However, in practice, it may actually reduce management capacity within government departments, which, according to Andrews and colleagues [13], implies that 'there could be a positive or a negative relationship between the relative agencification of a public organization and overall capability' [13: 6]. Moreover, Höpfl [14] claims that agencification attempts to sharpen the distinction between the ministers 'driving the reform agenda ... and civil servants responsible for performance, implementation (...) in a quasi-contractual 'public service agreement' or 'framework document' specifying the respective roles of 'sponsoring' departments and the chief executives of 'delivery agencies', whose performance is audited and measured, and who are in this sense accountable' [14: 42–43].

The *cultural* perspective sheds light on how reforms and change in public organizations trigger an institutionalization process that gradually introduces the 'core informal norms and values' that set the organizations on a path of cultural change and distinction. The fact that different countries and government institutions have different historical-cultural backgrounds means that their reforms follow a 'path dependent' course that gives each national reform a distinct complexion. The proposed reform of a public organization must be put to the test of 'cultural compatibility' [8]: 'reform initiatives that are incompatible with established norms and values in organizations will be rejected, while parts that are compatible will be implemented; controversial parts will be adapted so as to be made acceptable' [8: 132]. Hence, the reforms are likely to be more successful when their underlying values are more optimally aligned with the values embedded in the existing administrative system.

Public organizations are said to dwell in a dual *environment*: the technical part, which mainly focuses on efficiency, production and exchange, and the institutional part [15], which is more about issues such as the appropriate organizational structure, internal culture, recruitment policy, etc. The institutional environment is a breeding ground for the reform myths that develop, spread to other organizations and give the public organizations their isomorphic personalities [8]. These myths 'window-dress' the organization's image and increase its legitimacy. 'From a myth perspective, reform initiatives that correspond with current doctrines about 'good' and 'modern' organizations will gain acceptance more readily than initiatives that diverge from what is thought to be modern. The greater the correspondence between, on the one hand, problem definitions and suggested solutions in reform programmes, and, on the other hand, the circumstances of organizations perceived as well-run models for other organizations, the easier it will be to gain legitimacy and endorsement' [8].

The above concepts will be used below to read and interpret the case study.

3   Research Approach

When the research questions are 'How?' and 'Why?', when the researcher has little control over the events, and when the focus is on what is currently happening in real-life contexts [16], the most indicated methodological approach is the case study. That is the method adopted here to respond to the research questions raised, which centre on how and why the agency in question has taken the direction observed and the role played by the peculiarities of Italy's public machinery.

The research questions presented above are addressed through a longitudinal case study of the government agency responsible for Italy's digital agenda from 1993 to 2014 (which, for reasons of simplicity and consistency, given the several name changes this public body has undergone, we shall also refer to as the 'digital agency'). The 1993-2014 timeframe captures the setting within which the Agenzia per l'Italia Digitale[1] (AgID), initially called the Autorità per l'informatica nella pubblica amministrazione[2] (AIPA), was created and evolved; 1993 was the year in which Italy embarked on the substantive administrative reforms that developed into a 'permanent cycle of reforms' [17: 787] and, in 2001, the AIPA was mandated to implement Italy's first ever national eGovernment plan. However, more recently, the tide of administrative reforms has been brought practically to a standstill, victim of the financial crisis that has rendered the economic climate uncertain and significantly eroded the public resources available to drive change. The current government issued the latest measure, which gave the AgID a new statute.

The relevant strengths of the various data sources (mainly official documents, regulatory measures and archival reports) were identified by triangulating the data collection and analysis results and were used to corroborate the study's findings and conclusions. The research team examined the main organizational and operational implications of each of the agency's diverse configurations and administrative reporting systems in order to reliably map the nature and limitations of each permutation, even though, for reasons of space, only a small part of that information can be presented here.

---

[1] Agenzia per l'Italia Digitale (AgID): Digital Agency of Italy *(our translation)*.

[2] Autorità per l'informatica nella pubblica amministrazione (AIPA): eGovernment Authority *(our translation)*.

4   From AIPA to AgID

Italy's first digital agency, the AIPA, was officially established on 12 February 1993—during a spate of particularly intense administrative reforms—to govern Italy's public-sector digital policies. It has since undergone a series of permutations that need to be set against the relevant events, background and environment in order to understand the evolutionary dynamics behind Italy's current digital agency, the AgID.

Mapping that journey, means starting at the very beginning, in 1992, when the Italian cabinet appointed a public body, the Department of Public Service (DPS), to govern the ICT-enablement of the public administration, but without vesting it with specific powers of intervention to develop a digital agenda. Its job, in fact, was purely to advise the government on the best way to coordinate the online PA, to research and design ICT development policies and to issue circulars and proposals on possible interventions.

Hence, in 1993, the government created the AIPA, the country's first national digital agency. Ten years later, in 2003, the AIPA was replaced, by the Centro Nazionale per l'Informatica nella Pubblica Amministrazione[3] (CNIPA). In 2009, CNIPA was succeeded by the Ente nazionale per la digitalizzazione della pubblica amministrazione[4] (DigitPA). The DigitPA was then subsumed, along with the functions of two other public bodies, into the AgID, the latest digital agency created in August 2012.

Rewinding to 1993: the AIPA 'operates under the aegis of the Italian cabinet, has technical and functional autonomy and shall form its own independent opinions'. In fact, Italy's first public-sector digital agency was tasked with both the oversight of the public ICT market (reporting on the technical-economic congruity of the biggest contracts signed by the State administrative bodies) and the promotion and realization of large-scale infrastructure projects (such as the RUPA[5] electronic PA network—completed in 2000 in accordance with the Department of Public Service's legislative and regulatory framework) or the building of networks to connect the information systems of the individual administrations. Other functions included monitoring public ICT programmes and producing annual reports for both the Government and Parliament. In early 1994, Chief Information Systems Officers were appointed at all the central administrations.

In 2000, external forces in the form of the global digital revolution and European momentum pushed the Italian government to sharpen its focus on ICT policies and approve the national eGovernment Action Plan. The aim was to give cohesive direction to the various attempts to improve the quality of public service. This was the first of several eGovernment plans to develop a network that interconnected the information systems of both the local and the central administrations; to implement online public services; to set up two web portal systems, one for citizens and one for business; to integrate the registry offices' databases; and to promote the use of electronic identity

---

[3] Centro Nazionale per l'Informatica nella Pubblica Amministrazione (CNIPA): National eGovernment Center *(our translation)*.

[4] Ente nazionale per la digitalizzazione della pubblica amministrazione (DigitPA): National Agency for a Digital Public Administration *(our translation)*.

[5] Rete unitaria della pubblica amministrazione (RUPA): Consolidated Electronic PA Network *(our translation)*.

cards and digital signatures. The federalist whirlwind that started to sweep Italy in 2001 (which lasted until 2007) then led Parliament to enact a special constitutional law, which put the local administrations (regional governments and municipalities) bang in the middle of the political action, making them the country's principal agents of change.

In 2001, the ruling centre-right party established the Ministry of Innovation and Technologies and its subordinate Department of Digital and Technological Innovation,[6] severing the administrative innovation policies from those of digitization. The appointment of the former head of IBM Italy, Lucio Stanca, as Minister of Innovation and Technologies was the clear opening of a door to the private-sector IT companies that previous governments had kept firmly shut. eGovernment thus became the means to get the different government levels to forge relations of effective institutional cooperation.

In 2002, the government issued a set of objectives that basically converged with those of the eGovernment Action Plan 2000.

In 2003, the downgrading of the AIPA to the CNIPA, with no change to either its institutional location or its mission, more or less put control back in political hands.

In 2004 and 2005, the lack of financial resources (budget cuts of more than 6 %) put the brakes on Italy's digital agenda and sent public-sector ICT spending back to the 1995 level. The government then introduced the regional competence centres to not only recognize and diffuse best practices, but also to get the local administrations to transfer and share their knowledge and skills.

In 2005, the Codice dell'amministrazione digitale (CAD), the Digital Administration Law, gave a legislative anchor and regulatory compass to the country's eGovernment policies and machinery. Basically, CAD aggregates the norms in a similar way to the Austrian law that allows the federal government to define standard products in the ICT field [18]. Also in 2005, Italy's Finance Act gave the CNIPA the task of preparing framework contracts for the procurement of standard ICT services applications (e.g. computer protocols or disaster recovery solutions) and made their use obligatory for the public administrations, except in demonstrable cases of alternative solutions that better meet their specific needs.

In 2006, Prodi's centre-left government remerged the Ministry of Innovation and Technologies into the Ministry of Public Service (a child of the previous centre-right government), bringing them under the leadership of one minister, an arrangement maintained by the successive centre-right executive, which launched yet another PA reform. In 2009, the CNIPA was replaced with the DigitPA, which was given design, technical and operating functions (including technical consulting for both the Prime Minister and the regions, local bodies and other public administrations) but had to contest with the persistent scenario of growing economic constraints. The change of the eGovernment guard from the CNIPA to the DigitPA further centralized the Italian cabinet's control over the country's ICT policies.

In 2012, the technocratic Monti government came to power and instituted the AgID on 7 August. The AgID replaced and absorbed all the various functions previously split across three different public bodies: the DigitPA; the Agency for the Diffusion of

---

[6] In Italian: Dipartimento per la digitalizzazione e innovazione tecnologica.

Innovation Technologies;[7] and the Department of Digital and Technological Innovation. However, the AgID did not inherit the DigitPA's role as sole operator of the PA network, which was transferred to CONSIP, the company set up by the Ministry of the Economy to manage the platform for the online purchase of goods and services. On 6 July 2012, the Monti government made e-procurement obligatory for the entire public sector.

The current centre-left government is increasingly turning the AgID into a technical creature of the executive. Indeed, the digital orchestra is conducted by a special steering committee chaired by the cabinet ministers' delegate; is responsible for identifying priorities of intervention and for monitoring implementation; and has the final say on the PA information systems strategic development model. The steering committee is made up of delegates from the Prime Minister's cabinet office, the Ministry of Economic Development, the Ministry of Education, Universities and Research, the Ministry of Public Administration, the Ministry of Economy and Finance, two delegates from the Conferenza Unificata Stato-Regioni,[8] and members of the newly formed Tavolo permanente per l'innovazione e l'Agenda digitale italiana,[9] an advisory body of innovation experts.

4.1 Outcomes

The eGovernment indices computed by the three transnational bodies of the UN, the OECD and the European Commission can be used to roughly measure and compare the outcomes of the combined actions of Italy's government policies and the interventions made by the Italian digital agency in its various guises.

The UN E-Government Development Index (EGDI) [19], based on a biannual survey, is split into three sub-indices: the Online Service Index (OSI), the Telecommunication Infrastructure Index (TII), and the Human Capital Index (HCI). As explained by the survey authors, the EGDI is not designed to track the development of e-government in absolute terms but to enable comparisons between different countries. Of the meta-regions, Europe, while far from homogeneous, posted the best results in 2014, with France, Holland and the United Kingdom heading up the world's top ten, compared with Italy at 23rd place, up from 32nd in 2012. It is important to note that of the three EGDI sub-indices, the HCI (which basically measures literacy and education) shows only a minimal gap between Italy and the best performers of comparable size (France and the UK), indicating that Italy's low ranking is mainly the fault of the other two indices, i.e., the TII and the OSI. The TII shows that Italy has a lower percentage of internet users (58 % versus 83 % in France and 87 % in the UK) and fewer wired broadband subscriptions per 100 inhabitants (22 versus 37 in France and 34 in the UK), while the OSI reveals an even bigger divergence, with Italy's online service uptake standing at 67 % compared with 88 % for France and 79 % for the UK.

---

[7] Agenzia per la diffusione delle tecnologie per l'innovazione: Agency for the Diffusion of Innovation Technologies *(our translation)*.

[8] Conferenza Unificata Stato-Regioni: State-Regions Unified Conference *(our translation)*.

[9] Tavolo permanente per l'innovazione e l'Agenda digitale italiana: Permanent Table for Innovation and the Italian Digital Agenda *(our translation)*.

The OSI result is especially significant because it concerns eGovernment itself, while the TII and the HCI can be seen as indicators of the preconditions needed to use the services. In fact, the survey built the OSI around six thematic sub-themes: whole-of-government, multichannel service delivery, bridging the digital divide, increasing usage, open government, and e-participation, which are precisely the areas that Italy worked hard to implement in 2012–2014, and that enabled it to leap nine rungs higher. Indeed, the OSI data of the earlier 2012 survey [20] shows Italy with 50 %, France 77 %, and the UK 85 %. Nevertheless, that big improvement demands closer scrutiny in order to understand, for example, the higher degree of internet use (the so-called degree of uptake) at which the citizens and firms of Italy interacted with the public authorities in 2014 compared with 2012.

On the other hand, the OECD data for 2011 [21] confirms Italy's unsatisfactory performance compared to France, the UK, and the OECD average generally, indicating that only those Italian firms with more than 250 workers used the internet to expedite PA business (e.g., obtaining information, downloading and sending forms, or completing administrative procedures and case handling) to a degree closer to France and the UK, and above the OECD average. That is well below the internet uptake target of around 75 % for all of Italy's firms, far lower than the OECD average (88 %) and nowhere near the 90 % of France and the UK. As the OECD itself points out, the index reveals a huge divergence in uptake between Italy's large and small enterprises (p. 154). Moreover, it underscores that Italian citizen uptake also fell far short of the OECD average in 2011, at approximately 25 % versus 65 % ([21], p. 157), a bottom-feeder in second-to-last place, beating only Chile.

The European Commission's 2014 data for Italy are similar to those of the UN. Notably, the Digital Economy and Society Index (DESI) 2015 [22] is a composite index that, unlike the EGDI, surveys not only a nation's eGovernment status, but also the overall digitization of both society and the economy. That said, one of the five indicators is Digital Public Services (DPS), which ranks Italy 15th in Europe (with France 8th and the UK 11th). Even though this result (0.42) was a tad short of the European average (0.47), it is the best indicator of all five of the sub-indices that make up DESI (which places Italy 25th). However, it is fairly meaningful that both the European Commission DPS index and the UN OSI, each designed to cover different dimensions, give similar rankings to all three countries.

In short, the transnational indices show that while Italy has improved its worldwide ranking and shortened the distance that sets it apart from France and the UK in the past two years, it still has much ground to cover. It should be noted also that the UN EGDI comprises indicators that are both complementary and "enabling" to eGovernment, which, as mentioned above, are more indicative of the *preconditions* needed to develop a digital government.

5   Discussion

We can identify three interrelated perspectives – structural-instrumental, cultural and environmental – that have affected the steering of Italy's digital agenda. The idea of setting up new arm's length bodies (or agencification) can be seen as a process of organizational differentiation meant as the variation in formal structure and orientation from one institution to another to deal with the variety of tasks in uncertain environments. In the case of AIPA, this organizational design choice was a deliberate change in response to an emergent issue, i.e., the steering of the ICT-enabled transformation of Italy's PA. The then ministers had assumed that 'going digital' meant not only the computerization of the public processes and services, but also the rewriting of the ground rules: 'rule-based information technologies alter the template on which service activities are conducted, and facilitate the application of ever more powerful computing tools to services that are often fundamentally information based' [23: 135].

In fact, in the early 1990s, a period in which only a few Italian PAs had embraced the digital culture, the AIPA was empowered by both the regulatory framework and the need to concentrate and develop the capabilities required to launch and govern the ICT strategies. Adopting an instrumental view confirms that a cross-cutting issue perceived as 'not working' by the political leaders of the time helped create 'a readiness to look for new solutions' [18: 10], including the birth of a single-purpose digital agency. This favourable climate and an autonomous statute enabled the legitimization of the AIPA and weakened the sovereignty of the ICT providers. The infrastructural projects and the diverse technical standards that enhanced the capacity of the administrations 'to share and integrate information across both traditional and new organizational boundaries' [24: 7] helped to spur the modernization of both the PA and the country itself.

Nevertheless, a predominantly technocratic approach, heedless of the domestic administrative and institutional context, is likely to fail [18, 25–27]. In fact, as soon as the realization dawned that the AIPA projects also promoted greater uniformity between the State's administrative apparatuses, it sparked a situation of opposition and conflict [8]. The strongly embedded culture of the government ministries often succeeded in defusing the external pressures applied by the agency and its successors to drive change, and, not surprisingly, although the less controversial of the planned changes (or those more compatible with the prevailing political-administrative culture and the established routines) were implemented, other of the digital agency's projects remained just that, and never even saw the light of day.

In more recent years, the myth perspective whereby a better-organized public sector corresponds to an ICT-driven public sector has gained legitimacy and, as a result, spurred eGovernment in Italy. For example, in June 2014 it became obligatory for all Italian PAs and their suppliers to use exclusively electronic systems for the billing and filing of accounting documents. Interestingly, this reform package meshed with a broader transnational project, the EU's payment-integration initiative for the simplification of bank transfers denominated in Euro (Single Euro Payments Area, or SEPA). Seen from an institutional-environmental perspective, a favourable culture and support from the environment can propel digital transformation.

5.1 The Different Political Takes on Modernization

The coming into power of a succession of governments, each with their own particular idea of how to modernize Italy's PA and bring the country into the 21st century, significantly increased the cast of ICT policy actors. The centre-left governments approached the reorganization of both the PA and the processes as a joint affair, mapping a long and complex journey towards the integration of the various back-offices. On the other hand, the centre-right governments saw the front-office services as a more immediate way to pluck the fruits of visibility and consensus.

The result of these significantly divergent approaches can be seen in the repeated merging and demerging since 2003 of the Dept. of Public Service and the Dept. of Digital and Technological Innovation, before both were ultimately abolished in 2012 and their mandates transferred to the AgID. The volatile institutional context has shifted and blurred the objectives and the priorities of the eGovernment plans, the implementation of which, given their nature and Italy's infrastructural shortcomings, otherwise would have been spread over the medium to longer term.

5.2 Multiple Roles and Motives of Misalignment

Despite being officially established as an authority, in reality the AIPA combined the features of a ministerial department with those of an agency. The multiple roles attributed to the AIPA shrouded it in ambiguity [28]. Indeed, it was at the same time the regulator tasked with redressing the imbalances of an oligopolistic market dominated by suppliers, the 'watchdog' of the PAs and the ICT providers, to reduce opportunistic behaviour (and possible collusion), and the front-line market operator sent into the field for particularly important interventions. As Halligan says in his Australian study [29: 448], each of these roles "captures an organizational imperative that is externally grounded and usually has a basis in the agency's empowering legislation. Each has a different external driver, respectively: customers, clients, competitors, and politicians". The friction caused by cramming four models into one organization invariably sparks tensions and conflicts.

There are three interrelated reasons for this misalignment between the various digital agencies and the individual PAs. *First*, the objectives set out in the government guidelines are either incredibly vague or, to the contrary, fix on a specific detail. The difficulty of identifying the objectives has been compounded by the difficulty of assessing the *ex-ante*, *in itinere* and *ex-post* effects of the ICT-enabling projects. In fact, the 1990s saw the AIPA struggle to monitor both the spending and the number of ICT platforms and services purchased by the various administrations. *Second*, the negative economic cycle has ruled out the use of financial incentives to get the PAs to invest in technological and organizational innovation. Moreover, not all the administrations had the capabilities needed to launch large-scale projects or were even interested enough to measure the results of the initiatives implemented. Hence, many of the "zero-cost" innovations promoted by the AIPA et al. remained on the drawing board [30]. *Finally*, even though each ministry had been asked to appoint a Chief Information Officer (CIO) to specifically facilitate matters with each PA, the role was never fully recognized, which left the digital agency without the liaison officers, i.e., the unique points of reference, it needed to fulfil its mandate.

Interestingly, the EU has had a clearly observable impact. The momentum that spurred Italy's digital agenda in 2000 coincided with the launch of the eGovernment plans formulated to meet the targets set by the European Commission's Lisbon strategy. Seen from a myth perspective, these projects were part of a more general trend that the 'old-style' [25: xiv] governments of the time were eager to embrace as a way to gain international legitimacy.

6 Final Remarks

The two original features of this paper are, first, the decision to investigate the combined effects of eGovernment and agencification at the public-sector macro level and, second, the adoption of a contextual lens [27] to study the evolution of an Italian public agency. Although the analysis of the arm's length body AIPA and its successors CNIPA, DigitPA and AgID has greatly enriched our knowledge of the digital government approach taken by Italy's political leaders, we will limit ourselves here to summing up the key findings. First, but by no means unexpected, is the fact that the single-purpose agency investigated in no way mirrors the ideal type advocated in the mainstream literature on agencification. Second, the digital agency had much more power to decide its objectives in the period 1993–1999, while the relative ministry's assessment of its performance and senior public managers was very low-key. After 1999, the AIPA and its successors gradually lost their autonomy and relevance, taking on more the guise of a government operational arm. Third, the article reveals a considerable rhetorical dimension among the many variables that shape the course and outcome of Italy's eGovernment policies [31], as well as the inability of the independent agency mandated to steer and reinforce the digital transformation of the public sector and, thus, to catalyze major change. Indeed, the actual steering action is so diluted that it bears no resemblance at all to the ICT-driven change boldly promised by each new Italian government, no matter their political affiliation.

Looping back to the first RQ *'What institutional responses has Italy's government come up with to ensure the governance of its public-sector ICT policies?'* we can say that the proliferation of the agencies was originally driven by the absolute strategic approach taken to the institutional design implementations from 1999 to the present. The analysis has shown that Italy has done very little to improve the effectiveness of its eGovernment policies. At the same time, the regulatory framework used to govern the public-sector ICT strategies has not only grown unwieldy, but places too much emphasis on the technological, instrumental aspects of digital government, ignoring the bigger picture of digital citizenship, to which all the governments in question have paid only fleeting attention.

To respond to the second RQ *'What explains the continuity and discontinuity of those responses?'* the main variables were analyzed using a theoretical lens sensitive to contextual factors [1, 32, 33]. Applying this interpretive key to the Italian case shows that the wobbly path of continuity and discontinuity that has taken the spin out of Italy's digital agenda can be attributed to specificities of a structural, cultural and environmental nature. What unique features were decisive in shaping the events that in many ways recur around the world? No general answer may be attempted here, even though, in a country like Italy with a decidedly Napoleonic administrative landscape, the absence of a permanent strategic body at the highest level is certainly a primary factor. The weakness shown in the early formative years has stunted the evolution and scope of action of the digital agency, which found itself in the unenviable position of having to run a strategically decisive process in the life of the country with a toolbox consisting of not much more than the power drill and screws needed to put up a framework of technical rules and regulations. However, the pre-eminently cognitive aim of the paper means that the analysis makes no attempt to correlate or map the dynamic interaction of the identified explicative variables, although we plan to redress that limitation in the next phase of this fledgling research path.

References

1. Pierre, J.: Context, theory and rationality: an uneasy relationship? In: Pollitt, C. (ed.) Context in Public Policy and Management, pp. 124–130. Edward Elgar, Cheltenham (2013)
2. Salamon, L.M. (ed.): The Tools of Government. A Guide to the New Governance. Oxford University Press, Oxford (2002)
3. Majone, G.: The agency model: the growth of regulation and regulatory institutions in the European Union. Eipascope **1997**, 1–6 (1997)
4. Wettenhall, R.: Agencies and non-departmental public bodies. Public Manag. Rev. **7**, 615–635 (2005)
5. Yin, R.K.: Case Study Research, 2nd edn. Sage, Thousand Oaks (1994)
6. Pollitt, C., Bouckaert, G.: Public Management Reform. A Comparative Analysis: New Public Management, Governance, and the Neo-Weberian State, 3rd edn. Oxford University Press, Oxford (2011)
7. Mele, V.: Innovation policy in Italy (1993–2002): Understanding the invention and persistence of a public management reform. Governance **23**, 251–276 (2010)
8. Christensen, T., Lægreid, P., Roness, P.G., Rovik, K.A.: Organization Theory and the Public Sector. Routledge, Abingdon (2007)
9. Christensen, T., Lægreid, P.: Complexity and hybrid public administration. theoretical and empirical challenges. Public Organ. Rev. **11**, 407–423 (2011)
10. Chikalov, I.: Introduction. In: Chikalov, I. (ed.) Average Time Complexity of Decision Trees. ISRL, vol. 21, pp. 1–14. Springer, Heidelberg (2011)
11. Yildiz, M.: Big questions of e-government research. Inf. Polity **17**, 343–355 (2012)
12. Dahl, R.A., Lindblom, C.E.: Politics, Economics, and Welfare. Transaction Publishers, Piscataway (1953)
13. Andrews, R., Beynon, M.J., McDermott, A.M.: Organizational capability in the public sector: a configurational approach. J. Publ. Adm. Res. Theory, 1–29 (2015)
14. Höpfl, H.: Bureaucratic and post-bureaucratic accountability in Britain: some sceptical reflections. In: Clegg, S., Harris, M., Höpfl, H. (eds.) Managing Modernity: Beyond Bureaucracy?, pp. 30–55. Oxford University Press, Oxford (2011)
15. Meyer, J.W., Rowan, B.: Institutionalized organizations: formal structure as myth and ceremony. Am. J. Sociol. **83**, 340–363 (1977)
16. Myers, M.D.: Qualitative Research in Business & Management. SAGE Publications, London (2009)
17. Capano, G.: Administrative traditions and policy change: when policy paradigms matter. The case of Italian administrative reform during the 1990s. Public Adm. **81**, 781–801 (2003)
18. Pollitt, C. (ed.): Governments for the Future. Ministry of Finance, Helsinki (2013)
19. United Nations: E-Government Survey 2014. United Nations, New York (2014)
20. United Nations: E-Government Survey 2012. United Nations, New York (2012)
21. OECD: Government at a glance. OECD, Paris (2013)

22. European Commission. Digital Agenda Scoreboard 2014 – Italy. http://ec.europa.eu/digital-agenda/en/digital-agenda-scoreboard (2014)
23. Zysman, J., Breznitz, D.: Double bind: governing the economy in an ICT era. Governance **25**, 129–150 (2012)
24. Pardo, T.A., Nam, T., Burke, G.B.: E-Government interoperability: interaction of policy, management, and technology dimensions. Soc. Sci. Comput. Rev. **30**, 7–23 (2012)
25. Margetts, H.: Information Technology in Government: Britain and America. Routledge, London (2012)
26. Casalino, N., Buonocore, F., Rossignoli, C., Ricciardi, F.: Transparency, openness and knowledge sharing for rebuilding and strengthening government institutions. In: WBE 2013 Conference, IASTED-ACTA Press Zurich, Innsbruck, Austria (2013)
27. Christensen, T., Lægreid, P.: Context and administrative reforms: a transformative approach. In: Pollitt, C. (ed.) Context in Public Policy and Management, pp. 131–156. Edward Elgar, Cheltenham (2013)
28. Natalini, A.: Le riforme amministrative tra vincoli istituzionali e processo di cambiamento: il caso dell'informatizzazione. Rivista Italiana di Politiche Pubbliche, pp. 105–132 (2006)
29. Halligan, J.: Advocacy and innovation in interagency management: the case of centrelink. Governance **20**, 445–467 (2007)
30. Sorrentino, M., De Marco, M.: Implementing e-government in hard times: when the past is wildly at variance with the future. Inf. Polity **18**, 331–342 (2013)
31. Kraemer, K., King, J.L.: Information technology and administrative reform: will e-government be different? Int. J. Electron. Gov. Res. **2**, 1–20 (2006)
32. Lenk, K.: Reform opportunities missed: will the innovative potential of information systems in public administration remain dormant forever? Inf. Commun. Soc. **1**, 163–181 (1998)
33. Depaoli, P., Sorrentino, M., De Marco, M.: E-services in the ageing society: an Italian perspective. J. e-Gov. **36**, 105–118 (2013)

E-Government Systems Design
and Implementation in Developed
and Developing Countries:
Results from a Qualitative Analysis

Catherine G. Mkude and Maria A. Wimmer[(✉)]

Institute for IS Research, University of Koblenz-Landau,
Universitätsstr. 1, 56070 Koblenz, Germany
{cmkude,wimmer}@uni-koblenz.de

Abstract. Developing countries continue to rely on solutions and research from developed countries as they strive for more successful e-government endeavours. Different authors argue that the transfer of solutions and expertise among developed and developing countries is not a straightforward task and the context of countries is a significant influencing factor. This paper investigates and compares e-government design and implementation approaches in developed and developing countries. Along the qualitative analysis, differences and similarities in the approaches are highlighted, and recommendations are brought forward. The paper adds value to current e-government developments, particularly in developing countries, by eliciting approaches applied in developed countries and their impacts to more successful e-government implementation.

Keywords: E-government design and implementation · Developed countries · Developing countries · Qualitative analysis

1 Introduction

The last United Nations (UN) e-government survey reveals that governments in developing countries have recognisably advanced in the area [14]. The contribution of mobile phones and technologies is highly acknowledged in such advancements, particularly in the provision and adoption of online public services by governments and citizens [9, 14]. To support developing countries in keeping pace with the innovations and developments of e-government and in realising more successful e-government implementation, the sharing and transfer of expertise, experiences, design approaches and solutions among developed and developing countries is crucial. However, a direct transfer of solutions is cautioned in literature because a country's context is not necessarily reflected in system designs [5]. Also, contextual factors of countries such as culture, infrastructure, economic growth and ICT capabilities ought to be considered when transferring solutions [2]. Sæbø points out that knowledge of e-government in developing countries, is "mainly based on research in developed countries" [12].

Following these arguments, this paper has two objectives to bridging the gap between developed and developing countries: (1) to investigate and compare e-government design

© IFIP International Federation for Information Processing 2015
E. Tambouris et al. (Eds.): EGOV 2015, LNCS 9248, pp. 44–58, 2015.
DOI: 10.1007/978-3-319-22479-4_4

and implementation approaches in developed and developing countries along differences, similarities and their impacts; and (2) to bring forward recommendations for more successful implementation of e-government endeavours in developing countries based on findings of (1). The term 'e-government approaches' is used throughout the paper in a general manner to incorporate methods of analysis, design, implementation and evaluation as well as overall frameworks (for distinct purposes such as strategic, legal, management, architecture, interoperability, technological development or evaluation) that are employed by governments to support better achievement of the envisaged objectives. The primary focus of study is the national level, and the research is guided by a strategic framework for e-government implementation as put forward in [7]. Practitioners of e-government - particularly of developing countries – can benefit from the insights and lessons of the qualitative analysis and from the recommendations put forward to successfully implement e-government.

The remainder of the paper is as follows: Sect. 2 presents the research design and methods used, followed by the analysis and comparison of approaches of e-government design and implementation employed in different countries (Sect. 3). Recommendations derived from the data analysis are synthesised in Sect. 4. In Sect. 5, we conclude with suggestions for future research.

2   Research Design

Comparing approaches of e-government design and implementation in developed and developing countries is grounded in qualitative research. This is because the objectives are not particularly geared towards generalisation and representativeness of samples in empirical research, which are among the key features of quantitative approaches [4, 10]. A qualitative approach is also selected because of its relatively smaller sample in which the researcher acquires a comprehensive overview of different contexts to draw conclusions rather than statistical measures of results ([10], p. 259). Based on the objectives, interviews and desk research were selected as research methods. The design of the interviews and the systematic analysis of literature through desk research were guided by the framework for strategic design of e-government suggested in [7]. The framework helped to identify the areas of investigation deemed important to e-government design and implementation at national level.

The strategic framework for designing e-government in [7] compares nine e-government approaches identified in literature and proposes five core activities of e-government implementation to better achieve the overall objectives: (1) developing a vision, (2) developing a strategy, (3) introducing programmes for implementing the strategy, (4) running concrete projects, and (5) evaluating the achievements of projects towards strategy and vision. The framework emphasises a clear relationship and feedback loop among the activities so policy makers are able to evaluate the achievement of objectives of each activity by the subsequent activity. Further literature review revealed the significance of e-government sustainability [1, 3, 6] as a key principle of strategic design of e-government. Accordingly, the principle is investigated in this paper, too.

The interview protocol consisted of 30 questions (mix of open and closed), which were grouped into six parts (A – F) grounded on the strategic framework for designing e-government. Part A consisted of demographic questions. Part B collected information about the existence of a vision and strategy in a country. Part C investigated the presence of programmes (see [7] for a definition of 'programmes') that support the implementation of the strategy. The purpose of part D was to find out what approaches countries employed for successfully implementing e-government projects. This part investigated aspects such as criteria for selection of projects, interoperability and development methods. Part E investigated evaluation and sustainability approaches. Part F inquired recommendations for successful implementation of e-government.

The interviews were conducted in person (at the IFIP EGOV conference in 2013) and via VoIP technologies to reach experts beyond the conference in developed and developing countries in the time span of end 2013 - mid 2014. The experts were selected from the pool of contacts of the authors – one per country, with a balance among developed and developing countries. The interviews took 40–60 min to allow in-depth interrogation. The transcribed interviews were sent to the interviewees for accuracy and additional comments. The authors ensured that the responses were recorded and verified to ensure accuracy and reliability of the findings as is suggested by Riege [11]. Data obtained from the interviews was analysed qualitatively to search for patterns, similarities and differences in the approaches.

Desk research was conducted in parallel to the interviews to triangulate and validate data collected from the interviews. The authors sought official documentations such as e-government strategies, interoperability frameworks and architectures and evaluation frameworks, and evaluated the suitability of documents with the interviewees so to address drawbacks of desk research such as access restrictions or lack of control over data quality (see [8, 13] for more details).

3   Analysis of e-Government Approaches in Developed and Developing Countries

3.1   Sample Selection and Demographic Information of Experts

The authors aimed at interviewing at minimum one person per country and at investigating a reasonable set of countries. A good balance of interviews from developed vs. developing counties was aimed at, with a minimum of five interviews per country group. However, the selection of countries was challenging because the interview required participants who are knowledgeable of e-government endeavours in their countries at the national level and that the interviewees bring 40–60 min of their time. These aspects presented a significant geographical constraint to approach the 'right and willing' participants. The candidates were selected from the pool of contacts in the e-government networks they are involved.

In total, 20 experts from developed and 21 from developing countries were approached. The developed countries are Australia, Austria, Czech Republic, Canada, United States of America, Denmark, Sweden, Malta, Saudi Arabia, United Kingdom, Germany, Netherlands, Russia, Singapore, South Korea, Japan, Finland, Greece, Norway and Poland. Eleven experts agreed to be and were interviewed.

The developing countries are Tunisia, Turkey, Sri Lanka, China, India, Kazakhstan, Mexico, Georgia, Lebanon, Jordan, Afghanistan, Brazil, Kenya, Egypt, Uganda, South Africa, Nigeria, Gabon, Ghana, Malawi and Rwanda. Seven experts agreed to be and were interviewed. Table 1 presents the demographic information of the interviewees.

Table 1. Interviewees' demographic information (part A of questionnaire)

Country (country code)	Domain of work	Research discipline/ thematic background	Years of experience
Developed countries			
1. Austria (AT)	Public sector	E-Government	>15
2. Canada (CA)	Public sector	E-Government	18
3. Denmark (DK)	Public Sector	E-Government	10
4. Germany (DE)	Academia and public sector	Information systems	10
5. Malta (MT)	Public sector	Computer science	20
6. The Netherlands (NL)	Academia	E-Government	12
7. Russia (RU)	Academia	E-Government	5
8. Saudi Arabia (SA)	Academia and public sector	E-Government	6
9. Sweden (SE)	Public sector	E-Government	5
10. Switzerland (CH)	Academia and public sector	E-Government, Computer science	5
11. United Kingdom (UK)	Public sector	E-Government, E-Participation	13
Developing countries			
1. Egypt (EG)	Public sector	E-Government	12
2. Georgia (GE)	Public sector	Jurisprudence and E-Government	5
3. Lebanon (LB)	Academia and public Sector	Computer science	7
4. Malawi (MW)	Academia	Information systems	5
5. Mexico (MX)	Academia	Public administration	12
6. Nigeria (NG)	Public sector	E-Government	6
7. Tunisia (TN)	Public sector	Public administration	5

3.2   Analysis of Results Along the Interview Protocol, Parts B - E

The results are presented along the five activities suggested in the strategic framework for e-government of [7], with the addition of sustainability (along evaluation). The italic entries with *Q:* correspond to the interview questions.

Part B: Vision and Strategy Formulation
Q: Is there an e-government vision and strategy at the national level?

10 out of 11 experts of developed countries and 6 out of 7 experts from developing countries confirmed the existence of a vision and strategy at the national level. In CA, the Digital Canada 150 was published in April 2014, which was after the interview, i.e. today, all 11 developed countries where we conducted interviews have a vision and strategy in place at national level. However, the respondent of CA stated that lacking a strategy at the national level led to the absence of a standardised approach and to non-exploitation of synergies across the country to implement e-government projects, which also led to high costs. The respondent argued further that solutions are not

interoperable due to the lack of a centralised approach. Furthermore, the respondent stated that "*this situation is worse to handle in a federal country because there is no standardised direction in coordinating vertical and horizontal level investments of the government*".

The formulation of a vision and strategy at the national level in NG is an on-going process. General guidelines for e-government implementation exist in ministries, departments and agencies. The respondent stated that the absence of the strategy results in a lack of a standardised approach across the country to implement e-government projects, presence of dismantled programs and projects with objectives that are not necessarily aligned, waste of resources and redundancy of solutions.

Q: Is the implementation of the strategy obligatory, optional but recommended or optional and not recommended to other government levels?

In developed countries, the implementation of the strategies is obligatory in MT, SA, DK and RU and optional but recommended in AT, CH, SE and DE. The implementation in NL and UK includes obligatory and optional but recommended facets depending on aspects addressed by the strategy. Respondents from CH, DE and NL revealed that the high level of autonomy in lower levels of the government contribute to the implementation of the strategies being not entirely obligatory. Respondents from AT, CH and DE also mentioned that the non-obligation is due to the federal structure of the governments. The respondent from AT explained that internal discussions, collaboration and common agreements among the federal government and lower levels of the government improve consistent and coordinated implementation of e-government.

In developing countries, the implementation of the strategy is obligatory in LB and GE, and optional but recommended in TN, MW and EG. The respondent from GE stated that the strategy has a legal force; therefore all government organisations are highly obliged to implement the objectives specified therein. The implementation of the strategy in MX includes obligatory and optional but recommended facets depending on aspects addressed in the strategy. The overall approach of implementing the strategies in TN and EG have been disrupted by political revolutions. For example, the respondent from EG commented that "*after the revolution, the national focus shifted from development aspects, particularly e-government implementation, to the turbulences and security. Therefore at the moment, ministries are not as obligated to implement the strategy as before*".

Q: What impacts does the answer in the previous question have to e-government systems design at national level?

All respondents, regardless if obligatory or optional but recommended, reported that the presence of an e-government strategy at the national level helps to enhance adoption, to ensure political support at the national level and to provide a national framework for implementation of strategic objectives. Table 2 sums up the impacts reported by experts on obligatory and optional but recommended facets of implementing the e-government strategy. As can be noted, the obligatory strategy has more positive impacts on implementing e-government than optional but recommended ones. In AT, where the strategy is optional but recommended, the presence of collaboration, internal discussions and common agreements among different levels of the government strengthen the implementation of effective, efficient and interoperable e-government solutions.

Table 2. Impacts of obligatory vs. optional but recommended e-government strategies

Impacts if obligatory strategy	Impacts if optional but recommended strategy
Cost savings due to a centralised structure of planning and implementing e-government;	Provision of more opportunities for bottom up initiatives that are not necessarily identified by the centralised strategy;
Comprehensive and consistent provision of public services across the country;	Lack of coordination in achieving the objectives of the strategy;
Enhanced assurance that the implementations are directed towards achieving the goals and objectives of the strategy;	Lack of standardised approach towards implementing e-government;
A unified approach towards implementing e-government;	Low cooperation among public sectors at different levels of government particularly in federal countries;
Enhanced coordination and collaboration in achieving the objectives of the strategy	Lack of clear alignment between strategy and projects implemented at different levels of government

Q: How do you ensure the alignment of the objectives of the strategy to the vision?
In 9 out of 10 developed countries and in 4 out of 6 developing countries, mechanisms are in place for ensuring that the objectives of the strategy are aligned to the vision. The following mechanisms were mentioned (with respective country indications):

- The same organisation is responsible to formulate both a vision and a strategy – AT, UK, CH, SE, NL, DE, SA, MT, DK, MX, MW, LB, GE
- Re-evaluation and feedback of how the strategy impacts and realises the vision – AT
- Constant negotiations and communications involving representatives of the government at different levels and use of alignment scenarios – NL

No specific mechanisms exist in RU, TN and EG.

Part C: Programmes Supporting the Implementation of Vision and Strategy
Q: Are there any programmes that support implementation of the strategy?

In 7 out 11 developed countries (AT, NL, SE, SA, MT, DK and RU) and in 4 out of 7 developing countries (TN, LB, EG and GE), respective programmes to implement the e-government vision and strategy are in place.
    Q: What is the impact(s) of the presence or absence of the programmes?

Table 3 indicates the impact of the presence or absence of programmes at the national level. Respondents from DE and CA, both federal countries, stressed on the resulting different approaches towards achieving the objectives of the strategy and lack of coordination as the most observed and significant impacts.

Table 3. Results regarding impacts of presence or absence of programmes

Impacts of presence of programmes	Impacts of absence of programmes
Holistic management of projects that they don't exist in silos;	Different approaches towards achieving objectives of the strategy;
Provide an end-to-end of projects to strategy and vision particularly in large scale implementations of the strategy;	Lack of clear alignment of projects to the objectives of the strategy;
Ensure coordination across the country in implementing the strategy;	Uneven distribution of e-government progress, particularly in federal governments;
Create transparency and shared understanding of the development efforts;	Lack of coordination in implementing the projects at national level
Benefits and value are the foci of programmes unlike projects which are often measured by objectives, deliverables and milestones;	
Concrete definition of measures and actions for implementing the strategy including setting of priority themes	

Q: How do you ensure the alignment of the programmes to the strategy?

8 developed countries and 3 developing countries have mechanisms in place for ensuring the alignment. The following mechanisms were named – with country indication:

- The same organisation is responsible for formulating the strategy and for defining the programmes – AT, DK, SE, MT, SA, LB, GE
- Constant communication among stakeholders involved in planning and implementing the programmes – AT, NL
- Top down approach of formulating the programmes by formulating the programmes from the objectives of the strategy – MT, RU
- Demonstrating alignment of programmes to the strategy by indicators – SE, EG

Part D: Implementation Through Projects
Q: How do you ensure the alignment of the projects to the programs?

All developed countries and 3 developing countries mention mechanisms for ensuring the alignment as follows (with respective country-indication):

- Assessment and evaluation of projects by experts based on their business cases to ensure that they are aligned to the programmes – AT, NL, DK, SE, RU, EG
- Presence of the same organisation/committee that formulated the strategy, identified the programmes and selected the projects – SE, AT, DK, MT, SA, LB, GE
- Collaborative meetings and discussions when selecting projects and transparency in implementation of projects – AT
- Presence of an e-government commission, which is responsible for cross-agency cooperation and coordination – GE

Q: Is there an e-government interoperability framework at the national level?

An interoperability framework exists in 9 out of 11 developed countries, except in CA and CH. Among the developing countries, an interoperability framework is in place only in NG (it is currently under review). However, all respondents in developing countries indicated that the development of the framework is on-going. Respondents from LB, MX, EG and GE reported that there are interoperability standards but they are developed in an ad hoc manner and are not institutionalised.

Q: Which challenges have you identified on organisational, legal, semantic and technical interoperability? What possible solutions exist to address these challenges?

A total of 13 challenges – 3 legal, 5 organisational, 2 semantic and 3 technical – were identified by the respondents with proposed solutions (except, CA and SA, where the expert did not provide answers to the question). Due to space limitation, only summaries and not the individual answers are reported here. The presence of legacy systems was identified as a technical challenge in developing countries and not in developed countries. All other challenges were mentioned by respondents from both groups. Respondents argued that legal and organisational challenges are more prominent than semantic and technical challenges because the latter are mostly resolved by high availability of advanced technologies to support semantic and technical interoperability. Legal and organisational interoperability challenges are e.g. grounded in different and long-term social circumstances and organisational structures and the long time required to change legislation compared to advancements made in e-government and innovative ICT. Respondents emphasised that the development of an interoperability framework that addresses the challenges is vital to ensure interoperable e-government solutions. Also, such a framework needs continuous improvement. Adding to this, the respondent from GE stated: *"given the significance of an interoperability framework in implementing e-government, we currently develop the framework with legal obligations attached to it"*.

Q: Is there a project development method at the national level? Is the method obligatory, optional but recommended or optional and not recommended to other government levels? What are its objectives?

6 out of 11 developed countries have a project development method in place, which is obligatory in DK, AT, MT and SA and optional but recommended in SE and UK. None of the experts of developing countries reported the existence of a project development method at the national level. Table 4 presents the methods and their objectives mentioned by experts (except by the expert of MT who could not provide details due to confidentiality reasons).

Q: What is the impact of the absence of a project development method at the national level?

Respondents from the countries that have no project development method at the national level pointed out that the impacts of this absence include among others a high fragmentation and heterogeneous solutions, a higher number of solutions that are not interoperable, a duplication of efforts and waste of money, a lack of learning from the projects' results by organisations, a lack of coordination in the development processes and in the use of required infrastructure, an increased uncertainty in the outcomes of the projects, and a lack of proper documentation in place.

Table 4. Summary of project development methods and objectives in use

Country: Method	Objectives
DK: Common government IT project model	Contribute to a better and more uniform planning, management and implementation of IT projects
SE: Method Development Coalition	Provide a common framework to ensure quality, meet common expectations and demands on development
UK: Agile method	Ability to better meet user needs;
	Improve quality and visibility of the method;
	Reduce cost to market
SA: YESSER software development life cycle	Assure predictability of work activities and achieving approximately the same deliverables with the same resources;
	Increase productivity and the probability that the deliverables produced will be the desired deliverables;
	Increase awareness of the required standards;
	Improve schedule and budget predictability;
	Increase quality and customers satisfaction
DE: V-Modell XT	Minimise project risks;
	Improve and guarantee quality;
	Reduce total cost over the entire project and system life cycle;
	Improve communication between stakeholders

Q: Is there an architecture repository at the national level? What are its objectives? What is the level of reusability of the artefacts?

Architecture repositories exist in 7 out of 11 developed countries (not in UK, RU and CA), while none of the developing countries have architecture repositories in place. However, the respondent from LB stated that there is a high emphasis of sharing and reuse of resources across the public sector.

The objectives of the repositories are to provide a reference point for project developments and architectural works, to provide consistency of the artefacts for reuse in new projects, to achieve synergies and sharing of artefacts, to promote reusability, to improve interoperability, to reduce costs by reducing duplication of artefacts and to improve quality in projects by providing quality assured artefacts.

The artefacts are extensively reused in NL and DK, reused in SA, DE, SE and AT, and rather not reused in MT (scale: extensively reused, reused, rather not reused, not reused). The respondent in MT stated that the repository is rather not reused because reuse is not institutionalised. The establishment of the repository in the UK is an on-going process. The UK respondent also stated that resource sharing is among the core technology codes of practice that *"must be demonstrated for the project to proceed"*. The sharing and re-use of ICT components and solutions across government is also emphasised in UK's Government Digital Service (GDS) design manual.[1]

---

[1] See: https://www.gov.uk/service-manual/technology/code-of-practice.html#the-technology-code-of-practice (last access: 2015/03/15).

Part E1: Evaluation *Q: Is there an evaluation framework at the national level? Is the framework obligatory, optional but recommended or optional and not recommended?*

At national level, 7 out of 11 developed countries apply evaluation frameworks (except in CA, SE and MT), which are obligatory for all except in AT where the framework is optional but recommended. 2 out of 7 developing countries have evaluation frameworks at the national level – LB (obligatory) and MW (optional but recommended).

Respondents from countries that lack evaluation frameworks at the national level reported impacts such as the lack of a possibility to determine whether the projects have achieved the objectives of the strategy or programmes, decentralised approaches to evaluation across the government, uncertainty whether the project outcomes are the desirable ones depending on time and financial investments, lack of possibility to measure the quality of the projects at the national level and low sustainability of the projects.

Q: Does the framework assess the alignment of the projects' objectives with the objectives of strategy and programmes?

Only in 2 countries, AT and SA, the evaluation frameworks include assessment of the alignment of project objectives with the objectives of both the strategy and programmes. The framework in CH and MW assesses the alignment of project objectives with strategic objectives since there are no programmes in CH and MW.

Part E2: Sustainability *Q: How important do you perceive sustainability to be addressed along project development? How is e-government sustainability ensured at the national level?*

All respondents considered e-government sustainability as a significant factor to be addressed in all e-government projects. A total of 24 sustainability factors were mentioned by respondents from country experts (see Table 5), except from CA, GE, LB and MX. The respondent from DE commented that the use of standards to ensure interoperability is particularly important in federal governments. Further to the sustainability factors identified, respondents were asked to recommend additional factors if the ones that are already in place are insufficient.

4   Recommendations

The results of the analysis of e-government implementation approaches in developed and developing countries reveal findings consistent with the literature and with international surveys: developing countries still lag significantly behind developed countries. We argue that developing countries can learn from experiences of developed countries for more successful e-government endeavours by applying a strategic framework for designing e-government as proposed in [7], and along this, by employing a set of measures to improve quality, efficiency, collaboration and success.

Recommendations for successful e-government implementation were put forward by the respondents in part F of the interview protocol. They are summarised in Table 6 and include political, economic, socio-cultural, technological and legal aspects as well

Table 5. E-government sustainability factors named by respondents

Sustainability factors	In place in (country)	Recommended in (country)
Government commitment to e-government implementation	UK, DK, SA, DE, GE	
Sufficient and continuous funding of e-government initiatives	UK, DE, CH, MT, GE	TN, EG, MW, LB
Continuous control and maintenance of solutions	CH, SA, NL, DE	TN, LB
Use of standards to ensure quality and interoperability	DE, UK, MT, RU	MW, NG, TN, GE, MX, EG, LB
Promote transparency in implementation and evaluation of projects	NL, AT	
Support the implementation of e-government with a legal framework	AT, DE, RU, GE	MX, NG, LB
Centralisation and coordination of e-government implementation at the national level through a centralised organisation	SA, GE	TN
Close linkage of e-government strategies with national development goals and policies in sectors such as health and education	DK, MX	UK
Yearly assessment of projects regarding outcome, prioritisation and sustainability by relevant stakeholders	AT	
Use of robust business cases	DK	
Use of robust guidelines for contracts, developments and implementation procedures of the projects	DK	
Development of reusable solutions	SE	
Ensure relationship and link between the strategy, programmes and projects, and also among different projects	NL	
Track usage of e-services and feedback of users	MT	
Ensure political support and commitment regardless the change in political leadership	DK	NL
Collect, use and disseminate knowledge on e-government implementation across the public sector	SE	
Ensure sufficient ICT infrastructure	RU	
Establish support from experts with a long-term perspective of e-government solutions		SE, EG, LB
Presence of a centralised evaluation framework		NG, MW, EG
Ensure sufficient ICT capacity in public sectors		GE, EG, MW
Ensure coalition and cooperation among ministries		DE, EG
Exercise accountability measures when projects are outsourced to private sectors		UK
Integrate knowledge between researchers and practitioners in public sectors		MT
Citizens' desire for the government to provide e-services		MX

as management aspects of implementing e-government. These recommendations provide a rich addition to current literature of e-government success factors.

Based on the insights from literature and data analysis, the following e-government design and implementation approaches have positive impacts on success e-government implementation and are therefore highly recommended for a transfer to developing countries:

Table 6. Recommendations for successful e-government implementation

Recommendations for successful e-government implementation	Country
Developed and developing countries	
Study and reflect the level of trust of citizens and their willingness in using e-government services when designing e-government strategies	UK, NL, RU, MX
Increase the understanding of the importance of coordination and collaboration in vertical and horizontal government relations in implementing e-government projects. Advantages of this must be made clear	SE, DE, SA, EG, MW, NG, LB, GE
Design e-government strategies whilst reflecting on the local settings of a country – PESTEL factors	NL, RU, UK, MX, EG, LB, TN, MW
Use user-friendly technologies and multi-channel delivery of services to cater the needs of all citizens including online and offline provision of services. Leverage on the opportunities brought by the widespread mobile market	NL, DK, MW, MX, TN
Establish a legal framework to support the implementation of e-government projects and increase an emphasis on data security and protection procedures	UK, EG, GE, MW
Ensure political support and commitment regardless the changes in political system to ensure e-government sustainability	NL, EG, MX, TN
Developed countries	
Use design thinking approaches and engage users in designing and providing e-services. Personalise services to users' conditions, skills and needs to increase the uptake of e-services by the users	UK, NL, CA, DE, RU, AT
Apply stakeholder management methods to ensure inclusion of dynamic groups of stakeholders in designing and implementing e-government solutions	CH, CA, MT
Change the government's role as a sole provider of e-services by encouraging other proprietors and societies to utilise open data and e-participation initiatives to provide public services	UK, CA
Assess the public value generated by the projects	UK, CA
Embed the use of ICT in the overall social welfare. Do not only migrate towards e-services but also use ICT to improve the quality of services provided via non-electronic media	UK
Policy and implementation are too far apart from each other therefore ensure advanced agreements among organisations to improve the implementation of cross-organisational projects	NL
Implementation of projects which are easier to manage and sustain	NL
Top management support in organisations	NL
Do not underestimate the importance of personal interactions e.g. in areas such as education and health. Personal	DK

(Continued)

Table 6. (*Continued*)

Recommendations for successful e-government implementation	Country
Developed and developing countries	
interactions should not be minimised but use ICT to improve the quality of those services	
Ensure obligated adoption of important aspects in e-government implementation for example interoperability standards and principles, evaluation methods and reusability of solutions	SA
Developing countries	
Use measures to ensure interoperability at all levels	GE, MW, LB, MX, EG, TN, NG
Formulate a centralised entity to coordinate, enforce and monitor e-government implementations	EG, LB, NG
Ensure human capacity in developing, implementing and maintaining e-government services and also for the side of users by providing continuous training	MW, NG, LB
Ensure accountability of public managers to the public and the parliament in the development and implementation of ICT solutions	TN

- *Define success factors for e-government that are customised to the country's circumstances.* Developing countries can benefit a lot by specifying success factors for their e-government strategies, programmes and projects, which are customised to their local circumstances in which they operate, and involving political, economic, socio-cultural, technological and legal conditions.
- *Mechanisms to ensure alignment between e-government strategies, programmes and projects.* Ensuring this alignment is significant to ensure that the objectives are achieved and consequently to evidence that resources are spent well. A total of 7 alignment mechanisms were identified mostly from developed countries.
- *Presence of government-wide interoperability frameworks.* Initiatives are already on-going in all developing countries investigated. However, developing countries need to ensure that their framework addresses the country's specific interoperability challenges and that continuous improvements of the national framework are ensured.
- *Presence of architecture repositories to avoid reinventing the wheel and to improve quality of design artefacts.* As architecture repositories promote reusability, improve quality of design artefacts and prevent redundant investments, developing countries can benefit from this opportunity of sharing and reusing.
- *Presence of evaluation frameworks at national level* to ensure that not only the objectives of the projects are achieved, but also contributions to the strategic objectives and the vision are made. Evaluation frameworks are particularly important for developing countries where funds are very limited. Also, transparency in evaluation and implementation of projects (sustainability factor) is important and recommended.

- *Implementation of project development methods at national level.* While no such methods are implemented so far in developing countries investigated, they can learn from developed countries particularly the objectives of methods, stages supported and adoption approaches across government. Only 6 out 18 countries studied implement such a method at national level. Interestingly, research on successful e-government project development methods and their impacts to the overall success in e-government implementation is scarce.
- *Include sustainability at strategy, programme and project levels.* Most of the 24 sustainability factors put forward are settled in developed countries while respondents from developing countries could only recommend them (as these are not yet applied in their countries). For example, a significant sustainability factor is a close linkage between e-government strategies and national development goals which is already applied in MX and DK and recommended in UK.
- *Learn from others and reuse concepts and solutions.* Experiences from developed countries can be a valuable and useful asset for developing countries to transferring concepts and solutions among developed and developing countries. Yet, capabilities of transferring and sustaining solutions from other countries have to be available, too.

5   Conclusion

This paper presented a qualitative analysis of e-government approaches in developed and developing countries based on a strategic framework for e-government design [7] to scope the areas of investigation: formulation of vision and strategy at the national level, selection of programmes, selection and implementation of projects, evaluation and sustainability. While literature cautions that the transfer of concepts and solutions is not a straightforward task and that the understanding of differences in the countries' contexts is important, this paper investigated the approaches of e-government development from 18 countries – 11 from developed and 7 from developing countries. Based on the analysis, recommendations were put forward for more successful e-government implementation in developing countries.

The findings highlight differences in the advancement of e-government implementation between developed and developing countries and, most importantly, the impacts of such advancements to successful implementation of e-government. The differences in implementing the approaches provided a rich ground in understanding the impacts of their presence/absence and for deriving recommendations to transfer best practices to developing countries.

Further research is required to assess the application of the recommended approaches in a particular country grounded with a good understanding of the context of the country, as recommended in the paper. Additionally, the studied approaches in this research call for richer investigations; for example, the contents and application of evaluation frameworks and project development methods at the national level demand for more details of understanding to operationalise transfer.

References

1. Aichholzer, G.: Scenarios of e-government in 2010 and implications for strategy design. Electron. J. e-Gov. **2**(1), 1–10 (2004)
2. Chen, Y.N., Chen, H.M., Huang, W., Ching, R.K.H.: e-government strategies in developed and developing countries: an implementation framework and case study. J. Glob. Inf. Manag. (JGIM) **14**(1), 23–46 (2006)
3. Dshusupova, Z., Janowski, T., Ojo, A., Estevez, E.: Sustaining electronic governance programs in developing countries. In: Klun, M., Decman, M., Jukić, T. (eds), Proceedings of ECEG 2011. pp. 203–212. Academic Publishing Limited, Reading (2011)
4. Guba, E.G., Lincoln, Y.S.: Competing paradigms in qualitative research. Handb. Qual. Res. **2**, 163–194 (1994)
5. Heeks, R.: Information systems and developing countries: failure, success and local improvisations. Inf. Soc. **18**(2), 101–112 (2002)
6. Kumar, V., Mukerji, B., Butt, I., Persaud, A.: Factors for successful e-government adoption: a conceptual framework. Electron. J. e-Gov. **5**(1), 63–77 (2007)
7. Mkude, C.G., Wimmer, M.A.: Strategic framework for designing e-government in developing countries. In: Wimmer, M.A., Janssen, M., Scholl, H.J. (eds.) EGOV 2013. LNCS, vol. 8074, pp. 148–162. Springer, Heidelberg (2013)
8. Oates, B.: Researching Information Systems and Computing. SAGE Publication, London (2006)
9. Ogunleye, O.S., van Belle, J.P.: Exploring the success, failure and factors influencing m-Government implementation in developing countries. In: Proceedings of IST-Africa Conference, pp. 1–10. IEEE (2014)
10. Punch, K.F.: Introduction to Social Research: Quantitative and Qualitative Approaches, 1st edn. SAGE Publications, London (1998)
11. Riege, A.M.: Validity and reliability tests in case study research: a literature review with "hands-on" applications for each research phase. Qual. Market Res. Int. J. **6**(2), 75–86 (2003)
12. Sæbø, Ø.: e-government in Tanzania: current status and future challenges. In: Scholl, H.J., Janssen, M., Wimmer, M.A., Moe, C.E., Flak, L.S. (eds.) EGOV 2012. LNCS, vol. 7443, pp. 198–209. Springer, Heidelberg (2012)
13. Saunders, M., Lewis, P., Thornhill, A.: Research Methods for Business Students, 3rd edn. Prentice Hall, Upper Saddle River (2003)
14. United Nations: United Nations e-government Survey 2014: e-government for the future we want. http://unpan3.un.org/egovkb/Portals/egovkb/Documents/un/2014-Survey/E-Gov_Complete_Survey-2014.pdf (2014). Accessed 20 Jan 2015

Theoretical Support for Social Media Research. A Scientometric Analysis

Laura Alcaide Muñoz[⊠] and Manuel Pedro Rodríguez Bolívar

University of Granada, Granada, Spain
{lauraam, manuelp}@ugr.es

Abstract. We seek to analyze the research into the field of social media implementation in public administrations, examining the theories that support the use of social media, the main use of this technology for public administrations and the trends and research innovations in this area in the future. In addition, a comparative study will be performed in order to identify differences of research, research gaps and interest on the different domains of this topic into different contexts. To achieve the aims, the scientometric methodology will be applied to a sample of papers published in journals listed in the fields of Public Administration, Information Sciences and Communication. In this sense, the research about social media has not been the same in all areas. Knowledge gaps and research opportunities are identified from these observations, which reveal changes in the research methods applied, reinforcing the development of a theoretical framework so that the application of social media may efficiently contribute to improving management in the public sector.

Keywords: Social media · Scientometric study · Research opportunities · Theories

1 Introduction

The e-strategies have been the key-elements for Governments in order to perform investment planning on Information Communication and Technologies (ICTs), and to manage social change [1]. In this regards, e-Government development has been characterized by a three stage process [2]. The first one is called the era of "direct government" and it is characterized by offering static, limited and basic information, such as links to ministries/departments, archived information, and regional/local government services (unidirectional government-to citizen (G2C) information flows). In the second stage, called "orthodox government", services tailored to individual needs, more joined-up government services connected government initiatives [3] and opportunities for a 'mixed economy' of service provision were promised. In fact, citizen to government interactions -C2G interactions- are present in this stage of development.

Finally, from 2005 to the present time, under the "transformational government", the government encourages participatory deliberative decision-making and is willing and able to involve the society in a two way open dialogue (Open Government Initiative) [4]. Under this third stage, governments must strengthen their capacity to assess the needs of

© IFIP International Federation for Information Processing 2015
E. Tambouris et al. (Eds.): EGOV 2015, LNCS 9248, pp. 59–75, 2015.
DOI: 10.1007/978-3-319-22479-4_5

users (both private and commercial) and involve user groups through the use of second generation web technologies (Web 2.0) in order to listen, to engage users in the design of services and in the production of policies and to forge collective initiatives and inter-action [5]. Indeed, social media, particularly internet social networking has profound effects on all facets of social life and has fundamentally altered the nature of social relations [6], changing the nature of political and public dialogue [7].

Continuing interest in the question is reflected in the large number of studies published in this respect in the last years. It draws upon various reference disciplines, including public administration, information science and communication. Since its appearance, social media researchers in public administration have mainly analyzed the usefulness of social media for different purposes such as political campaigns [8], the disclosure of greater volume of information to a wider range of citizens [9] and the citizen coproduction initiatives [10]. The first two of these aspects concern the trans-parency and visibility of local government actions, while the second, in addition, favors more participative management.

In order to understand the construction of theoretical support underpinning the question of social media, it is of critical importance to explore its intellectual core, by analyzing the cumulative body of knowledge rather than looking at individual works [11]. Therefore, comprehensive reviews are needed, to integrate contributions and to provide a critical outlook on work in this field, to improve our understanding of e-Government and to gain a broad view of the current situation and of possibilities for future research. For this purpose, we propose a scientometric methodology [12] that has been comprehensively tested in the field of information science [13]. This specific approach has been used, among other reasons, as an attempt to understand the identity of a scientific discipline in a particular academic area [14]. In this paper, the underlying assumption of our approach is that the theoretical framework of a scholarly discipline is built upon the high quality body of knowledge published in the leading channels established for this purpose. Nevertheless, to date prior research has not analyzed this item in social media field of knowledge.

To fill this gap, the objective of the present paper is to analyze the research into the field of social media implementation in public administrations, examining the theories that support the use of social media, the research topics that have found in theories a fundamental pillar for building knowledge in the social media area, the relation between the use of theories and field of knowledge as well as the association between the use of theories and the quality of the journal in which research on social media is published. In addition, a comparative study will be performed in order to identify differences of research, research gaps and interest on the different domains of this topic into different contexts. The ultimate objective of this paper is to build fundamental pillar for the research area of social media as well as for assisting researchers in the development and direction of future analysis in the implementation of social media in public administrations into different contexts.

2 Background

The advent of social media using Web 2.0 technologies has opened up unprecedented new possibilities of engaging the public in government work and has changed the public's expectations about how government work should be done [15]. Indeed, social media applications provide channels not just for mass dissemination but also for mass production and collaboration, and have become acceptable information and communication channels in governments [16], playing an important role in implementing open government and in rendering online public services.

In this regard, driven by rising citizen expectations and the need for government innovation, social media has become a central component of e-Government in a very short period of time [17]. Nonetheless, the introduction of social media in public administration requires a thorough analysis of theoretical support in relation this role in the innovation of social communication between public administrations and citizens. Indeed, previous research shows that an effective review of theories creates a firm foundation for advancing knowledge [18]. It facilitates development of knowledge and scientific research, closes areas where a plethora of research exists, and uncovers areas where research is needed [19, 20].

In addition, as evidenced previous studies, the implementation of NPM models [21] and the evolution of e-Government [22] have been implemented worldwide but in widely varying forms. These differences are due to the bureaucratic structures and legal systems as well as differences in administrative cultures [23, 24]. Therefore, it would be interesting to know whether this theoretical basis differs in relation to the knowledge area or countries that have investigated about social media.

Therefore, with the aim at analyzing the contribution of social media to the sphere of public administrations, and analyze the degree of maturity it would be necessary to undertake scientometric analyses, which seek to help organize the information available to consolidate research and to highlight useful areas for future research. In addition, this analysis could help to know the theoretical underpinnings of the use of social media into the public sector environment.

Nonetheless, to date, scientometric projects in social media in public administrations have not been examined. This absence of comprehensive scientometric studies could mean that an interesting aspect of social media research has remained unexamined [25], despite the fact that social media, in terms of the use of information technology, has been studied from diverse standpoints. Therefore, it would be interesting to analyze the research published in the main fields of knowledge [26] and thus acquire different perspectives of social media research. Our first research question is:

RQ1 How many social media articles have been published in JCR journals in the fields of Public Administration, of Information Science & Library Science and of Communication?

As noted above, scientometric projects seek to identify a discipline, to structure the information available and to highlight potential areas for future research [27]. In this regard, the analysis of the most commonly published questions in the field of social media could inform researchers of the state of the art and highlight research gaps. In addition, the analysis of the use of the one to support research topics and the field of knowledge in which the research is published could be very useful for assisting scholars in future research. In other words, this analysis could be valuable as a tool guiding social media research [28]. Therefore, the following research question is proposed:

RQ2   How many articles used theories in order to support their findings?

Journals allow researchers to directly communicate their ideas to a wider audience, become aware of recent developments, learn about seminal works, accumulate references, and preserve the scientific body of knowledge for the future generations of scholars and practitioners [29]. Therefore, in the field of e-Government research, it could be interesting to analyze the leading high quality journals which include social media as one of their areas of interest. Accordingly, the third research question addressed is:

RQ3   Which journals publish such papers most frequently?

It could be of interest to analyze if the use of theories to support social media research is focused, or not, in concrete countries because it could indicate the different perspective in public management in these countries. In addition, a study of different social media experiences around the world could enhance our understanding of the instruments used to promote the social media implementation in public affairs and thus facilitate a resolution of democratic deficits [30], improving the efficiency, acceptance and legitimacy of political processes. In addition, the different interests of researchers in this field of knowledge could be the result of the universities to which they belong to, and could be a reflection of the concerns of the country in which social media is analyzed by the universities. The following research question is therefore derived:

RQ4   What are the countries analyzed when academic researchers used theories in their articles?

Previous research show that social media is a highly multi-disciplinary domain of research [25, 31], so, it is necessary more search to better understand the social media concept. Hence, we think that it could be interesting to analyzed different perspectives in which the social media is to examine, because it is revealed hidden structural characteristics which will help understand the structural differences among theories [28]. In addition, these perspectives may reflect the possibility of publishing in a journal with greater or lesser impact. Similarly, we want to examine whether these differences occasionally to the way in which each knowledge area addresses the problem of research. The following research question is therefore derived:

RQ5   Is there any relationship between the use of the theories to support the findings of the studies and the ranking of the journal published? Is there a trend in terms of academic area analyzed?

Also, we propose the following general and specific hypotheses for each area of knowledge.

H_0 There is a relationship between the use of theories in articles to support the findings and the impact factor of journals where they are published

H_{1A} There is a relationship between the use of theories in articles to support the findings and the impact factor of communication journals where they are published

H_{1C} There is a relationship between the use of theories in articles to support the findings and the impact factor of public administration journals where they are published

To address these research questions, we conducted a descriptive scientometric study [13] of social media articles published in the Journal Citation Report-listed (JCR) international journals in the areas of "Information Science & Library Science", "Communication" and "Public Administration", as described in the methodology section of this paper – Table 1.

Table 1. Articles about social media and journals that are published (chronological evolution)

JOURNALS*/YEAR	2008	2009	2010	2011	2012	2013	TOTAL**
COMMUNICATION							
Journal of Communication	-	-	-	-	4	1	5
New Media and Society	-	1	1	4	11	1	18
Journal of Computer-Mediated Communication	-	-	-	-	-	1	1
Telecommunication Policy	-	-	-	-	1	1	2
International Journal of Press-Politics	1	-	-	-	-	1	2
International Journal of Public Opinion Research	-	-	-	-	1	-	1
Public Relations Review	-	-	-	-	1	4	5
Information, Communication and Society	-	-	-	2	-	2	4
European Journal of Communication	-	-	-	1	1	2	4
TOTAL	1	1	1	7	19	13	42 (38.18%)
INFORMATION SCIENCE							
Scientometrics	-	-	-	-	1	-	1
Government Information Quarterly	-	-	2	2	10	16	30
Journal of Computer-Mediated Communication	-	-	-	-	-	1	1
Information and Management	1	-	-	-	-	-	1
Telecommunication Policy	-	-	-	-	1	1	2
Social Science Computer Review	-	-	-	8	1	8	17
Online Information Review	-	-	-	-	2	1	3
Aslib Proceedings	-	1	-	1	-	1	3
TOTAL	1	1	2	11	15	28	58 (52.73%)
PUBLIC ADMINISTRATION							
Journal of Public Administration Research and Theory	-	-	-	-	-	1	1
Policy Studies Journal	-	-	-	1	-	-	1
Public Administration Review	-	-	-	1	-	1	2
International Review of Administrative Science	-	-	-	-	2	-	2
Australian Journal of Public Administration	-	-	1	-	1	-	2
Administration and Society	-	-	-	1	-	-	1
Transylvania Review of Administrative Sciences	-	1	-	-	-	-	1
TOTAL	-	1	1	3	3	2	10 (9.09%)
TOTAL	2	3	4	21	37	43	110

Source: Authors
*NOTE: This table shows only those journals that have published articles about social media in public administration.
**NOTE: There are two journals –*Journal of Computer-Mediate Communication and Telecommunication Policy*- that are classified in Communication and Information Science, so they appear in both areas.

3 Research Methodology

The Scientometric methodology allows scholars to identify the historical roots of a determined field of study [18], to identify prospects for future research, and to decide the right direction in which to focus subsequent research [32]. Therefore, this article not only serves as a synopsis of existing research, but also as an identifier of emerging trends, gaps, and areas for future study.

This tool has been widely used in research field such as communication about the internet and new media [25, 31], allowing the knowledge of the evolution of this interdisciplinary field, journals taken as a reference by researchers, the input knowledge, research gaps, trends and future opportunities.

All these studies focus on social media in general terms. However, in previous literature, there are no scientometric studies which have analyzed the research into the field of social media implementation in public administrations, examining the theories that support the use of social media, the main use of this technology for public administrations and the trends and research innovations in this area in the future. Therefore, this article tries to cover this gap in the academic literature.

3.1 Sample Selection

3.1.1 Journals Analyzed

In order to provide a complete review of the current state of research into social media in public sector management context, previous studies have indicated that this topic is one of the main research topics of e-Government [33] and papers about this topic are mainly published in two areas: "Information Science & Library Science" and "Public Administration". Nonetheless, with the aim of avoiding potential errors in search, we carried out a systematic research, entering the descriptors "social media", "electronic government", "e-Participation", "e-Democracy" into the ISI Web of Knowledge database. This first search enabled us to examine the main academic areas that provide most contributions on this topic and it also provided the articles that would be included in our database.

The results of this search showed that more than 42.53 % of the articles on social media were published in journals listed in the fields of "*Information Science & Library Science*", "*Public Administration*" and "*Communication*". The rest of papers about social media are published in other areas such as paediatrics or medical analysis, but these areas are not related to the field of public sector management and they also can be considered as residual areas of analysis because none of them concentrated a high volume of papers. Also, papers published in other areas such as Computer Science or Information Systems are also residuals and, mainly, of very technical nature without a clear link to public sector management. Therefore, our study research is focused on papers published in the above mentioned fields.

This study is focused on analyzing journal publications, in the view that they constitute a resource that is often used by academics as a source of new knowledge and as a medium for its disclosure [34], and at the same time, as an indicator of scientific productivity [34]. In addition, with the aim of analysing high quality contributions to the field of social media, we have used objective criteria [35] to select the journals. This way, based on prior research [36], only journals indexed in the Institute for Scientific Information (ISI) in the above-mentioned sample areas for the year 2013 were selected for analysis. Therefore, e-Government, e-Participation or e-Democracy journals were excluded from our analysis if they were not listed in the ISI index. In addition, prior research has indicated that total citations and the impact factor of journals are considered indicators of research quality [37, 38]. Thus, we excluded listed journals of marginal importance, i.e. those with an impact factor of less than 0.25 or with fewer than 50 total citations [39].

We analyzed all journals and articles that met the exclusion-inclusion criteria. In consequence, our sample was comprised of 27 journals listed in the area of Communication, 45 journals listed in the area of Public Administration and 69 journals listed in the area of Information Science & Library Science, indexed in the ISI Web of Knowledge for the year 2013. However, not all of these journals have published articles on social media. Therefore, Table 1 lists only the journals that, within the sample, have published articles on social media in public administration.

3.1.2 Articles Selected

In determining the articles to be included in the sample, we analyzed all the articles published in the journals that met the above-described criteria for inclusion. To do this, we first examined the title and the keywords of each one [36]. If the keywords offered were generic, we then read the abstract, to obtain a better view of the article. If doubts remained, we then read the introduction to identify the research goals and to determine the main factors analyzed. As a result, we obtained a database composed of 107 articles published during the period 2000–2013, although the first article that we have found was published in 2008 (see Table 1).

3.1.3 Collection and Data Encoding

In order to achieve our research goals, each of the articles included in our database was manually examined and catalogued, using MS Excel software, by the journal title, the country in which the study was carried out, the main topic addressed, the principal methodology used, and the theories used by the author to support the knowledge.

In order to determine the research topics analysed in each study, we based our initial classification on the topics used in previous public administration research [40]. However, since e-Government and social media are research fields that have only recently appeared to a considerable degree in conferences, journals and books, we encountered some research topics that could not be classified under any of the descriptions offered in previous studies, especially for issues related to improving e-democracy, promoting citizens' participation in public affairs, the supply of public services through the internet, increasing access to information through greater transparency, and enhanced accountability [33]. In consequence, we included some new additional categories – see Table 2.

To determine these new research topics, we carried out an exploratory content analysis of each of the articles in the sample [40]. Keywords are derived from the literature review. During this phase of the study, QSR NVivo v.10 software was used to automate the coding of the articles [41, 42]. This coding was conducted using the

Table 2. Research topics, subject areas and theories used

Theories /research topics*	Disclosure information			Delivery public services			Regulatory aspects			Social media in general terms			Organizational theory			E-campaign			DEMOCRACY AND PARTICIPATION		
	COM	IS	PA	COM	IS	PA	COM	IS	PA	COM	IS	PA	COM	IS	PA	COM	IS	PA	COM	IS	PA
Agenda setting theory																	2.7 % 6.7 %				
Cognitive dissonance theory																	2.7 % 6.7 %		2.7 % 5.9 %		
Commodity theory	2.7 %** 5.9 %***																				
Communication privacy management theory	2.7 % 5.9 %																				
Convergence culture theory																			2.7 % 5.9 %		
Democratic theory																			2.7 % 5.9 %	5.4 % 13.3 %	
Development theory																			2.7 % 5.9 %		
Domestication theory																			2.7 % 5.9 %		
Equalization and normalization theory																2.7 % 2.9 %					
Exemplification theory																2.7 % 5.9 %					
Framing theory																	2.7 % 6.7 %				
Galbraith's information-processing theory						2.7 % 25.0 %															
Gatekeeping theory	2.7 % 5.9 %	2.7 % 6.7 %																			
Habermas theory	2.7 % 5.9 %																		5.4 % 11.8 %		
Informal learning theory																				2.7 % 6.7 %	

(Continued)

Table 2. (*Continued*)

Theories /research topics*	Disclosure information			Delivery public services			Regulatory aspects			Social media in general terms			Organizational theory			E-campaign			DEMOCRACY AND PARTICIPATION		
	COM	IS	PA	COM	IS	PA	COM	IS	PA	COM	IS	PA	COM	IS	PA	COM	IS	PA	COM	IS	PA
Inglehart's postmaterialist theory																			2.7 % 5.9 %		
Innovation diffusion theory			2.7 % 25.0 %		2.7 % 6.7 %												2.7 % 6.7 %				
Lasswell's policy sciences																					2.7 % 25.0 %
Theory of affordances											2.7 % 6.7 %										
Mediatization theory																	2.7 % 6.7 %				
Merkl-Kelsen's theory									2.7 % 6.7 %												
New Media theory																			2.7 % 5.9 %		
New public management theory					5.4 % 11.8 %																
Political communication theory																			5.4 % 11.8 %		
Political engagement gateway theory																				2.7 % 6.7 %	
Post-Habermasian theories		2.7 % 6.7 %																			
Priming theory																	2.7 % 6.7 %				
Principal- agent theory			2.7 % 25.0 %																		
Public sphere and representation theories																2.7 % 5.9 %				2.7 % 6.7 %	
Social information processing theory																					

(*Continued*)

Table 2. (*Continued*)

Theories /research topics*	Disclosure information			Delivery public services			Regulatory aspects			Social media in general terms			Organizational theory			E-campaign			DEMOCRACY AND PARTICIPATION		
	COM	IS	PA	COM	IS	PA	COM	IS	PA	COM	IS	PA	COM	IS	PA	COM	IS	PA	COM	IS	PA
Social network theory						2.7 % 25.0 %													2.7 % 5.9 %		
Social-technical systems theory											2.7 % 6.7 %										
Software platforms and ecosystems theory					2.7 % 6.7 %																
Strategic business alignment approach														2.7 % 6.7 %							
Two step flow of communication						2.7 % 25.0 %														2.7 % 6.7 %	
Transactions cost theory						2.7 % 25.0 %															
Wicked problems theory					2.7 % 6.7 %																

Source: Own Elaboration

*NOTE: There are articles that support their findings on more than one theory.

**NOTE: This percentage is based on the total of articles with theory.

***NOTE: This percentage is based on the total of articles in each area.

random tags option of the software, which enabled us to obtain a hierarchical concept structure to group and adapt this published research on e-Government.

In this encoding phase, the researchers held several meetings to decide the labels to be assigned and the topics to be included (see Table 2). Subsequently, each of the articles incorporated in the study sample was encoded separately, and any disagreements concerning the definition of the categories to be analyzed were discussed and resolved.

4 Analysis of the Results

RQ1 How many social media articles have been published in JCR journals in the fields of Public Administration, of Information Science & Library Science and of Communication? **RQ3:** Which journals publish such papers most frequently?

Public administration have adopted different Web 2.0 tools, which have attracted the interest of researchers and scholars, and this has been reflected in a gradual increase in the number of studies published in international journals since 2011 (see Table 1).

In this sense, most of these articles were published in *Information Science & Library Science* journals (52.73 %), followed closely by *Communication* journals (38.18 %), while the rest (9.09 %) are set out in *Public Administration* journals. At this regard, 81.03 % of the articles (47) are published in two journals in *Information Science & Library Science – Government Information Quarterly* (GIQ) (51.72 %; 30/58) and *Social Science Computer Review* (SSCORE) (29.31 %; 17/58)-. Meanwhile, in the case of *Communication* journals, Table 1 show that 42.86 % of the articles published correspond to a single journal, *New Media and Society*, which accounts for 18 of the 42 article included in this knowledge are. Finally, in the case of *Public Administration*, there is no exist clear preference for published articles about social media.

RQ2 How many articles used theories in order to support their findings?

Regarding theories, there are 66.36 % (71/107) published articles that do not use theories to support their findings, only 33.64 % (36/107) of the articles use theories – see Table 4, and these are varied to analyze the same topic, which seems to be a common indicator of research topic of social media, regardless of where it is analyzed [30] – see Table 2. Similarly, the same theory is used to analyze different research topics.

Hence, it appears the social media is still far removed from establishing its theoretical foundations. In this sense, we can observe that Innovation Diffusion Theory is used for explaining the studies' findings about different research topics in the field under study, such as disclosure information, delivery public services and e-campaign, or Cognitive Dissonance Theory is used for supporting the empirical findings about e-campaign and democracy and participation. Similarly, communication researchers used Habermas Theory for analyzing disclosure information and democracy and participation phenomena. On the other hand, communication and information science academics used Democratic Theory and Gatekeeping Theory for finding evidence about democratic and participation and disclosure information, respectively.

RQ4   What are the countries analyzed when academic researchers used theories in their articles?

In this sense, the main studies on social media focus on analyzing this phenomenon in countries of United States of America and Europe, followed distantly by Australia (Table 3). In addition, these studies are usually carried on for universities of their countries. Hence, it seems likely that these countries will be able to initially invest heavily in research institutions, attract top faculty and provide research support to further research in this area. This in turn facilitates the production of more scholarship in those selected countries, resulting in an hegemony of a few elite scientific nations [30].

On the other hand, the USA and European academics used a variety of theories to analyze and support studies on social media. However, we can observer that in the case of Arab World studies are focused on production, dissemination, procession and effects of information both through media and interpersonally, within a

Table 3. Countries and theories used

COUNTRIES	THEORIES	ARTICLES*
AFRICA		2
Agera – Libyan - Mauritania – Morocco – Somalia – Sudan- Tunisia	- Political Communication Theory	1
Egypt	- New Public Management Theory	1
ASIA		5
South Korea	- Priming theory	1
	- Framing theory	1
	- Agenda-setting Theory	1
	- Mediatization Theory	1
Bahrain – Iran – Iraq – Jordan – Kuwait – Oman – Saudi Arabia – UAE – Yemen	- Political Communication Theory	1
AUSTRALIA		3
	- Lasswell's policy sciences	1
	- Communication in Society	1
	- Pos-Habermasian Theories	1
EUROPE		12
European Union Countries	- Development Theory	1
	- Democratic Theory	1
Finland	- Equalization and Normalization Theory	1
Greek	- Inglehart's Postmaterialist Theory	1
Holland	- New Public Management	1
	- Strategic Business Alignment Approach	1
Slovenia	- Merki-Kelsenrs Theory	1
Sweden	- Habermas Theory	1
	- New Media Theory	1
	- Social Network Theory	1
United Kingdom	- Democratic Theory	1
	- Public Sphere and Representation Theories	1
SOUTH AMERICA		1
Colombia	- Social Information Processing Theory	1
UNITED STATE OF AMERICA		28
	- Cognitive dissonance Theory	2
	- Commodity Theory	1
	- Communication Privacy Management Theory	1
	- Convergence Culture	1
	- Democratic Theory	2
	- Domestication Theory	1
	- Exemplification Theory	1
	- Galbraith's Information Processing Theory	1
	- Gatekeeping Theory	2
	- Habermas Theory	2
	- Informal Learning theory	1
	- Diffusion Innovation Theory	3
	- Interorganizational Networks Theory	1
	- Theory of Affordances	1
	- Political Communication Theory	1
	- Political engagement gateway theory	1
	- Principal Agent Theory	1
	- Socio-Technical Systems Theory	1
	- Software Platforms and Ecosystems Theory	1
	- Transactions Cost Theory	1
	- Two step flow of communication	1
	- Wicked Problems Theory	1

Source: Own elaboration

*NOTE: There are articles that support their findings on more than one theory and country political contest, thus researchers usually used Political Communication Theory. It seems to be that academics are trying to analyze if it is producing social and political changes towards greater democracy and transparency of information in these countries. Hence, these articles deal with the studies of information media, the analysis of speeches by politicians and those that are trying to influence the political process, and formal and informal conversations among members of the public, among other aspects.

RQ5   Is there any relationship between the use of the theories to support the findings of the studies and the ranking of the journal published? Is there a trend in terms of academic area analyzed?

In this regard, Table 4 shows that the articles are usually published in first quartile journals (top journals), regardless the use, or not, of theories to support their findings. As there is not clearly perceived a certain trend in publishing articles that support their findings with theories, we performed a regression analysis to confirm o not this research question. Furthermore, we do not know if there is a trend based on a specific academic area.

The results of this regression analysis are showed in the Table 5. They show that there is a positive and not statistically significant relationship between use of theories in articles and the impact factor of journals, in general terns ($r = 0.1167$; $\rho > 0.10$), i.e. it seems to be that when the articles used theories are more likely to be published in journals with higher impact factor. However, this is not a behavior that extends to all analyzed subjects. In the case of *Communication*

Table 4. Articles with and without theories, and quartiles of journals

Quartiles journals	Articles with theories	Articles without theories
Journals in first quartile	30–83.34 %	49–69.01 %
Journals in second quartile	3–8.33 %	9–12.68 %
Journals in third quartile	3–8.33 %	13–18.31 %
Total	36–33.64 %	71–66.36 %

Table 5. Hypothesis test results

HYPOTHESIS	SPEARMAN CORRELATION	Significance
H_0: There is a relationship between the use of theories in articles to support the findings and the impact factor of journals where they are published	$r = 0.116$ $N = 107$	0.234
COMMUNICATION		
H_{1A}: There is a relationship between the use of theories in articles to support the findings and the impact factor of Communication journals where they are published	$r = 0.370$ $N = 42$	0.016
INFORMATION SCIENCE AND LIBRARY SCIENCE		
H_{1B}: There is a relationship between the use of theories in articles to support the findings and the impact factor of Information Science and Library Science journals where they are published	$r = -0.019$ $N = 58$	0.889
PUBLIC ADMINISTRATION		
H_{1C}: There is a relationship between the use of theories in articles to support the findings and the impact factor of Public Administration journals where they are published	$r = 0.050$ $N = 10$	0.890

subject, this relationship is positive and statistically significant ($r = 0.370$, $\rho < 0.05$), thus, the findings made in the studies under this area of knowledge are usually supported by theories if they would be published in high-impact journals. In the case of *Information Science and Library Science* area, the relationship is negative and not statistically significant ($r = -0.019$; $\rho > 0.10$), therefore, under this area of knowledge the articles published in high-impact journals do not have to be supported by theories. Finally, in the case of *Public Administration* area, the relationship is positive but not statistically significant ($r = 0.050$; $\rho > 0.10$), which leads us to conclude that there are more options to publish an article in a top *Public Administration* journal, when it takes a theoretical framework to support its findings.

5   Conclusions and Discussion

According to our results, there are an increasing number of papers published in JCR journals about the use of social media in public administrations and it is growing in the last years (RQ1). In fact, social media in public administrations has mainly attracted the attention of researchers in the last three years. It is a reflection of the increasing incorporation of these technologies in the social life of people and the need of public administrations of implementing these technologies in the public affairs.

Nonetheless, the research about social media implementation, and similarly their use in public administrations, has not been the same in all fields of knowledge (RQ1) or in the journals in which they are published (RQ3). Indeed, whereas the electronic participation has been the main research theme published in the communication and information science fields of knowledge – mainly in the journals of GIQ and SSCORE-, the delivery of public services is increasingly being the key theme in the public administration area – no preference for publishing in a particular journal in this field exists-. This result highlights the different perspective of the fields of knowledge analyzed in this paper, and it also reflects the concerns of social media in its implementation in public administrations. In fact, results indicate that the electronic participation has been the first concern of public administrations in implementing these new technologies. It seems that governments have tried to take advantage of Web 2.0 technologies as other channels for a wider representation of the government actions or the elected political party into the Internet.

On the other hand, this new field of research needs grounded theories to support social media application into public administrations (RQ2). Our review indicates that several different theories have been called to be applied in the application of social media in public administrations. But which one of them prevails? Many of them are embedded from other areas of study. In this regards, is social media a field of knowledge that need a deep analysis of theories or can it embedded theories from other fields of knowledge? Why? Does your application depend on contextual factors or training of research? All these questions remain currently without appropriated answer. Therefore, future research could undertake theoretical studies on this issue.

In addition, the main studies on social media focus on analyzing this phenomenon in countries of USA, Europe and Australia. However, it is increasingly common that the main university of these countries invest in research about Arab World and developing countries (RQ4). These studies are focused on political affair and public debate, which are theories used in political science about processes and effects of the media communication in a political context.

Finally, the regression results show that there is relationship between use of theories in articles and the impact factor of journals, specially, in *Information Science and Library Science* subject (RQ5). It appears that the social media concept has a higher theoretical support in this area, although this phenomenon is a relatively new one [31], because it brings in revolutionary paradigms for information science research and practical use. So, a main research question to be answered by future research could be: are there journals classified inside certain academic areas that are more attracted to articles based on theoretical foundations?, i.e., when you base your research on theoretical foundations, is it more likely to publish your research in journals cataloged in certain areas with higher theoretical roots?

To conclude, the review presented in this paper provides a comprehensive summary of the research into social media within the fields of Communication, Information Science and Public Administration, highlighting the main research topics and theories used. Explanations and clarifications are given whenever possible. Knowledge gaps and research opportunities are identified from these observations, which reveal changes in the research methods applied, reinforcing the development of a theoretical framework so that the application of social media may efficiently contribute to improving management in the public sector. Nonetheless, future research could analyze other journals different from those included in the sample selection of this paper such as, for example, those not listed in the ISI index or those included in other different fields of knowledge, with the aim of completing the whole picture of social media regardless its link to public sector management.

Acknowledgements. This research was carried out with financial support from the Regional Government of Andalusia (Spain), Department of Innovation, Science and Enterprise (Research Project No. P11-SEJ-7700).

References

1. Anthopoulos, L., Fitsilis, P.: Trends in e-strategic management: how do governments transform their policies? Int. J. Public Adm. Digit. Age (IJPADA) 1(1), 15–38 (2014)
2. Taylor, J.A.: The information polity: towards a two speed future? Inf. Polity Int. J. Gov. Democracy Inf. Age 17(3/4), 227–237 (2012)
3. United Nations: E-Government Survey 2010. Leveraging e-Government at a time of financial and economic crisis, United Nations, New York (2010)
4. Peedu, G.: Enhancing public service user experience in information society. Master Thesis, Tallinn University, Estonia (2011)
5. OECD: Denmark: Efficient e-Government for Smarter Service Delivery. OECD Publishing (2010). http://dx.doi.org/10.1787/9789264087118-en

6. Li, D.: Online social network acceptance: a social perspective. Internet Res. **21**(5), 562–580 (2011)

7. Osimo, D.: Web 2.0 in Government: Why? and How?. Institute for Prospective Technological Studies, Joint Research Centre, European Commission. Office for Official Publications of the European Communities, Luxembourg (2008)

8. Williams, C.B., Gulati, G.J.: Social networks in political campaigns: facebook and the congressional elections of 2006 and 2008. New Media Soc. **15**(1), 52–71 (2013)

9. Bonsón, E., Torres, L., Royo, S., Flores, F.: Local e-Government 2.0: social media and corporate transparency in municipalities. Gov. Inf. Q. **29**(2), 123–132 (2012)

10. Linders, D.: From e-Government to e-Government: defining a typology for citizen coproduction in the age of social media. Gov. Inf. Q. **29**(4), 446–454 (2012)

11. Holsapple, C.W.: The pulse of multiparticipant systems. J. Organ. Comput. Electron. Commer. **18**(4), 333–343 (2008)

12. Neufeld, D., Fang, Y., Huff, S.: The IS identity crisis. Commun. Assoc. Inf. Syst. **19**, 447–464 (2007)

13. Cocosila, M., Serenko, A., Turel, O.: Exploring the management information systems discipline: a scientometric study of ICIS, PACIS, and ASAC. Scientometrics **87**(1), 1–16 (2011)

14. Straub, D.: The value of scientometric studies: an introduction to a debate on IS as a reference discipline. J. Assoc. Inf. Syst. **7**(5), 241–245 (2006)

15. McDermott, P.: Building open government. Gov. Inf. Q. **27**(4), 401–413 (2010)

16. Mergel, I.: Social media adoption and resulting tactics in the U.S. federal government. Gov. Inf. Q. **30**(2), 123–130 (2013)

17. Bertot, J.C., Jaeger, P.T., Hansen, D.: The impact of policies on government social media usage: Issues, challenges, and recommendations. Gov. Inf. Q. **29**(1), 30–40 (2012)

18. Peng, T.Q., Zhang, L., Zhong, Z.J.: Mapping the landscape of internet studies: text mining of social science journal articles 2000-2009. New Media Soc. **15**(5), 644–664 (2012)

19. Webster, J., Watson, R.T.: Analyzing the pas to prepare for the future: writing a literature review. MIS Q. **26**(2), 13–23 (2002)

20. Woolcock, M., Narayan, D.: Social capital: implications for development theory, research, and policy. World Bank Res. Observer **15**(2), 225–249 (2000)

21. Rodríguez Bolívar, M.P., Caba Pérez, M.C., López Hernández, A.M.: Cultural contexts and government digital reporting. Int. Rev. Adm. Sci. **72**(2), 269–290 (2006)

22. Rodríguez Domínguez, L., García Sánchez, I.M., Gallego Álvarez, I.: Determining factors of e-Government development: a worldwide national approach. Int. Public Manage. J. **14**(2), 218–248 (2011)

23. Rodríguez Bolívar, M.P., Alcaide Muñoz, L., López Hernández, A.M.: Determinants of financial transparency in government. Int. Public Manage. J. **16**(4), 557–602 (2013)

24. Rodríguez Bolívar, M.P., Navarro Galera, A., Alcaide Muñoz, L.: Governance, transparency and accountability: an international comparison. J. Policy Model. **37**(1), 136–174 (2015)

25. Khan, G.F.: Social media-based systems: an emerging area of information systems research and practice. Scientometrics **95**, 159–180 (2013)

26. Tomasello, T.K., Lee, Y., Baer, A.P.: New media research publication trends and outlets in communication, 1990-2006. New Media Soc. **12**(4), 531–548 (2010)

27. Khan, G.F., Moon, J., Park, H.W.: Network of the core: mapping and visualizing the core of scientific domains. Scientometrics **89**(3), 759–779 (2011)

28. Serenko, A., Jiao, C.: Investigating information systems research in Canada. Can. J. Adm. Sci. **29**(1), 3–24 (2012)

29. Nabatchi, T.: Addressing the citizenship and democratic deficits: the potential of deliberative democracy for public administration. Am. Rev. Public Adm. **40**(4), 376–399 (2010)

30. Coursaris, C.K., Van Osch, W.: A scientometric analysis of social media research (2004-2011). Scientometrics **101**(1), 357–380 (2014)
31. Löfstedt, U.: E-Government –assessment of current research and some proposals for future direction. Int. J. Public Inf. Syst. **1**(1), 39–52 (2005)
32. Rodríguez, M.P., Alcaide, L., López, A.M.: Trends of e-Government research. contextualization and research opportunities. Int. J. Digit. Acc. Res. **10**, 87–111 (2010)
33. Rodríguez, M.P., Alcaide, L., López, A.M.: Scientometric study of the progress and development of e-Government research during the period 2000-2012. Inf. Technol. Dev. doi:10.1080/02681102.2014.927340
34. Gordon, M.D.: Citation ranking versus subjective evaluation in the determination of journal hierarchies in the social sciences. J. Soc. Inf. Sci. **33**(1), 55–57 (1982)
35. Forrester, J.P., Watson, S.S.: An assessment of public administration journals: the perspective of editors and editorial board members. Public Adm. Rev. **54**(5), 474–482 (1994)
36. Rodríguez Bolívar, M.P., Alcaide Muñoz, L.: Comparative scientometric analysis in social media: what can we learn? and what is next?. In: Reddick, C.G., Anthopoulos, L. (eds.) Information and Communication Technologies in Public Administration. Innovations from Developed Countries, pp. 97–124. CRC Press, Washington, USA (2015)
37. Garfield, E.: Citation analysis as a tool in journal evaluation. Science **178**(6), 471–479 (1972)
38. Vocino, T., Elliott, R.H.: Journal prestige in public administration: a research note. Adm. Soc. **14**(1), 5–14 (1982)
39. Plümber, T., Radaelli, C.M.: Publish or perish? Publications and citations of Italian political scientists in international political science journals, 1990-2002. J. Eur. Public Policy **11**(6), 1112–1127 (2004)
40. Lan, Z., Anders, K.K.: A paradigmatic view of contemporary public administration research: an empirical test. Adm. Soc. **32**(2), 138–165 (2000)
41. Krippendorff, K.: Content Analysis: An Introduction to Its Methodology. Sage Publications, Inc., USA (1980)
42. Fraser, D.: QSR Nvivo. NUDIST Vivo. Reference Guide. Malaysia. QSR International Pty. Ltd, Melbourne (2000)

Open and Smart Government

Big and Open Linked Data (BOLD) to Create Smart Cities and Citizens: Insights from Smart Energy and Mobility Cases

Marijn Janssen[✉], Ricardo Matheus, and Anneke Zuiderwijk

Delft University of Technology Faculty of Technology, Policy and Management,
Jaffalaan 5, 2628 BX Delft, The Netherlands
{m.f.w.h.a.janssen,r.matheus,
a.m.g.zuiderwijk-vaneijk}@tudelft.nl

Abstract. Smart cities focus on using existing resources in a better way to improve the urban environment. At the same time Big and Open Linked Data (BOLD) can be used to better understand the use of the resources and to suggest improvements. The objective of this paper is to investigate the complementariness of the smart cities and big and Open Data research streams. Two inductive cases concerning different aspects of smart cities, energy and mobility, are investigated. The idea of using BOLD for smart cities seems initially straightforward, but the cases show that this is complex. A taxonomy for forms of collecting and opening data is derived. A major challenge is to deal with data distributed over various data sources and how to align the data push with the citizens' needs. This paper highlights a continuous scale between open and closed data and emphasizes that not only Open Data but also closed data should be used to identify improvements. BOLD can contribute to the 'smartness' of cities by linking and combining data or employing data or predictive analytics to improve better use of resources. A smart city only becomes smart when there are smart citizens, businesses, civil servants and other stakeholders.

Keywords: Open Data · Big Data · Big open linked data · BOLD · Smart city · E-government · Open government · Smart energy · Smart mobility

1 Introduction

Open Data can be used as fuel for the creation of smart cities [1]. Open urban data and technology can be used to develop services for citizens through open and people-driven innovation models [2]. Web applications can assist in monitoring, analyzing and visualizing social, economic and environmental phenomena [1]. Data-driven initiatives can focus on various types of value [3]. The ability to effectively and efficiently combine, link and share data will determine such data's value [4].

Big Open and Linked Data (BOLD) is a recent and rapidly evolving field in technology driven business world. The volume of data is growing exponentially. Big Data is formed of large, diverse, complex, longitudinal, and distributed data sets generated

© IFIP International Federation for Information Processing 2015
E. Tambouris et al. (Eds.): EGOV 2015, LNCS 9248, pp. 79–90, 2015.
DOI: 10.1007/978-3-319-22479-4_6

from various instruments, sensors, Internet transactions, email, video, click streams, and other sources, whereas open linked data focusses on the opening and the combining of data. The data can be released both by public organizations and by private organizations or individuals. Big Data analytics can be used to promote better utilization of resources and improved personalization [5].

Smart cities is a concept that is gaining more attention over time. Smart cities refer to types of technology-supported innovation in urban spaces and city governments [6]. The term smart cities is rapidly replacing the original concept of sustainable city [7], however, whereas 'sustainability' has a clear scope, the term 'smart' is more loaded and unclear. Furthermore, other terms such as intelligence, knowledge, information and ubiquitous city are used [7]. What actually constitutes 'smart' is rather unknown [8].

While various studies have been conducted on Big Data [5] and Open Data [9–11], there are only few studies that combine these two concepts [e.g., 1, 12]. Existing research leaves a void in how BOLD can be used to create smart cities and how they contribute to their 'smartness'. In BOLD, organizational implications have been given limited attention [13]. Hence the objective of this paper is to investigate the relationship between the smart cities and BOLD. The contribution of the paper originates from the integration of two strands of research in e-government, namely the open and Big Data literature and the smart city literature and by investigating what the organizational implications of BOLD are.

This paper is organized as follows. First, we define the key concepts of this study, including smart cities and BOLD. Subsequently, the research approach of this study is presented. We followed an inductive method and investigated the patterns derived from two case studies. Next we describe the inductive cases followed by a discussion of the challenges and opportunities for combining smart city and BOLD literature, and, finally, we draw conclusions about how the two research streams can be combined and what can be learned from this.

2   Research Background

In this section we provide a brief account of the concepts of smart cities (Sect. 2.1) and BOLD (Sect. 2.2).

2.1   Smart Cities

Smart cities are a response to the challenges that cities face in meeting objectives regarding socio-economic development and quality of life [14]. The smart city concept has been defined in different ways [2, 15], where definitions vary from smart urban space to environmentally healthy smart cities [7]. Others attempt to characterize smart cities and use dimension including (1) management and organization, (2) technology, (3) policy, (4) governance, (5) people and communities, (6) economy, (7) built infrastructures, and (8) the natural environment [16]. Six key dimensions for defining smart cities are a smart economy, smart mobility, a smart environment, smart people, smart living and smart governance [17]. There has been an inflation of the concept of smart cities and every ICT applications can be said to be smart. The concept of 'smartness' is often hardly defined and/or ill explained. A city can be called 'smart' "when investments in human and social capital and traditional (transport) and modern (ICT) communication infrastructures fuel sustainable economic growth and a high quality of life, with a wise management of natural resources, through participatory governance" [17, p. 70]. In our opinion, smartness does not refer to the bricks and mortar in the city, but to the mechanisms to improve the use of resources in the city. Furthermore, in our opinion a city can only become smarter when the inhabitants are empowered and thus also become smarter.

2.2 Big and Open Linked Data (BOLD)

Size is only one aspect of Big Data [18]. Big Data are commonly characterized with three or more Vs: Volume, Velocity, Variety [19], and additionally Value, Variability and Veracity [18]. Big Data and Big Data analytics refer to "datasets and analytical techniques in applications that are so large (from terabytes to exabytes) and complex (from sensor to social media data) that they require advanced and unique data storage, management, analysis, and visualization technologies" [20, p. 1166]. Big Data and Open Data are closely related, yet they are not the same. While Big Data is characterized by its size, Open Data is characterized by its free availability, although there is discussion about the level or volume that is necessary to make data big and the level of openness to deserve the name Open Data.

For the processing of data, data analytics play a role by providing deep insight and influence the decision making processes of public organizations and citizens often affecting the usage of resources in creating products and services in smart cities. Big Data Analytics are characterized by the requirement of advanced data storage, management, analysis, and visualization technologies, which traditional business analytics are not able to offer. These technologies include, among others, interfusion of various data sources, real-time analysis, online analytical processing, business performance management, data mining, machine learning, cloud computing, distributed processing, parallel algorithms, and parallel Database Management Systems (DBMS) [18].

3 Research Method

This paper aims to investigate the complementariness of the smart cities and big and open data research streams. The research approach for attaining this objective is as follows. Since this study aimed at enhancing our understanding of how research on BOLD and Smart Cities can complement each other, a qualitative, case study-based approach was used [21, 23] to inductively arrive at the results. Inductive approaches combine theory and practice and are especially appropriate for dealing with ill-defined problems and theory development. This study uses theoretical sampling to select the cases, which is appropriate for exploring a relatively new field and stimulate the extension of emergent theory and provide examples [22] as is our objective. The following criteria were used for the selection of the cases:

- The cases employ large cities that have started Smart City initiatives and that have already established a BOLD infrastructure;
- The cases employ predictive analytics for the use of BOLD;
- The cases concern data on different societal topics;
- The cases represent BOLD and Smart City initiatives in different countries;
- The cases represent cities of different size;
- Case study information should be available and accessible.

We opted for comparing BOLD and Smart City initiatives on different topics, from different countries, and for cities of different size, to obtain insights from the comparison of these contexts. Based on the selection criteria, we selected the following cases:

Smart Energy. This case study examined a Smart City and BOLD initiative of the city of Amsterdam in the Netherlands. Amsterdam has approximately 800,000 inhabitants. The case focused on the topic of energy saving, and more specifically, on using smart grids and open data on energy to obtain insights about how energy can be saved in the Amsterdam New West district.

Smart Mobility. This case concerned the Smart City and BOLD initiative of the city of Rio de Janeiro in Brazil. Rio de Janeiro has 6.5 million inhabitants. The case focused on the topic of mobility, and, more specifically, on using open public transport and traffic data to obtain insights in how the public transport and traffic can be improved in Rio de Janeiro.

Various information sources were used to investigate the cases. The information sources used to study the cases encompassed reports, documents, applications, websites and observations. From the case study we inductively arrived at the results by comparing the smart cities and BOLD aspects and deriving how both of them were used. The inductively derived concepts and theory can then be used together with other theories as an initial theory in further research.

4   Case Studies: Smart Energy and Smart Mobiliy

This section provides the findings from the two case studies concerning smart energy (Sect. 4.1) and smart mobility (Sect. 4.2).

4.1   Energy Savings in Amsterdam

The city of Amsterdam developed an open data portal which currently contains 416 datasets and a number of APIs. The infrastructure is available via http://www.amsterdamopendata.nl/home. The infrastructure contains data about 18 different themes, including public space, traffic, economy and energy. There is also a reference to an application which provides so-called Smart City Data (http://amsterdam.smartcityapp.nl/), for instance about energy usage, windmills and purchase prices of residences. To become a smart city, the municipality and a number of other partners founded the Amsterdam Smart City (ASC) initiative in 2009. In the ASC initiative, companies, governmental agencies, knowledge institutions and citizens collaborate to make Amsterdam a smarter city. ASC focuses on five key areas, namely smart mobility, smart living, smart society, smart areas and smart economy. The envisioned smart city is one where social and technological networks provide solutions for increased sustainable economic growth, so that the quality of living in the city improves. ASC involves more than 100 partners and more than 75 projects. The projects deal with topics such as budget monitoring, sustainable electric vehicles, air quality, parking, noise pollution, digital road management for emergency services, and energy saving and sustainability [24].

Various ASC projects are focused on energy saving. One of the ASC projects is called "City-zen - Smart Grid" [25]. The project is centered around the development of a smart grid for approximately 40,000 households in the Amsterdam New West district. In addition to the smart meters and solar panels that are already used in this district, computers and sensors are placed in the grid to monitor current and voltage. The electricity grid should reduce the number and duration of power outages, allow for feeding consumer-produced electricity back to the grid, better support electric-powered vehicles, prevent large price increases for electricity transmission and assist in active participation in sustainable energy provision [25].

Liander, the organization maintaining the infrastructure for energy supply in Amsterdam, provides open data about energy usage, including electricity and gas consumption, power outages, and smart meter usage [26]. It offers datasets on energy usage per year, per type of residence, per day, and other detailed data [27]. The data can be accessed and used free of charge. These open data offer energy monitoring opportunities for Amsterdam. For example, based on a combination of datasets from Liander and various simple data analytics, visualizations were created displaying the average monthly usage of electricity and gas among Amsterdam's zip code regions, as well as information about the energy labels for each building. Open data from the municipality of Amsterdam regarding solar panels and regarding the potential of solar panels can be added to this [28]. The combination of these datasets may be interesting not only to the municipality, but also to companies. For instance, a home isolation company that is looking for potential customers could identify residences with high gas usage and a low energy sustainability label, since these residences might suffer from limited home isolation. The isolation company may then target promotion campaigns at these residences. Another application for a company that sells solar panels could be to approach the owners of buildings with a high electricity usage and with high potential to use solar panels, so that the buildings with most energy saving potential are addressed first.

The foregoing shows that the Smart City initiative of Amsterdam can be complemented through open data, that need to be analyzed with data analytics. However, the use of a single dataset is not sufficient to obtain useful insights for energy monitoring purposes in the city. Various datasets from different organizations need to be combined to be able to draw useful conclusions. At the same time, some of the required energy data is not yet available as open data. For instance, the Smart Grid project focused on the Amsterdam New West district. At the time that we conducted this study, open electricity usage data was lacking for certain parts of the city. To allow for the use of open data in the ASC projects, relevant datasets need to be opened and used to make the city 'smarter'.

4.2   Mobility in Rio de Janeiro

The City of Rio de Janeiro in Brazil developed one of the biggest BOLD infrastructures in the world. It has over thirty thousand datasets and seven APIs for real time data – www.data.rio.rj.gov.br. The data is coming from three different places. First, the Center of Operations Rio was created in 2011 and aims to promote the improvement of public service delivery in real time. This includes events such as car accidents or big events that change the routine of the city (e.g., the FIFA World Cup in 2014, Réveillon 1st January and Olympics games in 2016). The second stream of data is collected by the Call Center 1746, where people complain about the public services and the situation of municipal infrastructure, and which can be used as public service maintenance planning. The third type of open data concerns general data from the city. For example, data about the weather and climate (e.g. rain, sea level, river level), health, education, social aid and transport.

The Smart City initiative of Rio de Janeiro was created to solve problems related to public transportation and traffic. With the ownership of one car for almost every two persons in the city (3 million cars for 6.5 million inhabitants), Rio is suffering from huge traffic jams all over the city. The Center of Operations has the operational control over the data collection, and collects everyday around 4 GB of data. However, planning for data collection in the long run was not its function and it did not have the expertise to do so. Therefore, a Big Data group called PENSA – Ideias Room – was created. Specialists in geography, engineering, public administration, physics and computer science started to use the data collected by the City Hall and connected it to the data from Social apps, such as Waze Social GPS.

The first result of this project was the re-dimension of the bus fleet used to transport two million people at the Copacabana beach during the Réveillon 1st January. In 2014, comparing 2013, some barrios had no bus routes, while social data collected in real time from cellphones showed that around 25 thousand people came from there to see the fireworks on the first day, which shows the misconnection of the bus routes with the number of people that wanted to make use of them. It was also found that for some routes the number of required buses was overestimated and they were not needed in reality.

The second result of the project concerned a partnership with the Waze application (http://waze.com). The Rio City Hall understood that not only the city has to be smart, but also citizens have to be assisted in making the best decisions and become smarter than they were before. A partnership with the Waze application was set up, which allows citizens to send real time information to the city about information about, for example, traffic conditions and accidents. The Rio City Hall, via the Center of Operations, also uses the application to send real time information about route changes, flood routes, traffic jams and car accidents to the citizens. The Waze application aimed to improve people's data access, in real time, to make the best decisions, diluting the problems over the city and improving the velocity of cars and buses in the city, measured by cameras and speed traps.

The third part of the project gathered all the data and put them online on some totems (video walls) of the Rio de Janeiro City Hall. They can be used to identify the condition of the traffic and how long cars take to arrive at their destination. The place of totems was planned in accordance with the Big Data analysis from PENSA taking in consideration the data of all apps and internal datasets, looking for the majority of traffic jams (and consequently, the highest number of people on the route). On those totems, the information displayed was a mixture of real time data from social apps of cellphones and the data from Rio (GPS buses).

Fourthly, the project encompassed a partnership with the social app MOOVIT. This application allowed people that used buses in Rio de Janeiro to see, in real time, the condition of bus traffic and how long it takes the bus to arrive at the bus stop and at the destination. It uses the GPS devices that were installed on the buses.

The foregoing shows that the Smart City initiative of Rio de Janeiro can be complemented through open data. The smart city initiative requires the analysis of BOLD with data analytics. Nevertheless, collecting data is hard due to some reasons. A large number of sensors needs to be available to collect data. The sensors are used to track the traffic in real time. Software and human resources have data processing and analytics expertise need to be available. Finally, political support is necessary to gain access to open data.

5   Discussion

In this section we discuss challenges and opportunities for combining smart city and BOLD literature, using the case studies as illustrations for our arguments.

5.1   Opening of Data Sources: Primary and Secondary Measurements

In the cases, datasets originating from different (public) organizations were combined to draw useful conclusions. At the same time, some of the required data was not yet available as open data in both cases. Despite the many datasets that are already opened a main challenge is still the identification of data sources and making data available for use. The lack of willingness to share information among agencies is often a failure factor [29]. Data is easily mistaken for fact, but the raw data is often full of mistakes and have low information quality which makes it unsuitable for direct processing. In both cases the data is used for drawing conclusions at the individual level which requires that the data quality is sufficient for this. Successful open data use strongly depends on the quality of open data [30]. Big Data has an even worse annotation as the term suggests assembling many facts to create greater insight, whereas combining many sources of low information quality might result even in less quality, although not necessarily. The veracity characteristics of big data refers to the need and ability to deal with imprecise and uncertain data [18]. These problems are widely known in the literature, however, with the opening and use of data these problems may become apparent [31] as the opened data might be used for decision-making. Only if the actual user needs is known beforehand it is possible to process data in advance and make the results available.

There are primary and secondary measurements of data used in the cases. *Primary measurement* means that what is measured is directly measured, such as the temperature outside or number of cars passing by. *Secondary measurement* means that a surrogate is measured to determine the measure, like the use of gas for determining the heating of a building. The heating is also dependent on the process of consuming gas into heat which might have various degrees of efficiency dependent on the transformation process design. Primary and direct measurement is often more factual, e.g. if sensors are used to measure directly what is going on, whereas using secondary measurement might give a view which might not always be correct. Smart phones might be used as proxies for the needs, but the use of smart phones varies among populations and might not be used by the owner all the time. Furthermore, data might be subjective, and data collected from smart phones or social media might not be representative for the entire population. For being representative a random sample from a population needs to be taken that has a sufficient size and in which the measurements are independent. These conditions necessary for using statistics often do not hold.

5.2   Fusing Open and Closed Data

Primary and secondary data can both encompass open and closed data. Open and closed data are often combined in the two cases and there is a thin line between open and closed data. In one case a closed dataset was bought by the government which allowed them to open the data for use by others. Also sometimes open and closed data were combined to provide more insight. The results of these combinations are open, but the source data remains closed. There are various reasons for now opening the data including privacy and unclear ownership. A continuous scale between open and closed data emphasizes that not only open data but also closed data should be used to identify improvements. This suggests that a too narrow view on data that is open only might not result in releasing the potential of smart cities.

Furthermore, the way the data is collected is very important and can be done in various ways as systematically described using a taxonomy for collecting and opening data in Fig. 1. In this figure the source of data at the left hand side, the users on the right hand side, and the process of opening data in the middle. At the bottom data push and pull is shown. *Data push* concerns the collection of the data and the subsequent storing of the information in a data storage. The data is collected and pushed to the storage. *Data pull* concerns the delivery of data based on user requests.

Raw data can be made available directly or can be enriched or processed before actual use. Often this is necessary to ensure privacy, to enhance quality or due to other requirements. There are various options for doing this. First, data can be *de-identified* by stripping of certain identifiers, such as names and addresses. Sometimes the identifiable data has been replaced and it is possible to link the data back to an individual, whereas in other cases the data is fully anonymized. Tracing back data might be suitable if recommendations need to be made at the individual levels, e.g. your house can be isolated resulting in a saving of money, whereas, sometimes this might be risky or unwanted, e.g. energy usage might be used by companies to make a commercial offer. Another way of anonymizing data is by *aggregating* data in which the individual data cannot be accessible anymore. If this is suitable depends on the need of the data user, as the aggregated data cannot be used to infer at a lower level of aggregation.

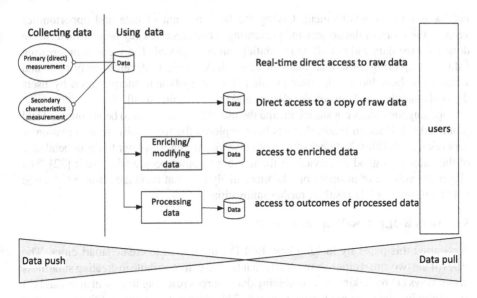

Fig. 1. A taxonomy for forms of collecting and opening data

A third way of dealing with data is to *make only the results of the processing available*. The disadvantage of only having the outcomes of the processed data is that there is no direct access to the source which might be necessary for interpretation or for determining alternative ways of processing data. The advantage is that individual data does not need to be opened.

5.3 Driving Innovations: Balancing Data Push and Pull

Creating innovations with data is a complex process in which both the available data and the users' demand need to be taken into account. The word 'data-driven' suggests that many efforts are data-driven rather than need-driven. In some cases we found that the actors started to think about how to create something that would be useful and attractive for the users, and thereafter the data was investigated. Also the reversed process was found in which data were first opened and thereafter data used to come up with new ideas. Often innovations were inspired by already existing examples which were transferred to the situations of the two smart cities. In the cases the actors examined an idea, and subsequently the potential and limitations of the data for the smart application were shaped. In Rio, for example, the traffic information was collected to improve bus routes which resulted in significant savings. In addition, the traffic information was used by the regional police system to improve the time of police work and to improve their security.

The innovations involved multiple actors, including experts with domain knowledge of the data, database specialists with knowledge about releasing data, analytics experts and people representing the needs of end-users. Having a multidisciplinary development team seems to be a key success, although the cases mainly included IT-people and did not focus on user involvement. Giving the huge amount of data and opportunities keeping the scope of the project and preventing scope creep is a key issue. Much can be done with the data and not all opportunities can be explored. The focus is on creating value by exploring those data that can be used. A trap is to develop many tools and websites without having the user in mind. Use of tools and interpretation by users demands that the gap between developers and users remains small.

Opening the data is not sufficient, and the use of the data needs to be encouraged and promoted [1]. Once an innovation has been explored the focus shifts to the creation of network externalities. Network effects or network externalities refer to the dependence of the value of a good or service on the number of other people who use it [32]. The bigger the volume of information, the more likely it is that users are attracted. A large volume of users might result in further innovation.

5.4 Does BOLD Result in Smartness?

We started this paper by looking how BOLD can be used to create smart cities. The cases of the two smart cities show clearly that BOLD can contribute to creating smartness in two ways (1) by linking and combining data sources resulting in new insights and (2) by employing data and predictive analytics. This does not rule out that there are other ways to create a smart city. For example, the availability of broadband is often considered as part of the smart city concept (e.g. [8]), but has nothing to do with BOLD. When we investigate the intelligence used to process the data, the algorithms used are relatively simple and straightforward. The challenge is often in making the data ready for use and combining them with other data.

The case studies showed that the development of services and applications for citizens requires the analysis of BOLD. The combination of data, data analytics and predictive analytics were used to create applications or to make sense of the data, especially when datasets from different organizations need to be combined to be able to draw useful conclusions. Predictive analytics can be used to seek to uncover patterns and capture relationships in data. Therefore, not only the data need to be available to their users, but also the tools to analyze the data need to be accessible and useful. Balancing the data-driven and user-driven innovation is a key aspect.

In both cases the role of the users is key to accomplish the improved use of resources. *A smart city only becomes smart when there are smart citizens, businesses, civil servants and other stakeholders.* In both cases participatory processes were used to involve the people in the cities. Connecting data and people is a key issue in which the people are able to make use of the data. In Amsterdam citizens can identify opportunities to safe energy and in Rio to improve their traffic planning. As such the concept of smart cities largely depends on what can be called smart citizens; citizens who are able to make advantage of the knowledge and to reduce the actual resource consumption, in this way accomplishing the objectives of smart cities.

6 Conclusions

The objective of this paper is to investigate the complementariness of the smart cities and big and open linked data research streams. Two case studies in smart energy and smart mobility are investigated in different countries. The main challenge of using BOLD for creating smart cities is the identification of data sources and making data available for use. For this purpose a taxonomy for forms of collecting and opening data was derived to support the collection of data. This taxonomy can be used by initiatives aimed at opening data to determine which way of opening data are appropriate. We recommend to further refine this taxonomy.

In both case studies a key element is that open data is linked to and mixed with closed data. This suggests that primarily focusing on open data is a too narrow view. In addition, in both cases data analytics are used to improve the resources in smart cities in which big and open data plays a pivotal role. BOLD enables the use of data and predictive analytics to improve the use of resources in the urban area. The data analytics used in both cases are rather simple. This shows that much can be accomplished using simple techniques. The linking and combination of data and the use of data analytics can result in improved decisions and better utilization of resources and in this way contribute the smartness of cities. Realizing the benefit is dependent on smart citizens; citizens who are able to make advantage of the knowledge and in this way better utilize resources. In the future more comprehensive and advanced data and predictive analytics might be employed to make even more better use of resources to make cities smarter.

Combining BOLD and smart cities proves to be a suitable combination and we plea for more research regarding the adoption, usage and impact of data for smart cities. A limitation of this conceptual study is that the findings are illustrated by only two case studies from different countries. We suggest to conduct more empirical research and to investigate the use of data analytics for creating smartness using a large sample.

References

1. Jaakola, A., Kekkonen, H., Lahti, T., Manninen, A.: Open data, open cities: Experiences from the Helsinki Metropolitan Area. Case Helsinki Region Infoshare www.hri.fi. Stat. J. IAOS J. Int. Assoc. Official Stat. **31**, 117–122 (2015)
2. Komninos, N., Pallot, M., Schaffers, H.: Special issue on smart cities and the future internet in Europe. J. Knowl. Econ. **4**, 119–134 (2013)
3. Jetzek, T., Avital, M., Bjørn-Andersen, N.: Data-driven innovation through open government data. J. Theor. Appl. Electron. Commer. Res. **9**, 100–120 (2014)
4. Janssen, M., Estevez, E., Janowski, T.: Interoperability in big, open, and linked data—organizational maturity, capabilities, and data portfolios. Computer **47**, 26–31 (2014)
5. Chen, Y.-C., Hsieh, T.-C.: Big data for digital government: opportunities, challenges, and strategies. Int. J. Public Adm. Digit. Age **1**, 1–14 (2014)
6. Scholl, H.J., AlAwadhi, S.: Pooling and leveraging scarce resources: the smart eCityGov alliance. In: HICSS, pp. 2355–2365. IEEE, Hawaii (2015)
7. de Jong, M., Joss, S., Schraven, D., Zhan, C., Weijnen, M.: Sustainable–smart–resilient–low carbon–eco–knowledge cities; making sense of a multitude of concepts promoting sustainable urbanization. J. Clean. Prod. Forthcoming (2015). http://ac.elscdn.com/S0959652615001080/1-s2.0-S0959652615001080-main.pdf?_tid=a1bbb6f0-2bb1-11e5-81f1-00000aab0f6b&acdnat=1437047942_1c4e6ccc6a45eb4425262876713afd55
8. Hollands, R.G.: Will the real smart city please stand up? City **12**, 303–320 (2008)

9. Barry, E., Bannister, F.: Barriers to open data release: a view from the top. Inf. Polity **19**, 129–152 (2014)

10. Veljković, N., Bogdanović-Dinić, S., Stoimenov, L.: Benchmarking open government: an open data perspective. Gov. Inf. Q. **31**, 278–290 (2014)

11. Parycek, P., Höchtl, J., Ginner, M.: Open government data implementation evaluation. J. Theor. Appl. Electron. Commer. Res. **9**, 80–99 (2014)

12. Lynggaard, P., Skouby, K.E.: Deploying 5G-Technologies in smart city and smart home wireless sensor networks with interferences. Wirel. Pers. Commun. **81**, 1399–1413 (2015)

13. Corbett, J., Webster, J.: Organizational sensemaking and big data frames: opportunity, control and data limitation In: HICSS2015, pp. 4772–4791. IEEE (2015)

14. Schaffers, H., Komninos, N., Pallot, M., Trousse, B., Nilsson, M., Oliveira, A.: Smart cities and the future internet: towards cooperation frameworks for open innovation. In: Domingue, J., Galis, A., Gavras, A., Zahariadis, T., Lambert, D., Cleary, F., Daras, P., Krco, S., et al. (eds.) The Future Internet. LNCS, vol. 3356, pp. 431–446. Springer, Heidelberg (2011)

15. Nam, T., Pardo, T.A.: Conceptualizing smart city with dimensions of technology, people, and institutions. In: Proceedings of the 12th Annual International Digital Government Research Conference: Digital Government Innovation in Challenging Times, pp. 282–291. ACM, College Park (2011)

16. Chourabi, H., Taewoo, N., Walker, S., Gil-Garcia, J.R., Mellouli, S., Nahon, K., Pardo, T.A., Scholl, H.J.: Understanding smart cities: an integrative framework. In: 2012 45th Hawaii International Conference on System Science (HICSS), pp. 2289–2297 (2012)

17. Caragliu, A., Del Bo, C., Nijkamp, P.: Smart cities in Europe. J. Urban Technol. **18**, 65–82 (2011)

18. Gandomi, A., Haider, M.: Beyond the hype: big data concepts, methods, and analytics. Int. J. Inf. Manage. **35**, 137–144 (2015)

19. McAfee, A., Brynjolfsson, E.: Big data: the management revolution. Harvard Bus. Rev. **68**(128), 60–66 (2012)

20. Chen, H., Chiang, R.H., Storey, V.C.: Business intelligence and analytics: from big data to big impact. MIS Q. **36**, 1165–1188 (2012)

21. Benbasat, I., Goldstein, D.K., Mead, M.: The case research strategy in studies of information systems. MIS Q. **11**, 369–386 (1987)

22. Eisenhardt, K.M.: Building theories from case study research. Acad. Manage. Rev. **14**, 532–550 (1989)

23. Yin, R.K.: Case Study Research. Design and Methods. SAGE publications, Thoasand Oaks (2003)

24. http://amsterdamsmartcity.com/

25. http://amsterdamsmartcity.com/projects/detail/id/17/slug/nieuw-west-smart-grid?lang=en

26. https://www.liander.nl/over-liander/innovatie/open-data

27. https://www.liander.nl/over-liander/innovatie/open-data/data

28. http://www.amsterdamopendata.nl/data?dataset=zonnepanelen

29. Peled, A.: Traversing Digital Babel. MIT Press, Cambridge (2014)

30. Behkamal, B., Kahani, M., Bagheri, E., Jeremic, Z.: A metrics-driven approach for quality assessment of linked open data. J. Theor. Appl. Electron. Commer. Res. **9**, 64–79 (2014)

31. Petychakis, M., Vasileiou, O., Georgis, C., Mouzakitis, S., Psarras, J.: A state-of-the-art analysis of the current public data landscape from a functional, semantic and technical perspective. J. Theor. Appl. Electron. Commer. Res. **9**, 34–47 (2014)

32. Katz, M., Shapiro, C.: Network externalities, competition and compatibility. Am. Econ. Rev. **75**, 424–440 (1985)

Open Innovation Contests for Improving Healthcare – An Explorative Case Study Focusing on Challenges in a Testbed Initiative

Siri Wassrin[✉], Ida Lindgren, and Ulf Melin

Department of Management and Engineering, Linköping University,
Linköping, Sweden
{siri.wassrin,ida.lindgren,ulf.melin}@liu.se

Abstract. Working with innovation is important in several sectors and industries. One emerging arena for innovation is the arrangements of innovation contests. The aim of the paper is to describe and characterize an open innovation contest for improving healthcare, and to address the challenges involved. The research is a qualitative, explorative and interpretive case study of a Swedish region providing publicly funded healthcare. The conclusions show the need to generate and analyze data from actors with several perspectives in the contest. Challenges identified include defining and precisely expressing the problem, separating and delimiting the different problems and achieving a joint view. Other challenges were identifying and attracting knowledgeable participants, to consider incentives, and communicating the contest. In the collaboration stage, challenges involved the contest design, enabling knowledge sharing, managing various agendas, and being open-minded to new ideas; and finally, assessing whether the problem is suitable for open innovation contests at all.

Keywords: Open innovation · Innovation · Innovation contests · Open innovation process · Healthcare · Testbed

1 Introduction

Public healthcare, and government agencies in general, seems to be subject to transformation – processes and technologies need to be updated and improved (e.g. [1]) in order to deliver quality services to a growing, more informed, demanding, and ageing population. In the Swedish setting, similar to several other countries, different actors are trying to contribute to this transformation, including the Swedish innovation agency Vinnova. In 2012 Vinnova launched a call for supporting county councils and regions providing publicly funded healthcare to set up organizations that can facilitate innovative IT-solutions and other preconditions for innovation. The purpose with that initiative was to support building and establishing structures for enabling innovations in healthcare; called 'testbeds'. These testbeds are meant to work as platforms for external businesses, as well as employees in healthcare, to test and implement various types of innovations in the healthcare system. As part of

© IFIP International Federation for Information Processing 2015
E. Tambouris et al. (Eds.): EGOV 2015, LNCS 9248, pp. 91–104, 2015.
DOI: 10.1007/978-3-319-22479-4_7

their testbed activities, several institutions have launched innovation contests. We regard such contests as examples of open innovation (OI). Piller and West [2] elaborate on OI and divide its process into four stages; defining, finding participants, collaborating, and leveraging. These stages are used to structure the analysis below.

In the Swedish context, the use of innovation contests for this purpose is still a novel phenomenon and many institutions are trying this out for the first time. Consequently, there are few empirical studies of these initiatives, and those that exist illustrate how problems experienced in healthcare are typically complex and seem to require in-depth knowledge. Perhaps these problems are too complex to be addressed through OI contests? For example, Hellberg's [3] study of an innovation contest involving the use of open data, organized by a Swedish county council, illustrates that "[t]o have the ability to take part [in the contest] there is first a need for knowledge on the subject. Not many have this, because in general people do not know what public data is. Secondly, there is a need for competence to understand and use the data" (p. 272).

This paper illustrates and discusses an OI contest organized by a Swedish region providing publicly funded healthcare. The aim of this paper is to: (1) describe and characterize an OI contest for improving healthcare, and (2) to address the challenges identified in this case. The identified challenges can be understood as aspects to address from a practical point of view when improving healthcare, and as an inspiration for further research.

The paper is organized as follows; first, the theoretical background of the paper is presented; second, the research approach is discussed; third, the case study is described; fourth, the analysis and discussion; and finally, the conclusions are presented.

2   Theoretical Background

Innovation is a buzzword echoing throughout public and private sector as well as academia. Although often vaguely defined, the etymological meaning of innovation refers to the introduction of novelties, alteration of established forms through the introduction of new forms or a change in something [4]. Traditionally, the innovation process has been firm-centric where producers innovate to compete on a market. Today, this process is often opened up by purposively letting knowledge flow in and out of a firm, called Open Innovation (OI) [5]. Chesbrough distinguishes between inbound and outbound OI. The former refers to internal use of external knowledge, whereas the latter refers to external use of internal knowledge. These can also be divided into pecuniary and non-pecuniary OI [6]. *Revealing* refers to non-pecuniary outbound OI, e.g. when an organization discloses internal resources to the environment. Its pecuniary equivalent is *selling* information or ideas. *Sourcing* refers to non-pecuniary inbound OI, e.g. when organizations scan the environment for external sources of innovation such as ideas and technologies that may be incorporated into the organization. Its pecuniary equivalent is *acquiring* these sources of innovation [6]. OI can be construed as an umbrella term [7] that includes many already existing innovation activities such as innovation contests. Hence, in this paper we consider innovation contests as an example of OI. The next section focuses on how an OI process can be construed.

2.1 Four Stages in the OI Process

Gassman and Enkel (in [2]) propose a mode of OI called *coupled process* where the inflow and outflow of knowledge and ideas are combined by "working in alliances with complementary partners" (p. 37). Piller and West elaborate on this concept and divide the process of coupled OI into four stages; (1) defining; (2) finding participants; (3) collaborating; and (4) leveraging.

The first stage of the OI process involves defining the problem to be addressed in the OI project. The problem, scope and performance criteria need to be expressed precisely, using vocabulary that is comprehensible for potential participants from different knowledge fields [2]. Nickerson and Zenger [8] draw on the ideas of Simon [9] and argue that problems can be *decomposable, nearly decomposable* or *nondecomposable*. Decomposable problems "can be subdivided into subproblems, each of which draws from rather specialized knowledge sets" [8] (p. 620). These subproblems are independent of one another, which mean that interaction is not needed between solvers of the various subproblems and hence are suited for outsourcing to a crowd or a market [8]. Nondecomposable problems, on the other hand, are ill-structured and not possible to divide into subproblems because of their "unexpected and unknown interactions among the potential different knowledge sets that make up the overall problems and the lack of definitive criteria for assessment of solutions" [10] (p. 1018). Instead, these problems call for a high level of interaction between people with various knowledge sets and, hence, knowledge transfer is of great importance. These complex problems are suited for problem-solving methods where people with different knowledge may interact and share their knowledge [8]. Nearly decomposable problems lie in between the two prior concepts. These problems may be divided into subproblems but interdependencies between the subproblems exist. This calls for a moderate level of interaction between knowledge sets [8]. Jeppesen and Lakhani [10] argue that most problems in real life fall into this last category. These are ill-structured problems that have been transformed and formalized so that they can be decomposed.

The second stage in the OI process involves finding suitable participants with relevant knowledge and skills. According to Piller and West [2], defining the problem is essential to attract participants and to identify relevant characteristics of possible contributors. However, Jeppesen and Lakhani [10] point out that problems are sometimes solved by nonobvious individuals with knowledge sets that at first sight do not seem to match the problem. They argue that new perspectives on a problem may lead to new and innovative solutions and hence, nonobvious and marginalized participants should be invited to partake in the OI project. When recruiting contributors, it is important to understand and strengthen participants' incentives to collaborate and share their knowledge. In the literature, incentives are often divided into monetary (e.g. prizes, selling or licensing information) and non-monetary (e.g. possibility to fulfill their own needs, career-visibility or social motives). In reality, this distinction is usually blurred and various participants are motivated both by monetary and non-monetary incentives [2]. The recruitment process is generally driven by the initiator of the OI project. Piller and West [2] distinguish between three recruitment strategies; *open call, selective open call* and *open search*. The first strategy is directed towards a broad and undefined group of participants (cf. crowdsourcing), whereas the second strategy pin-points suitable groups of participants (e.g. experts, market segments) and directs the call towards these. In the third strategy, the initiator actively engages in identifying suitable participants and invites them to collaborate.

The third stage in the OI process involves the interactive collaboration between the initiator and external participants. Piller and West [2] argue that this is "[t]he key value creation process" (p. 40) in which new innovations are created. The initiator has to create and implement structures for collaboration to monitor and manage the value creation and also define the span of control and influence given to external participants. Participants who are given a high level of freedom become engaged but this gives the initiator less power to control the processes. Also, internal attitudes and competences should be addressed to facilitate collaboration, e.g. the willingness to open up for sharing and exchanging information and knowledge. These ideas are also echoed in the literature on innovation contests. This kind of events can be designed to support competition or collaboration to varying degrees. Lampel et al. [11] argue that contests with only one award nurtures a winner-takes-it-all mindset whereas a more collaborative approach usually has several prizes to recognize different participants' contributions and cultivate a culture of knowledge sharing, networking and learning from each other through interaction. Furthermore, innovation contests may range from having broad to narrow goals and organizers and participants join the contest with different agendas. These agendas affect the goal and process of the contest [11].

The final stage concerns the leveraging and exploitation of the collaboration results, e.g. through integrating the new knowledge into the organization and commercializing the innovation. This stage is not within the scope of this paper.

3   Research Approach

The empirical data in this paper was collected as part of a research project designed to study and document the formation and evolution of a testbed initiative in a region in Sweden. The testbed initiative is based at a regional university hospital, is funded by Vinnova, and was approved with the exclusive criteria that researchers had to be part of the development, set-up and the evaluation of the testbed. Hence, our research project is financed as a part of the particular testbed initiative in focus. The research project is managed by the university and runs through 2013–2015. The overall research questions addressed in the project include exploring: (1) What constitutes a testbed in this particular organization? (2) How is the testbed organized and coordinated? and (3) What stakeholders are involved and managed by the project management? The project group responsible for the testbed organized an innovation contest in 2014.

As a part of the project we were allowed to study the contest, generating empirical data through semi-structured face-to-face interviews and participatory observation during the process. We conducted seven interviews with an average duration of approximately 40–45 min. The interviews included conversations with the project manager, two clinic representatives and one development director on the regional level. We also attended ten meetings with the average duration of 90 min per meeting. The meetings contained actors from the project team, a competing team in the innovation contest, and one external researcher from The Swedish National Road and Transport Research Institute (VTI). The meetings were distributed in time and along the planning and executing process of the innovation contest. They covered the introduction, different stages of the contest, coordination, and the finale. On one occasion, a meeting was videotaped and analyzed by the researchers at a later stage. The interviews took place between April and October 2014; the meetings took place the same year between February and October.

One researcher from the research project was present at the meetings, and one or two researchers conducted the interviews. The qualitative data have been analyzed using a hermeneutic approach [12]. The research presented in this paper is hence conducted as a qualitative case study and is built on interpretive assumptions of the world [13]. For the theoretical foundation, hermeneutic literature reviews were conducted [14]; focusing on key terms such as innovation, open innovation, innovation contests. The overall testbed initiative can be classified as action research, whereas the research activities focused in this paper can be understood as a qualitative and interpretive case study.

4   The Case – The Innovation Contest

This section describes the contest and its context, and gives an account of what happened before, during, and after the contest. In addition, it presents a number of challenges encountered during the innovation contest.

4.1   Before the Contest

The innovation contest was led by a project team consisting of a project manager from the region's testbed organization, two other members from the same setting and a chief physician and two occupational therapists from a medical clinic. The problem that was to be solved in the contest was introduced by employees at one of the region's medical clinics, who worked with assessments of patients with brain injury and their ability to drive a vehicle. According to the staff at the clinic, proper methods to assess people's ability to drive and the deterioration of intellectual abilities that may occur after brain injury were missing. The methods available were a driving simulator and paper-based psychological tests, but these methods were not perceived as sensitive and reliable enough. The technology was seen as old and unpredictable as the computers often broke down. Hence, the staff at the clinic saw a need to develop a simple, yet secure, method to assess a person's driving ability after brain injury.

The project team came up with a contest design that was rather complex, containing multiple stages, (including ideation, lo-fi prototyping and executable prototyping) and two tracks – an open track and a conventional track. The open track was meant to focus on open innovation and ideation where the work of the participants was to be presented openly after each stage. The conventional track was meant for firms that wanted to compete but that did not wish to disclose their product development or other internal business secrets. At the last stage in the contest, the two tracks were meant to be merged and all entries were to compete against each other. The project team also specified evaluation requirements for assessing the solutions resulting from the contest. These were expressed in a list of 14 requirements, e.g., ecological validity, reliability, possibility to configure the solution after current needs. There were no criteria concerning what problem the solution should solve. The competing teams' solutions were to be assessed by the project team.

The innovation contest was meant to be open for everyone, e.g. individuals, students, associations, organizations and firms, and people were allowed to compete alone or in teams. In order to attract contestants, the project team organized three introductory meetings to inform people about the contest. Information about these meetings was communicated through their webpage, e-mail to companies and educational programs at the university, the region's twitter account, and to some extent in local media. Wanting to attract anyone who could be interested in the contest, the project team did not articulate any special target group for their communication. Nonetheless, during internal meetings, they discussed e.g. cognitive science, medicine, programming, technology and psychology as possible target groups. Concerning incentives for participating in the contest, the team reflected only slightly on what the contest could offer to the participants. They concluded that contestants could make a civic contribution and create a product, or business idea.

The day of the first introductory meeting, no one showed up. Interestingly, no participants showed up for the second or third introductory meetings either. The team concluded that reaching out to participants was a bigger challenge than what they had thought. Because of the lack of participants, the whole contest was rescheduled and redesigned from three stages and two tracks to only focus on two stages; ideation and lo-fi prototyping. The project team wanted to find a contestant that could be interested in spending a lot of time on the task at hand and in cooperating also after the contest. For these reasons, the idea to only work with the first two parts of the contest was seen as a good way to continue. Thereafter, a fourth introductory meeting was held and six individuals showed up to this meeting. These were all personally invited by the project manager and they represented various organizations, e.g. IT and management consultancy firms and departments in the region. None of these participants decided to join the contest.

4.2 During the Contest

Only one team signed up for the contest by the registration deadline. This was an IT consultancy firm that had been contacted directly by the project team, encouraging them to join the contest. Thus, the contest contained only one competing team. Now that the contest had a contestant, the first part of the contest (ideation) was launched. The competing team presented their work and explained that they had started their process by talking to the medical staff, gathering information and forming an understanding of the problem at hand. They also visited the Swedish National Road and Transport Research Institute (VTI), an organization that develops driving simulators and performs research on these issues. The team's solution was a scalable and modular technology platform that was meant to fill the needs in primary healthcare; a platform that can be used as a first screening device by simple tests on a tablet, but that can also be used at the specialist clinic using full scale simulators. Note however that the competing team pointed out that they did not have the competence to develop the medical tests to put into the platform. Instead, they asked for help to choose an existing test that they could turn into a tablet application.

After the ideation stage, the project team evaluated the proposed solution together with the director of research from VTI and concluded that the scalability was a good feature. They also concluded that the competing team had included more features in the solution than was outlined in the specification of requirements. These new features were seen as good, but raised the question of what should be put into the prototype. The project team thought that a solution of the problem was missing in the contestant's presentation and wanted a dynamic test in which cognitive and meta-cognitive abilities were taken into consideration. The researcher from VTI pointed out however, that metacognition is very difficult to measure.

The next step in the contest was the prototyping stage. The project team and the competing team discussed what content could be put into the platform as a first prototype. The project team emphasized that the competing team should focus on the screening instrument, and not the other features that was presented in the first stage. The competing team concluded that they needed help from VTI to choose what types of cognitive tests that could be developed for the platform.

By the end of the contest, the competing team presented their perception of the problem area once more, followed by a description of their solution. They pointed out that they did not know how to produce tests that could measure cognitive abilities, but that their approach instead was to create a whole technical concept around the problem. Their prototype built on a cognitive test suggested by VTI that had been translated from a paper form to a test on a tablet. After the presentation, the project team adjourned to discuss whether or not the competing team had met the requirements of the contest. The project group concluded that the solution was not novel, but just a matter of digitalization of a paper form. In addition, the test that was chosen had not been tested in relation to driving and was therefore not properly validated. The tablet solution did have some advantages however, in terms of enabling instant feedback and creating possibilities for digitizing additional tests into the tablet that could be useful when screening patients. Despite these flaws in the solution, the project team found that most of the 14 requirements had been fulfilled; resulting in a situation where the competing team's solution was deemed to fulfill the contest requirements despite the fact that the solution did not solve the problem at hand. The competing team was chosen as winners of the contest and all participants agreed that they wanted to continue cooperating after the contest. After a prize ceremony, the contest was perceived as finished.

4.3 After the Contest

All involved actors were overall content with their part in the contest, but had different views on the outcome of the contest. The testbed representative thought that they had learnt a lot from trying out a new work format; they had realized how much work it took to communicate such an event and that it was difficult to attract participants. In turn, the competing team was happy with their achievements in the contest. They had made an executable prototype, which was not even required by the contest rules. However, they thought that the project team was not open to a new approach and broader problem formulation. The competing team felt that the clinic would rather just have their old technological equipment replaced by new technology but with similar features. Last, the representative from the clinic was disappointed that the problem had not been solved, meaning that the challenges in their work at the clinic were still prevalent. One of the clinic staff argued that a replacement of the old technology would have solved their problem at the specialist clinic, but that this solution would not have been considered innovative. Even though the participants disagreed on the success of the outcome, all of the participants wanted to continue their cooperation to develop the solution further.

4.4 Challenges Encountered During the Contest

Many challenges were encountered during the contest. In this section, we discuss some of these challenges in relation to three themes identified in the empirical data; (1) the contest's problem formulation; (2) the participants' expectations and goals; and (3) cooperation, communication and competence.

First, an obvious challenge illustrated in the description above concerns the problem to be solved by the contest. The problem that contestants were to solve in the contest was formulated differently throughout the information that was disseminated by the project team. For instance, the problem was phrased as follows: A way/method/appropriate tool to easily/reliably/cost-effectively assess/measure/identify a person's ability/ condition/cognitive skill to safely drive in traffic after brain injury. Furthermore, the cognitive abilities that the clinic wished to assess, measure or identify were described differently in the written, versus oral, presentations of the problem. When reflecting on their problem formulation, the project team argued that few people could understand what the problem entailed. In the framing of the problem, the project team was also unclear concerning in what medical context the test was to be applied. The solution that the project team was searching for was to be applied in primary healthcare, and not in the specialist clinic. The competing team, however, thought that the solution was to be implemented at the specialist clinic.

The contest's problem formulation was also expressed differently by its various participants. For example, the project manager emphasized certain aspects of the problem, whereas the representatives from the clinic emphasized other aspects. A possible reason to the uncertainties concerning the problem formulation, given by the project manager, was that the complexity of the problem was unveiled for the project management members as the contest progressed. As a result of the vague problem description, the competing team came up with their interpretation of the problem. Their interpretation of the problem was more general, and more focused on the technical platform of the test, rather than the test in itself. Based on their interpretation of the problem, the competing team changed the focus of the contest to create a modular framework. They argued that they did not know how to develop the tests per se, instead their solution was to create a whole concept in which tests can be incorporated in different platforms within the framework.

Concerning the second theme, the participants' expectations and goals with the contest varied. From the clinic's point of view, the goal was to find a solution to their problem. One person from the clinical staff expected that the contest would lead to a new product that could be used at the clinic. The testbed representatives, on the other hand, wanted to try out innovation contests as a work method, but also to create opportunities to cooperate with researchers, innovators, and firms in other ways than public procurement. The competing team expected to get access to the clinic and problem owners in order to discuss the problem and come up with a good solution. They also anticipated new business opportunities and relationship building with the region, since these were customers they wished to work with.

Concerning the last theme, both the representative from the clinic and the competing team thought that the level of cooperation between the two parties had been fairly low during the contest and that more cooperation would have been necessary for a better solution. The competing team felt that they did not get access to the knowledge and cooperation that they had expected. One reason for this was that the clinic did not want to reveal too much information since they thought that this would steer or bias the competing team and hence inhibit their innovative ability. The clinic representative said that they did not want to tell them to replace their old technology but that it was difficult to describe what they were looking for. Last, there were some additional communication problems. The competing team repeatedly said that they did not have the skills to develop medical tests, but the clinic did not become aware of this until late in the contest. The competing team argued that they could only develop the technological parts of a test if they were told what the test was to consist of. At the same time, the clinic repeatedly stressed that they needed help to develop the tests. When asked who had the competence to develop tests, the competing team referred to VTI, researchers and the chief physician at the clinic, whereas the clinic representative referred to occupational therapists and VTI, rather than to physicians. However, both parties thought that the cooperation and communication would become more clear and unambiguous now that the contest was over.

5 Analysis and Discussion

The aim of this paper is to: (1) describe and characterize an open innovation contest for improving healthcare, and (2) to address the challenges identified in our case. The former section described an open innovation contest; in this section we turn to the identified challenges in the light of theory.

5.1 Challenges Related to the Problem Definition Stage

Piller and West [2] emphasize the importance of defining the problem to be solved in OI processes. This was a major challenge in the innovation contest. For instance, the problem was expressed in many different ways in the written information and by the participants; there were no criteria for assessing the chosen solution, i.e. what problem the solution should solve; and there were confusion concerning whether the solution should be applied in the specialist clinic or in primary healthcare. Furthermore, many cognitive abilities were mentioned as important when assessing people's ability to drive.

Metacognitive abilities were also pointed out as complex and difficult to measure. These examples imply that the problem formulation was ambiguous, ill-structured and complex. It is however hard to tell if the problem was nondecomposable or if it just had not been thoroughly formalized and divided into subproblems. The major challenges in the definition stage in this particular innovation contest were to define and precisely express the problem; to separate and delimit different actors' problems (i.e. the specialist clinic's problem versus primary healthcare's problem), to communicate the problem(s) and to achieve a (fairly) joint view of it.

5.2 Challenges Related to the Stage of Finding and Attracting Participants

To identify and attract suitable participants proved to be a major challenge in the innovation contest. The project team used the strategy *Open call* [2] by opening up their problem to a broad and undefined crowd. The team wanted the contest to be open to anyone, as they forecasted opportunities for innovation by putting people with heterogeneous competences together. However, there was little funding for communicating the contest as an event and the project team thought that it would be sufficient to inform about the contest through the organization's website and through e-mails. Hence, it was difficult to spread information about the contest in order to ensure participants. When realizing that the chosen communication strategy was not effective, they switched to an *Open search* [2] approach where they actively searched for and invited 'head hunted' participants. Furthermore, the project group seems to have overestimated the interest and the incentives for participating in the contest; they only managed to find *one* participating team. Our analysis shows that the issue of incentives was not discussed by the project group to any greater extent. However, previous research shows that it essential to take possible participants' incentives into consideration [2]. This difficulty is also illustrated by Hellberg [3], who argues that it is hard to get the right people interested in participating in contests like these. Our research clearly supports these difficulties.

Another part of the challenge to find and attract participants had to do with identification of relevant knowledge sets and competence that could help to solve the problem. In the studied contest, the problem was not solved partly because important knowledge sets were missing. The clinic initiated the contest because they did not have the appropriate skills, knowledge and competence to solve their problem internally. The competing team also articulated that the knowledge about how medical tests should be developed was missing in the contest. This indicates that crucial knowledge sets for solving the problem were not present in the contest. One explanation for this could be that the ambiguous, ill-structured and complex problem formulation, as mentioned above, made it difficult to assess what knowledge sets and competence that were needed to find a solution. This may not be apparent even with a well-defined problem, since solutions can come from people with unexpected competences [10] – but when it is evident that knowledge is missing, new sources of knowledge should be searched for. To conclude, the major challenges in this stage were to identify and attract participants with relevant knowledge sets, to consider participants' incentives, to choose and communicate an effective recruitment strategy.

5.3   Challenges Related to the Collaboration Stage

The problem to be solved in an OI process should fit the contest design [8] and the design and structure will also affect the collaboration between the initiator and external participants [2]. Without a clear picture of the problem it is difficult to make informed decisions about contest event design – whether the problem calls for interaction between people with different knowledge sets or if it is more suitable for crowdsourcing where interaction is less crucial. A challenge in this particular innovation contest was to fit the design of the contest to the problem at hand, or vice versa, to formulate a problem that suited the contest design. As mentioned above, it is hard to tell whether the contest's problem is decomposable and, thus, suited for the open contest design, or whether the problem is truly nondecomposable and that the design should have emphasized more collaboration [8]. Our analysis shows that there are indications that more collaboration was needed. For instance, all participants wanted to collaborate *after* the contest and several participants expressed that collaboration would be easier when the contest was over. Again, if the problem is nondecomposable, a design that enables interaction between knowledge sets and accelerates knowledge transfer is preferable [8].

Interaction can be managed by designing structures for collaboration which enables the OI initiator to steer these processes [2]. The vague problem formulation in the contest made it possible for the competing team to reinterpret, broaden and even redefine the problem from their perspective. Hence, the ambiguous problem definition opened up for a broad control span for the contestants [2]. In this sense, the structures for collaboration were loose and the possibility for the project team to monitor and manage this process was partly 'given away' [2]. However, that contestants interpret the contest's problem from their own perspective can probably not be, nor should be, avoided. On the contrary, Jeppesen and Lakhani [10] point out that disparate and marginal perspectives can open up for new solutions paths – the major reason of opening up the problem-solving process in the first place. This means that different interpretations do not have to be negative, but in this case the new perspective that the competing team suggested did not solve the problem; it was rather seen as out of scope by the project team. Thus, it seems like the initial ambiguity in the problem formulation contributed to further ambiguity in the contest, in line with Piller and West's [2] idea of 'ambiguity in, ambiguity out' and that the problem formulation is one tool for the initiator to steer the collaboration process.

The collaboration process was also influenced by the participants' various agendas; the clinic wanted to solve their problems at the clinic and in primary healthcare, the testbed wanted to try out the innovation contest as a new way of working and to find and attract new partners to cooperate with. The competing team, on the other hand, wanted to get access to the clinic, establish new relationships and open up new business opportunities. The various goals of the participants also echoed in their views of the contest's outcome. Those with a narrower goal, to find a solution for the clinic, were more disappointed than those who had broader goals. This indicates challenges to manage various agendas and expectations in the contest and to create and implement structures for collaboration that meet these needs. Different forces will affect the contest design and if the 'wrong' goals are allowed to dominate the contest, this can lead the contest off track. In this particular contest, it seems that the goals to try out innovation contest as a work form and to create relationships were met, whereas the goal that initiated the contest was not fulfilled. Hence, the ambiguity echoing through the contest also affected the interaction and collaboration processes.

Another challenge in the studied open innovation contest was to be open. In the light of theory, the contest can be understood as a case of *outbound open innovation that is non-pecuniary,* i.e. *revealing* [6]. Initially, the project team aimed at revealing a problem, information and other internal resources such as the opportunity to talk to the staff at the clinic, to get access to clinical and technical competence, get support to advance and evaluate the winning entry. The revealing strategy is used when it is too difficult or expensive to develop something in-house [6]. However, the project team did not want to reveal too much of their thoughts and ideas since they did not want to limit the competing team's innovative ability. They did not want to 'bias' the competing team by telling them to replace the old technology. The competing team, who used a sourcing strategy, i.e. *non-pecuniary inbound open innovation* [6], wanted more collaboration and knowledge exchange with the clinic to be able to develop their solution. Hence, the 'openness' of the OI initiative was limited since they did not fully commit to their chosen strategy. This, in turn, limited the level of cooperation in the contest. A similar challenge was for the project team to be open-minded to new interpretations and to seriously consider new perspectives. For instance, the competing team did not feel that their new approach was taken into serious consideration. However, to facilitate collaboration, attitudes and willingness to open up need to be addressed [2].

A final challenge identified in our analysis of the empirical data was to assess whether the problem is suitable for open innovation contests at all, or if another project or event design would be better. There are some indications that the wish to be 'innovative' and to organize an innovation contest impeded the problem solving process in this particular case. As mentioned above, the level of revealing information and knowledge transfer was inhibited because the clinic did not want to 'bias' the competing team's innovative ability. Collaboration was inhibited for the same reasons although both parties thought that collaboration was needed to solve the problem. It was also made clear that a replacement of the old technology would have solved the problem, but since this was not considered innovative enough, it was out of the question. Before designing and launching an innovation contest it could be useful to think about whether the innovation really is needed to solve the problem at hand, or if 'innovation' acts as an institutional pressure (e.g. [15]) to act as a modern and innovative organization in line with dominating norms. To uncover underlying assumptions of innovation processes can also be useful, i.e. whether innovative ideas occur in isolation (e.g. do not 'bias' the contestants), or if they occur through collaboration (e.g. design for interaction).

To conclude, challenges regarding the collaboration stage include fitting contest design and problem to one another, creating structures for collaboration to enable knowledge sharing and manage various agendas, being open by sharing knowledge and information and to be open-minded to new ideas, and finally, to assess whether the problem is suitable for open innovation contests at all.

6   Conclusions

The challenges identified in the analysis and discussion above can be summarized as follows based on the different stages in an open innovation contest; (1) In the definition stage, the major challenges were to define and precisely express the problem, to separate and delimit the different problems and achieve a (fairly) joint view of it. (2) In the stage of finding participants, the major challenges were to identify and attract participants with relevant knowledge sets, to consider participants' incentives, to choose a suitable recruitment and communication strategy. (3) In the collaboration stage, challenges involved fitting the contest design and problem to one another, creating structures for collaboration to enable knowledge sharing and manage various agendas, being open by sharing knowledge and information and to be open-minded to new ideas, and finally, to assess whether the problem is suitable for open innovation contests at all.

We have studied open innovation in a public healthcare case in this paper, but claim that the challenges are possible to generalize analytically to other public or private sector cases and setting. Analyzing the data in the previous section in the light of the theory supports this claim. However, it may be some aspects of a public organization providing healthcare such as power, politics and strong professional groups affecting e.g. the different aspects of the problem definitions and solutions, and the norms discussed above that can be domain specific.

The conclusions show the need to generate and analyze data from actors with several perspectives in the innovation contest. The identified challenges in this paper can also be viewed as an inspiration for further research directions and aspects to address from a practical point of view regardless of sector. Some practical implications that can be drawn based on this explorative study is that there is a need to address the problem space of an innovation contest thoroughly since this affects many other areas such as contest design, collaboration and the possibility to identify and attract participants.

References

1. Nograšek, J., Vintar, M.: E-government and organisational transformation of government: black box revisited? Gov. Inf. Q. **31**, 108–118 (2014)
2. Piller, F., West, J.: Firms, users, and innovation: an interactive model of coupled open innovation. In: Chesbrough, H., Vanhaverbeke, W., West, J. (eds.) New Frontiers in Open Innovation, pp. 29–49. Oxford University Press, New York (2014)
3. Hellberg, A.-S.: Policy, process, people and public data. In: Janssen, M., Scholl, H.J., Wimmer, M.A., Bannister, F. (eds.) EGOV 2014. LNCS, vol. 8653, pp. 265–276. Springer, Heidelberg (2014)
4. innovation, n.: http://www.oed.com/view/Entry/96311?redirectedFrom=innovation
5. Chesbrough, H.W.: Open Innovation: The New Imperative for Creating and Profiting from Technology. Harvard Business Press, Boston (2006)
6. Dahlander, L., Gann, D.M.: How open is innovation? Res. Policy **39**, 699–709 (2010)
7. Huizingh, E.K.R.E.: Open innovation: state of the art and future perspectives. Technovation **31**, 2–9 (2011)
8. Nickerson, J., Zenger, T.: A knowledge-based theory of the firm: the problem-solving perspective. Organ. Sci. **15**, 617–632 (2004)

9. Simon, H.A.: The Sciences of the Artificial, 3rd edn. The MIT Press, Cambridge (1996)
10. Jeppesen, L., Lakhani, K.: Marginality and problem-solving effectiveness in broadcast search. Organ. Sci. **21**, 1016–1033 (2010)
11. Lampel, J., Jha, P.P., Bhalla, A.: Test-driving the future: how design competitions are changing innovation. Acad. Manag. Perspect. **26**, 71–85 (2012)
12. Klein, H.K., Myers, M.D.: A set of principles for conducting and evaluating interpretive field studies in information systems. MIS Q. **23**, 67–93 (1999)
13. Walsham, G.: Interpretive case studies in IS research: nature and method. Eur. J. Inf. Syst. **4**, 74–81 (1995)
14. Boell, S.K., Cecez-Kecmanovic, D.: A hermeneutic approach for conducting literature reviews and literature searches. Commun. Assoc. Inf. Syst. **34**, 257–286 (2014)
15. DiMaggio, P.J., Powell, W.W.: The iron cage revisited: institutional isomorphism and collective rationality in organizational fields. Am. Sociol. Rev. **48**, 147–160 (1983)

Public Accountability ICT Support: A Detailed Account of Public Accountability Process and Tasks

Rui Pedro Lourenço[1,2(✉)], Suzanne Piotrowski[3], and Alex Ingrams[3]

[1] INESC Coimbra, Coimbra, Portugal
[2] Faculty of Economics, University of Coimbra, Coimbra, Portugal
ruiloure@fe.uc.pt
[3] School of Public Affairs and Administration, Rutgers University-Newark, Newark, USA
spiotrow@scarletmail.rutgers.edu, alex.ingrams@gmail.com

Abstract. A key objective of open government programs is to promote public accountability by using Information and Communication Technologies (ICT) to release data on the internal working of public agencies. However, it is not clear how actual accountability (such as sanctions or rewards) may be achieved from the data disclosed. Nor it is clear how ICT in general should support it. To better understand how ICT can support open data initiated accountability processes in achieving their goal, this paper considers the three phases (information, discussion, and consequences) usually used to describe such processes. Defining ICT support for these major phases is a difficult effort, since each phase encompasses different tasks and support requirements. This paper aims to address this problem by providing a detailed account of the tasks associated with the whole public accountability process. This may be used by those responsible for open government programs to design and deploy comprehensive ICT support platforms using a task-technology fit perspective.

Keywords: Open government · Accountability · ICT · Task-technology fit

1 Introduction

A central pillar of open government initiatives is the active disclosure of data held by public agencies. The creation of open data portals (e.g. Data.gov) has subsequently become associated with the expression Open Government Data (OGD). In the context of open government, the release of data might serve two main purposes [1]: (1) allowing the re-use of such data to enable the creation of new products and services by the private sector; or (2), *transparency for accountability*, where public agencies disclose data about their internal works allowing the general public to monitor their actions and performance [2, 3].

Despite the apparent success and high impact of open data portals, Yu and Robinson [4] draw attention to the ambiguity of the expression Open Government Data as it may convey two very different meanings: (1) the disclosure of politically relevant data, whether or not using information technology or (2) the usage of technological platforms to facilitate access to government held data, whether or not politically relevant. Yu and

© IFIP International Federation for Information Processing 2015
E. Tambouris et al. (Eds.): EGOV 2015, LNCS 9248, pp. 105–117, 2015.
DOI: 10.1007/978-3-319-22479-4_8

Robinson [4] also point out that these initiatives focus "more on technological innovation and service delivery" and public agencies "have tended to release data that helps them serve their existing goals without throwing open the doors for uncomfortable increases in public scrutiny."

Despite the doubts raised by Yu and Robinson [4], OGD portals may be considered as an example of how ICTs may support public accountability. Even so, as Bovens [5] notes, transparency as data disclosure is certainly a pre-requisite for public accountability but the latter also requires the scrutiny of the data provided and the possibility to award rewards or sanctions accordingly. Therefore, OGD portals could, at most, be considered as a technology that supports the initial phase (data disclosure) of the whole public accountability process which comprises three main phases: information/transparency, debate, and consequences.

The discussion on how ICTs might help to support public accountability needs to look beyond OGD portals and data disclosure, and a Task-Technology Fit (TTF) [6] perspective may be useful to frame such discussion. TTF was advanced in the context of Computer-Mediated Communications (CMC) and Group Support Systems (GSS) to stress the importance and impact of a good fit between the task to be performed by groups and technologies used, on the effectiveness of group support (CMC, GSS). To determine a 'good fit' it is necessary to consider both the attributes of task(s) to be performed and the relevant technology characteristics.

The problem of finding the 'best fit' technologies to support public participation, in part or as a whole process, is also illustrated by Robinson et al. [7] who, when describing a set of ICT tools that have the potential to support data presentation and visualization, ended their analysis with this sentence: "Exactly which of these features to use in which case, and how to combine advanced features with data presentation, is an open question." To design a complete public accountability platform that goes beyond simple data disclosure it is necessary to consider:

- What tasks need to be supported along the whole public accountability process?
- What type of support is required for each task?
- What kind of applications have the potential to support each task?
- How to design, develop and implement a comprehensive public accountability platform by selecting and combining the 'best fit' applications and technologies to meet the requirements?

We identify and characterize the tasks performed in the context of a public accountability process (providing an answer to the first question) and therefore provide the solid ground upon which a TTF approach might be used. We start by characterizing public accountability (Sect. 2), including its main phases and parties involved. In Sect. 3, the three main phases of the public accountability process are further analyzed and divided into discrete tasks according to the literature. Within Sect. 4, we identify a set of abstract data patterns performed along the process which already indicate the type of ICTs adequate to support them. By the end of Sect. 4, each public accountability task is associated with one or more abstract task patterns thus providing a starting point to design a comprehensive public accountability support platform under a TTF approach.

2 Public Accountability

The concept of accountability is complex ("an ever-expanding concept" [8]) and is subject to many interpretations and disagreement about its meanings [9–11]. Several authors have advanced definitions of accountability [5, 12, 13], and have proposed accountability typologies [5, 12, 14, 15] (see also Steccolini [16, p. 332] - Table 1 for a list of such typologies). In this paper we will consider Bovens' definition:

> "Accountability is a relationship between an *actor* and a *forum*, in which the actor has an obligation to explain and to justify his or her conduct, the forum can pose questions and pass judgement, and the actor may face consequences." [5]

Moreover, our focuses is on *public accountability*, that is, the accountability of organizations or officials exercising public authority, from a perspective concerned with democratic control over those institutions and individuals [5]. Figure 1 illustrates the simplified accountability model considered here (inspired by [5], p. 454; Fig. 1), depicting the main stages and main parties involved in public accountability process.

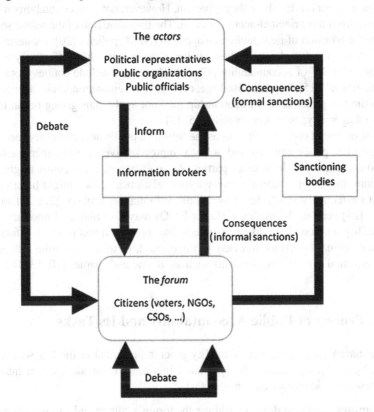

Fig. 1. Public accountability model considered (inspired by [5], p. 454; Fig. 1).

The main stages depicted in Fig. 1, usually considered in any public accountability processes [5, 17], are:

1. *Information*, sometimes also equated to *transparency* [18] or data disclosure, where the 'actor' discloses the information needed to account for its actions ("to explain and to justify his or her conduct");
2. *Debate*, during which the information gathered is processed by the 'principal' [10], who has the right to ask for additional information and justifications under the principle of 'answerability' [18];
3. *Consequences*, during which the 'principal' passes judgment based on the information analyzed, and decides whether or not to sanction or reward the 'actor' for his or her actions.

Figure 1 also depicts the main parties involved in public accountability. Representative democracies may be considered as "a concatenation of principal-agent relationships" [19] between citizens (the *forum*), their elected political representatives, and public officials (the *actor*) to whom actual administrative actions are delegated and who have an obligation to account for their actions to whom they represent. However, not all accountability relationships derive from this principal-agent principle. The fragmentation of the public sector as a result of the adoption of new public management (NPM) policies [20], for instance, led to an increase in the complexity of these chains of delegation which effectively turn into 'networks' or 'webs' of accountability [19, 20]. These may include entities from "third-party government" [15], "decentralised agencies" [21] or semi-autonomous agencies [13] to whom the full principal-agent relationship may not apply, thus giving origin to horizontal and diagonal types of accountability [5, 13].

Even if we might consider citizens as the 'ultimate public accountability forum' and public agencies, public officials and political representatives as the general actor, we must also consider the role of other parties. As an example, while courts might not fit directly into this 'actor'-'forum' accountability relationship, they might be crucial for citizens to effectively apply legal sanctions. Information brokers [22, 23] or info-mediaries [24] such as the media, CSOs or NGOs may also play an important role in accountability relations by helping to collect data, process it and produce information in a format ordinary citizens find easy to understand, or to reinforce the influence of indirect, informal sanction mechanisms such as 'blame and shame' [10, 13, 18].

3 The Process of Public Accountability and Its Tasks

From the macro view of the accountability process presented in the last section, it is possible, by analyzing accountability related literature, to break it down into more discrete tasks. We identified eleven such tasks:

1. **Voluntary disclosed data.** To address the forum's "direct and passive information rights" [10], actors need to voluntarily and proactively [18] disclose accountability related data. The data organization should facilitate analysis and re-usability according to the objectives of open government [1].

2. **Requested and disclosed data.** Voluntarily disclosed data might not be sufficient for forums to hold public agents accountable. Forums may therefore need to request additional data from public agencies according to "demand-driven access" to information [18].

3. **Data from other sources.** But even when public agencies make available additional data as a response to requests from the accountability forum, it still may not be sufficient. Therefore it may be necessary for the forum to collect data from other sources. This task can include searching for data, collecting data in hard copy and converting it to digital format [25], collecting data in digital format from other sources, or even asking third-parties (such as audit offices) to disclose it.

4. **Distribute and increase visibility of data.** Peixoto [26] explicitly refers to the "publicity condition" (publicized transparency) which implies the existence of a free press and a facilitated access to the internet as a preferred means to distribute information. While these publicity conditions exist in contemporary representative democracies, there may still be necessary additional efforts on the part of the accountability forum to further improve data visibility [25] and therefore "reach the intended public" [26].

5. **Data quality and suitability.** Not all data releases through open government data portals are relevant for accountability [4]. Fox [18] reinforces this perspective and uses the expression "opaque or fuzzy transparency" to designate the "dissemination of information that does not reveal how institutions actually behave", but also "to information that is divulged only nominally, or which is revealed but turns out to be unreliable." Some OGD platforms explicitly state that all disclosed data adheres to some kind of quality assurance policy.[1]

6. **Process and merge data.** The result of previous tasks is a repository of accountability relevant, complete and high quality data. This task in the accountability process is to organize it, merge it, process it and produce new data and information [25]. This requires accountability forums such as NGOs, CSOs, or ordinary citizens to possess the time, personnel, competence, and technical capabilities to process the available data [10, 26].

7. **Interpretation and identification of an issue.** The end result of the previous tasks is reliable information. In this task the forum continuously monitors and interprets the information to identify and characterize potential accountability issues. This has been described as arriving "at a shared definition of the problem", including determining "why and how the current situation has arisen" [17].

8. **Request additional information and ask for justifications.** Having fully characterized the accountability issue, including the identification of the relevant accountability actors involved, it should be possible for the forum to further interrogate the actor and question the legitimacy of conduct [5], ask for additional information [13], pose follow-up questions [11], and demand explanations [18]

---

[1] "All information accessed through Data.gov is subject to the Information Quality Act (P.L. 106–554). … each agency has confirmed that the data being provided through this site meets the agency's Information Quality Guidelines." From Data.gov (https://www.data.gov/data-policy) last visited in 30/10/2014.

concerning a specific issue. This task marks the beginning of the debate phase between the forum and the actor [13] which might be considered as a transition between transparency and accountability [18].

9. **Clarify and justify.** Still part of the debating phase, actors are expected to explain their behavior and justify their actions in response to public reaction and questioning [5, 11, 26].

10. **Assess and judge.** At some point the debate between the forum and the actor involved in a particular issue should reach an end. All available information is considered by the forum [11] in order reach a concluding judgment about the actor's actions regarding a particular issue under analysis [5, 11].

11. **Select and apply sanctions.** If there is a decision to sanction the actor, the task is now to select which of the available sanction mechanisms should be used [13]. The array of possible options depends on the accountability issue type, the type and nature of the actor, and the nature of the accountability involved.

(a) *Negative publicity ('blame and shame').* In the spectrum of accountability sanctions, negative publicity or 'blame and shame' sanctions are considered an indirect and informal sanctioning mechanism [10, 11]. This sanction mechanism might be easier to apply since it depends mostly on the forum's ability to make visible or 'shame' the actor involved. However, in practice, the 'shaming' power depends on how other information brokers, mass media or specialized forum such as policy or public administration networks, deal with and publicize such issues [13, 18]. To reinforce the impact of a sanction mechanism, accountability forums might partner with media to regularly report on the issues, use social media to publicize the sanction in social networks and forums, or use notification mechanisms to increase citizens' awareness.

(b) *Seek legal sanctions.* When deemed appropriate, the accountability forum might consider the possibility of taking the actor (agency or public official responsible) to court. Again, the success of this sanctioning option would depend on third parties (in this case, the judicial system). Recognizing this, it is considered an indirect sanctioning mechanism [10].

(c) *Influence supervisory or sanctioning bodies.* Just like the courts, supervisory and sanctioning bodies have the possibility to directly enforce sanctions on public officials and public agencies. Accountability forums may try to indirectly influence these bodies through the press using 'blame and shame' or directly influence them through petitions or research support [25].

(d) *Influence hierarchy.* One possible 'weak' accountability arrangement available to accountability forums outside the actors' hierarchical structure includes influencing and appealing to agencies or public officials in higher positions to apply sanctions which may include cutting budgets and bonuses, termination of contracts, tightened regulations, fines, discharge of management or increase control and reduce independence [11, 13].

(e) *Influence political and electoral sanctions.* Elections are a powerful sanction mechanism for political representatives who anticipate the retrospective control and sanctions of future electoral moments and act in order to maximize their reelection possibilities [27]. In order to effectively apply these types of sanctions, accountability platforms need to increase the impact of 'blame and shame' on voters, political parties, campaign donors and alike by keeping an up-to-date record of the issues discussed and decisions reached.

(f) *Influence participative forums.* Some actors (public agencies) promote internal participatory forums. These might function themselves as accountability forums with privileged access to data and hierarchy, and possibly with the power to impose sanctions directly. In this case, an external accountability platform might function as an internal analysis support tool, or as a way to pressure these forums to initiate accountability processes and impose sanctions.

4   Abstract Task Patterns

The tasks presented in the previous section define the high-level requirements to develop a comprehensive accountability support platform. This section aims to contribute to a platform design proposal, inspired by TTF theory and Collaboration Patterns ("classify group activities based on the changes-of-state they produce") [28], by suggesting a set of abstract task patterns already linked to some examples of elementary technologies and applications:

1. **Disclose, organize and link data.** Traditionally, public agencies have been using their own web sites to publish accountability related data.[2] However, many public agencies now publish in one-stop government data portals such as Data.gov or Data.gov.uk [29]. These portals are at the core of what Schillemans et al. [17] designate as "dynamic accountability" which allows citizens to monitor government in near real-time Accountability forums outside governmental control might find it difficult to perform some of the tasks identified previously when using government platforms such as portals, which seems to indicate that 'independent' platforms may be needed. One important aspect to consider is the adoption of the principles of Linked Data: "data published on the Web in such a way that it is machine-readable, its meaning is explicitly defined, it is linked to other external data sets, and can in turn be linked to from external data sets" [30].

2. **Rate and categorize (data, issues, and sanctions).** There is a need to properly categorize data in order to help distinguish accountability related data (and their different topics) from other type of data that coexist in today's open data government portals. Rating mechanisms might also help to improve the impact and influence of accountability processes on the general public, particularly when there is a time lapse between the moment of discovery and discussion of an issue and the actual sanctioning moment (at elections, for instance). One way to complement official quality assurance and categorization mechanisms finds inspiration in crowd

---

[2] See [38] for a list of online transparency assessment efforts based on individual website analysis.

sourcing - "using the collective wisdom of a large group of people to help solve problems" [31].

3. **Notify and increase awareness.** Even in high profile open government portals, accountability relevant data may be 'hidden' by the sheer amount of datasets available. It is therefore necessary not only to create specific organizing structures within those general purpose portals [32] to increase this data visibility but also to use awareness mechanisms (such as Real Simple Syndication – RSS – and social networks – e.g. Twitter).

4. **Communicate (directed).** In some cases open government data portals offer the possibility to request additional datasets (using request forms or email) and even allow users to monitor the request process by providing request status information.[3] Yet in other situations, 'traditional' Freedom of Information Act mechanisms and channels may be used to request such data.[4] Accountability forums and information brokers should facilitate such requests by providing seamless communication channels and independent monitoring of the whole process.

5. **Search and discover.** Independent platforms run by accountability forums can play a crucial brokerage role by providing a single interface to accept data requests and look for the data or, at least, find out where it can be obtained. Platforms might use crowdsourcing efforts for that purpose, complemented by technical resources like search engines or web crawlers to identify potential databases of interest and thus catalogue data resources.

6. **Process data (format and analyze).** Business Intelligence and Analytics systems [33] may provide the necessary tools, including Extract, Transform and Load (ETL) capabilities, to produce a data repository adequate for further processing and analysis. In general, accountability platforms (such as governmental portals or those privately maintained) should offer data mining and statistical analysis capabilities including the possibility to build new "mashup" datasets, to build and compare data-based performance indicators or to identify 'peculiar' cases.

7. **Decide (issue, sanction and sanction type).** Several tasks associated with the accountability process require users from the accountability forum to characterize an emergent issue, to decide whether or not to sanction an actor or to choose from a set of possible sanction types. In a broader context, such tasks might be considered as "Evaluate" and "Build Commitment" tasks of group collaboration efforts [28] or may be referred to, in social media contexts, as "Crowd voting" [31].

8. **Discuss and debate.** Several tasks require members of the accountability forum to debate among themselves while other tasks would require debating with the involved actors, similar to the divergent phase of groups strategic planning activities [34] and the 'generate' collaborative patterns [28]. These discussions are crucial to identify potential accountability issues, to formulate new questions, or to precede the elaboration of 'blame and shame' documents.

---

[3] See, for instance, the New Zealand data portal (https://data.govt.nz/latest-data-requests/).

[4] "How do I make a FOIA Request?" (http://www.foia.gov/how-to.html).

9.   **Reduce, filter and clarify (issue and question).** In some cases, the discussion is just part of a process for defining new issues or new questions to ask accountability actors. In this case it is necessary to filter the whole pool of suggestions and ideas (removing inappropriate questions, for instance) and to consolidate similar or redundant ideas into a single one. Care must be taken so that this would not constitute a form of censorship eliminating opposing points of view.

10. **Create ('blame and shame' document, legal document, or petition).** Producing accountability documents from a divergent pool of ideas resulting from the debate phase is a challenge and it is considered the "convergent" part of any group cognitive task [34]. In general, web collaborative writing tools such as wikis might provide support for this task, while blikis [35] may provide a bridge between the discussion (divergent) phase and the collaborative writing (convergent) phase.

Table 1. Stages, tasks and abstract task patterns in the public accountability process

Stages	Tasks	Abstract task patterns
Information	1	1
	2	4, 1
	3	5, 6, 1
	4	1, 3
	5	2
Debate/ Discuss	6	6, 1
	7	8, 9, 7, 11
	8	8, 9, 4
	9	4
Conse- quences	10	8, 7
	11	8, 7
	11.a	10, 2, 3
	11.b	12, 10, 11, 3
	11.c	10, 3
	11.d	10, 3
	11.e	10, 2, 3
	11.f	6, 10, 3

11. **Manage progress (issues, legal processes).** When the forum decides that sanctions should be awarded in the form of a legal process, it is important to know at each moment and for each legal process, what its status is. To accomplish this, workflow systems or issue tracking systems (used in software engineering, for instance) might be adopted.
12. **Obtain specialized resources.** Throughout the accountability process several tasks require resources, such as specialized skills and competences or financial resources, which an isolated citizen might not possess. To support the forum in obtaining such resources (and account for their usages), the accountability platform can adopt crowdsourcing tools.
13. **Supporting the overall process: facilitation.** In group settings, facilitation is understood as "a set of functions or activities carried out before, during, and after a meeting to help the group achieve its own outcomes" [36]. It may be performed without any technology support ("human facilitation"), solely by technology ("automated facilitation"), or by human facilitators with technological support [37].

Table 1 links each accountability task and process stage with several predominant abstract task patterns. Together with the illustrative technology examples provided, this detailed account of abstract task patterns occurring during the complete public accountability process forms a contribution to a tentative support platform design proposal. The abstract task patterns proposed above are now more easily associated with particular supporting technologies in a TTF perspective and provide an answer to the first two questions elaborated in the Introduction section.

5   Conclusion

The potential of Information and Communication Technologies (ICT) to support democratic processes (eDemocracy) and governmental service provision (eGovernment) has been recognized for quite some time now. Recently, scholars and practitioners have turned their attention to open government and, specifically, to governmental transparency and public accountability. Open government efforts led to the creation of dataset portals such as data.gov which enable open data initiated accountability processes.

The internet and social media applications, for instance, have also been generically recognized as having the potential to support data disclosure and dissemination, and public debate. But this recognition does not take into account all accountability process stages, or the specific requirements of each stage. To go beyond such generic descriptions of the ICT potential to support public accountability it is necessary, first and foremost, to have a detailed and comprehensive account of the tasks performed by the different parties involved in the process. Only then a Task-Technology Fit approach might be used to select the appropriate technology or application needed to support each individual task and therefore, provide a comprehensive public accountability support platform.

This paper contributes to the design of a comprehensive public accountability support platform by considering the three main stages of the accountability process and, supported by relevant research literature, details them into more specific tasks. Then, inspired by the collaboration patterns used to support group tasks, identifies a set of abstract task patterns occurring along the accountability process whose description is now suitable for a Task-Technology Fit approach. As such, this work answers the first two questions elaborated in the Introduction section. Further research is needed to fully answer the remaining two questions, and it is expected that scholars and practitioners use the proposed detailed account of a public accountability process as a solid foundation to design and develop comprehensive accountability support platforms.

Acknowledgements. This work has been partially supported by the Fundação para a Ciência e a Tecnologia (FCT) under project grant UID/MULTI/00308/2013.

References

1. Linders, D., Wilson, S.C.: "What is open government? one year after the directive. In: 12th Annual International Conference on Digital Government Research (Dg.o 2011), pp. 262–271 (2011)
2. Grimmelikhuijsen, S., Porumbescu, G., Hong, B., Im, T.: The effect of transparency on trust in government: a cross-national comparative experiment. Public Adm. Rev. **73**(4), 575–586 (2013)
3. Meijer, A.: Understanding the complex dynamics of transparency. Public Adm. Rev. **73**(3), 429–439 (2013)
4. Yu, H., Robinson, D.: The new ambiguity of 'Open government'. UCLA Law Rev. Discl. **59**, 178–208 (2012)
5. Bovens, M.: Analysing and assessing accountability: a conceptual framework. Eur. Law J. **13**(4), 447–468 (2007)
6. Zigurs, I., Buckland, B.K.: A theory of task/technology fit and group support systems effectiveness. MIS Q. **22**(3), 313–334 (1998)
7. Robinson, D., Yu, H., Zeller, W.P., Felten, E.W.: Government data and the invisible hand. Yale J. Law Technol. **11**, 160 (2009)
8. Mulgan, R.: 'Accountability': an ever-expanding concept? Public Adm. **78**(3), 555–573 (2000)
9. Koppell, J.G.S.: Pathologies of Accountability: ICANN and the Challenge of 'multiple accountabilities disorder'. Public Adm. Rev. **65**(1), 94–108 (2005)
10. Biela, J., Papadopoulos, Y.: Strategies for assessing and measuring agency accountability. In: Conference Paper Presented at the 32nd European Group for Public Administration (EGPA) Annual Conference, Toulouse, France, Sept 2010
11. Brandsma, G.J., Schillemans, T.: The accountability cube: measuring accountability. J. Public Adm. Res. Theory **23**(4), 953–975 (2013)
12. Sinclair, A.: The chameleon of accountability: forms and discourses. Acc. Organ. Soc. **20**(2/3), 219–237 (1995)
13. Schillemans, T.: Accountability in the shadow of hierarchy: the horizontal accountability of agencies. Public Organ. Rev. **8**(2), 175–194 (2008)
14. Behn, R.D.: Rethinking Democratic Accountability. Brookings Institution Press, Washington, D.C. (2001)

15. Dubnick, M.J., Frederickson, H.G.: Accountable agents: federal performance measurement and third-party government. J. Public Adm. Res. Theory **20**(suppl 1), i143–i159 (2010)

16. Steccolini, I.: Is the annual report an accountability medium? an empirical investigation into italian local governments. Financ. Account. Manage. **20**(3), 327–350 (2004)

17. Schillemans, T., Van Twist, M., Vanhommerig, I.: Innovations in accountability. Public Perform. Manag. Rev. **36**(3), 407–435 (2013)

18. Fox, J.: The uncertain relationship between transparency and accountability. Dev. Pract. **17**(4–5), 663–671 (2007)

19. Bovens, M., Curtin, D., Hart, P.T.: Towards a more accountable EU: retrospective and roadmap. Amsterdam Centre for European Law and Governance (2010)

20. Scott, C.: Accountability in the regulatory state. J. Law Soc. **27**(1), 38–60 (2000)

21. Busuioc, M.: Accountability, control and independence: the case of european agencies. Eur. Law J. **15**(5), 599–615 (2009)

22. Rutherford, B.A.: Developing a conceptual framework for central government financial reporting: intermediate users and indirect control. Financ. Account. Manage. **8**(4), 265–280 (1992)

23. Heald, D.: Fiscal transparency: concepts, measurement and UK practice. Public Adm. **81**(4), 723–759 (2003)

24. Carter, B.: Transparency and accountability. GSDRC (2014)

25. van Zyl, A.: How civil society organizations close the gap between transparency and accountability. Governance **27**(2), 347–356 (2014)

26. Peixoto, T.: The uncertain relationship between open data and accountability: a response to Yu and Robinson's the new ambiguity of 'open government'. UCLA Law Rev. Discl. **60**, 200–213 (2013)

27. Elster, J., Przeworski, A.: Introduction. In: Elster, J. (ed.) Deliberative Democracy, pp. 1–18. Cambridge University Press, Cambridge (1998)

28. Briggs, R., Kolfschoten, G., Gert-Jan, V., Douglas, D.: Defining key concepts for collaboration engineering. In: Twelfth Americas Conference on Information Systems (AMCIS 2006), p. 17 (2006)

29. Kalampokis, E., Tambouris, E., Tarabanis, K.: A classification scheme for open government data: towards linking decentralized data. Int. J. Web Eng. Technol. **6**(3), 266–285 (2011)

30. Bizer, C., Heath, T., Berners-Lee, T.: Linked data – the story so far. Int. J. Semant. Web Inf. Syst. **5**(3), 1–22 (2009)

31. Pedersen, J., Kocsis, D., Tripathi, A., Tarrell, A., Weerakoon, A., Tahmasbi, N., Jie, X., Wei, D., Onook, O., de Vreede, G.J.: Conceptual foundations of crowdsourcing: a review of IS research. In: 2013 46th Hawaii International Conference on System Sciences (HICSS), pp. 579–588 (2013)

32. Lourenço, R.P.: Open government portals assessment: a transparency for accountability perspective. In: Wimmer, M.A., Janssen, M., Scholl, H.J. (eds.) EGOV 2013. LNCS, vol. 8074, pp. 62–74. Springer, Heidelberg (2013)

33. Hsinchun, C., Chiang, R.H.L., Storey, V.C.: Business intelligence and analytics: from big data to big impact. MIS Q. **36**(4), 1165–1188 (2012)

34. Orwig, R., Chen, H., Vogel, D., Nunamaker, J.F.: A multi-agent view of strategic planning using group support systems and artificial intelligence. Gr. Decis. Negot. **6**(1), 37–59 (1997)

35. Lourenço, R.P.: A bliki model to support political discourse formation. In: 2008 International Symposium on Wikis (WikiSym 2008) (2008)

36. Bostrom, R.P., Anson, R., Clawson, V.K.: Group facilitation and group support systems. In: Jessup, L.M., Valacich, J.S. (eds.) Group Support Systems: New Perspectives, vol. 8, pp. 146–168. Macmillan, New York (1993)
37. Seeber, I., Maier, R., Weber, B.: Opening the black box of team processes and emergent states: a literature review and agenda for research on team facilitation. In: 2014 47th Hawaii International Conference on System Sciences (HICSS), pp. 473–482 (2014)
38. Lourenço, R.P.: Data disclosure and transparency for accountability: A strategy and case analysis. Inf. Polity 18(3), 243–260 (2013)

Mediating Citizen-Sourcing of Open Government Applications – A Design Science Approach

Mai Abu-El Seoud and Ralf Klischewski[✉]

German University in Cairo, New Cairo 11835, Egypt
{mai.abuelseoud,ralf.klischewski}@guc.edu.eg

Abstract. A design science approach is followed to develop architectural blueprints for implementing platforms to source open government applications from citizens. Zachman framework is initially used as a guide to categorize and develop the artefacts. After designing the blueprints, their usefulness is demonstrated through prototype implementation, and their potential for problem solution is evaluated from the development perspective as well as communicated to governmental peers. Contributions to research and practice include a set of blueprints covering the top levels of a platform's enterprise architecture, a reusable sourcing platform prototype, set of validated test cases for following up the implementation process, as well as success factors and lessons learned from the government perspective.

1 Introduction

Since the introduction of the open government concept in 2009, many governments started to follow this path. However, intermediate monitoring revealed that governments still need to exert much more effort to utilize the emerging technologies in the service of open government [33], one of which citizen-sourcing, among other Government 2.0 technology supports [3, 35]. Citizen-sourcing is defined as the adoption of crowdsourcing principles and technologies in the public sector [22], and crowdsourcing is well-established in the private sector as an instrument for supporting customer participation and knowledge sharing [13].

The focus of this research is on enabling citizen-sourcing of open government applications because (a) applications are needed to harness the benefit of available open data [33], and (b) governments mostly do not have the capacity to develop such applications to serve citizens' needs. While citizen-sourcing could be the solution to address this shortage, the research gap is perceived as the lack of sufficient knowledge of how to efficiently and effectively develop citizen-sourcing platforms that enable citizens to share self-developed web applications to support open government. In this regard, the research question is: Which architectural artefacts are needed to develop an open government application sourcing platform? Accordingly, this research aims to develop, validate, demonstrate, test, and communicate the appropriate architectural artefacts that are required and could be easily replicated for developing open government application sourcing platforms. As being concerned with developing new innovative artefacts and testing them in real world context, a design science approach has been followed.

© IFIP International Federation for Information Processing 2015
E. Tambouris et al. (Eds.): EGOV 2015, LNCS 9248, pp. 118–129, 2015.
DOI: 10.1007/978-3-319-22479-4_9

After discussing the extant literature on citizen-sourcing and open government applications (Sect. 2), the applied design science process is introduced and subsequently the main activities and results of each phase are presented (Sect. 3). Finally, the conclusion (Sect. 4) summarizes the findings and points to future research.

2   Citizen-Sourcing of Open Government Applications

Private organizations always seek for new innovative approaches that help in improving their customers' engagement and participation [2, 23]. Recently, governments worldwide are following similar strategies in attempting to enhance citizen participation and collaboration. Moreover, the unremitting evolution of ICTs has changed the way governments interact with their citizens [9]. The concept of citizen-sourcing relates to and integrates several other well-established concepts [15, 25]:

- *Citizen engagement* reveals the main objective of citizen-sourcing [22, 26]. Citizen engagement is not only about governments being transparent and gaining support from citizens in return, but it is also concerned with changing the traditional and often insufficient ways of exchanging information between governments and citizens [8, 20]. Moreover, with the acceleration of citizens' demands, governments have started to realize the importance of adopting a citizen-centric approach to understand citizen demands towards government transformation [15, 24].
- *Crowdsourcing* as a term has been first coined by Jeff Howe [16, 17] as the act of an institution or a company to perform a function or a task that was once performed by the employees. It provides a number of benefits to companies such as the ability to gain access to a very huge community of current workers in the requested field, save cost and time, enhance quality of the provided solution or idea [18, 26, 34]. The task should be outsourced to an undefined network of people which is referred to as the crowd. Accordingly, Hilgers and Ihl [15] defined citizen-sourcing as the governmental adoption of the crowdsourcing principles and techniques in the public sector. Citizen-sourcing is seen as a new approach that (re-)shapes the relationship between governmental agencies and citizens based on evolving practices from the private sector [15, 22].
- *Open government* as a term dates back to the initiative of U.S. President Obama having announced a new era of participation, transparency, and collaboration in 2009. Since then widely adopted, this concept embraces new approaches to further involve citizens and external parties in governmental processes [15]. Yet, the ambiguity regarding open government expectations largely remains, and definitions in the literature (e.g. [5, 35]) mostly rely on three principles which are: availability of regularly updated governmental information for citizens (transparency); citizen engagement across all the levels of government, non-profit organizations, and businesses (collaboration); and improving effectiveness in government and enhance decision-making quality through citizen engagement (participation). Challenges in open government implementation and evaluation are manifold and still subject to research.

While there are many efforts directed to serve open government initiatives worldwide, most of these initiatives have been restricted to tackling the ability of the governments to present their data to the public in the form of open data such as Data.gov platform [7]. Hence, it was claimed that governments need to direct more efforts in utilizing the emerging technologies in the service of open government [33]. Moreover, to be able to make best use of open data, either web or mobile applications are needed to harness the benefit of the availability of this available open data. Notably, the Obama administration gave citizen-sourcing superiority among other Government 2.0 technologies [3, 25]. Yet, there is still very limited research directed towards utilizing citizen-sourcing in an open government context [26, 29].

From the research perspective no unique definition of open government applications has been coined on the basis of which their scope and expected deliverables could be identified. Hence, for the time being, we refer back to the definition of web-based applications. A web-based application can be considered as an application that is developed to be executed in a web-based environment [4, 11], i.e. enables information processing functions to be initiated remotely from a web browser and executed partly on a web server, application server, and/or database server [4]. Based on this, an open government application is considered as a web-based application that serves the purpose of open government by serving its above mentioned principles. In the current research, open government applications are envisioned to be provided through a platform-based citizen-sourcing process.

3   A Design Science Approach for Platform Development

The platform development assumes the following scenario: The citizen-sourcing process starts by an application request in the form of an open call. The requester can be representatives from the government, non-government organization, or citizens. This request is then published on an online platform that acts as an intermediate between the requesters and providers. The skilled citizens are the providers who submit applications that fulfil the published requests. An intermediate in the form of an online platform facilitates the process between the requesters and providers. Citizens can also act as testers and evaluate the submitted applications by reviewing them, posting possible enhancements to the developers, providing a rating etc. After testing the uploaded web applications, the requesters can choose applications that match best the call requirements and proceed with setting these applications into productive mode either on the intermediate or on another platform.

Based on this scenario Fig. 1 depicts the main actors, concepts, and their interrelations as perceived within the frame of this research. Since the research gap is concerned with the lack of knowledge with regards to efficiently and effectively developing open government application sourcing platforms, the creation of the appropriate architectures as reusable blueprints is considered essential (samples of architecture blueprints are depicted lower part; see Sect. 3.1 for more details). Since the research is aiming for developing new artefacts to solve a given problem, a design science methodology was found to be the most appropriate.

The literature has put forward several schema variations of the design science processes from which the widely cited approach by Peffers et al. [27] has been adopted

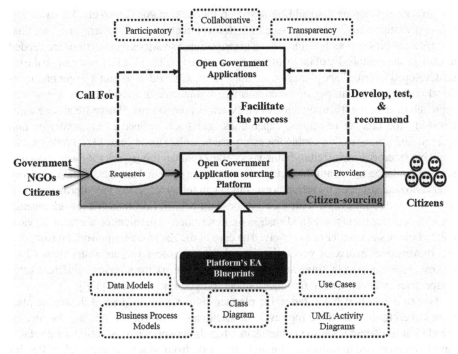

Fig. 1. Research model

in the current research. This design science process consists of six main phases with the different possible entry points for the research: identifying problem and motivation, defining objectives for a solution, design and development, demonstration, evaluation, and communication. This research has started the nominal process from the second phase as the research problem has been identified from previous literature and governmental documents on the status of open government (see Sect. 2). For each of the remaining five phases the main activities (stretching from April 2014 until January 2015) as well as the results are described in the following subsections.

3.1 Defining Objectives for a Solution

Objectives for a solution should be inferred from the problem definition. The problem is perceived as (1) the governmental necessity to utilize new technologies, especially citizen-sourcing, in the favour of open government, (2) the need to make use of the available open data through web applications, (3) the need of enhancing the relationship between citizens and their governments through enhancing citizen engagement (see Sect. 2). All of this can be achieved by engaging citizens in the development of open government web applications. Using a citizen-sourcing process will not only help governments achieve a new level of citizens' engagement but also provide governments with a wide range of developed and tested web applications at minimal cost.

Artefact development should be based on theories and/or constructs. Research has frequently emphasized the importance of high-level integration, alignment, and coordination between different architectures in an organization, as various architectures are needed to manage the complexity of large information systems [1, 12, 14, 21]. Even though the to-be developed intermediary platforms are not a priori assumed to be part a larger organizational context, using an enterprise architecture framework is considered an appropriate approach to ensuring the integration of all system's components. Enterprise architectures transform the broader principles, capabilities, and goals defined in the strategies into systems and processes that enable the enterprise to realize these goals [32]. From various available enterprise architecture frameworks, the Zachman framework [36] was chosen to provide guidance for identifying relevant information systems' artefacts. The framework offers a logical structure by which organization can follow to ensure the information flow architectures are integrated with their business units [10]. Zachman framework ensures accurate and consistent results and enables the description of the architecture from the view point of every stakeholder respectively. The core of the Zachman framework consists of a two dimensional matrix of which the six columns represent various abstractions (data, process, location, people, time, and motivation) and the six rows indicate different actor perspectives (planner, owner, designer, builder, programmer, and user) [36].

One of the authors has acted as the planner, owner, and designer of the online platform covering the first three top levels of Zachman framework, following the recommendation to elaborate on the columns in a top-down approach. A variety of artefacts have been proposed to satisfy Zachman framework, from which the approach of Pereira and Sousa [28] has been employed for identifying the artefacts of this research. Most of these proposed deliverables have been developed except for those strongly requiring contextualization (i.e. all artefacts related to location as well as to people and motivation from the designer's view).

3.2 Blueprint Design and Development

This phase is mainly concerned with developing and designing the artefacts. Each blueprint is developed following certain design notations, for example unified modelling language (UML) for activity diagrams, crow's foot notation for entity relationship diagram, and business process modelling notation (BPMN) for business process modelling. Requirements were elaborated from analysing existing crowdsourcing processes, extended through applying open government principles as far as feasible. See Table 1 for the type and number of blueprints developed, and Fig. 2 depicts a sample of the developed blueprints from the owner's view: the entity relationship diagram, one of the business process models, and the app developer's use case diagram (all artefacts are available on request).

After developing the initial set of the blueprints, an expert panel has been conducted consisting of four academics from the Information Systems field (one associate professor and three senior assistants) as well as three software developers working in the software development industry. Although the participants were selected upon convenience, it was ensured that they all have sufficient knowledge and experience regarding development and use of architectural models.

Table 1. Summary of developed artefacts

Level	Abstractions	Current research deliverables
Level 1 – objectives/scope planner's view	Data (What)	List of important data
	Function (How)	List of important business process
	People (Who)	List of stakeholders – stakeholders' analysis
	Time (When)	List of important events
	Motivation (Why)	List of the business goals
Level 2 – business conceptual model owner's view	Data (What)	Entity relationship diagram (ERD)
	Function (How)	Business process models (5)
	People (Who)	Use case diagrams (5)
	Time (When)	Event process chain diagrams (5)
	Motivation (Why)	Platform's rules
Level 3 – system model designer's view	Data (What)	Class diagram
	Function (How)	Activity diagrams (17)
	Time (When)	State diagram

The participants were first presented with the project scope, all the developed artefacts, and the notations used. Subsequently they were asked to review the compatibility of the artefacts with Zachman framework, the clarity and correctness (logic) of the artefacts, and the artefacts notations, as well as to suggest ways to enhance the artefacts and recommend new artefacts that might be missing.

Feedback was collected through one-to-one sessions with each panel expert. All feedback has been taken into consideration and accordingly some of the artefacts have been modified and enhanced. Most of the artefacts (such as the activity diagrams, use case diagrams) have only been slightly altered to improve the wording to be clearer for readers. However, the entity relationship diagram was significantly changed in terms of adding more entities and relationships between them for a better database design. Since the development of the class diagram considers the entity relationship diagram as an input, it was also modified with the new changes. For the framework compatibility, the feedback showed that the presented artefacts are compatible with Zachman's description of each cell.

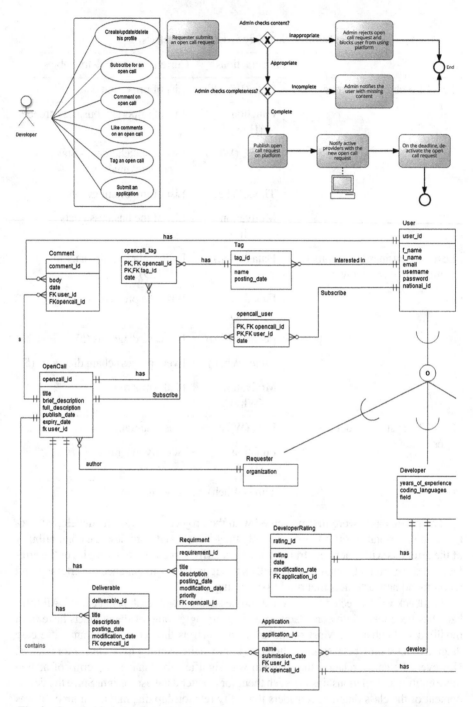

Fig. 2. Sample blueprints: app developer's use cases, process of call request, ERD (cropped)

3.3 Demonstration: Blueprints Used for Prototyping

In this stage, the artefacts are utilized in a suitable context to solve one or more instances of the originally identified problem. According to [27], this could take the form of experiments, case study, or any appropriate form. In this research, a simplified version of the platform has been developed based on the enhanced version of the designed arte-facts from the previous stage, now used as blueprints. A prototype is considered a simple version that implements the core features of the intended system to be developed quickly and to be used for early evaluation [30]. According to [31], prototypes take the archi-tectures, designs, features, and functionalities of the system as an input and demonstrate them through the implementation of the prototype.

The prototype development has been outsourced to a computer science graduate who has been working in a reputable software development company for two years. The developer was chosen based on his qualifications, development skills, availability, and willingness to develop the platform. The development process took about six weeks. The developer was provided with all the enhanced artefacts. All the core features are implemented except some supporting features such as the 'forgot password'. The outcome of this phase is an implemented prototype based on the blueprints. The proto-type has some limitations such as it only runs on Firefox internet browser, the user interface is very basic and simple, and the uploaded applications should be coded with the same language as the prototype. Two dummy applications were developed to be used in the prototype testing.

3.4 Evaluation of Effectiveness and Efficiency

The artefacts in use should be observed and measured for their effectiveness and effi-ciency to solve the problem. In this phase, a comparison between the objectives of the solution and the actual results should take place. At the end of this phase, the researcher can choose either to iterate back to the design and development phase to improve the artefacts or to continue to the last phase and leave the improvements to future research and projects [27].

In general, effectiveness is the extent to which the stated objectives are met. To be able to test the effectiveness of the blueprints in developing open government application sourcing platforms, the researcher has initially generated 110 test cases to test each blueprint through the prototype. Each blueprint was used to generate success and failure test cases to be used for evaluation by a testing committee. For example, using an activity diagram, test cases are generated that ensure the prototype is following the same sequence as the design etc.

A test case is a specific input including procedures that the tester will do to test the software at hand [19]. The main purpose of the test cases is to detect the faults in the software against the design and requirements. This is considered a black box testing as it is concerned with the external functionalities of the platform, not the coding design and style [6]. Accordingly, the test cases were validated by a certified software tester (chosen based on convenience) who works in the website testing field for almost three years. The tester was provided with all the developed artefacts plus the generated test scenarios and asked to validate the wording of the test cases, the test cases in accordance with the artefacts, the classification of the test cases, and to identify missing test cases.

After the validation, four new test cases were added to the initial pool to result in 114 cases to be executed. Upon execution 105 passed test cases were found as well as 9 failed cases. Accordingly, the pass rate is calculated to identify the percentage of passed test cases, reflecting the quality of the implemented software and how far it meets the objectives and designs. Since a pass rate of the total test cases above 90 % is claimed to be acceptable for many software development projects [6], a pass rate of more than 92 % in this research is considered satisfactory.

Second, efficiency is doing the work with fewer resources. The resources utilized to develop the prototype (e.g. time consumed to understand and use the blueprints) are identified and a set of three efficiency measurable variables are used to evaluate efficiency. A simple questionnaire (to be answered by the prototype developer) had been developed to test each of these variables using a 5-point Likert scale. The prototype developer agreed that the blueprints meet the clarity, time, and accuracy standards; this confirms a positive feedback after using the blueprints as a base for implementing the application sourcing platform.

3.5 Communication: Architecture Review by the Egyptian Government

The problem, the developed artefacts, and their solution capability should also be communicated to researchers and other relevant audiences (professionals, other stakeholders). This research has been communicated through presenting the research problem, artefacts, prototype, and evaluation results to selected citizens, including academics, and representatives of the ministry that is responsible of electronic government in Egypt with the main objective to employ ICTs in implementing and improving e-government services. As the Egyptian government has started to consider open government and recently announced an open data initiative,[1] feedback from these stakeholders was considered essential. The vice minister has been contacted and interviewed as well as a project manager and the software quality assurance manager who are mainly interested in improving the electronic services which the Egyptian government offers to the citizens. The interviews were mainly directed towards the applicability of such technology within the Egyptian context and whether the government can consider the architectures as a first step of implementing citizen-sourcing to develop open governments web applications or not.

During the interviews, the representatives from the Egyptian government have shown serious interest in such projects, highlighting that this is what they actually need now in terms of citizens engagement and participation. However, Egypt is still at a very early stage having an open data initiative. After some discussion about the readiness of the government to consider the research artefacts, it was agreed that some prerequisites should be met before implementing such technology: (a) current regulations prevent the government from acquiring software solutions except from a few contracted software vendors – this would have to change when implementing the application sourcing platform as the providers will be citizens expected not to belong to one of these vendors;

---

[1] http://www.egypt.gov.eg/english/general/Open_Gov_Data_Initiative.aspx.

(b) the availability of governmental open data for the citizens is considered a first step before implementing this application sourcing platform – yet multiple efforts are still needed to achieve this in the near future; (c) the availability of skilled citizens who can develop and test the open government applications should be ensured – this can be achieved through establishing partnerships with different university, research centres, and software development start-ups.

4   Conclusion

After reviewing the extant literature on the related concepts and identifying the research gap, this research has developed the needed architectures for developing a platform for sourcing open government applications from citizens. Subsequently, these architectures were validated through an expert panel upon which the architectures were enhanced. These architectures were then demonstrated by implementing a prototype of the online application sourcing platform by a third party. Test cases had been developed and applied to evaluate the effectiveness of the blueprints based on the implemented prototype, and a simple questionnaire was conducted to evaluate the blueprints' efficiency in developing the application sourcing platform. Finally, the research has been communicated namely to governmental representatives, leading to identification of success factors of platform utilization.

The contribution of this research is both practical as well as theoretical. Firstly, a set of validated, demonstrated, tested, and communicated software architectures for developing open government application sourcing platforms is provided as blueprints for reuse. Secondly, the prototype developed based on these architectures can be further enhanced and used by governments or other stakeholders to adopt citizen-sourcing for open government applications. And the set of validated test cases can be used as a base for generating more test cases for testing a fully functioning platform. Moreover, the government feedback may serve as input for developing action plans and roadmaps when implementing such citizen-sourcing projects. As contribution to e-government research can be considered the adoption of Zachman's framework to develop and categorize application sourcing platforms architectures as well as the systematic approach of utilizing architectures to bring out an e-government solution intended for replication.

Limitations of time and other resources have caused also several limitations in research such as: limited number of high-level expert panellists; the prototype was only implemented for Firefox internet browser; the efficiency questionnaire was simple and not validated nor piloted; only dummy application were uploaded ("sourced") and no sourced application was set into production mode; only one developer was recruited to actually use the artefacts to implement the prototype. Especially the last limitation raises concerns about generalization of the efficiency evaluation results.

Beyond overcoming these limitations, future research is suggested to address the following questions: How to ensure security of the submitted applications as well as property rights? How to integrate the developed applications with the already available governmental infrastructure? How to publish the open government applications on the platform and link them with governmental public databases? What kind of open government tests are appropriate as pre-defined test cases executable on the application sourcing platform? And on the infrastructure level: what is the role of architectures in developing, disseminating, and managing e-government solutions in a distributed environment? After all, the application sourcing platform is only an intermediary which could be replicated in many countries and contexts. However, what the principles of open government mean in a given context and what quality benchmarks are to be applied, this should be subject to an ongoing government-citizen dialogue.

References

1. Barros, O., Julio, C.: Enterprise and process architecture patterns. Bus. Process Manage. J. **17**(4), 598–618 (2011)
2. Boudreau, K.: Open platform strategies and innovation: granting access vs. devolving control. Manage. Sci. J. **56**(10), 1849–1872 (2010)
3. Brabham, D.C.: Using crowdsourcing in Government. Collaborating across Boundaries Series, IBM Center for the Business of Government (2013). http://www.businessofgovernment.org/sites/default/files/Using%20Crowdsourcing%20In%20Government.pdf
4. Bruno, V., et al.: Characteristics of web applications that affect usability: a review. In: 17th Australia Conference on Computer-Human Interaction: Citizens Online: Considerations for Today and the Future, pp. 1–4. Computer-Human Interaction Special Interest Group (CHISIG) of Australia (2005)
5. Chun, S.A., et al.: Government 2.0: making connections between citizens, data and government. Inf. Polity **15**(1), 1–9 (2010)
6. Desikan, S., Ramesh, G.: Software Testing: Principles and Practice. Pearson Education, India (2006)
7. Ding, L., et al.: Data-gov Wiki: towards linking government data. In: AAAI Spring Symposium: Linked Data Meets Artificial Intelligence, vol. 10 (2010)
8. Dobos, Á., Jenei, Á.: Citizen engagement as a learning experience. Procedia Soc. Behav. Sci. **93**, 1085–1089 (2013)
9. Dutil, P.A., et al.: Rethinking government-public relationships in a digital world: customers, clients, or citizens? J. Inf. Technol. Politics **4**(1), 77–90 (2007)
10. Ertaul, L., Sudarsanam, R.: Security planning using Zachman framework for enterprises. Proc. EURO mGOV **2005**, 153–162 (2005)
11. Finkelstein, A.C., et al.: Ubiquitous web application development-a framework for understanding (2002). http://www0.cs.ucl.ac.uk/staff/A.Finkelstein/papers/uwa.pdf
12. Frankel, D.S., et al.: The Zachman framework and the OMG's model driven architecture. A White Paper by the Business Process Trends (2003)
13. Geiger, D., et al.: Managing the crowd: Towards taxonomy of crowdsourcing processes. In: 17th American Conference on Information Systems, Detroit, Michigan, 4–7 Aug 2011
14. Gregor, S., et al.: Enterprise architectures: enablers of business strategy and IS/IT alignment in government. Inf. Technol. People **20**(2), 96–120 (2007)
15. Hilgers, D., Ihl, C.: Open governance and citizensourcing: applying the idea of open innovation to the public sector. Int. J. Public Participation **4**(1), 67–88 (2010)
16. Howe, J.: The rise of crowdsourcing. Wired Blog Network: Crowdsourcing (2006a). http://www.wired.com/wired/archive/14.06/crowds.html
17. Howe, J.: Crowdsourcing: a definition. Wired Blog Network: Crowdsourcing (2006b). http://crowdsourcing.typepad.cpm/cs/2006/06/crowdsourcing_a.html

18. Iren, D., Bilgen, S.: Methodology for managing crowdsourcing in organizational projects. In: Modeling and Analysis of Novel Mechanisms in Future Internet Applications. Würzburg University (2012). http://www3.informatik.uni-wuerzburg.de/events/summerschool2012/proceedings/Iren.pdf
19. Keyvanpour, M.R., et al.: A classification framework for automatic test case generation techniques for web applications. J. Inf. Process. Manage. 4(3), 26–39 (2013)
20. Klein, W.R.: Building consensus. In: Hoch, C.J., Dalton, L.C., Frank, S.S. (eds.) The Practice of Local Government Planning, pp. 423–438. ICMA, Washington, D.C. (2000)
21. Lankhorst, M.: A language for enterprise modeling. In: Lankhorst, M. (ed.) Enterprise Architecture at Work, 3rd edn, pp. 75–114. Springer, Berlin Heidelberg (2013)
22. Lukensmeyer, C.J., Torres, L.H.: Citizensourcing: citizen participation in a networked nation. In: Yang, K., Bergrud, E. (eds.) Civic Engagement in a Network Society, pp. 207–233. Information Age Publishing, Charlotte (2008)
23. Majchrzak, A., Malhotra, A.: Towards an information systems perspective and research agenda on crowdsourcing for innovation. J. Strateg. Inf. Syst. 22(4), 257–268 (2013)
24. Medeni, D.T., et al.: The demand for development of E-government service and gateway in turley taking citizens perceptions and suggestions into account. In: Shareef, M.A., Kumar, V., Kumar, U., Dwivedi, Y.K. (eds.) Stakeholder Adoption of E-Government Services: Driving and Resisting Factors, 1st edn, pp. 116–135. Hershey, Information Science Reference (2010)
25. Nam, T.: Suggesting frameworks of citizen-sourcing via government 2.0. Gov. Inf, Q. 29(1), 12–20 (2012)
26. Nam, T.: Citizens' attitudes toward open government and government 2.0. Int. Rev. Admin. Sci. 78(2), 346–368 (2012)
27. Peffers, K., et al.: A design science research methodology for information systems research. J. Manage. Inf. Syst. 24(3), 45–77 (2007)
28. Pereira, C.M., Sousa, P.: A method to define an enterprise architecture using the Zachman framework. In: Proceedings of the ACM Symposium on Applied Computing, pp. 1366–1371. ACM (2004)
29. Prest, E.: Citizensourcing (Doctoral dissertation, Central European University) (2012). www.etd.ceu.hu/2012/prest_emma.pdf
30. Sabale, R.G., Dani, A.R.: Comparative study of prototype model for software engineering with system development life cycle. J. Eng. 2(7), 21–24 (2012)
31. Scacchi, W.: Process models in software engineering. Encyclopedia of Software Engineering (2001). http://www.ics.uci.edu/~wscacchi/Papers/SE-Encyc/Process-Models-SE-Encyc.pdf
32. Tamm, T., et al.: How does enterprise architecture add value to organizations? Commun. Assoc. Inf. Syst. 28(1), 141–168 (2011)
33. The White House: The Obama's administration commitment to open government: status report (2011). http://www.whitehouse.gov/sites/default/files/opengov_report.pdf
34. Whitla, P.: Crowdsourcing and its application in marketing activities. Contemp. Manage. Res. 5(1), 15–28 (2009)
35. Yu, H., Robinson, D.: The new ambiguity of' open government (2012). http://papers.ssrn.com/sol3/papers.cfm?abstract_id=2012489
36. Zachman, J.: A framework for information systems architecture. IBM Syst. J. 26(3), 276–292 (1987)

Processing Linked Open Data Cubes

Efthimios Tambouris[1,2], Evangelos Kalampokis[1,2(✉)],
and Konstantinos Tarabanis[1,2]

[1] University of Macedonia, Thessaloniki, Greece
[2] Information Technologies Institute, Centre for Research and Technology – Hellas,
Thermi, Greece
{tambouris,ekal,kat}@uom.gr

Abstract. A significant part of open data provided by governments and international organizations concerns statistics such as demographics and economic indicators. The real value, however, of open statistical data will unveil from performing analytics on top of combined datasets from disparate sources. Linked data provide the most promising technological paradigm to enable such analytics across the Web. Currently, however, relevant processes and tools do not fully exploit the distinctive characteristics of statistical data. The aim of this paper is to present a process that enables publishing statistical raw data as linked data, combining statistics from multiple sources, and exploiting them in data analytics and visualizations. Moreover, the capability of existing software tools to support the vision of linked statistical data analytics is evaluated. We anticipate that the proposed process will contribute to the development of a roadmap for future research and development in the area.

Keywords: Linked data · Data cubes · Open data · Statistics · Data analytics

1 Introduction

Open data refer to the idea that certain data should be freely available for re-use for purposes foreseen or not foreseen by the original creator [1]. This data can be an important primary material for added value services and products, which can increase government transparency, contribute to economic growth and provide social value to citizens. As a result, governments and organisations launch portals that operate as single points of access for data they produce or collect [2]. A major part of this open data concerns statistics such as demographics and economic indicators [3]. For example, the vast majority of the datasets published on the open data portal[1] of the European Commission are of statistical nature.

Statistical data is often organised in a multidimensional manner where a measured fact is described based on a number of dimensions, e.g. unemployment rate could be described based on geographic area, time and gender. In this case, statistical data is

---

[1] http://open-data.europa.eu.

© IFIP International Federation for Information Processing 2015
E. Tambouris et al. (Eds.): EGOV 2015, LNCS 9248, pp. 130–143, 2015.
DOI: 10.1007/978-3-319-22479-4_10

compared to a cube, where each cell contains a measure or a set of measures, and thus we onwards refer to statistical multidimensional data as data cubes or just cubes [4].

Linked data has been introduced as a promising paradigm for opening up data because it facilitates data integration on the Web [5]. In the case of statistical data, linked data has the potential to create value to society, enterprises, and public administration through combining statistics from various sources and performing analytics on top of integrated statistical data [6, 7].

During the last years various processes have been introduced to enable an understanding of how (a) governments open up their data for others to reuse (e.g. [8]) and (b) data providers publish their data according to the linked data principles to facilitate data integration on the Web (e.g. [9]). However, recent developments suggest that statistical data present distinctive characteristics and thus the vision of linked data cube analytics requires the introduction of new processes and software tools [10, 11].

The aim of this paper is to present a process that enables publishing statistical raw data as linked data cubes, combining cubes from multiple sources, and exploiting them in data analytics and visualisations. Towards this end, we interviewed employees from public and private organizations that (a) produce and open up statistical data, (b) publish linked data cubes, or (c) consume statistical data to make decisions. The proposed linked data cubes process is employed to evaluate the capability of existing software tools to support the vision of linked data cube analytics. The evaluation results provide interesting insights into the software tools that are required so that to make possible the vision of linked data cube analytics.

The rest of the paper is structured as follows: Sect. 2 sets the background of our work and explains the need for a linked data cubes process. Section 3 presents related work regarding processes for linked and open data. In Sect. 4 the approach we followed is described while in Sect. 5 the proposed process is presented. In Sect. 6 we apply the process to evaluate the capacity of existing tools to support the linked data analytics vision. Finally, Sect. 7 draws conclusions.

2 Motivation

A data cube is specified by a set of dimensions and a set of measures. The dimensions create a structure that comprises a number of cells, while each cell includes a numeric value for each measure of the cube. Let us consider as an example a cube from Eurostat with three dimensions, namely time in years, geography in countries, and sex, that measures the percentage of population that is involved in lifelong learning. An example of a cell in this cube would define the percentage of males involved in lifelong learning in Denmark in 2014.

A fundamental step towards the exploitation of data cubes in Linked Data is the RDF data cube (QB) vocabulary, which enables modelling data cubes as RDF [12]. Centric class in the vocabulary is *qb:DataSet* that defines a cube. A cube has a *qb:DataStructureDefinition* that defines the structure of the cube and multiple *qb:Observation* that describe each cell of the cube. The structure is specified by the abstract *qb:ComponentProperty* class, which has three sub-classes, namely *qb:DimensionProperty*, *qb:MeasureProperty*, and *qb:AttributeProperty*. The first one defines the dimensions of the cube, the second the measured variables, while the third structural metadata such as the unit of measurement.

At the moment, a number of statistical datasets are freely available on the Web as linked data cubes. For example, the European Commission's Digital Agenda[2] provides its Scoreboard as linked data cubes. An unofficial linked data transformation[3] of Eurostat's data, created in the course of a research project, includes more than 5,000 linked data cubes. Few statistical datasets from the European Central Bank, World Bank, UNESCO and other international organisations have been also transformed to linked data in a third party activity [15]. Census data of 2011 from Ireland and Greece and historical censuses from the Netherlands have been also published as linked data cubes [13, 14]. Finally, the Department for Communities and Local Government (DCLG) in the UK also provides local statistics as linked data[4].

The real value, however, of linked data cubes is revealed in the case of combining statistics from disparate sources and performing analytics on top of them in an easy way. Following the previous example, let us consider a cube from Digital Agenda measuring internet usage that is structured based on the same three dimensions, i.e. time in years, countries, and sex. If we combine these two cubes from Eurostat and Digital Agenda, we can perform a regression analysis and derive some interesting results like the plot of Fig. 1. In this case, the value is present when all needed steps can be easily performed using relevant online tools.

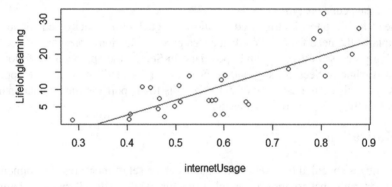

Fig. 1. Combining and analysing data cubes from Eurostat and digital agenda

During the last years, a few research endeavors focused on performing statistical analyses on top of combined linked data cubes [16–18]. These endeavors mainly proposed ad hoc solutions that use specific datasets in order to prove the applicability of the approach. We believe, however, that a common understanding of the whole process of creating and exploiting linked data cubes is required in order to apply the concept of linked data analytics at a Web scale.

---

[2] http://digital-agenda-data.eu/data.
[3] http://eurostat.linked-statistics.org.
[4] http://opendatacommunities.org/data.

3   Related Work

According to the literature, open data processes specify the steps that governments should follow to set their data free for others to reuse [8, 19–21]. For example, the process introduced by Janssen and Zuiderwijk [8] involves five steps, namely creating data, opening data, finding open data, using open data, and discussing and providing feedback on open data. Moreover, a few processes have been recently proposed in the literature to describe the steps that are followed in publishing and consuming linked data [9, 22–25]. For example, Auer et al. [9] present a process comprising eight steps: (i) transform data to RDF, which includes the extraction of data from sources (structured or unstructured) and its mapping to an RDF data model, (ii) store and index data efficiently and using appropriate mechanisms, (iii) manual revise, extend and create new structured information according to the initial data, (iv) establish links to different sources that regard the same entities but are published by different data publishers (v) enrich data with high-level structures so as to be more efficiently aggregated and queried (vi) assess data quality using data quality metrics available for structured information such as accuracy of facts and completeness, (vii) repair data so as to encounter data quality problems identified in the previous step, and (viii) search, browse and explore the data in a fast and user friendly manner.

However, these processes are general and need to be specialised for accommodating statistical data modelled using linked data technologies. In particular, these generic processes present the following limitations when applied to linked data cubes:

- They focus on the publishing part of linked data and they do not provide details on the exploitation, which is usually summarised at the last step of the process. In our case, however, the possible statistical analyses are well defined in the literature (e.g. OLAP analysis, statistical learning etc.) and thus should be further elaborated particularly as they can also provide feedback to the publishing steps of the process.
- Typically, data integration in the Web of Linked Data is facilitated by establishing *owl:sameAs* links [26], which indicate that two URI references refer to the same thing. However, in the case of cubes these links are applicable only at the metadata level that define the structure of the cube and not at the observation level. As a result, integration of data cubes is not currently properly accommodated in existing linked data processes.
- The use of the QB vocabulary introduces considerable complexity that calls for specific requirements in the publishing steps.

4   Approach

In order to understand the requirements of a linked data cube process we interviewed employees from public and private organisations that work with open data, linked data, and statistical analysis. More specifically, the following appointments were made per area:

- Open data: The head of the open data team of the Flemish government.
- Linked data: Two employees from an international Swiss Bank.
- Statistical data: 16 employees of the Irish Central Statistics Office (CSO). The interviewees were chosen as a cross-section of CSO staff from different functional areas and different levels of seniority, with particular focus on staff involved in data dissemination and IT operations. One of CSO's major statistical datasets is Census 2011, which has been already published as Linked Data[5].
- Open/linked data: Three employees from the Research Centre of the Government of Flanders; a government having as mission statement to conduct research in the fields of demographics, macroeconomics and social-cultural developments.
- Open/linked data: Three employees from the Assistant Deputy Director of Strategic Statistics in the UK Department for Communities and Local Government (DCLG). DCLG currently produces 53 main statistical datasests and is commited to routiely release its data as linked open data. It also maintains a data portal that currently contains more than 150 datasets[6].

The interviews along with the relevant literature resulted in the series of consecutive steps that structure the linked data cube process presented in Sect. 5.

5   A Process for Linked Data Cubes

This section presents the proposed process for creating value through linked data cubes. This process comprises three phases, namely (a) Creating Cubes, (b) Expanding Cubes, and (c) Exploiting Cubes. The first phase involves creating linked data cubes from raw data, the second supports the expansion of a cube by linking it with other cubes on the Web, and the last one enables the exploitation of the cubes in data analytics and visualisations. The three phases further split up into a number of steps. A depiction of this process is presented in Fig. 2. In the rest of the section the steps of each phase are outlined.

5.1   Step 1.1: Discover and Pre-process Raw Data

This step enables stakeholders to discover, access, view and process raw data cubes. At this step, data cubes come in various data formats such as CSV files, XLS files, RDBMS or RDF files. In addition, cubes can be formatted in various structures such as rectangular data, tree data and graph data.

In this step, stakeholders are able to browse raw data and perform activities aiming to improve the quality of raw data (e.g. data sorting, filtering, cleansing, transformation). This step could also include raw file or raw data storage in a local repository or database system. In this case, metadata regarding the provenance of raw data may be also stored along with the actual data.

---

[5] http://data.cso.ie.
[6] http://opendatacommunities.org/.

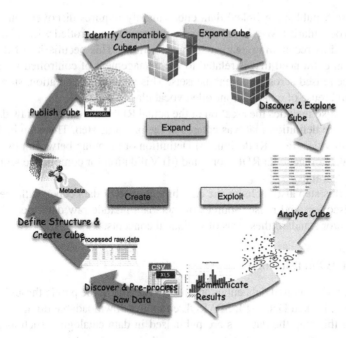

Fig. 2. The linked data cubes process

5.2 Step 1.2: Define Structure and Create Cube

An important step in linked data creation regards the definition of the structure of a model that the data will be mapped to. Initially, a conceptual model that drives the development of the structure of the linked data cube is created. This specifies:

- The dimensions of the cube, which define what the observation applies to.
- The measured variables (i.e. what has been measured) along with details on the unit of measure or how the observations are expressed.

As reusing widely accepted vocabularies is considered to be of high importance in linked data, defining the structure of the model also requires importing and reusing existing linked data vocabularies. In the case of data cubes, the *RDF Data Cube (QB) vocabulary* constitutes the main framework to model data cubes as RDF graphs. In addition, other linked data vocabularies can be also used to define the values of the dimensions, measures and attributes of the cube. Common statistical concepts can be reused across datasets e.g. dimensions regarding age, location, time, sex etc. or the values of specific dimension (e.g. the countries of Europe). These concepts are defined in linked data vocabularies that standardise dimensions, attributes and code lists. The most widely accepted is the SDMX-RDF vocabulary[7], which is based on the statistical encoding standard SDMX.

---

[7] https://code.google.com/p/publishing-statistical-data/.

As a result, publishing linked data cubes mainly requires discovery and reuse of controlled vocabularies. We should also note that reusing controlled vocabularies could be considered as reconciling against such collections. This peculiarity of data cubes introduces an extra need that is related to the management of controlled vocabularies that could be reused across different datasets. This includes the creation, store, search, discovery and reuse of existing controlled vocabularies.

This step also includes the creation of the actual RDF data out of the raw data based on the structure definition that was created at the previous step. This step includes the following activities: (a) URI design, (b) Definition of mapping between raw and RDF data, (c) Data storage to an RDF store, and (d) Validation for compliance with schema or values constraints.

Finally, this step also includes the enrichment of RDF data cubes with metadata to facilitate discovery and reuse. Sources of metadata include raw data files, the cube's structure and/or standard thesaurus of statistical concepts.

5.3   Step 1.3: Publish Cube

In this step, the generated data cubes are made available to the public through different interfaces e.g. Linked Data API, SPARQL endpoint, downloadable dump etc. In addition, during this step the datasets are publicised in data catalogues such as Europe's public data portal[8] or other national portals (e.g. data.gov.uk or data.gov.gr), the datahub platform[9] or the Linking Open Data cloud[10].

Metadata that describe the dataset should be also published along with the actual data. The produced metadata are usually shared across multiple platforms and implementations. As a result, stakeholders need to be able to import or export metadata related to data cubes.

5.4   Step 2.1: Identify Compatible Cubes

This step supports the identification of compatible to join cubes in order to enable expanding linked data cubes. The identification of compatible cubes is performed through two processes:

- Search on an existing collection of linked data cubes and evaluate the compatibility of a cube at hand with every cube in the collection. The compatibility evaluation is based on (a) the structure of the cubes i.e. dimensions, measures, levels and hierarchies, and (b) the desired type of join. For example, a cube is compatible to join in order to add a new measure to an original cube if: *(i)* both cubes have the same dimensions, *(ii)* the second cube has at least the same values in each dimension of the original cube, and *(iii)* the second cube has at least one measure that does not exist at the original cube.

---

[8] http://publicdata.eu.
[9] http://datahub.io.
[10] http://lod-cloud.net.

- Create a set of compatible cubes from an initial linked data cube by computing aggregations across a dimension or a hierarchy. In the case of aggregating data across a dimension, 2^n new cubes are created where n is the number of the dimensions of the cube. In the case of aggregating data across a hierarchy, a new cube is created that contains observations for all values of a dimension at every level. Special attention should be paid on the types of measures and dimensions and the aggregation function (i.e. sum, count, min, max etc.) that can be used.

This step can also include the establishment of typed links between compatible to join cubes. These links will enable, at a later stage, identifying linked data cubes that can be combined in order to perform enhanced analytics on top of multiple linked data cubes. For this reason, it is important to define compatibility of cubes and develop tools that could search on large collections of cubes and discover cubes that can potentially be combined.

5.5   Step 2.2: Expand Cube

Expanding cubes enables adding more data into a cube. We assume that a cube can be expanded by increasing the size of one of the sets that defines it. Therefore, a cube can be expanded by adding one or more elements into the set of measures, the set of concepts in a dimension and the set of dimensions. This can be done by merging a cube with a second one, which is compatible with the initial cube. The links that have been established at the previous step can be exploited towards this end.

Following the same example, we see that we have two cubes that describe two different measures (i.e. unemployed people and crime incidents) based on the same dimensions (i.e. time and geography), and with the same concepts (i.e. 2010 for time and the European countries for geography). These two cubes are compatible to merge and thus a new cube with two measures can be created out of the initial ones.

We should note that the expanded cube could be either created and stored or just conceptually defined in order to be used along with a data analytics tool.

5.6   Step 3.1: Discover and Explore Cubes

At this step, stakeholders aiming to consume data exploit the mechanisms set up at the previous step in order to discover the appropriate cubes for a task at hand. For example, we consider a researcher that needs to study the relation between unemployment and criminality and thus needs to analyse data that describe unemployment and criminality in different geographic areas or time periods.

In general, the discovery of linked data cubes could be done through:

- A data catalogue that allows exploring the available data cubes based on (a) generic metadata records stored inside the catalogue platform that describe the cube as a whole, and (b) Cube-specific metadata that provide information about the concepts that formulate the cube i.e. dimensions and measures.
- Full-text search that enables discovery of data cubes not only by metadata but also by the actual content of the cubes.

In our example, we suppose that the researcher identifies two cubes:

- A cube presenting the number of unemployed people in three dimensions i.e. countries, years and age groups.
- A cube presenting crime incidents in two dimensions i.e. countries and time (quarters of the year).

At this stage, we consider that the researcher is also able to browse the cube in order to better understand the data and proceed with further analysis. This enables the researcher to view data based on different dimensions or measures. For example, if the data describes the unemployment rate at different European countries in different years then stakeholders could view either the unemployment rates of a particular country throughout the years or the unemployment rates of a specific year across different countries. This would enable stakeholders also to sort or filter the data based on the values of the dimensions or the actual values of the observations.

5.7   Step 3.2: Analyse Cube

In this step the data cubes that were resulted from the previous step are employed in order to perform analytics through (a) OLAP operations, (b) computing simple summaries of the data, and (c) creating statistical learning models.

The transformation of linked data cubes at the previous step will enable stakeholders to perform the following OLAP operations:

- *Dimension reduction:* This would enable users to select part of a data cube by removing one of the dimensions. In the unemployment rate example this would enable, for example, removing the age group dimension and thus keeping only the time and location dimensions.
- *Roll-up* and *drill-down* operation: These OLAP operations allow stakeholders to navigate among levels of data cube by stepping down or up a concept hierarchy. Following the previous example, stepping down a concept hierarchy for the dimension time could perform this OLAP operation. If we consider the concept hierarchy "month<quarter<year" then drill down would present unemployment rate of different age groups at different countries for every quarter.

The stakeholder could also select to produce either quantitative (i.e. summary statistics) or visual (i.e. simple to understand graphs) summaries. As regards the quantitative summaries, a stakeholder in this step will be able to describe the observations across a dimension using descriptive statistics. For example, this step would enable the calculation of the mean and standard deviation of the unemployment rate of European countries in a particular year. Moreover, stakeholders would be able to calculate statistics (e.g. Pearson's correlation coefficient) that estimate dependences between paired measures described in disparate but compatible cubes. Paired here is used to denote that the measures share at least one common dimension and thus can be compared.

Finally, the types of visualisation charts that can be used in this step include scatter plots, bar charts, pie charts, histograms, geo charts, timelines etc.

Following the example of the previous steps, the researcher use the cubes created after the last step in order to perform the following:

- Create a scatter-plot presenting unemployed people against crime incidents across European countries.
- Calculate Pearson's correlation coefficient between number of unemployed and number of crimes.

In this step, the cubes that were created in the previous steps could be also used in machine learning and predictive analytics in order to produce learning or predictive models. At the same step, the models that were created could also be published into the Linked Data Web and thus feedback the lifecycle at the first step.

Following the example of unemployment and criminality, we consider that the researcher now wants to create a model in order to be able to estimate future crime rates based on unemployment rates. Towards this end, the researcher exploits the results of the previous step and the data cubes in order to select an appropriate data mining method (e.g. Support Vector Machines) and build a model. The researcher goes back to the previous steps in order to also identify data to evaluate the model.

5.8   Step 3.3: Communicate Results

This step involves the visualisation of results. This step may feed back to the first step of the process if the results of the analyses performed in the previous steps indicate a need for further analyses requiring additional data. Towards this end, the analysis proceeds with the first step of the process in order to discover new raw data, transform them to RDF and eventually perform a comparative analysis with existing RDF data cubes.

6   Tools

The exploitation of linked data in statistics requires specialised software tools that (a) are generic and thus applicable to all datasets that use the QB vocabulary, and (b) support each step of the linked data cube process. Therefore, existing linked data tools should be evaluated to determine their capability to fully support the process steps.

In this section, we evaluate nine widely-used open data, linked data, and statistical analysis tools, namely:

1. OpenRefine[11]
2. PoolParty[12]
3. CSVImport (LOD2 project)[13]
4. TabLinker[14]
5. SILK[15]

---

[11] http://openrefine.org.

[12] http://www.poolparty.biz.

[13] https://github.com/AKSW/csvimport.ontowiki.

[14] https://github.com/Data2Semantics/TabLinker.

[15] http://wifo5-03.informatik.uni-mannheim.de/bizer/silk/.

6. Pubby[16]
7. CubeViz (LOD2 project)[17]
8. SPARQL R[18]
9. RapidMiner (LOD)[19]

Table 1. Evaluating the capacity of 9 tools to support the 8 steps of the process

	1	2	3	4	5	6	7	8	9
Step 1	F	N	P	P	N	N	N	N	N
Step 2	P	P	P	P	P	N	N	N	N
Step 3	N	N	P	P	N	P	N	N	N
Step 4	N	N	N	N	P	N	N	N	N
Step 5	N	N	N	N	N	N	N	N	N
Step 6	N	N	N	N	N	N	N	N	N
Step 7	N	N	N	N	N	N	P	P	P
Step 8	N	N	N	N	N	N	P	P	P

In Table 1 the results of our analysis are presented. The horizontal axis presents the tools while the vertical the process steps. In each cell a letter indicates whether the tool (F)ully, (P)artially or N(ot) covers the functionality required by a step of the process. The analysis that we performed revealed that the following important functionalities are not currently supported by existing tools:

- Transform raw data to linked data cubes (as existing tools for RDF creation are difficult to use in the case of the QB vocabulary).
- Materialise cubes by computing aggregations across dimensions and hierarchies. This functionality is important for enabling OLAP browsing.
- Identify cubes with similar structure that could potential integrate.
- Create integrated views of multiple linked cubes on the Web. This will enable performing analytics on top of multiple cubes at a Web scale.
- Browse a linked data cube and perform advanced OLAP operations such as drill-down and roll-up.

Some tools, such as R and RapidMiner, with their extensions for importing RDF data can be also used for enabling performing data analytics on top of linked data cubes. We should, however, note that these generic RDF importers are difficult to use in the

---

[16] http://wifo5-03.informatik.uni-mannheim.de/pubby/.
[17] http://cubeviz.aksw.org.
[18] http://cran.r-project.org/web/packages/SPARQL/.
[19] http://dws.informatik.uni-mannheim.de/en/research/rapidminer-lod-extension/.

case of cubes because of the complexity that the QB vocabulary introduces. Our analysis revealed that linked data cube specific extensions are needed.

7 Conclusions

During the last years the open data movement has been introduced evangelising the need for certain data to be freely available for re-use. A major part of open data concerns statistics that is structured as multi-dimensional data cubes. Linked data technologies have the potential to realise the vision of combining and performing analytics on top of previously isolated cubes at a Web scale. However, a common understanding of the whole process of creating and exploiting linked data cubes is required in order to be able to apply the concept of linked data cube analytics at Web scale. Existing processes for linked and open data are general and need to be specialised for accommodating statistical data modelled using linked data technologies.

In this paper, we introduced a process that enables publishing statistical raw data as linked data cubes, combining cubes from multiple sources, and exploiting them in data analytics and visualisations. The process comprises the following eight steps: (i) discover and pre-process raw data, (ii) define structure and create cube, (iii) publish cube, (iv) identify compatible cubes, (v) expand cube, (vi) discover and explore cube, (vii) analyse cube, and (viii) communicate results.

The proposed process was applied to evaluate the capability of existing tools to support the vision of linked data cube analytics. The results revealed that tools need to be specified and developed to support the easy creation of linked data cubes, the identification of linked data cubes with similar structure, the integration of linked data cubes, and the easy statistical analysis (e.g. OLAP analysis) of integrated cubes. We anticipate that the proposed process will contribute to a better understanding of linked data cube analytics and to the development of a roadmap for future research and development in the area.

Acknowledgments. This work is funded by the European Commission within the 7th Framework Programme in the context of the project OpenCube (http://opencube-project.eu) under grand agreement No. 611667. The authors would like to thank the whole OpenCube consortium that interviewed employees from private and public organisations as well as Mr. Konstantinos Tsiftsis who analysed linked data from Eurostat and Digital Agenda and created Fig. 1.

References

1. European Commission: Open data: an engine for innovation, growth and transparent governance. In: Communication from the Commission, COM (2011) 882 final, Dec 2011
2. Kalampokis, E., Tambouris, E., Tarabanis, K.: A classification scheme for open government data: towards linking decentralized data. Int. J. Web Eng. Technol. **6**(3), 266–285 (2011)
3. Cyganiak, R., Hausenblas, M., McCuirc, E.: Official Statistics and the Practice of Data Fidelity. In: Wood, D. (ed.) Linking Government Data, pp. 135–151. Springer (2011)
4. Datta, A., Thomas, H.: The cube data model: a conceptual model and algebra for on-line analytical processing in data warehouses. Decis. Support Syst. **27**(3), 289–301 (1999)

5. Bizer, C., Heath, T., Berners-Lee, T.: Linked data - the story so far. Int. J. Semant. Web Inf. Syst. **5**(3), 1–22 (2009)
6. Kalampokis, E., Tambouris, E., Tarabanis, K.: Linked open government data analytics. In: Wimmer, M.A., Janssen, M., Scholl, H.J. (eds.) EGOV 2013. LNCS, vol. 8074, pp. 99–110. Springer, Heidelberg (2013)
7. Abello, A., Darmont, J., Etcheverry, L., Golfarelli, M., Mazon, J.-N., Naumann, F., Pedersen, T., Rizzi, S.B., Trujillo, J., Vassiliadis, P., Vossen, G.: Fusion cubes: towards self-service business intelligence. Data Warehouse. Min. **9**(2), 66–88 (2013)
8. Janssen, M., Zuiderwijk, A.: Open data and transformational government. Transforming Government Workshop. Brunel University, United Kingdom (2012)
9. Auer, S., Lehmann, J., Ngonga Ngomo, A.-C., Zaveri, A.: Introduction to Linked Data and Its Lifecycle on the Web. In: Rudolph, S., Gottlob, G., Horrocks, I., van Harmelen, F. (eds.) Reasoning Weg 2013. LNCS, vol. 8067, pp. 1–90. Springer, Heidelberg (2013)
10. Kalampokis, E., Nikolov, A., Haase, P., Cyganiak, R., Stasiewicz, A., Karamanou, A., Zotou, M., Zeginis, D., Tambouris, E., Tarabanis K.: Exploiting Linked Data Cubes with OpenCube Toolkit. In: Proceedings of the ISWC 2014 Posters and Demos Track a Track within 13th International Semantic Web Conference (ISWC2014), vol. 1272, 19–23 Oct 2014, Riva del Garda, Italy, CEUR-WS (2014)
11. Ermilov, I., Martin, M., Lehmann, J., Auer, S.: Linked open data statistics: collection and exploitation. In: Klinov, P., Mouromtsev, D. (eds.) KESW 2013. CCIS, vol. 394, pp. 242–249. Springer, Heidelberg (2013)
12. Cyganiak, R., Reynolds, D.: The rdf data cube vocabulary: W3C recommendation. W3C, Technical report (2014)
13. Petrou, I., Papastefanatos, G. Dalamagas, T.: Publishing census as linked open data: a case study. In: Proceedings of the 2nd International Workshop on Open Data, Ser. WOD 2013, pp. 4:1–4:3. ACM, New York, NY, USA (2013)
14. Meroño-Peñuela, A., Ashkpour, A., Rietveld, L., Hoekstra, R., Schlobach, S.: Linked humanities data: the next frontier? In: A Case-study in Historical Census Data. Proceedings of the 2nd International Workshop on Linked Science 2012, vol. 951 (2012)
15. Capadisli, S., Auer, S. Riedl, R.: Linked statistical data analysis, ISWC SemStats (2013). http://csarven.ca/linked-statistical-data-analysis
16. Zapilko, B., Mathiak, B.: Performing statistical methods on linked data. In: International conference on Dublin Core and Metadata Applications, pp. 116–125 (2011)
17. Capadisli, S., Meroño-Peñuela, A., Auer, S., Riedl, R.: Semantic similarity and correlation of linked statistical data analysis. In: Proceedings of the 2nd International Workshop on Semantic Statistics (SemStats 2014), ISWC. CEUR (2014)
18. Kämpgen, B., Stadtmüller, S., Harth, A.: Querying the global cube: integration of multidimensional datasets from the web. In: Janowicz, K., Schlobach, S., Lambrix, P., Hyvönen, E. (eds.) EKAW 2014. LNCS, vol. 8876, pp. 250–265. Springer, Heidelberg (2014)
19. van Veenstra, A.F., van den Broek, T.: A community-driven open data lifecycle model based on literature and practice. In: Case Studies in e-Government 2.0, pp. 183–198. Springer International Publishing (2015)
20. Curtin, G.G.: Free the data!: E-governance for megaregions. Public Works Manage. Policy **14**(3), 307–326 (2010)
21. Hyland, B., Wood, D.: The joy of data - a cookbook for publishing linked government data on the web. In: Wood, D. (ed.) Linking Government Data, pp. 3–26. Springer, New York (2011)

22. Edgard, M., Shekarpour, S., Auer, S. Ngomo, A-CN.: Large-scale RDF dataset slicing. In: 2013 IEEE Seventh International Conference on Semantic Computing (ICSC), pp. 228–235. IEEE (2013)
23. Villazón-Terrazas, B., Luis, M.V.B., Oscar, C., Asunción, G.-P.: Methodological guidelines for publishing government linked data. In: Wood, D. (ed.) Linking Government Data, pp. 27–49. Springer, New York (2011)
24. Ding, L., Peristeras, V., Hausenblas, M.: Linked open government data [guest editors' introduction]. IEEE Intell. Syst. **27**(3), 11–15 (2012)
25. Alani, H., Dupplaw, D., Sheridan, J., O'Hara, K., Darlington, J., Shadbolt, N.R., Tullo, C.: Unlocking the potential of public sector information with semantic web technology. In: Aberer, K., Choi, K.-S., Noy, N., Allemang, D., Lee, K.-I., Nixon, L.J., Golbeck, J., Mika, P., Maynard, D., Mizoguchi, R., Schreiber, G., Cudré-Mauroux, P. (eds.) ASWC 2007 and ISWC 2007. LNCS, vol. 4825, pp. 708–721. Springer, Heidelberg (2007)
26. Schmachtenberg, M., Bizer, C., Paulheim, H.: Adoption of the linked data best practices in different topical domains. In: Mika, P., Tudorache, T., Bernstein, A., Welty, C., Knoblock, C., Vrandečić, D., Groth, P., Noy, N., Janowicz, K., Goble, C. (eds.) ISWC 2014, Part I. LNCS, vol. 8796, pp. 245–260. Springer, Heidelberg (2014)

Scrutinizing Open Government Data
to Understand Patterns
in eGovernment Uptake

Helle Zinner Henriksen[1,2(✉)]

[1] Copenhagen Business School, Frederiksberg, Denmark
hzh.itm@cbs.dk
[2] University of Agder, Kristiansand, Norway

Abstract. Research on open government data focuses mainly on standards for publishing data and access to data. In this study of the uptake of Digital Post in Denmark open data is applied in the analysis of the course of events leading up to the implementation of the mandatory digital mail-box. The study reflects on the impact of communication via local print media and discusses the body of literature which focuses on print media as a vehicle for communication to citizens. The study opens for a discussion of how open government data-sets give new opportunities for generating scholarly insights but also how it can challenge the position of researchers.

Keywords: Open data · Print media · Mandatory e-government services

1 Introduction

Digital self-services in public sector have been discussed extensively in the e-government literature for more than a decade. Empirical studies have explored various angles of usability [25], impact, transformation [20], and access [13] just to mention a few. The digital self-services have been seen as a tool of efficiency in public administration and further an alternative channel to service provision and communication with public sector. Most e-government studies are optimistic and enthusiastic about the digital agenda. However, some contributions have raised concerns and skepticism [6, 16, 20]. Access or digital divide [19] was one of the core concerns and counter argument to the more techno-optimistic accounts in the early stage of academic research on digital self-services provided by public sector. The first contributions in the digital divide literature focused on those groups in society without access to computers and Internet [12, 19]. With the fast diffusion of Internet in society the discussion shifted from the have/have-not dichotomy to a more multifaceted view involving social, institutional and political factors along with the availability of technology [12]. Another dimension in the digital divide debate which has pinpointed potential weaknesses to the digital agenda relates to digital literacy [4]. With the massive diffusion of Internet to the majority of the grown population in the Western societies the core issue in the ability to use digital self-services is not access to the services but rather the ability to read and understand the content of the digital services. Administrative literacy is crucial [4].

© IFIP International Federation for Information Processing 2015
E. Tambouris et al. (Eds.): EGOV 2015, LNCS 9248, pp. 144–155, 2015.
DOI: 10.1007/978-3-319-22479-4_11

The issue of administrative literacy has been highlighted in the digital immigrant/digital native discussion where it has been argued that the digital natives have limited digital capabilities [24]. These factors can influence the uptake and use of the digital self-services [24] but have on the other hand not hindered a constant development and implementation of digital self-services among governments throughout the globe. From a citizen perspective the mitigating circumstances have been that uses of digital self-services so far have been voluntary. The reported study presents an initiative which makes eGovernment use mandatory unless the citizen actively opts out. Danish Citizens are digital by default. The digital by default strategy is the final goal of 15 years of digital strategies for the Danish public sector. It is materialized in a mandatory digital mailbox for all citizens +15 years of age. The digital mailbox will be used for all communication from public sector to a citizen and does replace most window envelopes from public sector to citizens. It is in principle a one-way communication from government to citizens which in some case initiates further interaction and thus represents the first step in digital self-service e.g. rectification or correction of tax statement, confirmation of waiting list, or application for subsidies.

The primary objective of this article is to initiate a discussion about the potential of using open government data-sets in (eGovernment) research and furthermore the implications of getting pre-packaged data-sets for research purposes. To illustrate the discussion the case of uptake of the digital mailbox in Denmark is presented. The uptake is analyzed using open data-sets from the Agency of Digitization combined with print media content. Open government data has received much attention in the eGovernment research community. Focus has mainly been on the overall PSI agenda [14] or the standards for publishing data and access to data [15]. The use of open data for the purpose of analyzing Governments' own actions has received little attention. And to the authors knowledge the implications of open data for scholarly knowledge generation has not received any attention yet. To set the scene for the analysis another type of open data is included. That is open data on the Parliamentary process. Data is included to illustrate the political discussions prior to the implementation of the law. The next section presents the content of these political discussions. Section 3 provides an introduction to media frames which is applied as the analytical lens of the open data-sets. Section 4 presents the research method, including handling of data, graphical illustrations of data, and interpretations of data. The final section offers some concluding remarks.

2   The Mandatory Public Mail Box

In the Danish context some digital citizen services have been implemented via direct legislation. In line with this strategy the Minister of Finance in 2012 proposed a law on mandatory digital post for all Danish citizens to the Danish parliament. The proposal was part of the implementation of a public digitization strategy outlined in collaboration between municipalities and central government [8]. The overall objective was to achieve a goal of making 80 % of all communication between citizens and public sector digital before end of 2015. The strategy stipulates "**End of paper forms and letters:** In their busy working life Danes should not waste their time filling paper forms at the local town hall. Tax-money should not be used on stamps and handling of paper, when we have digital solutions which can solve things more efficient" [8, p. 3]. The quoted passage from the digitization strategy reflects the optimistic discourse presented in a large share of annual reports from International associations such as WEF, UN, and OECD and the e-government literature including proceedings of the EGOV conferences over the years.

2.1   The Preparation and Passing of the Law

In the Danish context the process of legislation is highly documented. Transcripts of Parliamentary sessions and documentation such as minutes from meetings, responses from hearings, and other relevant data from the preparation and negotiation in parliament is open and easily searchable via a portal hosted by the Danish Parliament.

The reading of the open archives of the Danish Parliament illustrates that throughout the parliamentary discussions and approval of the law elected politicians and associations, which had contributed with responses via public hearings, primarily discussed three themes: the possibility of opting out of the mandatory digital post, privacy and security challenges, and the infrastructure supporting the digital post. The infrastructure consists of a digital signature, the "NemID" and a postbox "e-boks". The infrastructure is hosted by a private provider "Nets" owned by two US based hedge funds and a Danish pension fund, which has a minor share. Some parliamentarians viewed the private ownership problematic due to the handling of sensitive and confidential information about citizens. However, the core of the discussion related to the possibility of opting out from the digital postbox. In order to accommodate for consensus in the Parliament the final law has specific paragraphs about how to opt out. The law and its respective documents reflect none discussions or debates about the financial rationale behind the implementation of mandatory digital mail for all citizens. It appears that there is a consensus among the elected politicians that the initiative is financially viable and reasonable in general. The political consensus is in line with other studies on eGovernment diffusion [18]. The passing of the law was subject to little discussion considering its far reaching implications for each and every Danish citizen +15 years. And further has huge implications for the daily routines of civil servants [2]. The law on mandatory digital post came into force on November 1st 2014. It was the Agency of Digitization which was in charge of the overall implementation of the law. To stimulate the competition among municipalities the agency created a high degree of transparency in the adoption process. Each week the Agency of Digitization published statistics on number of citizens who had signed up for the digital post box and also number of citizens who had asked for exemption from the law. Municipalities have the most direct interaction with citizens and were in charge of getting citizens on board through local initiatives and campaigns. It became a measure in itself for municipalities to harvest the honor of being the winner of the week by being the "weekly top performer" measured by the increase in percentage of citizen enrollment or to be among the Top 5 digital municipalities.

The Agency of Digitization prepared campaigning material for municipalities and orchestrated campaigns to promote the Digital Post prior to November 1st. Templates for Web-banners, pamphlets and flyers, posters, and other material was developed and distributed to municipalities. The effects of information campaigns are well researched in social science and leave a mixed picture of the effect of the hypodermic model [9]. The hypodermic model suggests that mass media have direct and powerful effects on a mass audience [23]. The model fundamentally suggests that citizens are passive recipients who are easy to manipulate [9] and that media are powerful instruments to create awareness of innovations among diverse groups of people [23].

3 Media as Vehicles of Public Information

Though there has been a decrease in the circulation number of newspapers there is still a strong interest in news among citizens [22]. The most recent cross-country analysis of media use reflects that Danes are consuming news on a daily basis. News is presented mainly via TV but also newspapers both printed and online whereas social media as a channel for news plays a less prominent role [22]. Media is a cornerstone in society and shape public opinion by their framing of events [7]. The framing is driven by various factors and represents "interpretive packages" [10]. Gamson and Modigliani [10] refer to media packages which "can be conceived as a set of interpretive packages that give meaning to an issue. The package has an internal structure. And its core is a central organizing idea, or frame, for making sense of relevant events," (p. 3) (Table 1).

Table 1. Components of frames

Framing devices	How to think about the issue
Metaphors	Imagined events which are intended to illuminate and enhance our understanding through powerful illustrations
Exemplars	Real events of the past or present
Catchphrases	The capture of essence in a single theme statement or slogan
Depictions	Characteristics in a particular fashion through some colorful string of modifiers
Visual images	Icons or other visual images
Reasoning devices	**What should be done about the issue**
Roots	Analysis of the causal dynamics underlying the strip of events
Consequences	Analysis of the consequences that will flow from different actions or interventions. Focus can be on the short or long term consequences
Appeals to principle	Rely on characteristic moral appeals and uphold certain general precepts

Adapted from Gamson and Modigliani [10]

The framing and media packages play a central role in the construction of the social reality. The media analysis as presented by [7, 9, 10] has as its starting point the *framing*. It is referred to as interpretive packages. Macro level issues in society have several interpretive packages each representing for example ideological or political stances. As such they represent the key dialectical principle of debate in the public sphere – every claim tends to generate a counter-claim [11]. The interpretive package consists of an overall frame and position that defines it (i.e. roots, consequences, and appeals to principles). A central part of the construction of the social reality relates to the lexical choice [11]. "The lexical choice and discursive practices are central components on how issues are rhetorically constructed and 'framed' and how in turn particular messages/meanings are conveyed and boundaries set for public understanding and public interpretation…" [11, p. 10].

The framing and the lexical choice constitutes the representation of for example Digital Post. Representation requires that the communicator takes a position. The far reaching example is the Orwellian news-speak from the 1984 novel. In the IT context the positions often range from the cyber-optimists to the cyber-pessimists with the cyber-realists in between [19]. The 'spin' to the framing of news stories appear to differ depending on the context [11] and from the reading of the sample of articles included in the analysis on the communication of Digital Post in local newspapers it appears that the content of the often very brief articles most often is informative rather than opinionated.

Media analysis has received attention within the area of public sector IT and policies. Examples include a critical analysis of Swedish ICT policy visions [21] and a content analysis of political speeches related to digital divide [17]. Kvasny and Truex [17] identify how the term digital divide is shifted to digital opportunities. They observe how the (US) presidential speeches present technology as a "magical force" which is a means for progress. They argue that governments play an important role in popularizing technology terms and in giving meaning to them. Yildiz and Saylam [26] reach similar conclusions in their content analysis of e-government discourses in Turkish newspapers. Yildiz and Saylam [26] suggest that "Media use for discourse production and reinforcement is critical because media outlets can be very effective in legitimizing initiatives such as e-government."

4   Research Method, Data Collection, and Data Representation

The Agency of Digitization has since 2011 published data on uptake per municipality on a weekly basis [1]. The data is published as open data in Excel format and can be downloaded at their web-site. The open data was used to identify patterns in uptake across the five Danish regions. The five Danish regions differ in population and number of municipalities. The "Region Hovedstaden" which is the region with the capital and its suburbs is the largest region measured in number of citizens and number of municipalities and at the same time the region which is most densely populated. Data on uptake eleven months prior to and one month after the effectuation of the law was mapped and combined with data on media coverage in local newspapers in the same period. The media base InfoMedia which indexes all public media was used to identify communication on the Digital Post in local newspapers. The search criteria used in the InfoMedia base was any article within a given week where the words "Digital Post" appeared. The argument for using local newspapers in the analysis is their embedd-edness in the local context. Their content apart from local advertisements is mainly news and announcements to the local community. Furthermore, the reasons for choosing the local newspapers for the analysis were: (i) it is freely distributed; (ii) to all households; (iii) it is assumed that it has a larger number of readers compared to subscription newspapers; and finally (iv) it gives an opportunity to analyze where and when information about the Digital Post was communicated. Data on the local com-munication was collected on a weekly basis for each of the Danish regions. A total of 1.222 articles which met the search criteria were published during the period 1.11.2013 to 30.11.2014 (Table 2).

Table 2. Basic information about the five Danish regions

Region	Share of population +15 years (n = 4,692,381)	Number of municipalities
Hovedstaden	31.23 %	29
Sjælland	14.54 %	17
Sydjylland	21.32 %	22
Midtjylland	22.52 %	19
Nordjylland	10.39 %	11
Total	100 %	98

The articles were registered per region and were mapped against the percentage of citizens which had actively signed up for digital post across the regions. The numbers are shown in Figs. 1, 2, 3, 4 and 5. The Figures show that there is a steady growth in number of citizens signing up for the digital post throughout the first eleven months analyzed. For all regions there is a jump in number of citizens enrolled after November 1st 2014. The reason for the steep increase is that citizens who did not sign up voluntary were automatically enrolled by November 1st unless they had actively opted out. It is beyond the scope of this analysis to discuss this phenomenon.

The initial analysis of numbers and graphs delivers a mixed message:

(a) media does not influence uptake, and
(b) media influences uptake.

4.1 Ad (a) Media Does not Influence Uptake

Figures 1, 2, 3, 4 and 5 show a steady and similar growth in enrollments in all regions. The steady growth and level of uptake is independent of the media coverage in local newspapers. Region Nordjylland (Fig. 5) published sparsely in local media whereas

Region Hovedstaden and Region Sjælland (Figs. 1 and 2) much more frequently published information about the Digital Post (notice that the measures on the y-axis differ across the regions). This pattern corresponds to a study of the uptake of Digital Post among citizens in 2012–13 by Berger and Hertzum [3]. This suggests that the hypodermic model [9, 23] was of little use in relation to the enrollment of citizens to Digital Post when taking into consideration that the diffusion curve had an almost identical trajectory in all five regions independently of local media exposure.

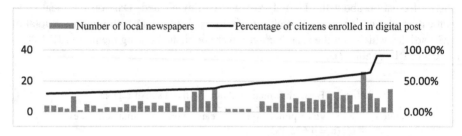

Fig. 1. Region Hovedstaden

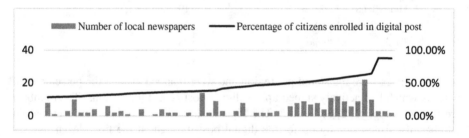

Fig. 2. Region Sjælland

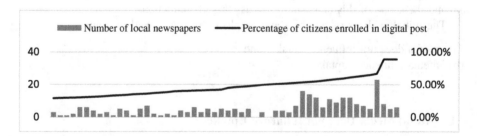

Fig. 3. Region Syddanmark

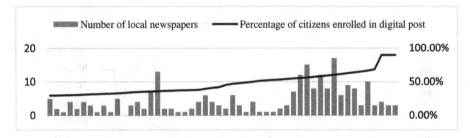

Fig. 4. Region Midtjylland

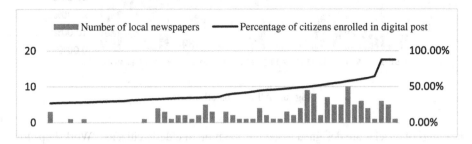

Fig. 5. Region Nordjylland

4.2 Ad (b) Media Influences Uptake

Figures 1, 2, 3, 4 and 5 show that there is a simultaneous increase in enrollment across all regions in week 22 (May 2014). What is remarkable is that there is an increase in number of articles in week 20. This could indicate that readers of the local newspapers have been influenced by the media coverage. The increase in enrollments from week 21 to week 22 is statistical significant (Chi-square statistics: $p < 0.01$) (Fig. 6).

To get further insight to the actual media communication in week 20 and to find frames related to Digital Post we now turn to content of the articles published in local media during that particular week compared to other weeks. There were 45 articles on Digital Post in local newspapers in week 20. To identify differences in the media communication prior to week 20 and after week 20 the 1.222 articles were analyzed using one of the simple text-filtering tools (WordItOut) available on-line. The 30 most frequent nouns, adjectives, and verbs were included. Given that the texts are in Danish the outcome of the analysis is presented as tag clouds to illustrate the three groups of texts.

Irrespective of the large variation in number of articles it is striking that the tag clouds do not differ significantly in their composition in the three clusters. From week 20 the words Digital and Post have a more prominent position. The word "fritagelse" which translates into opting out does appear in the week 20 tag and not in the prior weeks of media coverage. This should however lead to that less people sign up for the Digital Post in the following weeks. The tag clouds illustrate that communication has been rather consistent throughout the period analyzed. However, there is one shift which is noticed from browsing through the three clusters of articles. Up to week 20 there is mainly focus on getting the elderly on board. From reading the articles it shows that in particular

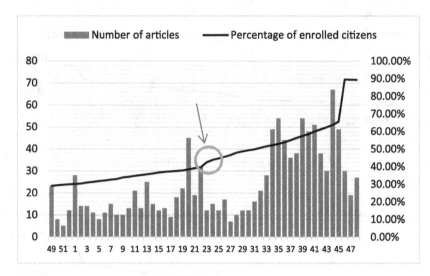

Fig. 6. All regions all articles

headings of articles are designed to get the attention of elderly citizens. "Workshops for elderly", "Assistance for elderly", "Help to IT-disabled" and similar headings are found across the articles relating to Digital Post. The articles after week 20 do however recognize that youth is the most challenging group to get on board (Fig. 7).

A cross-check in the InfoMedia base in relation coverage on Digital Post in National and Regional newspapers in week 20 shows a different pattern. National newspapers had only 3 articles the particular week and Regional newspapers had 24 articles. The coverage in Regional newspapers differs substantially from the local coverage. The Regional newspapers have in general very negative headings e.g. "Digital terror", "Digital disadvantages", and "More Citizens will opt out". The majority of articles are letters to the editor where citizens air their frustration. In comparison do the Local newspapers have headings such as "Join the Internet café" and "Workshop on Digital Post", reflecting a helpful and cozy atmosphere. The articles are with no exception written by the journalists affiliated with the newspapers.

Fig. 7. Tag clouds of articles

To get a closer understanding of the content of the media coverage in local newspapers the next step is to identify the framing of Digital Post. First of all it is striking to see how well the overall campaign is infused in the local media is across the 98 Danish municipalities. The message is homogeneous across the 1.222 articles with a similar lexical choice [11] leading to similar framing across time and regions. The framing across municipalities and their respective local outlets leave little room for interpretation. Though it is possible to identify counter arguments in the public debate from the Regional newspapers the overall framing presented in the Local newspapers is consistent over time. It is a framing which is not questioning the phenomenon of Digital Post. Instead the campaign establishes a competition where municipalities encourage citizens to enroll to help the municipality to win the race. A large number of municipalities even chose to introduce a prize for signing up for the digital post-box. There were identified 120 articles which encouraged citizens to sign up for Digital Post and thus be part of a prize draw. In the time-spirit and in line with the overall goal of digitizing the prize was an iPad (Table 3).

Table 3. Digital Post frames

Framing devices	How to think about the issue
Metaphors	The same just more convenient. Digital Post is more secure and much easier. Paper-based letters get replaced with digital messages.
Exemplars	n.a.
Catchphrases	"Are you ready for Digital Post"
Depictions	With Digital Post can you read messages from public sector – independently of location. You get rid of paper and binders, and your letters never get lost.
Visual images	eGovernment is difficult to communicate via visual images. But the Agency for Digitization has designed an image which has been shown everywhere. The image has similarities to an Apple product and almost gives the silky feel of the packaging of Apple products.
Reasoning devices	What should be done about the issue
Roots	Educate non-users and solve the problem of non-acceptance: If you have not yet signed up then attend a workshop where you learn how to navigate on the Internet and get confident with technology.
Consequences	n.a. (municipalities wrote physical letters to all citizens who did not sign up before November 1st and enrolled them automatically)
Appeals to principle	n.a.

Adapted from Gamson and Modigliani [10]

The analysis on citizen enrollment to Digital Post solely focused on the weekly increase at regional level. The open dataset is much richer with data on the individual municipality including gender, age and socio-economic status of citizens enrolled. The superficial use of the data-set does however illustrate the potential for gaining insights and showing trends on eGovernment uptake. But does it tell the full story?

5 ... and Some Reflections

In their essay on deconstruction of IS texts Chiasson and Davidson [5] raises the question of the practical relevance of scrutinizing texts. Their answer to the question is that breakthrough innovations often require the overturning of the taken-for-granted assumptions. The taken-for granted assumption in the case of Digital Post as it is presented in local media is that Digital Post is a positive step towards e-government implementation, which is positive too.

The data used to illustrate the case of uptake of Digital Post is based on a quantitative open government data-set including the total population combined with qualitative data from the open archives of the Parliament and on-line information from the Agency of Digitization. As stated in the introduction the primary objective of this paper is to "initiate a discussion about the potential of using open government data-sets in (eGovernment) research." The quantitative open data-sets often excel by including the total population contrary to the situation where research is based on sampling and methodological stances of the researcher in charge of designing the instruments for data collection. And it is beyond discussion that the openness "enable public access and facilitate exploitation" [15]. But do they make field research obsolete? The sources included in the paper illustrate the richness in open government data but also the potential for multiple interpretations which are highly dependent on specific knowledge about the context. The highly interpretative framework on media frames [10] was added to illustrate that we can scrutinize open government data and get parts of the story on uptake but to understand patterns in eGovernment uptake we still need a contextual qualitative data which need a human (researchers') touch in order to make sense of the massive body of information generated by public sector institutions.

References

1. Agency of Digitization: Open data-set on citizen enrollment. https://www.borger.dk/for-myndigheder/Sider/Kampagnematerialer-2014.aspx?NavigationTaxonomyId=fa911c07-f84c-4def-8218-6d52a8200433. Accessed Mar 2015
2. Berger, J.B.: Mandatory e-government has arrived: the silent protest from staff calls for the committed scholar – resistance must never be futile! In: Proceedings of the 25th Australasian Conference on Information Systems (ACIS), Auckland (2014)
3. Berger, J.B., Hertzum, M.: Adoption patterns for the digital post system by danish municipalities and citizens. In: Proceedings of the Twenty Second European Conference on Information Systems (ECIS), Tel Aviv (2014)
4. Belanger, F., Carter, L.: The impact of the digital divide on e-government. Commun. ACM 52(4), 132–135 (2009)

5. Chiasson, M., Davidson, E.: Reconsidering deconstruction in information systems research. Eur. J. Inf. Syst. **21**(2), 192–206 (2012)
6. Coursey, D., Norris, D.F.: Models of e-government: are they correct? An empirical assessment. Public Adm. Rev. **68**(3), 523–536 (2008)
7. De Vreese, C.H.: News framing: theory and typology. Inf. Des. J. Doc. Des. **13**(1), 51–62 (2005)
8. E-government Strategy: e-government strategy 2011–15 (2011). http://www.digst.dk/Servicemenu/English. Accessed Mar 2015
9. Gamson, W.A.: The 1987 distinguished lecture: a constructionist approach to mass media and public opinion. Symbolic Interact. **11**(2), 161–174 (1988)
10. Gamson, W.A., Modigliani, A.: Media discourse and public opinion on nuclear power: a constructionist approach. Am. J. Sociol. **95**, 1–37 (1989)
11. Hansen, A.: Communication, media and environment: towards reconnecting research on the production, content and social implications of environmental communication. Int. Commun. Gaz. **73**(1–2), 7–25 (2011)
12. Helbig, N., Ramón Gil-García, J., Ferro, E.: Understanding the complexity of electronic government: implications from the digital divide literature. Gov. Inf. Q. **26**(1), 89–97 (2009)
13. Jaeger, P.T., Bertot, J.C.: Responsibility rolls down: public libraries and the social and policy obligations of ensuring access to e-government and government information. Public Libr. Q. **30**(2), 91–116 (2011)
14. Janssen, K.: The influence of the PSI directive on open government data: an overview of recent developments. Gov. Inf. Q. **28**(4), 446–456 (2011)
15. Kalampokis, E., Tambouris, E., Tarabanis, K.: A classification scheme for open government data: towards linking decentralised data. Int. J. Web Eng. Technol. **6**(3), 266–285 (2011)
16. Kraemer, K., King, J.L.: Information technology and administrative reform: will e-government be different? Int. J. Electron. Gov. Res. (IJEGR) **2**(1), 1–20 (2006)
17. Kvasny, L., Truex, D.: Defining away the digital divide: a content analysis of institutional influences on popular representations of technology. In: Realigning Research and Practice in Information Systems Development, pp. 399–414. Springer, New York (2001)
18. McNeal, R.S., Tolbert, C.J., Mossberger, K., Dotterweich, L.J.: Innovating in digital government in the American states. Soc. Sci. Q. **84**(1), 52–70 (2003)
19. Norris, P.: Digital Divide: Civic Engagement, Information Poverty, and the Internet Worldwide. Cambridge University Press, Cambridge (2001)
20. Norris, D.F., Reddick, C.G.: Local e-government in the United States: transformation or incremental change? Public Adm. Rev. **73**(1), 165–175 (2013)
21. Olsson, T.: Appropriating civic information and communication technology: a critical study of Swedish ICT policy visions. New Media Soc. **8**(4), 611–627 (2006)
22. Reuters: Reuters institute digital news report 2014 (2014). https://reutersinstitute.politics.ox.ac.uk
23. Rogers, E.M.: Diffusion of Innovations. Free Press, New York (2003)
24. Selwyn, N.: The digital native–myth and reality. In: Aslib Proceedings, vol. 61, no. 4, pp. 364–379, July 2009
25. Venkatesh, V., Chan, F.K., Thong, J.Y.: Designing e-government services: key service attributes and citizens' preference structures. J. Oper. Manage. **30**(1), 116–133 (2012)
26. Yildiz, M., Saylam, A.: E-government discourses: an inductive analysis. Gov. Inf. Q. **30**(2), 141–153 (2013)

Advancing e-Government Using the Internet of Things: A Systematic Review of Benefits

Paul Brous[1,2(✉)] and Marijn Janssen[1]

[1] Delft University of Technology, Delft, The Netherlands
{P.A.Brous,M.F.W.H.A.Janssen}@tudelft.nl
[2] Rijkswaterstaat, Delft, The Netherlands

Abstract. The Internet of Things (IoT) has been given scant attention in e-government literature, whereas promises are high. The IoT describes a situation whereby physical objects are connected to the Internet and are able to communicate with, and identify themselves to, other devices. These devices generate a huge amount of data. When it is possible to combine data from devices and other systems, new insights may be created which may provide important benefits. In this paper we explore the expected benefits of IoT for e-governance by investigating case studies at the Directorate General of Public Works and Water Management of the Netherlands. The results show that IoT has a variety of expected political, strategic, tactical and operational benefits which implies that IoT enables effective knowledge management, sharing and collaboration between domains and divisions at all levels of the organisation, as well as between government and citizens.

Keywords: Internet of things · E-governance · Smart cities · Benefits · Advantages

1 Introduction

The Internet of Things (IoT) describes a situation whereby physical objects are connected to the Internet and are able to communicate with, and identify themselves to, other devices [1–3]. IoT refers to the increasing network of physical objects that feature an IP address for internet connectivity, and the communication that occurs between these objects and other Internet-enabled devices and systems. These devices and the communication between these devices can benefit e-government by providing enough quality data to generate the information required to make the right decisions at the right time. E-governance is a technology-mediated relationship between citizens and their governments with respect to communication, development of policy and expressions of public will [4]. The term has very broad implications with regards to policy formulation, economic development, and the search for new ways to connect people with the political process [5]. This research explores the expected benefits of the IoT for e-government purposes by means of real world case studies.

The IoT is important because a physical (or sensor) object that is able to communicate digitally is able to relate not only to a single entity, but also becomes

© IFIP International Federation for Information Processing 2015
E. Tambouris et al. (Eds.): EGOV 2015, LNCS 9248, pp. 156–169, 2015.
DOI: 10.1007/978-3-319-22479-4_12

connected to surrounding objects and data infrastructures. This allows for a situation in which many physical objects are able to act in unison, by means of ambient intelligence [6]. The object becomes a part of a complex system in which the whole is greater than the sum of its parts [7]. For example, using networked sensors and cameras to analyse traffic flow, it is possible to determine the position and length of traffic jams, and to monitor trends, variations, and relationships in the road network over time. According to Xia et al. (2012), IoT will increase the ubiquity of the Internet by integrating every object for interaction via embedded systems [8]. This will enable a highly distributed network of objects communicating with human beings as well as other objects. For example, in the Netherlands, sensors installed in buoys in countrywide network of sensors monitor the water levels in Dutch rivers and in the North Sea. The system automatically sends reports to the storm surge barriers such as the "Maeslantkering" and to their managers if water levels exceed the defined thresholds. Early predictions of rising water levels can be made and the storm surge barriers can be automatically closed to prevent major flooding. Also, combining information from devices and other systems using expansive analysis, may provide new insights for managers of public infrastructure. For example, it is possible to embed wireless sensors within concrete foundation piles to ensure the quality and integrity of a structure. These sensors can provide load and event monitoring for the projects construction both during and after its completion. This data, combined with data from load monitoring sensors designed to measure weights of freight traffic, may provide managers of physical infrastructure with new insights as to the maintenance requirements of the infrastructure.

Applications such as these imply that IoT has much potential; however, the benefits and barriers of IoT for e-governance, especially with regards to the management and maintenance of large physical infrastructure, have not been investigated systematically and remain largely anecdotal. There is a need to address the potentially unanticipated impacts of technology on governance structures and processes [4] and to investigate the impact of IoT in a systematic manner [9].

The methodology used in this research is described in Sect. 2. On the basis of state of the art literature and two explorative case studies at the Directorate General of Public Works and Water Management of the Netherlands, the potential benefits of IoT will be presented in Sect. 3. The Directorate General of Public Works and Water Management of the Netherlands is commonly known within The Netherlands as "Rijkswaterstaat", often abbreviated to "RWS", and is referred to as such within this research. RWS is part of the Dutch Ministry of Infrastructure and the Environment and is responsible for the design, construction, management and maintenance of the main infrastructure facilities in the Netherlands. The results of the literature review and the case studies, and the expected benefits of IoT for asset management will be discussed in Sect. 4. The results show that IoT has a variety of potential strategic, tactical and operational benefits which implies that IoT enables effective knowledge management, sharing and collaboration between domains and divisions at all levels of the organisation, as well as between government and citizens. Finally conclusions will be drawn in Sect. 5.

2   Research Method

To determine the expected benefits of IoT we followed two main research steps. First the common benefits of IoT were identified from a rigorous review of literature. The keywords: "Internet of Things", "benefits" ("advantages"), and "e-governance", returned zero hits within the databases Scopus, Web of Science, IEEE explore, and JSTOR. When we replaced the keyword "e-governance" with "governance", we had one hit in Web of Science and IEEE Explore, two hits in Scopus and four hits in JSTOR. The query [all abstract: "benefits" "internet of things" "e-governance"] searching between 2000 and 2015 returned ninety-eight hits in Google Scholar. We found a great deal of these articles mentioned IoT as being a potential facilitator for achieving the goal of a Smart City, but few articles mentioned how IoT would benefit this ideal. We then filtered these results and performed a forward and backward search to select relevant articles based on the criteria that they included a theoretical discussion on the benefits of IoT.

The second main research method was that of explorative case study to identify potential benefits of IoT within e-governance applications. Two cases were studied. The cases selected were both located within the context of RWS, which allowed the researchers unlimited access to subject matter experts and internal documentation for all the cases. This helped ensure the construct validity of the case studies [10]. The cases were selected based on their use of IoT for e-governance purposes – the unit of analysis being programmes within RWS which use and develop IoT for e-governance purposes. According to the United Nations e-government survey (2014) [5], The Netherlands is an e-participation leader. This contributes to the validity of the cases as being good representations of e-governance. The cases under study were selected from different domains within RWS in order to ensure diversity and external validity through replication logic [10, 11], in which each case serves as a distinct experiment that stands on its own as an analytic unit. The domains selected were road management and water management respectively.

We studied two separate cases to refine and extend the list of benefits from literature. In the Netherlands there is a sharp divide in how processes are managed between the "wet" or, water management domain and the "dry", or road management domain. We felt it necessary to select cases from both these domains in order to gain a more rounded perspective of the implementation of IoT within e-government in the Netherlands. The cases selected were: 1. Sensor information gathered for the purpose of road management; 2. Sensor information gathered for the purpose of water management. The first case deals with sensor information gathered by RWS with regards to traffic and road management. The second case study deals with sensor information gathered by RWS with regards to water and levee management. The case studies were explorative in method and descriptive in nature. Unstructured interviews were held with managers, subject matter experts, and consultants within RWS. Internal documentation was also studied. Finally, the results of the cases were shared with and verified by subject matter experts within RWS. The common benefits of IoT found in literature were listed and were compared with the evidence of benefits of IoT for e-governance found in the case study analysis. There were several iterations throughout the research as each case introduced new potential benefits. The expected benefits of the IoT for e-governance are expressed in italics within this paper.

3 Literature Background

The main enabling factor for the IoT is the blending integration of several technologies and communications solutions such as identification and tracking technologies, wired and wireless sensor and actuator networks, enhanced communication protocols (shared with the Next Generation Internet), and distributed intelligence for smart objects [1], Radio Frequency Identification technology, Electronic Product Code technology, and ZigBee technology [12]. IoT uses sensors and actuators to enable ubiquitous sensing, enabling ability to measure and infer and understand environmental indicators, from delicate ecologies and natural resources to urban environments [13]. IoT includes all devices connected to the Internet and to each other, generating sensor-based signals. By installing apps on a mobile phone or tablet the device can become a sensor in a large network. For example, accelerometers can be used to detect potential potholes when persons are cycling or driving. Cameras and microphones can be used to collect evidence when there is a robbery or a riot and devices can measure the concentration of fine particles. The resulting data from these sensors are often stored in databases. Sensors can be used for enabling public safety and compliance to regulations for example. In this way it may provide a more effective control mechanism [1, 12–15].

Public and private organizations are increasingly turning to the IoT as new sources of data, derived from continuously monitoring a wide range of things within a variety of situations, becomes available. These data can be used in many various ways, such as determining one's position or sensing the temperature to ensure that gauges are configured correctly and that temperatures remain within accepted norms. New vehicle technologies and applications can have a positive effect on traffic management systems by helping to improve the efficiency of the traffic network [16], and improving health and safety by reducing accidents and helping to reduce emissions [14, 16].

IoT results in a large amount of big data which can be opened to the public. Literature shows that this might have two important benefits for e-governance [17]. Firstly, making data and information available to the public greatly improves government transparency [17]. Increased openness and transparency helps ensure proper oversight and reduces government waste. Secondly, enabling consumer self-service in this way can empower citizens and business to take decisions through better access to information by making use of the vast amount of data collected by IoT and the collective wisdom of the crowds [1, 2, 12–14, 16, 18]. The IoT gives intelligent advice to users. For example, in intelligent transportation systems such as in-car intelligent driving systems and smart highways, route planning assists drivers by considering constraints related to traffic, time, and cost [6, 16].

Fleisch (2010) identifies seven value drivers for the IoT which result in potential business benefits [2]: 1. The "simplified manual proximity trigger" increases job satisfaction, empowers consumers by enabling consumer self-service, reduces labour costs and improves data quality; 2. the "automatic proximity trigger" reduces fraud related costs, process failure costs, and labour costs, and provides high granularity data for improved efficiency through process improvement; 3. the "automatic sensors trigger" helps improve service quality by providing individual and prompt process control, increases process efficiency and effectiveness, and provides an additional level of data quality for identifying potential areas for further process improvement; 4. automatic product security reduces cost of process failure due to fraud, reduces the cost of process security and helps increase consumer trust; 5. simple, direct user feedback improves service efficiency and effectiveness by helping processes become more accurate, more flexible, and faster; 6. extensive user feedback improves trust by ensuring new customer contact, providing new advertising opportunities and supporting additional service revenues; 7. mind changing feedback allows for the identification of trends, enabling new product features and new services, and enables an active selection of attractive customer segments [2].

Another view of possible IoT application classification is provided by Chui et al. [15]. Chui et al. [15] define two broad categories for IoT applications, Information and Analysis and Automation and Control. In Information and Analysis, decision making services are improved by receiving better and more up to date information from networked physical objects which allows for a more accurate analysis of the current status-quo with regards to tracking, situational awareness, and sensor-driven decision analytics. In Automation and Control, outputs received from processed data and analysis are acted upon to improve efficiency, effectiveness and to enforce compliancy.

Haller et al. [9] draw on the work of Subirana et al. [19] and identify two major paradigms from which business value can be derived: real-world visibility, and business process decomposition. Haller et al. [9] believe that with real-world visibility, sensors make it possible for a company to better know what actually is happening in the real world. The use of automated identification and data collection technologies such as RFID enables an increased accuracy and timeliness of information about business processes and provides competitive advantages through improved service efficiency in terms of process optimisation [20]. In business process decomposition, the decomposition and decentralization of existing business processes increases service flexibility and service effectiveness, allows better decision making and can lead to new revenue streams [9]. This implies not only real-world data flows to the business processes so that they can optimize their execution, but also the capability to delegate functionality to devices. This may allow for more system flexibility in which the system is better able to react to dynamic changes [20].

In short, IoT can deliver a variety of benefits related both to the real-time measurement and analyses of sensor data as to trend analysis of historical data over time. We list the possible benefits of IoT according to strategic/political, tactical and operational divisions. This is a popular divisioning [21, 22], suitable for e-governance research. Possible benefits of the IoT are: *1. Political and Strategic - improved forecasting and trend analysis, promoting government transparency, improved citizen empowerment; 2. Tactical - improved planning with regards to management and maintenance, more efficient enforcement of regulations, improved health and safety measures, cost reduction; 3. Operational - improved efficiency of services, improved effectiveness of services, and improved flexibility of services.*

4   Case Studies

The goal of the case study research was to refine and extend the list of expected benefits from literature and to understand the real life benefits of IoT in the most complete way possible. For this reason, the case study research involved the use of multiple methods for collecting data. The cases were selected from the primary processes of RWS. In RWS there is a sharp divide in how processes are managed between the water management domain and the road management domain. In order to gain a rounded perspective of the benefits of IoT within RWS, we believed it necessary to select cases from both these domains.

4.1   Case Study 1: Road Management Data Collection at RWS

RWS builds, manages and maintains the Dutch national highways. Correct data is required to do this effectively. Over the years, RWS has developed several methods for obtaining the necessary data from the highways it manages, collecting, processing and making the data available to traffic and road management teams. Measurements are generally made by placing sensors in the road in many different locations. These sensors produce large amounts of data which is mainly used in *mid-term planning*, *long term projections*, air quality predictions and noise calculations which have an impact on *health and safety measures* as well as the *environmental impact*, and improving *service efficiency* with regards to road works management.

During the winter months, RWS performs preventive scattering of salt on the highways to ensure that highways remain safe to drive on. Salt lowers the freezing point of water, thawing snow or ice. The nationwide slipperiness alarm system (SAS) automatically alerts RWS when potential hazardous situations arise with regards to the slipperiness of the road surface. SAS measures, among other things, the temperature of the road surface, air humidity and the salinity on the road. RWS decides whether or not to scatter salt based on the information provided by this system. This decision also takes into account the weather and the amount of salt that is possibly already under way. The improved efficiency and flexibility of this system means that only two hours are required before salt is scattered on the roads. Furthermore, the system contributes to the effectiveness of the service by helping RWS scatter salt in the correct places.

At present, RWS estimates that at least 15 % of freight traffic on the Dutch national road network is overloaded. Overloading of heavy vehicles causes road pavement structural distress and a reduced service lifetime [23, 24]. Effectively reducing overloading reduces the damage to the road infrastructure, lengthening the road's lifetime and reduces the frequency of maintenance. RWS has to deal with the negative effects of overloaded freight traffic. The damage to pavements and installations by overloaded trucks in 2008 was estimated to be at least 34 million euros per year. In addition, the extra maintenance required creates a significant amount of traffic disruptions. These disruptions are estimated to cost several million euros per year. The ambition of RWS is to increase the effectiveness of the approach of overloading. In 2010, RWS decided to tackle the overloading problem through structural cooperation. This decision was recorded in a protocol to reduce the current rate of infringement of overloading from 15 % to less than 10 %. Based on this objective, the estimated annual reduction in maintenance requirements of the damage to structures and pavements was calculated at a magnitude of 11 million Euros per year.

To facilitate enforcement of regulations, and reduce costs, RWS has created a national network of monitoring points, the "Weigh in Motion" network. This network, consisting of measurement points in the road on which the axle loads of heavy traffic is weighed, is used to support the enforcement of overloading by helping the enforcement agency to select overloaded trucks for weighing in a static location. In addition, the enforcement agency collects information regarding each truck. This provides access to the actual load of the main road, about peak times when it comes to overcharging and it provides RWS with the ability to collect information concerning the compliance behaviour of individual carriers. This forms the basis for business inspections and legal follow-up programs. According to RWS, the critical success factors for the deployment of the "Weigh In Motion" network are the strategic choice of locations and weighing the reliability of the measurement points. This tool has proved to be very effective in addressing overloading, especially because of the perception of probability and the enhanced effect of enforcement.

Inductive loops embedded in the road surface remain a key technology for traffic detection. An inductive loop is a simple and reliable way to detect the movement of vehicles over a road surface and is extensively used in traffic responsive traffic signal systems to collect traffic data to optimise signal timings accordingly [16]. Such loops provide data on traffic density, flows and speeds for trend analysis as well as providing a key input to real-time traffic models which predict queues or delays. RWS has implemented a system of induction loops for monitoring traffic flows. Traffic signalling is indicated by Motorway Traffic Management (MTM) and is installed on several highways in the Netherlands. MTM is a fully automated network management system and is used for automatic incident detection (due to road works or situations regarding defective infrastructure, for example) in order to improve the efficiency, effectiveness and flexibility of the services provided, as well as the enforcement of speed infractions and other control measures.

Traffic congestion is a major problem in the Netherlands. Recent years have seen a shift towards tackling the problem by managing the existing capacity rather than the traditional concept of more road building [16], requiring more efficient traffic management tools integrated within a wider traffic management environment. Within the Roads to the Future programme, RWS is undertaking a pilot project called 'Guide on the road' [25]. The pilot project 'Guide on the road' is looking to develop a system in which the motorist is presented with all the relevant road information in their car in real time. This system will collect data from various sources, process and manage the data and use this information to implement various measures to manage traffic. In its ultimate form, this could lead to a situation in which there are no road signs or other physical media along the way – the "Smart Highway". All information such as (maximum) speed limits, parking opportunities, the next gas station, passing zones and current route information is delivered directly to the motorist, in the car, in the form of picture, text or sound. The system provides driving assistance in the car, from warning for sharp turns, to traffic (management) information. RWS is attempting to develop and test the concept of the Smart Highway on the basis of a pilot study with regards to the usability and deployment aspects of these technologies.

Improving safety by reducing accidents is one of the spearheads of RWS. According to RWS, more than 12.5 % of all traffic jams on Dutch roads are caused by accidents [26]. Improving traffic safety can in this way also make a direct contribution to reducing congestion, which improves the efficiency of the road network. Accidents and traffic jams are often caused by unsafe driving practices such as tailgating and speeding. Traditionally, traffic management practices have focused on enforcing regulations. Within the "Roads to the Future" programme, RWS are also investigating how rewarding desired behaviours (as opposed to enforcing compliancy) such as keeping a safe distance and complying with the applicable maximum speed improves the behaviour of motorists. In cooperation with business, RWS has developed a field trial in which participating lease drivers are rewarded for good behaviour. Drivers' behaviour is recorded by a system in the car. This system includes a display which provides continuous feedback to the motorist while driving with regards to his following distance and speed. RWS expects that this approach will have a positive effect on road safety and traffic flow.

The expected benefits of the IoT for road management identified within this case are: *1. Political and Strategic - improved forecasting and trend analysis, promoting government transparency, improved citizen empowerment; 2. Tactical - improved planning with regards to management and maintenance, more efficient enforcement of regulations, improved health and safety measures, and cost reduction; 3. Operational - improved efficiency of services, improved effectiveness of services, and improved flexibility of services.*

4.2   Case Study 2: Water Management Data Collection at RWS

In the innovative "LiveDijk Utrecht" project RWS, water board the Stichtse Rijnlanden, The IJkdijk Foundation, and the Province of Utrecht are working together to develop knowledge and experience gained by the application of sensors for the inspection and testing of levees (smart levees) in levee management [27, 28]. The major benefit identified by the project is that the smart levee philosophy will lead to significant *cost savings* and deferred investments for water management authorities in the Netherlands. In its supervisory capacity the Province of Utrecht is already using knowledge gained by these tests for improving the *efficiency* of integral water management and water *safety*.

In The Netherlands, levees are inspected at regular intervals, usually two to three times a year and more frequently at high tide. Drought sensitive levees such as the Grechtdijk are inspected more frequently in periods of drought [27]. Traditionally, these are visual inspections of the external levee walls. This task is time consuming and provides little information about the internal conditions of the levees. According to the IJkdijk Foundation, sensors have been buried in the Havendijk levee in Nieuwegein and the Grechtdijk levee in Woerden. These sensors continuously monitor the water pressure in the two dykes. The more water a dike absorbs, the more the sand and pebbles can move the weaker the dike becomes. The water pressure in the embankment is therefore a measure of the stability of the embankment [29].

The sensors embedded in the levees supply a wide range of data. This data is centrally stored and used for the real time visualization of the measurements in a dashboard displaying the sensor results. The data is then directly interpreted for detection and warning systems. These sensors are increasingly being used for the management and monitoring of water barriers. This has resulted in a huge growth in the amount of (digital) data collected for this purpose. With regards to the LiveDijk programme, the participating organizations have ensured that the data is available for distribution via the Dike Data Service Centre, which is managed centrally by the IJkdijk Foundation [27]. The Dike Data Service Centre is a platform built up around a national database for the storage of measurement data in and around dikes and water barriers. This involves both real time and historical data. Linking the data of several levee management organizations makes it possible to compare the data of similar dikes in time. Examples of data that is measured include: height measurements, subsidence (in x, y, z direction), water and ground water levels, soil saturation, temperature, infrared and radar scans.

The National Water Measurement Network, at RWS known as "Landelijk Meetnet Water" (LMW), is a facility that is responsible for the acquisition, storage and distribution of data for water resources. LMW has more than 400 data collection points using a nationwide system of sensors. The data is then processed and stored in the data centre and is made available to a variety of systems and users. The LMW was created from the merger of three previous existing monitoring networks: the Water Monitoring Network, which monitored inland waterways such as canals and rivers; the Monitoring Network North, which monitored North Sea oil platforms and channels; and the Zeeland Tidal Waters Monitoring Network which monitored the Zeeland delta waterways. Four main types of measurement activities can be identified: water quantity, water quality, meteorological data and control information on infrastructure. The LMW measures a wide variety of hydrological data such as water levels, flow rates, wave heights and directions, flow velocity and direction, and water temperature. The LMW also measures meteorological data such as wind speed and direction, air temperature and humidity and air pressure amongst others. This meteorological data is collected in close collaboration with the Dutch Royal Meteorological Institute. The LMW provides a complete technical infrastructure for gathering and distribution of data and delivers the data to various stakeholders within and outside RWS. This distribution of data greatly improves the *transparency* of the decisions and actions taken by RWS such as when to close the storm surge barriers. This decision has a major impact on the Dutch economy, as it means closing access to the Dutch harbours.

The LMW is essential for the *efficient* management of the primary processes of RWS, especially with regards to water management (including the regulation of water levels), *planning* of construction, management and maintenance of infrastructure, improved efficiency, effectiveness and flexibility of shipping management and improved enforcement of regulations, more detailed weather forecasts for shipping and aviation, more efficient and effective warning services and improved *long term trend analysis*, such as rising sea levels. An important use of this sensor data is for the management of the storm surge barriers with regards to *safety*. Storm surge barriers are movable dams in estuaries, waterways and estuaries. They protect sensitive areas from flooding. RWS water defences are huge, imposing structures that protect The Netherlands at high tide. The LMW makes it possible to automate this process based on accepted norms and using well tested models, greatly reducing the time required to act in emergency situations. The LMW data is also used by, among other things: hydro-meteo centres, municipal port companies (including the Port of Rotterdam), storm warning services, energy corporations, meteorological institutions, and flood Information and warning systems.

The expected benefits of the IoT for water management identified within this case are: *1. Political and Strategic - improved forecasting and trend analysis, promoting government transparency; 2. Tactical - improved planning with regards to management and maintenance, more efficient enforcement of regulations, improved health and safety measures, and cost reduction; 3. Operational - improved efficiency of services, improved effectiveness of services, and improved flexibility of services.*

5   Discussion

The objective of this research was to identify potential benefits of the IoT for e-governance purposes. The IoT is important because a physical (or sensor) object that is able to communicate digitally is able to relate not only to a single entity, but also becomes connected to surrounding objects and data infrastructures. This allows for a situation in which many physical objects are able to act in unison, by means of ambient intelligence [6]. These devices and the communication between these devices can benefit e-government by providing enough quality data to generate the information required by government and citizens to make the right decisions at the right time.

We used two main research methods: (1) a literature review, (2) an analysis of two data infrastructure case studies. The literature review provided us with an overview of the existing body of knowledge, allowing us to analyse where gaps in knowledge or focus occur. It also provided definitions for the key concepts and helped develop a broader knowledge base in the research area. Case study research is a widely used qualitative research method in information systems research, and is well suited to understanding the interactions between information technology-related innovations and organizational contexts [30]. Following the advice of Yin [10], the protocol used in the case study included a variety of data collection instruments. In order to counter the possible influences of bias, multiple research instruments were employed to ensure construct validity through triangulation [8].

The results of the literature review and the case studies demonstrate that the IoT provides a variety of expected benefits with regards to e-governance which correlate with benefits identified in the literature review. Table 1 below lists the main benefits of IoT, differentiating between strategic, tactical and operational benefits.

Table 1. Benefits of IoT for e-governance in relation to the case studies.

	Benefits	**Case 1**	**Case 2**
Strategic	Improved forecasting and trend analysis	✓	✓
	Improved citizen empowerment	✓	
	Promoting government transparency	✓	✓
Tactical	Improved planning with regards to management and maintenance	✓	✓
	More efficient enforcement of regulations	✓	✓
	Improved health and safety measures	✓	✓
	Cost reduction	✓	✓
Operational	Improved efficiency of services	✓	✓
	Improved effectiveness of services	✓	✓
	Improved flexibility of services	✓	✓

Strategic benefits exert a decisive influence on an organization's likelihood of future success. Formulating strategy requires defining major goals and initiatives based on consideration of resources and an assessment of the internal and external environments in which the organization competes [30]. IoT provides a continuous stream of "trusted" data which managers can use to make informed, data-based decisions based on reliable forecasting and trend analysis. But although sustainable development has changed significantly over the past decades [5], RWS is still largely organised in "silos", in which departments and their managers tackle issues through a domain related perspective as opposed to a collaborative one. At the same time, Dutch citizens and businesses are demanding more open, transparent, accountable and effective governance. The case studies suggest that IoT is enabling effective knowledge management, sharing and collaboration between domains and divisions at all levels of the organisation as well as between government and citizens. This has improved the empowerment of citizens as well as promoting government transparency helping to improve the inclusivity and accessibility of government services provided by RWS.

Tactical benefits assist the administrative process of selecting among appropriate ways and means of achieving a strategic plan or objective. Tactical planning is short range planning that emphasizes the current operations of various parts of the organization [31]. Obtaining field information primarily through manual measuring experience or judgment in requires extensive labour costs and data quality is often low. The case studies back up suggestions made by Chen and Jin [12] that collecting information accurately and in real time allows managers to exploit resources reasonably, reduce production costs, improve the ecological environment, and improve products.

A primary use of IT in government is to improve the efficiency of government operations [17]. As with many other organisations [2] RWS uses IoT as a tool in industrial automation, in which simple manual tasks such as opening and closing bridges are automated. This reduces very low-level coordination work that was previously executed by humans. In this regard, IoT reduces the cycle time of the operational management "Deming" cycle [32] at RWS. This allows a continuous comparison of actual values with expected norms and enables the early detection of faults such as suggested by

Fleisch [2]. Constant checks such as those performed by the "weigh in motion" system at RWS, enable information systems to automatically detect relevant events. This allows RWS to manage operations by exception, in which systems deal with various known situations independent of human intervention. IoT is also important for quality of government services as suggested by Castro [17]. IoT improves the quality of RWS services through improved effectiveness, such as that displayed by the distribution of salt on slippery roads, and improved flexibility of services such as that of the LMW which is able to deliver data for a wide variety of applications.

6 Conclusion

The IoT makes it possible to access remote sensor data and to monitor and control the physical world from a distance. Furthermore, combining and analysing captured data also allows governments to develop and improve services which cannot be provided by isolated systems. This paper represents one of the first papers on IoT and e-governance. Although there has been limited research in the field of e-government about IoT, there is much potential as expressed by the potential benefits. This research provides a systematic insight into the expected benefits of the IoT for e-government purposes by means of case study analysis and a review of literature. The research shows that benefits range from the political to the operational level. Specifically benefits for e-government can be attributed to improved efficiency, effectiveness and flexibility of services; reduction of costs; improved citizen empowerment; improved government transparency; more efficient enforcement of regulations; improved planning and forecasting; and improved health and safety measures. It is clear that IoT will have a major impact on e-government services in the future and will bring a variety of benefits for e-government at all levels. However, potential barriers and negative influences of the IoT for e-government remain unclear and we recommend more research on addressing these issues.

Acknowledgements. We acknowledge and thank the people of the Rijkswaterstaat who gave of their time and expertise during the case study research. This research is funded by Rijkswaterstaat.

References

1. Atzori, L., Iera, A., Morabito, G.: The internet of things: a survey. Comput. Netw. **54**, 2787–2805 (2010)
2. Fleisch, E.: What is the internet of things? An economic perspective. Econ. Manage. Financ. Markets **5**, 125–157 (2010)
3. Kopetz, H.: Internet of Things. Real-Time Systems, pp. 307–323. Springer, New York (2011)
4. Marche, S., McNiven, J.D.: E-government and e-governance: the future isn't what it used to be. Can. J. Adm. Sci. Rev. Can. Sci. Adm. **20**, 74–86 (2003)
5. United Nations, Department of Economic and Social Affairs: United Nations E-government Survey 2014: E-government for the Future We Want. United Nations, New York (2014)
6. Ramos, C., Augusto, J.C., Shapiro, D.: Ambient intelligence-the next step for artificial intelligence. IEEE Intell. Syst. **23**, 15–18 (2008)

7. Miller, J.H., Page, S.E.: Complex Adaptive Systems: An Introduction to Computational Models of Social Life: An Introduction to Computational Models of Social Life. Princeton University Press, Princeton (2009)

8. Xia, F., Yang, L.T., Wang, L., Vinel, A.: Internet of things. Int. J. Commun Syst **25**, 1101–1102 (2012)

9. Haller, S., Karnouskos, S., Schroth, C.: The internet of things in an enterprise context. In: Domingue, J., Fensel, D., Traverso, P. (eds.) FIS 2008. LNCS, vol. 5468, pp. 14–28. Springer, Heidelberg (2009)

10. Yin, R.K.: Case Study Research: Design and Methods. SAGE Publications, Thousand Oaks (2003)

11. Eisenhardt, K.M.: Building theories from case study research. Acad. Manage. Rev. **14**, 532–550 (1989)

12. Chen, X.-Y., Jin, Z.-G.: Research on key technology and applications for Internet of Things. Phys. Procedia. **33**, 561–566 (2012)

13. Gubbi, J., Buyya, R., Marusic, S., Palaniswami, M.: Internet of things (IoT): a vision, architectural elements, and future directions. Future Gener. Comput. Syst. **29**, 1645–1660 (2013)

14. Boulos, M.N.K., Al-Shorbaji, N.M.: On the internet of things, smart cities and the WHO healthy cities. Int. J. Health Geogr. **13**, 10 (2014)

15. Chui, M., Löffler, M., Roberts, R.: The internet of things. McKinsey Q. **2**, 1–9 (2010)

16. Hounsell, N.B., Shrestha, B.P., Piao, J., McDonald, M.: Review of urban traffic management and the impacts of new vehicle technologies. IET Intell. Transp. Syst. **3**, 419–428 (2009)

17. Castro, D.: Digital Quality of Life: Government. Available SSRN 1285002 (2008)

18. Coetzee, L., Eksteen, J.: The internet of things - promise for the future? An introduction. In: IST-Africa Conference Proceedings 2011, pp. 1–9 (2011)

19. Subirana, B., Sarma, S., Fleisch, E.: High-resolution management. IESE Alumni Mag. **3**, 8–13 (2006)

20. Spiess, P., Karnouskos, S.: Maximizing the business value of networked embedded systems through process-level integration into enterprise software. Presented at the second international conference on pervasive computing and applications (2007)

21. Ivanov, D.: An adaptive framework for aligning (re)planning decisions on supply chain strategy, design, tactics, and operations. Int. J. Prod. Res. **48**, 3999–4017 (2010)

22. Ackoff, R.L.: Towards a system of systems concepts. Manage. Sci. **17**, 661–671 (1971)

23. Mulyun, A., Parikesit, D., Antameng, M., Rahim, R.: Analysis of loss cost of road pavement distress due to overloading freight transportation. J. East. Asia Soc. Transp. Stud. **8**, 1020–1035 (2010)

24. Bagui, S., Das, A., Bapanapalli, C.: Controlling vehicle overloading in BOT projects. Procedia Soc. Behav. Sci. **104**, 962–971 (2013)

25. Rijkswaterstaat: Wegen naar de toekomst. http://www.wegennaardetoekomst.nl/

26. Rijkswaterstaat: Feiten en cijfers. http://www.rws.nl/wegen/feiten_en_cijfers/statistische_verkeersgegevens/index.aspx

27. Stichting Ijkdijk: livedijk-utrecht. http://www.ijkdijk.nl/nl/livedijken/livedijk-utrecht

28. RTV Utrecht: Proef met dijksensoren in Woerden en Nieuwegein. http://www.rtvutrecht.nl/nieuws/859256/proef-met-dijksensoren-in-woerden-en-nieuwegein.html

29. Stichting Ijkdijk: Innovatief meetsysteem houdt Utrechtse dijken in de gaten. http://www.ijkdijk.nl/nl/nieuws/118-persbericht-innovatief-meetsysteem-houdt-utrechtse-dijken-in-de-gaten

30. Nag, R., Hambrick, D.C., Chen, M.-J.: What is strategic management, really? Inductive derivation of a consensus definition of the field. Strateg. Manage. J. **28**, 935–955 (2007)

31. Tactical planning vs strategic planning. https://managementinnovations.wordpress.com/2008/12/10/tactical-planning-vs-strategic-planning/
32. Deming, W.E.: Quality, Productivity, and Competitive Position. Massachusetts Institute of Technology Center for Advanced Engineering Study, Cambridge (1982)

Understanding Public-Private Collaboration Configurations for International Information Infrastructures

Bram Klievink[✉]

Delft University of Technology, Delft, The Netherlands
a.j.klievink@tudelft.nl

Abstract. Collaboration between the public and the private sector is seen as an instrument to make governance smarter, more effective, and more efficient. However, whereas there is literature on public-private collaboration, very little of it addresses how these collaborations can be shaped to make use of the huge potential that technological innovations in ICT may offer. To address this gap, this paper addresses public-private collaborative development of digital information infrastructures (IIs). Drawing on a combination of literature on public-private partnerships and on digital information systems or infrastructures, this paper studies an initiative for exchanging information among international trade supply chain partners and between the businesses and government (e.g. for declarations, compliance, border control). Specifically, it explores what would be the Dutch end of such an II, to understand the interplay between the technological innovation and partnerships that form the social context thereof.

Keywords: Information infrastructure · e-government · Public-private collaboration · International trade · Public-private information infrastructures · Collaborative governance

1 Introduction

To address the complexity of today's problems in networked societies, governance needs to be organised in a smarter way. In literature on innovation and improvement of the public sector, one of the proposed answers is that governments should strengthen the collaboration with societal actors, and include private partners in the strategy to realise public goals [1–4]. Smarter government can leverage information and communication technologies (ICTs) to enable governments to do more with less [5]. However, the role that ICTs can play in public-private collaboration to facilitate smarter, collaborative governance, is rarely studied. Studies focusing on the role of public-private collaboration, and on the public sector in general, tend to not really accommodate technological change [6]. Hence, to understand how public-private collaborations can take shape in an information infrastructure (II), insights from these studies will need to be combined with knowledge on how information infrastructures are shaped.

© IFIP International Federation for Information Processing 2015
E. Tambouris et al. (Eds.): EGOV 2015, LNCS 9248, pp. 170–180, 2015.
DOI: 10.1007/978-3-319-22479-4_13

In this paper, we combine a number of insights from literature on public-private partnerships with insights from literature on information systems or infrastructures. Using this analytical background, a case is described in which a public-private information infrastructure is developed for the domain of international trade. This case is interesting to study as a complex governance challenge as due to the international setting, there is no principal actor to realise IIs in this domain.

In international trade lanes, the system through which information is shared between stakeholders is deficient. For commercial reasons (e.g. to not disclose commercially sensitive information), supply chain actors do not always fully inform the next actor in the chain about who the original shipper is, and what precisely is in a container. Hence, the data found in transport documents and (based thereon) also in official declarations, are often not from the originator; i.e. not from the actor that really knows the specific goods being shipped [7]. Key parties such as buyers, customs and other authorities, have to manage and supervise the supply chain with second-hand information that is frequently inaccurate [7].

The original and correct information is present in the information systems of the various actors involved in international trade. ICT innovations enable electronic connections and information exchange between these systems and thereby access and re-use of these original trade data by other actors in the supply chain [8]. These developments can be considered a re-arrangement of the information infrastructures in international trade. Adapting the information infrastructures in international trade concerns the evolution and dynamics of existing information systems of supply chain actors, existing processes and procedures, and all the diversity in systems and relationships present therein [9–12]. Over the past few years, multiple initiatives have been undertaken to connect systems from all over the globe to each other in a standardized way, to capture data from their original source and to facilitate the exchange of data.

Information infrastructures (II) concern heterogeneous sociotechnical systems [10], which are systems that involve both complex (physical) technical systems and networks of interdependent actors [13]. Within such a sociotechnical system, questions arise on the technological system and standards used, but also on aspects such as responsibilities and ownership. Balancing the need that the infrastructure works for commercial parties and simultaneously for the community and the government is challenging. These questions have to be addressed collaboratively by the key stakeholders that are to build, finance, operate, use and facilitate the II. Hence, setting up such II goes beyond the technical challenges (e.g. interconnecting diverse information systems) and yields questions that have to be addressed by looking at the *socio* side of these developments (e.g. the partnerships that have to make this work). It is a collaborative setting in which autonomous actors control their own information systems, information sources and links with the II. It is a federated system that is largely built and operated by businesses. To avoid monopolization by single business actors and to ensure that public values are realised, governments must actively participate in the stakeholder community working on these innovations.

In public management literature, more is known tools of governance for public-private collaborations. There is much literature on public sector reform and innovation that in various ways argue for collaboration between the public and the private sector, also as a way to realise public goals [4, 14–16]. Partnership and collaboration are presented as new forms of governance, giving new legitimacy to government by combining the efficiency of the private sector with an involvement of society and other stakeholders [17]. The idea behind partnership is the notion of collaborative advantage [18].

Probably neither the public sector field nor the information systems field has the complete picture when it comes to understanding how public-private information infrastructures are or could be developed. Even when public-private collaborations live up to their promise of mutuality, a key question remains how government actions can accommodate the requirement of accountability when using infrastructural components, original business data, and shared functionality in an II. This paper focuses on challenges of partnership for II; the idea of bringing together public and private nodes in a form of partnership to play a role in something that is (partially) a public service or asset.

In this paper, we first discuss the background of two main challenges of partnership, which also serves as the main contribution of the paper. For illustration, in section four we look at how these challenges play out in a specific initiative for creating the Dutch end of an II for international trade, in the form of a Port Community System.

2 Background

This paper focuses on public-private collaboration; these partnerships do not conform to one organisational type, but could include combinations of involving private parties in the design, building, owning and operation of public sector assets or services by the private sector, or to transfer public sector assets to the private sector altogether [19]. In partnership terms, the II of study could be considered a 'Build-Own-Operate' type, in which the private sector finances, builds and operates the information infrastructure. An open question is to what extent and which parts of the information infrastructure can indeed be seen as a public sector asset. Strictly speaking, it is a partnership that concerns the integration of various private sector assets and public sector assets, in a way that needs to fulfil the public goals and has to make business-sense.

The insights from studies on public-private partnerships (PPPs) seem relevant to this set-up, and PPPs are one of the most studied forms of public-private collaboration, and include empirical studies. However, a lot of emphasis in PPP literature is on the contracts, the process of setting up PPPs (e.g. finding contractors), payment, performance monitoring, etc. That is not entirely the same as trying to build an II in which (new and existing) private sector IT assets will largely be the main building blocks.

One of the viewpoints offered by literature on PPP that seems relevant in assessing II is the distinction between the various analytical contexts and the way they are reflected in the governance of the partnership. For example, Johnston and Gudergan [19] distinguish between the technical-rational context, the social context and risk as an overarching governance consideration. They find that the rational-technical context and processes assume logical and linear decision-making and are typically reflected in legal contracts that define a partnership. This becomes the 'de facto' primary governance system [19]. However, contracts are based on limited, biased or otherwise imperfect knowledge and expectations that were prevalent at the time of drafting the contract, but not at the time of actual implementation or operation. As these contracts are therefore likely to be incomplete (and rationally bounded) and can or do not take into account contingencies, this is unlikely to be an effective governance instrument for a partnership [19]. Even if the technical-rational context works well for the contract, there is often an implicit social contract and problems related to that may threaten a 'rational' approach, especially at later points in the partnership. In other words: even if one could manage the technical complexity completely, the actor-related complexity has its own dynamics. Here, a project approach to managing a partnership would be insufficient, and process management seems required as social and political risks are far more difficult to control than project risks [20]. Johnston and Gudergan [19] argue that a risk assessment method is needed that looks at social risks in the partnership as much as at the defined technical-rational risks. A "strong dysfunction in the social organisation dimension of governance [cannot] be contained by the rational logics of contract" [19] (p. 580).

When assessing literature on public-private collaboration and literature on II (or its conceptual predecessor; IOS) from the perspective of these contexts, two insights on the challenges of partnership come up that seem relevant to understand the public-private collaboration for the international trade II.

2.1 Conflicting and Converging Goals: Parties 'Hidden' Agenda's in the Collaboration

The ideal for partnership is that partners agree on a common and agreed upon set of aims [18]. Also Hailey [21] thinks that a clear and shared vision on the purpose and objectives of partnership is necessary to drive a partnership based on a clear purpose. However, just agreeing on the goals of the partnership is only part of the story; partnerships are usually set-up because the partners are different, have different resources and have different purpose [22]. The idea of collaborative advantage is that bringing them together would be a source for advantage. Partners can agree to such advantage at a generic level, but they have different reasons for getting involving in the partnership (e.g. trading partner pressure). Agendas (both organisational and individual) might be hidden at the initiation of the partnership, but when the partnership gets specific, there is the danger that "irreconcilable differences will be unearthed", that weren't obvious yet when the aims were "vague enough that none of the parties involved can disagree with it" [22] (p. 296).

Partnerships take place in context and not in isolation, further adding to the complexity [18]. Because in an II for international trade a host of private parties are involved that also have dealings with each other beyond the collaboration, they may (officially) seek *collaborative advantage* in the partnership, but traditionally, ICTs are often used to gain a *competitive advantage* [23, 24]. Once common goals are translated to actual implementations, the status quo and legacy (both organisational and technical) may mean that the strategies that partners would like to follow for realising the shared goals differ greatly for different partners [25]. In the context of an II, we expect to see that parties try to maximise their control over the II [26] and wish to minimise the degree of vulnerability the II and the collaboration may bring [27].

The strategy will look different for different parties; IT solution providers and existing information brokers could aim to become a leader in the information infrastructure and seek input control (i.e. control what functionality may be offered via the infrastructure) in an attempt to maximise control and minimise dependency on others. To those parties, the II function is their core resource, which they would not want to govern collaboratively, but want to keep within their control [28]. Such a strategy is incompatible with the II as a collaborative endeavour [10] and will divvy up the business community, as parties that are involved from the physical handling of goods in international trade will seek benefits from an open II and fear getting locked-in by the IT solution providers [29]. For them, they seek to minimise potential homing and switching costs. Homing costs are the costs of being involved with a certain II and include costs of adoption, operation and opportunity costs [26]. If these costs are high, parties are less inclined to link with an II, especially if there are multiple II solutions they have to connect to (which lead to multi-homing costs, see Eisenmann et al. [30]). These costs that parties have to make to connect to a system of II increased their dependence and vulnerability on IT solution providers [31]. They have invested in a connection and might face switching costs or additional investments if different II providers do not adhere to the same (open) standards. That is a major barrier to collaboration between logistical parties and IT solution providers. In general, a lack of standards hampers adoption because parties might not be able to make use of their investments made in connecting with one to re-use in connections with others [32]. This is also the rationale for open standards (also to avoid lock-in and to facilitate re-use).

Based on this, we would expect to see two blocks in the private sector involved in the II: the parties with a big role in logistics, and parties with a big role in the II. That will mean that governments (as a third block) will have play a role in building trust and dealing with problems related to the social context, making the government a third party in the mix. Hence, even if they don't want to [33], government will sooner or later find itself in a position where they have to ensure the collaborative aspect, because the idea of having a partnership is that the II has an open architecture, which (given the dependencies this might bring to parties) requires a form of bidirectional control and possibly shared ownership [26].

2.2 Trust and Vulnerability: Technological Convergence and Dynamics in the Playing Field

Trust among partners is an important ingredient for making partnerships work [18]. When trust and reciprocity exist, it is much easier to "negotiate issues, resolve problems and work towards a common purpose" [21]. Trust facilitates communication, and sharing of sensitive information, but there are many obstacles to getting there. These obstacles include the existing power relationships, the involvement of parties for the reason that government wants them to be involved, parties with necessary resources that threaten to leave a partnership, parties with limited power, but with resources essential to the partnership (e.g. access to communities, markets, data) [18]. As not all aspects to a partnership can be covered in a contract [19], parties perceive the risk that any future partner (or change in direction or leadership of a company) may not "honour the many unwritten aspects of the initial agreement" [18]. Trust is needed, but the social context [19] might result in a situation (e.g. a lack of history between partners) that is ill equipped for forming trust.

Developing trust in the collaborative development of II is potentially even more difficult, as the interdependencies that such an II will bring, are a source of (perceived) vulnerability for the parties involved [27]. Especially developments like technological convergence threaten parties playing a role in existing II's, especially those that offer parts of the II (e.g. infrastructure components, databases, functionality). Whereas the role of parties in the physical logistics process is not as easily threatened, each information function that parties have and the power they derive from that, is threatened by the fact that technical components increasingly become integrated and providers of technological solutions increasingly have the opportunity to expand into this domain. This may tilt the power balance in favour of parties without a primarily information function, as they have an (be it implicit or explicit) threat of moving away from the II if the others (especially the IT solution providers) do not do more to meet their interests and demands. Following both public-private collaboration and information system literature, explicitly using such power would have negative consequences on the collaboration as this hampers the development of trust [18, 19, 27]. However, technical-rational instruments like contracts and project management cannot control this. Mitigating such a situation is hard, as there are power differences, but no actor with hierarchical authority to enforce action [18]. Without an approach to initiate a 'trust-building loop' [18], the result might be that the private sector is unable to collaboratively develop the II, calling for a bigger role of government, either as mediator [19] or in an active role in setting-up and governing the II. Pressure from the environment (both trading partners and government) and trust (also in the regulatory regime) are considered important antecedents to the adoption of an information system [31].

3 Research Approach

The empirical part of the paper is based on a study of a Dutch initiative to support innovations in logistics (Topsector Logistics). Part of this initiative is the development of an II called the Neutral Logistics Information Platform (NLIP, see www.nlip.org). This II is still under development and aims to support information exchange in international supply chains. The starting point in the NLIP are the Port Community Systems (PCSs) in mainports in the Netherlands, and build from there. As a case study we picked a specific PCS which is one of the building blocks of the national II. As part of the case, we made a detailed mapping of the process and data flows in various services that could become part of the NLIP, to enable the identification of issues in the current situation. These mappings and descriptions are based on interviews with the PCS, a branch organisation representing a large group of shippers/consignees, a carrier, a terminal operator, and Dutch Customs. Furthermore, documentation on services, processes and pricing also were used in the analysis. To ensure that our understanding of the current situation was correct, we discussed our descriptions with our interviewees or sent them for checking.

4   Case Description

One of the main challenges for international trade information infrastructures is how the diverse and (also geographically) dispersed business community can be joined-up to support visibility solutions that cross many international trade lanes, but to do this without a single lead actor with the power or jurisdiction to decide on a solution. A potential answer to this challenge found in a European project is that the business communities that make up a trade lane select a solution provider to which they open-up their data. As part of this, also parties with low levels of IT maturity and parties with legacy information systems, are connected to the system by the solution provider.

However, as the 'last leg' of the information infrastructure - connecting to a wide variety of businesses and local and national government agencies - is so difficult, the current role of PCSs come into view. A PCS (port community system) is an information hub, through which the business community in the port can exchange information that they need as part of their logistical processes. Through this function, a PCS has custody of much information that is relevant in the port environment. A PCS also plays a role in much of the data exchange between businesses and government, although companies can exchange information with government directly. The electronic exchange of data reduces the administrative burden, and saves operational costs (e.g. on personnel and couriers).

Apart from exchanging information among business actors, PCSs are often the linking pin between the business community, the port authority and government inspection agencies such as customs. In fact, many PCSs have originally been set-up or at least initiated by a government organization [34]. This is because much of the reporting towards government contains data of multiple actors. For example, in the clearance process at export, data need to be combined from (amongst others) the exporter (the export declaration), from the terminal (on which vessel goods were loaded), and the port authority (confirmation of vessel departure). By combining these data through a PCS, customs knows that goods have been exported and a confirmation of exit can be provided to the business.

This PCS role is a specific one, also in the context of international IIs, as in a (geographically limited) port community, a specific situation exists, with smaller and local companies, high interdependence and specific rules and regulations. This results in many 'thick' links between parties, which makes it hard to apply an open architecture. In some countries, such as the Netherlands, the idea is that because PCSs have these 'thick' connections with many parties – public and private – these PCSs are the existing systems that are well equipped to form the basis for bigger-scale information platforms at a national or supranational level.

However, a PCS is primarily a clearing house [35], which can and must rely on contracts with all kinds of actors, and agreeing on individual services and uses of data and is therein supported by having a specific role and data structure. As a result, the PCS relies on data contributors and does not have a clear incentive to move to an open architecture or to help the global IT solution providers in supporting their II, as that would threaten their 'monopoly' on acting as a clearing house for a specific geographically confined trade hub. At the same time, this makes data contributors (e.g. carriers, terminal operators) vulnerable, as their data are handed over to a party under financial pressure that can only be resolved by re-using that data for more commercial functionalities. Furthermore, as most international companies have dealings with multiple ports, every port having its own proprietary solution increases multi-homing costs.

The current design of the PCS is that of a public-private collaboration. In that design, data are handed over to the PCS but are still owned by the individual actors submitting the data. This enables government to access the data, and enables the PCS to optimize port operations by enabling companies operating in the port to share data without losing control of it. The PCS's revenue currently comes from subscriptions and a fee-per-message method. The core community services are funded through general funds of the shareholders, which are public or semi-public organisations.

Looking at it from a technical-rational perspective, a PCS adds value to the community as a whole, and specifically in the interactions with government. However, an open II for global trade would be open to many powerful parties, also those with a strong information function. To survive in that setting, a PCS will have to offer more, in the sense of more services, bigger scale, more parties, smarter combinations, etc. The ties to specific localised communities may not be enough for globally acting players to continue to prefer a PCS over business solutions. In the public-private structure of the PCS, the public component makes it difficult for a PCS to focus on commercial services and compete with business solutions. National governments do not have the jurisdiction or capacity and the business community is too fragmented to make the decisions, the long-term commitments and the ICT investments. Hence, an II can only be realised if the parties collaborate. Governments will have to facilitate (e.g. incentivise) and support (e.g. develop a Single Window, provide digital government building blocks, and ensure a level playing field) and businesses need to find sustainable businesses models and build the II.

5   Discussion and Conclusion

In a public-private partnership approach to an II based on PCSs, the public component makes it difficult for a PCS to focus on commercial services and compete with business solutions. Much of the data that would be the basis for those commercial services, are gotten because of the community role. When discussing re-use of the data that is needed for this core functionality in order to provide additional services, this community or public role gets obscured and parties object to a growing role of the PCS. However, now that due to austerity the general funds of the PCS are decreasing, some kind of additional sources of income for the PCS are needed. Increasing the fees for their services is one of the few instruments they have, next to developing new (business) services based on the data they have. If businesses consider this to be misuse of data provided for compliance purposes they could move to building direct links between various actors (e.g. send electronic messages to customs systems directly), and if government agencies argue that a PCS is optional because direct data provisioning to e.g. customs is also possible, all of them risk that the core flow of data that the PCS bases its services on dries out. The consequence may be that cascading inefficiencies in operations due to suboptimal data exchange, lead to depriving the entire port community of the benefits, which might make the port less interesting for globally operating players. The total set of core functionalities is without a very clear beneficiary community (other than the government), but our study shows that they are needed to offer the services that makes the port community as a whole more efficient and attractive to trade. When developing an NLIP in which the government aims for a role in the background, the question is if such a platform would ultimately provide the core functionality, for which a business model is so hard to find.

This creates a tension that is not easily resolved. Ungoverned use of community functionality and the data that follows from that for business services may lead to a slippery slope; the barrier between community and commercial functionality and assets becomes vague and the fear is that community data will be used to make more than just enough money to cover all costs of the system. However, when depriving a PCS of the option to use their infrastructure and the data that they have in custody to offer value-added services, which is one of their few ways to make money, the PCS as one of the main building blocks (at least in the short to intermediate term) of NLIP may run into difficulty sustaining itself. Either way, whether because the source of data dries out (if a few key providers of data do not wish to contribute to the PCSs business services) or whether the source of funding dries out (if no new sources of revenue are found), without a solution to this tension, it will be very difficult to find a sustainable model for creating NLIP as a platform of existing community systems.

Hence, in line with the theoretical background of the paper, the technical-rational approach that the actors followed resulted in tensions that block the enactment of the II. The role of the 'social' complexity proved to be large and measures were taken to address this type of complexity, primarily in the form of establishing a committee dealing with governance of the platform. The existing first steps towards a governance model for NLIP primarily concern governance as a process. In other words; it focuses on facilitating that the right people decide on how decisions are going to be made about combinations of public and private data. However, in this way many of those parties optimise for their own part of the operations, risking suboptimal decisions and configurations at the community (e.g. port community or supply chain) level. Small issues are easily resolved, but that does not solve that cascading issues lead to large costs for some parties, which, in line with the background, leads to a situation in which parties are reluctant to be actively involved. Simultaneously the perceived presence of hidden agenda's and additional vulnerabilities were not resolved by the governance model. Based on the theory, we suggest that to make NLIP work, it is vital that the community jointly decides that certain services and level of service should be considered community functionality and therefore also community funded. Our theoretical background suggests that this will involve a large government support, and even steering, whilst leaving some parts to the responsibility of the businesses. In any case, novel public-private governance models for decision-making on IIs should be further investigated.

In this case, all parties agree on the common goals, but have different underlying agenda's for the collaboration. What is clear is that due to the interdependence among the actors when it comes to data sharing, the fear for the agenda's of others, leads to actions to decrease additional vulnerabilities. As a result, solutions that should work well from a technical-rational perspective (e.g. an open infrastructure, separation between commercial and community functionality, a joint decision making structure), ultimately fail because of the social context in which the technical-rational solutions are perceived as potentially leading to new vulnerabilities (e.g. being locked-in, or being cut out of the information chain). Although the parties have long had dealings with each other as part of their role in the physical logistics flow, the existing relationships do not have sufficient trust basis to accommodate these vulnerabilities that follow from changes in the data position and role in the information infrastructure.

Acknowledgements. This work is part of the research project "Governing public-private information infrastructures", which is financed by the Netherlands Organisation for Scientific Research (NWO) as Veni grant 451-13-020.

References

1. Dunleavy, P., Margetts, H., Bastow, S., Tinkler, J.: New public management is dead - long live digital-era governance. J. Public Adm. Res. Theory **16**, 467–494 (2006)
2. Milward, H.B., Provan, K.G., Fish, A., Isett, K.R., Huang, K.: Governance and collaboration: an evolutionary study of two mental health networks. J. Public Adm. Res. Theory **20**, i125–i141 (2010)
3. Salamon, L.M.: The Tools of Government: A Guide to the New Governance. Oxford University Press, New York (2002)
4. Stoker, G.: Public value management: a new narrative for networked governance? Am. Rev. Public Adm. **36**, 41–57 (2006)
5. Scholl, H.J.: Five trends that matter: challenges to 21st century electronic government. Innov. Public Sect. **20**, 107–117 (2013)
6. Pollitt, C.: Mainstreaming technological change in the study of public management. Public Policy Adm. **26**, 377–397 (2011)
7. Hesketh, D.: Weaknesses in the supply chain: who packed the box? World Cust J. **4**, 3–20 (2010)
8. Tan, Y.-H., Bjørn-Andersen, N., Klein, S., Rukanova, B. (eds.): Accelerating Global Supply Chains with IT-Innovation. ITAIDE Tools and Methods. Springer, Heidelberg (2011)
9. Hanseth, O., Monteiro, E., Hatling, M.: Developing information infrastructure: The tension between standardization and flexibility. Sci. Technol. Human Values **21**, 407–426 (1996)
10. Hanseth, O., Lyytinen, K.: Design theory for dynamic complexity in information infrastructures: the case of building internet. J. Inf. Technol. **25**, 1–19 (2010)
11. Henningsson, S., Henriksen, H.: Inscription of behaviour and flexible interpretation in information infrastructures: the case of European e-customs. J. Strateg. Inf. Syst. **20**, 355–372 (2011)
12. Tilson, D., Lyytinen, K., Sørensen, C.: Digital infrastructures: the missing is research agenda. Inf. Syst. Res. **21**, 748–759 (2010)
13. De Bruijn, J.A., Herder, P.M.: System and actor perspectives on sociotechnical systems. IEEE Trans. Syst. Man, Cybern. - Part A Syst. Humans **39**, 981–992 (2009)
14. Agranoff, R., McGuire, M.: Collaborative public management: new strategies for local governments. Georgetown University Press, Washington, D.C. (2003)
15. Christensen, T., Lægreid, P.: The whole-of-government approach to public sector reform. Public Adm. Rev. **67**, 1059–1066 (2007)

16. Goldsmith, S., Eggers, W.D.: Governing by network - the new shape of the public sector. Brookings Institution Press, Washington, D.C. (2004)
17. Teisman, G.R., Klijn, E.-H.: Partnership arrangements: governmental rhetoric or governance scheme? Public Adm. Rev. 62, 197–205 (2002)
18. Huxham, C., Vangen, S.: What makes partnerships work? In: Osborne, S. (ed.) Public-Private Partnerships: Theory and Practice in International Perspective, pp. 293–310. Routledge, London (2000)
19. Johnston, J., Gudergan, S.P.: Governance of public–private partnerships: lessons learnt from an Australian case? Int. Rev. Adm. Sci. 73, 569–582 (2007)
20. de Bruijn, H., ten Heuvelhof, E., in 't Veld, R.: Process management: Why Project Management Fails in Complex Decision Making Processes. Springer, Heidelberg (2010)
21. Hailey, J.: NGO partners - the characteristics of effective development partnerships. In: Osborne, S. (ed.) Public-Private Partnerships: Theory and Practice in International Perspective, pp. 311–323. Routledge, London (2000)
22. Vangen, S., Huxham, C.: The tangled web: unraveling the principle of common goals in collaborations. J. Public Adm. Res. Theory. 22, 731–760 (2011)
23. Johnston, H.R., Vitale, M.R.: Creating competitive advantage with interorganizational information systems. MIS Q. 12, 152–165 (1988)
24. Huxham, C., Vangen, S., Huxham, C., Eden, C.: The challenge of collaborative governance. Public Manag. Rev. 2, 337–358 (2000)
25. Klievink, B.: Unravelling Interdependence: Coordinating Public-Private Service Networks. Delft University of Technology, Delft (2011)
26. Tiwana, A., Konsynski, B., Bush, A.A.: Research commentary—platform evolution: coevolution of platform architecture, governance, and environmental dynamics. Inf. Syst. Res. 21, 675–687 (2010)
27. Hart, P., Saunders, C.: Power and trust: critical factors in the adoption and use of electronic data interchange. Organ. Sci. 8, 23–42 (1997)
28. Klein, S.: The configuration of inter-organizational relations. Eur. J. Inf. Syst. 5, 92–102 (1996)
29. Wareham, J.D.: Information assets in interorganizational governance: exploring the property rights perspective. IEEE Trans. Eng. Manag. 50, 337–351 (2003)
30. Eisenmann, T., Parker, G., Van Alstyne, M.W.: Strategies for two- sided markets. Harv. Bus. Rev. 84, 12 (2006)
31. Robey, D., Im, G., Wareham, J.D.: Theoretical foundations of empirical research on interorganizational systems: assessing past contributions and guiding future directions. J. Assoc. Inf. Syst. 9, 497–518 (2008)
32. Markus, M.L., Steinfield, C.W., Wigand, R.T., Minton, G.: Industry-wide information systems standardization as collective action: the case of the U.S. residential mortgage industry. MIS Q. 30, 439–465 (2006)
33. Klievink, B., Janssen, M., Tan, Y.-H.: A stakeholder analysis of business-to-government information sharing: the governance of a public-private platform. Int. J. Electron. Gov. Res. 8, 54 (2012)
34. Romochkina, I.: Cluster Perspective on Inter-Organizational Information Systems. Erasmus University Rotterdam, Rotterdam (2011)
35. Kubicek, H., Cimander, R.: Three dimensions of organizational interoperability. insights from recent studies for improving interoperability frame-works. Eur. J. ePractice 6, 1–12 (2009)

Services, Processes and Infrastructure

Inter-organizational Public e-Service Development: Emerging Lessons from an Inside-Out Perspective

Marie-Therese Christiansson[1(✉)], Karin Axelsson[2], and Ulf Melin[2]

[1] Department of Information Systems, Karlstad University, Karlstad, Sweden
marie-therese.christiansson@kau.se
[2] Department of Management and Engineering, Information Systems,
Linköping University, Linköping, Sweden
{karin.axelsson,ulf.melin}@liu.se

Abstract. E-service development has grown to become a daily practice in most public organizations as a means for realizing digital agendas and e-government initiatives on different levels (local, regional, national and transnational governmental levels). Public e-service development is often an inter-organizational (IO) effort with multiple actors and organizations involved in the multi-faceted dimensions of design, development and delivery decisions. Still, there is a lack of research focusing on IO public e-service development practices in particular. In order to address this lack we elaborate on reported challenges and their implications for IO public e-service development in practice. By returning to two empirical cases of IO public e-service development, the IO dimension is evolved. Our purpose is to highlight challenges in IO public e-service development with implications for research and practice. Findings are presented as eight emerging lessons learned from an inside-out perspective related to phases in IO public e-service development processes.

Keywords: Public e-service · Inter-organizational · IO e-service development · IO dimension · Government · IS development

1 Introduction

Many initiatives and efforts in the public sector are aiming to foster citizen engagement and provide useful and meaningful e-services to citizens and businesses. Previous studies have reported on challenges (barriers and shortcomings) in terms of participation, such as low sustainability, poor citizen acceptance, coordination difficulties, lack of understanding, and failure to assess impact (e.g. [35]). Reported challenges and critical success factors of e-government adoption by Rana et al. [34], are highlighting that technological barriers, lack of security and privacy, lack of trust, lack of resources, a digital divide, poor management and infrastructure, lack of awareness, legal barriers, lack of IT infrastructure, and resilience were among some of the most commonly experienced aspects. Corresponding factors for the success of e-government initiatives were citizens' satisfaction, information accuracy, security, and privacy. Hence, several issues are identified in relation to what should be taken into consideration, managed

© IFIP International Federation for Information Processing 2015
E. Tambouris et al. (Eds.): EGOV 2015, LNCS 9248, pp. 183–196, 2015.
DOI: 10.1007/978-3-319-22479-4_14

and achieved in e-government. Nevertheless, there is not much published in the past years of research regarding challenges in inter-organizational (IO) e-service development processes. Recent studies are not focusing on the development process per se, but on concepts that can be useful when designing projects [15], collaboration competency and partner match [40] and questions the initiator needs to answer in advance [39].

In Sweden the government's strategy for a digital collaborative public administration [13], like in many other countries, is a driver. The strategy is a demand for agencies to increase their ability to collaborate across organizational borders as well as across geographical, legal, functional, technical, operational, and cultural boundaries, and a part of the realization of the national digital agenda [14]. Objectives behind strategies for e-government are many and expressed on different governmental levels. In Sweden, – the primary empirical domain in this paper – these are the national, regional and local levels together with the European level [12]. Hence, the daily practice, regardless of national differences, of public e-service development has many stakeholders and involves private, public and non-profit actors working to realize multiple digital strategies and agendas. Chun et al. [8] discuss forces in public collaboration in terms of citizen-, value-, economic/cost- and technology-driven projects. Thus, IO e-service development should respond to one or multiple drivers in each partaking organization. In addition, the IO development process involves actors from different sectors and roles on different levels with different objectives.

The purpose of this paper is to further elaborate on the understanding of challenges in IO public e-service development processes with the aim of generating lessons for such development. Our approach is to explore research on challenges in e-government and IO collaboration onto IO public e-service development practice. In addition, critical success factors identified by research are not always to be found in practice [9]. For that reason, we revisit the development practice in two IO public e-service development cases, to achieve summative reflections on IO challenges, justifying and validating findings of lessons learned.

Qualitative and interpretive case studies (one regional and one national case) are used (cf. [23, 30, 41, 42] and the study is classified as retrospective with a reflective follow-up on incentives, objectives, and performance. Incentives and objectives behind e-services are emphasized in our lessons learned (constrains and affordances [11]) in order to discuss impacts on development issues. Our role in the cases ranged from "insiders" as action researchers (e.g. [38]) to "outsiders" as more critical and reflective researchers [31]. Based on that we use the concept of an inside-out perspective, defined as the (IO) developing practice involving stakeholders in providing, and delivering a public e-service. Hence, the work practice performed by multiple stakeholders to identify pre-conditions, analyzing business processes and systems requirements, development, tests and maintenance issues. We use the inside-out perspective as a vehicle to analyze the roles and actors partaking in the design of an e-service and the delivery in terms of providing and using it. In reverse, an outside-in perspective can be viewed as a user receiving value from the e-service provision. Besides empirical sources such as semi-structured interviews, informal conversations, internal and external documents, project meetings and seminars, business process models, user tests of a web portal prototype and e-services under development were also used in data collection. The empirical data generation was guided from IO challenges identified in our literature review. In order to search for literature with an explicit IO focus (in purpose, research design and findings), we used terms such as "challenges" (barriers/success), "inter-organizational", "public e-service", "collaborative e-government initiatives", and "multiple organizations" when searching in Scopus, ScienceDirect and Google Schoolar. Madsen et al. [25] confirms our limited hits of publications, as only one paper out of 50 in their study addressed the developing practice.

Studies reported on e-service challenges and success in e-government are not focusing on the IO dimension [2, 19, 34] in the end-to-end development process [15, 33, 39, 40]. In order to learn from challenges in the development work practice, two IO public e-service development case studies are revisited. The analysis was performed based on phases in the development process and IO dimensions to achieve summative reflections in lessons.

In the following the paper is outlined as follows: First we discuss challenges and successes in IO public e-service development. Our inductively generated lessons are then discussed in relation to the IO dimension identified in previous research. In the concluding section, we summarize our conclusions with implications for practice and research, limitations and suggestions on future research.

2 IO Public e-Service Development

Governments are constantly in a state of change and adjustments, in relation to their environments, i.e. political, social, economic and cultural settings [9]. Political directives with the objective of increasing service and grade of transparency and effectiveness drive continuous improvement at the level of public administration. Multiple channels for digital contact, communication and interaction are used in order to provide and meet overall goals and agendas for digitalization. Messages from the EU level concern efforts to improve citizens' interactions, provide more efficient and effective administrations, and increase the transparency of government to enhance a more democratic society [44]. Public e-services are essential in governmental use of digital channels. Providing information systems with online services based on automated end-to-end processes or to some extent replacing manual case handling. Hence, public e-services are services for both external and internal use in a governmental and political setting [23]. The complexities and challenges of IO public e-service development are discussed below in terms of pre-conditions, design, and development and delivery phases in the process.

2.1 Pre-conditions for e-Service Development

Resource allocations, the future-readiness of innovations, and influences from institutional and environmental issues have been identified as crucial for incentives and goals in public e-service development [9]. In addition, Iskender and Özkan [19] relate identified success factors to net benefits in terms of cost savings, expanded communication channels to users, expanded service portfolio, increased information retrieval, and time savings. Moreover, their research reports on systems quality (adaptability, availability, reliability, response time, and usability), information quality (completeness, ease of understanding, personalization, relevance and security), service quality (assurance, empathy and responsiveness), use (nature of use, navigation patterns, number of site visits and transactions), and user satisfaction (repeat use, visits and experiences). To identify possible projects should be the first activity (c.f. [18]).

If we analyze the IO dimension of e-service development more closely, actors in IO development processes in general assume a responsibility of their own for results and also express a need and a willingness to collaborate through personal investments, commitments, and a joint use of resources in a win-win relationship [1, 4]. The latter might briefly be described as the work practices where activities are performed by the organizations with the best capability to provide the resources (e.g. competence, time, technology, and information) and performance required in delivery. Stakeholders might differ in their possibilities to collaborate and in their expectations of outcomes. Nonetheless, initiatives and decisions could be explained as driven by several rationales [5]. The most common is cost reduction; others include the possibility to gain access to adequate and competent resources, and to improve business process performance [1]. Hence, these rationales clearly match e-government goals to improve citizen interaction to make the administration more efficient and effective, and to increase transparency.

In the forecasting phase, the factors to consider in order to avoid failures are: the organization's behavior in relation to service innovation, idea generation sources and actions as well as organizational structure and resource allocation impact, that is internal and external value [2]. The IO public environment is related to the many involved stakeholders; for instance private, public and non-profit actors involved in the design, development and delivery of e-services [9]. The degree of in-house versus external resources varies and might include vendors and suppliers [4] acting together. Organizations collaborate in order to facilitate and perform actions across such boundaries, as well as the boundaries between sectors when private parties take the roles traditionally performed by government organizations [21]. Those involved are stakeholders in e-service design, development and delivery, actors affecting the development, and actors affected by the result [22]. Guha and Chakrabarti [15] argue for a better understanding of issues such as the politics of partner selection, the achievement of network goals, institutionalization processes, network structuring, and incentive design. Tsou's [40] findings show that collaboration competency and partner match relate positively to knowledge integration, which in turn relates positively to e-service innovation. Organizational compatibility and a prior history of business relations are critical elements of partner match. Furthermore, the study indicates the importance of similar management styles and cultures (ibid.). The underlying theme is that the public sector requires closer working relationships between government stakeholders [16: 539]; "The development of meaningful and effective relationships between central government, individual government agencies and users of public e-service are critical to the success of e-service".

2.2 Design and Development of e-Services

E-service development can be viewed as the digitalization of business processes to design and develop information systems (IS) with a front-end interface towards the user and back-end business logics, systems and channels. Tasks and issues identified as important for success are defining the scope, staffing, setting of realistic deadlines, reconstruction of processes, requirements, technologies, usability tests, anchoring of solution, hosting, maintaining, training, and problem management [2, 3, 27, 34, 40]. Thus, appropriate skills for the design and development of e-services range from project management, analysis and design, development, integration, tests and to systems maintenance. In addition, Iskender and Özkan [19] relate their findings on success factors (the inverse side of reported challenges) in e-government to the technical base (compatibility, accessibility, standards, interoperability, integrity, maintainability, ease of use), the social base (awareness, intention and education among stakeholders, digital divide and riskless environment), the organizational dimension (visionary leaders, accountability, organizational transformation plans, management support, institutional support and culture, IT investment, transparency and citizen centric) as well as the political and the legal base (political support, macro transformation plans and consistent regulatory framework). Political decisions need to be implemented in development and politicians need to be convinced of the necessity of investing in enabling technology, as well as to ensure the individual and political rights and obligations of citizenship. The public dimension, on the other hand, means to ensure access to services for all citizens, in all channels, to provide diversity, accessibility and usability [22]. Hence, the political, public and personal character of e-services (e.g. My Pages) might be a driver or a barrier in e-service development.

A number of factors have been identified as important in IO public e-service development, such as collaboration and partner match, complex or straight-forward development process, appropriate in-house/in-team skills, the coordination of parallel projects, laws and regulations for interdependencies/data interchange/definitions/ structure, infrastructure and resilience [3, 15, 27, 40]. In addition, transformation of strategies into the right policy measures and practical actions is crucial [33].

Strategic business and IT alignment, in the context of e-service development, is a multi-level task and a complex challenge which involves many concerns [10]. Angelopoulos et al. [2: 103] indicate that "… success or failure is not the result of managing one or two activities very well; rather it is the result of a holistic approach, managing several aspects competently and in a balanced manner". Managing e-service development includes striving for alignment, not only with the political, business and individual levels (i.e. the social and intellectual dimensions). The (IO) collaboration in terms of the political, business and individual levels of each participating organization, as well as the general domain must also be considered. Moreover, e-service development might be conducted in transnational, national, regional and local government levels, at the same time. With a decision of 25 new e-services on one level (in a transnational project) and the development and implementation of the same e-services on another level (the local), problems occur if the mandate to demand the required resources for implementation is lacking [26]. Decisions about e-services might be driven by internal needs and the opportunity-driven "build it and they will come" strategy [20] or, on the other hand, be made on the basis of demand-driven development putting the external target group in focus with its needs and behavior [43]. The strategy adopted by Swedish agencies working with e-government [37: 86] states: "The development of e-services should be based on individuals and business needs". However, support for performing user-driven e-service development is still in its infancy. Aiming for IT (e.g. e-services) to be aligned with business and striving for a mutual alignment of business and IT are two different perspectives [24]. IT should not only be regarded as a support function for the organization. Instead, IT can both enable and drive change depending on the situation (ibid.). Another perspective concerns the alignment on non-strategic levels. Alignment between strategies is important in order to achieve successful organizations; in addition the intellectual and social dimension of alignment is crucial to address. It includes aspects such as shared understanding, a common language, a shared domain of knowledge, and interaction quality between business and IT [36].

2.3   IO e-Service Delivery

The IO e-service delivery and business process changes should be part of analysis and design. There is a need to re-organize back-office processes in order to provide e-services of high quality and improve IO coordination and integration [29]. Millard et al. [28] show that interoperability is easiest achieved between agencies with a tradition of cooperation. Thus, a long-term collaborative relationship is viewed as a source of success. The management challenge increases relative to the scope and number of stakeholders, for example services at tourism destinations including local people, visitors, private enterprises, the public sector, and intermediaries [33]. Thus, end-to-end processes are hard to overview from the user perspective and difficult to grasp with an "ecosystem view" of e-services. With social media as part of the delivery, it is difficult to predict where the e-service starts and who are involved in the delivery. Hence, the scope and processes might involve many internal and external actors and are more or less complex to survey, manage and orchestrate. Furthermore, employees' willingness to recommend e-services in their daily business as well as citizens' adoption and use are prerequisites for benefits to arise [39].

   In delivery, the essential factor is supporting users with information content to find, understand and use the e-service [6] through website layers [7], and web-related technologies [33]. In addition, skills related to intrapersonal and interpersonal communication [33], business process management and the ability to communicate e-services in terms of information content management [6] are crucial. Thus, the ability to achieve local business and IT alignments are a multiple task across departments involved in the e-service delivery. Government officials, who both provide services and benefit from them in their public exercise of duty, are to be viewed as co-producers of service delivery together with external users (citizens, businesses, non-profit organizations, and visitors). Hence, the IO public e-service development is both an internal IO business development across administrations and at the same time across organizations. Specifying requirements is therefore a complex task, balancing demands on fully online services with many actors to agree on the business logic, legal, functional and technical solutions. Tseng and Hu [39] stress the fact that the social construct of e-services does matter, report on many e-service items not suitable for full online services, and point out that in addition, users are not demanding these services. Angelopoulos et al. [2], note that e-government efforts are contingent upon the willingness of the citizens to use e-services which, according to Nam [32] consist of service use, information use, and policy research (the latter is more engaged and concerned with society, neighbors and government). However, direct contact between citizens and the government is relatively rare according to Heeks [17] referring to Millard who presents an average of 1.6 times per year in Europe. Hence, development efforts measured on number of e-services, site visits and repeated use are not as adequate as measures on value in relation to both internal and external users.

2.4   Challenges in IO Public E-Service Development Phases

Based on the literature review above, IO-related challenges in public e-service development phases are presented in a summary, see Table 1.

Table 1. Challenges (C) in IO public e-service development phases

Pre-conditions

- To get a functional partner match with private/public/non-profit actors with multiple forces, rationales, goals, expectations, awareness, intention and grade of willingness (C1)
- To identify actors' behavior in relation to innovation, idea generation sources and development actions together with their possibilities for IT investment, resource allocation impact and market impact (C2)
- To identify in-house/in-team/external know-ledge, skills resources and environments by participation actors (C3)
- To staff a number of well-known and/or new actors with the same or different size of agencies, styles, cultures and collaboration competence (C4)

Design and Development

- To co-ordinate between stakeholders' own and common goals. Goals can exists on local/regional/national/EU level and should be aligned and achieved in intra- and inter-business process design (C5)
- To align decisions, multiple skills and actions in and between levels of involved actors. To achieve win-win situations and mutual responsibility for the technical base, design, development, resilience and maintainability (C6)
- To work with more or less political support, visionary leaders, plans and regulatory/legal frameworks by involved actors (C7)

Delivery

- To co-ordinate stakeholders' intra- and inter-business processes and channels (C8)
- To communicate and co-ordinate employees' intra- and inter-organizational actions with different degree of automated service delivery and channel choices (C9)
  To communicate multiple organizations' expectations on e-service quality with adequate measurements (C10)

3 Findings: Challenges in IO Public e-Service Development

The national e-service case aimed at developing an e-service for automated decisions of provisional driving license applications, i.e. to support case officers with cases that did not call for an extensive manual handling process). Benefits aimed for in the project were automatic handling of "unproblematic" applications, cost reduction, and faster decisions for citizens. By implementing the e-service, the agency should be able to save and reallocate resources to support more complex applications. An e-service like this also provided an opportunity to standardize the application handling processes across the nation and the 21 county administration boards. Prior to the project, the agencies had high expectations concerning the quality of data provided by citizens. The use of an e-service when applying for a provisional driving license made it possible to check the quality and the completeness of data automatically. Another advantage with the e-service was that the underlying IT system directs the citizen to the appropriate county administrative board – instead of having citizens wondering which board they belong to. The development project was hosted by Sweden's County Administrations but consisted of members from the Swedish Road Administration and several external IT consultancy firms delivering project services and IT applications.

In *the regional e-service case* the IO development participants include the county IT board, 16 local municipalities, one supplier and a national platform community. The objectives are to use standard e-services based on interpretative business rules without legal barriers in a shared technical infrastructure to reduce cost, increase service quality, increase access and easier contact for the citizens, save time and reallocate resources to more complex errands. The IO collaboration provides the ability to use financial resources better, to share competences and require, design and host e-services together. The "e-Office", made up of three employees lead the joint development and supports the municipalities with methods, testing, anchoring and training besides national and regional coordination. One e-service representative from each municipality is the local driver of development as well as coordinating the local service performance. Each local administrative unit is responsible for requirements and service delivery; both issues are difficult to coordinate without a defined role. Hence, the ability, expectations and willingness of the representatives vary, as well as skills and motivation. One challenge is to empower administrations to accept their e-service ownership responsibility. The e-Office acts as a "broker" in the political environment with a pedagogic challenge to align politics, business, and IT in order to explain needs versus technical drivers. Decisions on e-government are made on national and regional level and turn into services on the local level were they are delivered and used. The local municipality administrations are responsible for the e-service and further improvements. However, even smaller changes might be difficult to make as a new version activates the implementation process with a great deal of work for involved parties. Thus, improvements depend on the supplier and the customers' network where development efforts on functionality are shared in a national, regional and local win-win.

In order to structure the IO challenges identified in literature and the empirical cases we use key lessons presented by Axelsson and Melin [3], see Table 2. The abbreviations N (the national e-service case) and R (the regional e-service case) are used.

Table 2. IO challenges in previous research and in the national and the regional case

Six key lessons	IO challenges in literature	IO challenges in cases
(1) An e-government project should be initiated based on someone's explicit need for the e-service – there should be a problem that the e-service would solve or a situation to facilitate	To get a functional partner match (C1) To identify actors' behavior in relation to innovation (C2) To get political and management support (C7)	To decide for develop without knowing if the citizens ask for the e-service (N1) To identify a local need when representatives are lacking motivation of e-service initiatives (R1)
(2) E-service development projects should be based on a thorough understanding of citizens' needs and requirements	To co-ordinate goals and drivers between levels: local, regional, national, EU (C5)	To align knowledge between levels and organizations without someone responsible (N2) To align needs and objectives between levels in value evaluation and prioritization (R2)
(3) The security and identification solutions chosen should be carefully examined in relation to the specific target groups of the e-service	Not found in the literature review	To choose an identification solution (eID) that was very difficult to get access to for a main target group of the e-service (N3)
(4) The e-service in itself cannot be the only scope of the project; the complexity of internal and IO process changes and the general context must also be understood	To co-ordinate stakeholders' intra- and inter-business processes (C8) To achieve win-win and mutual responsibility (C6) To communicate stakeholders' expectations in relation to quality and adequate measurements (C10)	To perform IO business process analysis with stakeholders who can motivate and realize business changes and design of service and support without ownership of e-services (R3)
(5) An e-government develop-ment project should be properly planned and staffed with persons with an appropriate competence	To staff a number of actors; size of agencies, styles, cultures and collaboration competence (C4) To identify knowledge, skills resources and environments (C3)	To ensure in-house development competence lead to a high dependence on consultants (N4) To ensure a process to co-ordinate the IO development when experience was lacking (R4)
(6) Analysis of legal pre-conditions for the e-service should be done in the very beginning	To communicate and co-ordinate different degrees of automated service delivery and channel choices (C9)	To highlight regulations and sections of the law when identifying a potential service to develop (N5 + R5)

According to the analysis in Table 2 an explicit need for the e-service is in an IO context based on participating partners' local levels (employees and external users) as well as the regional and national levels in terms of re-use solutions in a broader sense. Thus, there is a challenge to motivate and support local e-service representatives to take the lead and identify local needs as well as to co-ordinate needs on a regional/national level. Hence, the partner match aspect is crucial in planning and staffing private/public/non-profit actors and their representatives. In addition, political and management support is needed as well as methodological support for instance for identifying and prioritizing whose needs should be served.

Basing the development of an e-service on a thorough understanding of citizens' needs and requirements is an ideal situation. However, to get users to express requirements for new services/solutions, in order to get an adequate user representation, is difficult. One way to identify requirements is to map the IO business processes with the external user in focus as well as the service impact on and demands for internal and external changes. However, before a business process mapping, the potential e-services to be developed need to be identified and prioritized. In this part of the work practice, regulations must be interpreted in the same way in order to develop an e-service to be used at a regional or national level.

The process design of the e-service delivery offers a possibility to co-ordinate resources and actions to achieve win-win and decide on mutual responsibilities. In addition, the expectations of organizations in relation to e-service quality can be based on measurements, such as the number of cases to handle, time-savings, channel choices and quality in performance instead of less adequate measurements like numbers of e-services, site visits and repeated use.

4 Conclusions

The purpose of this paper has been to further elaborate on challenges in IO public e-service development with the aim of generating lessons for such development. Our conclusions are based on the key lessons formulated by Axelsson and Melin [3], but put in an explicit IO focus in this paper, also revisiting the cases in the section above, and the analysis in the previous section. The major contribution is to further develop the reported lessons through adding an explicit IO dimension of e-service development. Eight emerging lessons learned (L), below, are related to different phases in the development process:

Pre-conditions for Public IO e-Service Development L1: E-service initiatives should be based on rationales connected to objectives at different levels (EU, national, regional, local) and the possibility to promote development corresponding to environment. **L2:** E-service design, development and delivery should handle the political, public and personal character of the e-service and its internal and external use based on a common decision between multiple stakeholders.

Design and Development of IO Public e-Services L3: E-service development should be initiated by someone's explicit need for the e-service (a problem to solve or a situation to facilitate) and based on expected (and evaluated) user value. **L4:** E-service development should be properly planned and staffed with persons with an appropriate partner match, competence, ability and responsibility defined with a mandate to act upon. **L5:** E-service design should be based on early-identified legal restrictions and the possibility to reach common regulations for e-service delivery provided by the involved stakeholders, that is service providers and users.

Delivery of IO Public e-Services L6: E-service delivery should be based on IO business process analysis and design.

L7: E-service security and identification solutions chosen should be carefully examined based on user types. **L8:** E-services should be delivered in relevant and multiple channel choices according to users' needs.

4.1 Implications and Future Research

In this paper eight emerging lessons corresponding to different phases in the development process were presented. We focused on the IO dimension of the e-service development process, but do not claim that all aspects of the challenges and emerging lessons are exclusive for the IO context. Actually, the case is rather the opposite; several of the challenges and lessons have been reported in previous research and practice. However, we would like to highlight the level of complexity with multiple stakeholders (for instance regarding objectives), challenges related to processes and staffing across organizational borders, and the choice of joint channels as particularly important aspects of IO e-service development. The implications for both practice and research are that the challenges that have to be handled at various stages need to be defined, and frameworks and methods developed in order to support the development practice. Our findings emphasize the importance of pre-conditions as a part of IO public e-service development in order to support alignment between strategic and business development at multiple levels with many issues to be handled from partner match to methodological support in the context of joint development. The IO dimension of multiple actors and levels is important to enable the design, development and delivery of public e-services.

One limitation in our work is the choice of two cases within the same national context. Future research can extend the national domain (for instance to include several countries within the European Union). Another possible avenue for further research is to use further analytically refine the lessons above, elaborate more on the design and development process as a point of departure for action and contextualization, and doing so as a means of validation and further improvement.

References

1. Alter, C., Hage, J.: Organizations Working Together. Sage, Newbury Park (1993)
2. Angelopoulos, S., Kitsios, F., Papadopoulos, T.: New service development in e-government: identifying critical success factors. Transforming Gov. People Process Policy 4(1), 95–118 (2010)

3. Axelsson, K., Melin, U.: Six key lessons for e-government projects. In: Proceedings of EGOV, pp. 93–103 (2009)
4. Axelsson, K., Melin, U.: An inter-organisational perspective on challenges in one-stop government. Int. J. Electron. Gov. 1(3), 296–314 (2008)
5. Axelsson, K., Melin, U., Lindgren, I.: Public e-services for agency efficiency and citizen benefit – findings from a stakeholder centered analysis. Gov. Inf. Q. 30(1), 10–22 (2013)
6. Christiansson, M.-T.: Improving citizens' ability to find understand and use e-services: communicating the social interaction dimension. Syst. Signs Actions 7(2), 177–204 (2013)
7. Christiansson, M-T., Wik, M.: Testing communicability in public e-services: process and outcomes. In: Proceedings of EGOV and Electronic Participation, pp. 244–253. IOS Press. doi:10.3233/978-1-61499-429-9-244 (2014)
8. Chun, S.A., Luna-Reyes, L.F., Sandoval-Almaza´n, R.: Guest editorial: collaborative e-government, transforming government. People Process Policy 6(1), 5–12 (2012)
9. Dawes, S., Eglene, O.: New models of collaboration for delivering e-government services: a dynamic model drawn from multi-national research. In: Center for Technology in Government, pp. 1–17 (2008)
10. Dawes, S.: Governance in the digital age: a research and action framework for an uncertain future. Gov. Inf. Q. 26(2), 257–264 (2009)
11. Gibson, J.J.: The theory of affordances. In: Shaw, R., Bransford, J. (eds.) Perceiving, Acting, and Knowing: Toward an Ecological Psychology, pp. 67–82. Lawrence Erlbaum, Hillsdale (1977)
12. Government Offices of Sweden: The Swedish model of government administration – three levels (2014). http://www.government.se/sb/d/2858
13. Government Offices of Sweden: Ministry of Enterprise, Energy and Communications, Swedish Government strategy on a digital collaborative public administration (2012). http://www.regeringen.se/sb/d/15700/a/206004
14. Government Offices of Sweden: Ministry of Enterprise, Energy and Communications, ICT for Everyone - A Digital Agenda for Sweden, N2011.19 (2011). http://www.government.se/sb/d/2025/a/181914
15. Guha, J., Chakrabarti, B.: Making e-government work: adopting the network approach. Gov. Inf. Q. 31(2), 327–336 (2014)
16. Hassan, H.S., Shehab, E., Peppard, J.: Recent advances in e-service in the public sector: state-of-the-art and future trends. Bus. Process Manage. J. 17(3), 526–545 (2011)
17. Heeks, R.: Benchmarking e-government: improving the national and international measurement, evaluation and comparison of e-government. In: Irani, Z., Love, P. (eds.) Evaluating Information Systems: Public and Private Sector. Elsevier Ltd, Amsterdam (2008)
18. Heeks, R.: Implementing and Managing eGovernment – An International Text. SAGE, London (2006)
19. Iskender, G., Özkan, S.: E-government transformation success: an assessment methodology and the preliminary results. Transforming Gov. People Process Policy 7(3), 364–392 (2013)
20. Jupp, V.: Realizing the vision of e-government. In: Curtin, G.C., Sommer, M.H., Vis-Sommer, V. (eds.) The World of E-government, pp. 129–145. Haworth Press, New York (2003)
21. Klievink, B., Janssen, M.: Challenges in developing public-private business models. Eur. J. ePractice 18, 9–23 (2012). http://www.epracticejournal.eu
22. Lindgren, I.: Public e-service stakeholders - a study on who matters for public e-service development and implementation. PhD thesis no. 580, Linköping University (2013)

23. Lindgren, I., Jansson, G.: Electronic services in the public sector: a conceptual framework. Gov. Inf. Q. **30**, 163–172 (2013)
24. Luftman, J., Rajkumark, K.: An update on business/alignment: a line has been drawn. MIS Q. Executive **6**(3), 165–177 (2007)
25. Madsen, C.Ø., Berger, J.B., Phythian, M.: The development in leading e-government articles 2001-2010: definitions, perspectives, scope, research philosophies, methods and recommendations: an update of Heeks and Bailur. In: Janssen, M., Scholl, H.J., Wimmer, M.A., Bannister, F. (eds.) EGOV 2014. LNCS, vol. 8653, pp. 17–34. Springer, Heidelberg (2014)
26. Magnusson, M., Christiansson, M-T.: Using goal modelling to evaluate goals for e- service development in government. In: ECIME, pp. 312–320 (2011)
27. Melin, U., Axelsson, K.: Managing e-service development – comparing two e-government case studies. Transforming Gov. People Process Policy **3**(3), 248–270 (2009)
28. Millard, J., Iversen, J S., Kubicek, H., Westholm, H., Cimander, R.: Reorganisation of Government Back-offices for Better Electronic Public Services – European Good Practices, Main report, European Commission, Brussels (2004)
29. Millard, J.: Are you being served? Transforming e-government through service personalisation. Int. J. Electron. Gov. Res. **7**(4), 1–18 (2011)
30. Myers, M.D.: Qualitative Research in Business & Management. SAGE Publications, London (2009)
31. Myers, M.D., Klein, H.K.: A set of principles for conducting critical research in information systems. MIS Q. **35**(1), 17–39 (2011)
32. Nam, T.: Determining the type of e-government use. Gov. Inf. Q. **31**(2), 211–220 (2014)
33. Paskaleva-Shapira, K., Azorin, J., Chiabai, A.: Enhancing digital access to local cultural heritage through e-governance: innovations in theory and practice from Genoa, Italy. Eur. J. Soc. Sci. **21**(4), 389–405 (2008)
34. Rana, N.P., Dwivedi, Y.K., Williams, M.D.: Analysing challenges, barriers and CSF of egov adoption. Transforming Gov. People Process Policy **7**(2), 177–198 (2013)
35. Sæbø, Ø., Rose, J., Skiftenes Flak, L.: The shape of eParticipation: characterizing an emerging research area. Gov. Inf. Q. **25**(3), 400–428 (2008)
36. Schlosser, F.: Mastering the social IT/business alignment challenge. In: Proceedings of the 18th Americas Conference on Information Systems, AMCIS, AIS Electronic Library, United States, pp. 1843–1849 (2012)
37. SOU: Strategi för myndigheternas arbete med e-förvaltning, (2009). http://www.regeringen. se/sb/d/11456/a/133813. (in Swedish)
38. Susman, G.: Action research: a sociotechnical perspective. In: Morgan, G. (ed.) Beyond Method: Strategies for Social Research, pp. 95–113. Sage Publications, Newbury Park (1983)
39. Tseng, K.-C., Hu, L.-T.: To cross or not to cross the boundaries? A reflection on electronic public service integration. In: Chen, Y.-C., Chu, P.-Y. (eds.) Electronic Governance and Cross-Boundary Collaboration: Innovations and Advancing Tools, pp. 2–22. IGI Global, Hershey (2012)
40. Tsou, H.T.: Collaboration competency and partner match for e-service product innovation through knowledge integration mechanisms. J. Serv. Manage. **23**(5), 640–663 (2012)
41. Van de Ven, A.H.: Engaged Scholarship: a Guide for Organizational and Social Research. Oxford University Press, Oxford (2007)
42. Walsham, G.: Doing interpretive research. Eur. J. Inf. Syst. **15**(3), 320–330 (2006)

43. E-delegation: Vägledning för behovsdriven utveckling, (2012). http://www. behovsdrivenutveckling.se. (in Swedish)
44. European Commission: Digital Agenda for Europe: A Europe 2020 Initiative, Scoreboard 2014 - Developments in eGovernment in the EU 2014, (2014). https://ec.europa.eu/digital-agenda/en/news/scoreboard-2014-developments-egovernment-eu-2014

What Is This Thing Called e-Service? Interoperability Challenges in e-Service Modelling

Svein Ølnes[1](✉) and Arild Jansen[2]

[1] Western Norway Research Institute, Sogndal, Norway
sol@vestforsk.no
[2] University of Oslo, Oslo, Norway
arildj@jus.uio.no

Abstract. Electronic service, or e-service, is a key concept in today's e-Government development. The availability and quality of electronic services are important indicators of e-Government maturity. However, we argue that our understanding of the concept e-service is poor and we show that the ambiguity surrounding the concept creates problems when building ontologies and thus makes it difficult to achieve better interoperability between systems. We thus propose a model for e-services building on a framework for categorizing services using some basic terms. In this way we can describe and model various types of communication between citizens and public agencies based on a consistent set of elementary categories. Our model also draws on EU's proposed Core Public Service Vocabulary (CPSV). The paper is conceptual and is mainly based on a literature review.

Keywords: Service · e-service · e-Government · Interoperability · Semantic web

1 Introduction

The service concept is widely used but involves much confusion. E-service is even worse; it is understood as almost all types of electronic communication between citizens and government [1, 2]. However, is the government offering us a "service" when we are paying taxes or a fine, just because we are using the Internet? In the rather vague terminology used within the e-Government field, almost all types of interaction between public authorities and citizens are regarded as services. Such confusions create difficulties also when defining ontologies that shall support electronic provision of services. Goldkuhl [3] questions the use of service in all governmental tasks, while Alter [4] points to the different definitions of service across communities, and Baida et al. [5] propose an ontology for describing services and service bundling. Following Alter [4] there is thus little consensus on the meaning of the concept e-service, and hence, the literature is full of synonymous terms and concepts as also Lindgren and Janson [2] point out.

Also Papadomichelaki and Mentzas [6] state that the subject of e-service quality is very rich in content of definitions, models, and measurement instruments but although there is agreement on e-service quality being a multidimensional construct, the content of what constitutes e-service quality varies across studies.

© IFIP International Federation for Information Processing 2015
E. Tambouris et al. (Eds.): EGOV 2015, LNCS 9248, pp. 197–208, 2015.
DOI: 10.1007/978-3-319-22479-4_15

A public service can be solely the electronic communication between a public agency and a user, as e.g. information provision, completing an application form etc., or it may be one part of a longer interaction sequence that also includes the provision of a physical service (e.g. applying for child care). The interaction may have been initiated by a user in order to obtain some value (good, benefit etc.), or it may be to fulfil a responsibility where we are obliged to provide information, e.g. when paying taxes, reporting various types of information to public authorities, etc. An electronic interaction can replace a former paper-based communication, or it can involve a new type of service, where the content in itself has a separate, original value, as e.g. an interactive digital map, an electronic book from the library etc. What is called an e-service can also include a set of separate interactions including case handling. On the other hand, public sector also has many functions which imply electronic interactions that should not qualify as services, as e.g. mandatory collection of information from businesses.

The research objectives of this paper is

- *to provide a better understanding of the e-service concept by analysing the relation between physical and digital parts of a service*
- *propose a model for describing (e-)services*

We do not intend to arrive at a definition of the concept e-service. Rather we will try to improve our understanding of the concept by analysing the different characteristics of the interaction between the government and its citizens and businesses, and by looking at the relation between physical and digital parts of a service and try to model these.

When discussing the concept e-service and its implications for interoperability it is important to be consistent in the use of words, and especially the distinction between concept, term and referent, as is described in the semiotic triangle [7].

The concept e-service is the idea or the mental understanding we have of it. The term is the specific label we apply to the concept, the name of the concept so to speak, and the concept e-service has several names (terms), e.g. "e-service", "digital service", or "online service". The referent is the actual e-service representing the concept, e.g. the concrete e-service applying for a student's grant.

The paper is structured as follows: The next chapter describes our method and we then move on to discuss the concepts of service and e-service and the interoperability challenges that arise. Next, we provide a relevant case from a recent project to shed light on the problems related to different definitions of the e-service concept. Based on the analysis of the service and e-service concepts and the different categories of interactions between government and citizens and businesses, we propose a simplified model for a service, in the form of an ontology.

2   Method

Our paper is primarily conceptual and exploratory, aiming to develop a model for describing public electronic services. The paper is rooted in the e-Government research field, but borrows from more general computer science, specifically semantic technologies and ontology development. The discussion of the concept of service is mainly drawn from business science and computer science, because there are few references to this in e-Government literature and not many papers rooted in the e-Government field discussing the service concept. As such we do not distinguish between service provision in a G2C or G2B manner.

The paper builds mainly on a literature review from different disciplines. Since the research question is how to understand the concept e-service, and hence how to model an e-service, a study of the use of the concept in different fields of science was seen as the best method. We also analysed a use case in order to bring experience from e-Government practice to the study.

The main source of literature is the extensive e-Government Reference Library, EGRL, which in the latest version 10.5 contains 7,237 of predominantly English-language, peer-reviewed work in the study domains of electronic government and electronic governance [8].

We also searched the Web of Science[1] for the topic phrase "e-service interoperability" which resulted in 60 papers of which seven was found to be relevant judged by the title and the abstract.

We have also used a case study approach and studied the Los case explained in Chap. 4 as an example of interoperability problems caused by the lack of understanding of the central concept e-service.

3 Understanding Service and e-Service

3.1 What Is a Service?

Service is a concept loaded with different meanings in different circumstances, mostly depending on who uses it. There exist a number of definitions of the concept service, both lexical and from other sources. Starting with encyclopaedia the word service comes from the Latin word "servus" which means slave [9]. A first definition of service is the occupation or condition of a servant, corresponding nicely to how service is understood in computer science: A program that offers a service to other programs through a well-defined user interface, as e.g. in service–oriented architecture (SOA).

From the above definition we can see that the concept service is used to indicate an action and also the type of action (the act or method). The definition also covers the output of a service (the quality) and the organization acting to carry out the service. Service first came into use in the 1930s in the U.S. Department of Commerce's Standard Industrial Classification (SIC) codes [10].

The European Parliament passed the Service Directive, also known as the Bolkestein Directive [11] in 2006. The directive refers to article 50 of the (Lisbon) Treaty [12] for a definition: "Services shall be considered to be "services" within the meaning of this Treaty where they are normally provided for remuneration, in so far as they are not governed by the provisions relating to freedom of movement for goods, capital and persons. "Services" shall in particular include: (a) activities of an industrial character;

---

[1] https://webofknowledge.com/.

(b) activities of a commercial character; (c) activities of craftsmen; (d) activities of the professions."

Hill [13] defines service this way: "A service is a change in the condition of a person, or a good belonging to some economic entity, brought about as the result of the activity of some other economic entity, with the approval of the first person or economic entity". Although not very precise, this definition has been adopted by the U. S. government. This definition puts weight on the action rather than the substance or the quality. Chesbrough and Spohrer [10] have called for a unified Service Science to integrate across academic silos and to advance service innovation. They also stress the conceptual confusion of 'services'. They argue that the change from products and tangible goods to more and more intangible assets calls for a broader perspective and the need for each party in the process to know the other party's knowledge in negotiating the service exchange. They also argue that service innovation is different from product innovation.

Maglio et al. in [14], also points to the diversity of perspectives involved in the understanding of what service is. They understand the term "services" to mean "service processes" and tries to bridge the different understandings of the service concept in his Unified Service Theory (UST). The UST defines services as production processes wherein each customer supplies one or more input components for that customer's unit of production The input dimension is considered to be unique to services. However, Sampson does not distinguish between e-services and services.

Baida [15] makes a distinction between an "elementary" service element and a "service bundle". A service bundle is a complex service element, including one or more service elements, any of which may be either elementary or a bundle. Service bundles can also be called compound services. A service element may be decomposed into smaller service elements, as long as the smaller elements can be offered to customers separately or by different suppliers. Once a smaller element represents a non-separable service element that is offered by one supplier, we call it an elementary service element.

Without fully adopting Baida's definitions, we believe the basic idea of elementary service elements is fruitful, and suggest that we make similar distinctions, which imply that we can develop an ontology of elementary public services, which may include both online and physical services and also make a distinction between the two, as indicated in the Los ontology shown in Fig. 1.

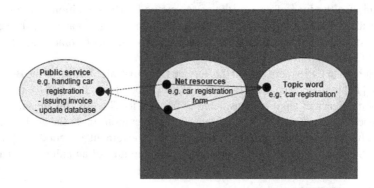

Fig. 1. Simplified Los ontology showing the example of registering a car.

3.2 What Is an e-Service?

Moving from the real world to the electronic representation, we question whether we can use the same definition of e-service as for service, the only difference being the means of how the service is delivered to the user? Is it just to add an "e"?

Goldkuhl [3] questions the use of service in all governmental tasks and he asks whether the service perspective is compatible with all kinds of public authority. More precisely, he questions whether a public e-service is a real service to the citizen, in a strict sense: in what ways is a citizen served through an e-service? A next question is what we mean by e-services. He ties these questions to a study of a child care service and the work with a requirement specification for an electronic child care service. He shows how the lack of a proper understanding of e-service led to problems with the requirement specifications and ultimately the e-service application itself. The citizen was mainly seen as an information provider and not as someone to serve.

Rust and Kannan [16] define e-services as general as "the provisioning of services over electronic networks", whereby electronic networks include not only the Internet but also electronic environments as ATMs. They discuss the e-service concept from a business science view and their e-service concept is tightly coupled with e-Commerce. They do not make any attempt to distinguish e-services from services and do not discuss the possible differences between services and e-services.

In an analysis of the e-service literature, Rowley [17] acknowledges that theory and practice of e-services is still in its infancy and that the result being the absence of an agreement on the definition. She thereafter goes on to define the concept 'e-services' as "...deeds, efforts or performances whose delivery is mediated by information technology. Such e-service includes the service element of e-tailing, customer support, and service delivery". Also this definition is based on a business science view, and it reflects the three main components involved: service provider, service receiver, and the channels of service delivery. However, she does not say anything about services and thus makes no attempt to relate or differentiate the two concepts.

O'Sullivan et al. [18] also ask "what is a service?" and recognize the difference between physical services and e-services, but without discussing them in depth. They assert that e-services exhibit minimal constraints on the time and location of request, contrary to most real-world services. They also emphasize the need to describe the non-functional properties (availability, channels, pricing strategies etc.).

Service quality is an important aspect of services and has also been attempted used to clarify the concept of public e-services, as pointed out by Buckley [19] and Zeithaml et al. [20]. But as Goldkuhl [3] points out, most often the underlying premises for the service concept seems to be taken for granted and not problematized.

Baida et al. [5] try to bridge the different definitions and approaches to the concept service from the three different communities of business science, information science, and computer science. Service and e-service as used in business science has a very different meaning than the same concepts used in computer science. The former community naturally puts weight on business transactions and see 'e-services' as a natural outgrowth of e-Commerce. From a strict technological point of view, (e-)services are web-delivered software functionality, often described as "web services".

Alter [4] also refers to three different disciplines, each with their own definitions of service: marketing, operations, and computer science. He proposes a service system as a useful fundamental unit for understanding, analysing, and designing services in all three disciplines. When discussing automated and non-automated services he emphasizes that the proposed frameworks for a service system does not make any assumptions about whether ICT is involved or not. From Alter's point of view ICT, or other technologies, can be part of the service system.

This is in line with this paper's view that although parts of a physical service are carried out online, that does not make the service necessarily an e-service. That is not to say that complete online services do not exist. In Norway the State Educational Loan Fund provides almost complete automated handling of most applications for grants and loans. Similarly, on-line declarations to the police, purchase of digital maps or retrieval of online books from a library are other examples of online services. Thus, many functions available from public websites are examples of "true" e-services in that they do not have a specific physical part.

3.3   e-Services and Interoperability Problems

A web service is, unlike the service and e-service concepts, fairly well defined. It denotes "a software system designed to support interoperable machine-to-machine interaction over a network" [21]. It is thus a much more precise and narrow definition than e-services. Tightly connected to web services is the Service Oriented Architecture, SOA, a popular framework in computer science. OASIS defines SOA as a paradigm for organizing and utilizing distributed capabilities that may be under the control of different ownership domains [22]. Furthermore, in SOA a service is understood as "as the capability to perform work for another or the specification of the work offered for another or the offer to perform work for another" [22].

Much effort has been put into developing more systematic vocabularies (ontologies) for describing public services, which is necessary to achieve better interoperability e.g. Wimmer [23], W3C [24], and OASIS [22]. In such work, there is a clear need for more precise definitions of the key concepts that can describe and model the different activities and processes involved, in other words develop an ontology. Shadbolt et al. define ontologies as "attempts to carefully define parts of the data world and to allow mappings and interactions between data held in different formats" [25], or as Gruber [26] puts it, "a specification of a conceptualization".

Semantic technologies call for a greater precision in defining concepts and their relations, what is usually called vocabularies or ontologies. Without such definitions machines will be unable to act on the information because of ambiguities in the definition of concepts. The service and e-service concepts are clear candidates for such ambiguities, which the case of Los described below clearly shows.

The Semantic Web is W3C's proposed method, based on the Resource Description Framework (RDF), for making machines on the Internet interpret and "understand" information so as to be able to act without specific instructions from the users [24]. The Semantic Web and semantic technologies in general are thought to have a profound influence on the future development of the Internet [27]. It will thus also have a significant influence on the future development of e-Government, not at least the challenging interoperability issues recognized as one of the major barriers to more seamless electronic applications and an area with a substantial gap between plans and realities [28].

The work with establishing a common model for public services has been brought about partly as a result of the work with a European Interoperability Framework (EIF). The first version of the EIF presented the much used three-level interoperability model with the technical, semantic, and organizational interoperability levels [29]. Version 2 of the EIF was published as an annex to the report "Towards interoperability for European public services" [30] and added the political and legal levels to the existing three levels of interoperability. It also put forward specific recommendations regarding the work with interoperable public services, among these:

> Public administrations should develop a component-based service model, allowing the establishment of European public services by reusing, as much as possible, existing service components (Recommendation 9)

Following up this recommendation, EU's programme for interoperability solutions (ISA) established a working group for the Core Public Service Vocabulary to develop a conceptual model for public services. A modified version of this model is shown in Chap. 5.

Our literature review shows that there is no coherent understanding of the service and 'e-services' concepts. Baida et al. [5] also underline that understanding the various interpretations of service is not enough to facilitate reasoning about services, as done in Semantic Web initiatives. They call for a shared conceptualization and formalization of describing services to allow for development of appropriate software. The important word here is "shared", and as we shall see in the next chapter problems arise when concepts that should be shared, are not understood in the same way.

4   Lost in Translation: The Case of Los

Los is the name of a system enabling automatic exchange of information between public organizations[2] [32]. The information exchange is based upon a controlled vocabulary (list of keywords and their relation) describing public services. The vocabulary is organized as a thesaurus following the ISO 2788 standard for monolingual thesauri construction [33] and expressed in Topic Maps, an ISO standard for structured metadata [34]. An important aspect of Los is the underlying semantics and the description of the key concepts. Experiencing interoperability difficulties as described above, it has been important to handle concepts like service and e-service carefully in Los and try to break these down into service elements and giving them unique names, e.g. a *service description*, a *form for printing*, a *form for electronic submission* etc. This is in line with Baida's

---

[2] The system is owned and developed by the national Agency for Public Management and e-Government in Norway (Difi – http://www.difi.no).

suggestions of separating the elementary services from a service bundle [15]. It also reflects the different categories of interaction between the Government and its citizens and businesses, as showed by Jansen and Ølnes [35].

The problems that can occur with ambiguous definitions were encountered during the test phase when the Los ontology was merged with the ontology for the Bergen municipality web portal. The municipality of Bergen, as one of the pilot users of Los, used a different definition of service than Los, which then caused a failure in the information integration process and resulted in a compromised system.

The municipality of Bergen's web portal was based on Topic Maps technology, as was the Los system, and the implementation of Los was therefore straightforward. An important feature in Topic Maps is that two concepts (called *topics* in Topic Maps) must be merged if they have the same name. The topic service from the Los vocabulary was therefore merged with the Bergen's own topic service and the result was a compromised system because the two systems relied on different definitions and understandings of the concept service. This is an interoperability conflict classified by Peristeras et al. [31] as a schema-isomorphism conflict.

In order to correct the situation, the Los ontology was revised, replacing the (e-)service concept with a new concept 'net resource' which is information about a service or methods of obtaining a service, e.g. an electronic form. Instead of naming everything a service (or e-service), a differentiation between different parts of a service was done, e.g. the service description, the electronic form(s) in use, other transaction types and so on.

The example above is from the public service of registering a car on a new owner. It shows the distinction and connection between online resources (inside purple box) and the physical part of a service provision (outside the box). This service could in principle be a complete e-service. However, in Norway only the registration form of the service is available online for citizens. The other interactions between the governmental agency and the citizens have to be carried out manually.

The Los case shows that a seemingly small detail in the definition of a concept can cause major problems when it comes to interoperability issues. In everyday language we can get away with imprecise use of concepts because of the pragmatic nature of human communication. Most often, we as humans will understand the meaning even if the concepts we use are not completely agreed upon at the beginning. However, when working with semantic technologies and making machines "understand" and act upon the information they process, unambiguity is an absolute necessity. Without having consistent terms and definitions we cannot solve the interoperability challenges when different systems are interacting. The lesson learned from the Los case is that we must define key concepts in consistent ways, which we will outline in the next section.

5   A Model for Conceptualizing e-Services

We most often fail to see the distinction between a physical service and an e-service, or at least any in-depth discussions. Also in measuring or benchmarking e-Government, e-service concepts are rarely discussed but taken for granted, as we can see from core e-Government reports from the EU and corresponding reports from other countries, e.g. Norway.

In striving for greater precision it is necessary to examine the different parts of a complete e-service and then identify and name these parts according to what they really are. We have to distinguish between the interface of a service, e.g. a form to apply for a service, and the service itself. If we call both things an "e-service", as is often the case today, we will face great challenges and difficulties when trying to achieve better interoperability.

Our model builds on a framework for describing e-services that has several dimensions [35], among them: (i) the purpose of the interaction such as execution of authority, fulfilling obligations as a citizen or a business, applying for a benefit or to provide information, (ii) the content or structure of the interaction, and (iii) the result or effect of the interaction. By using the ISA working group on public service vocabularies [36] as a starting point and incorporated the understanding of the categories of interaction between government and citizens and businesses, we propose this simplified model of a service (Fig. 2).

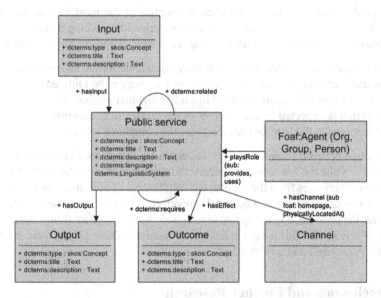

Fig. 2. A simplified service model expressed as a UML class diagram, based on CPSV

The different classes and relations of the UML diagram above are described in more detail in the table below (Table 1).

Table 1. Description of the different classes in the model

Class	Description
Input	The prerequisite for obtaining a service; structured information given in a form and often digitally represented
Public service	The physical or digital service offered to citizens or businesses
Agent	Service provider, citizen, business
Output	The information acquired by the client of the service after initiating the process and after the service provider has handled the case
Outcome	Change in status, e.g. if applying for a driver's license and passing the tests, the citizen has obtained the right to drive a car (or a vehicle)
Channel	The medium which the service is provided through. Also used to distinguish between digital and physical delivery

The model above has been simplified to emphasize the most important parts. A service model is more complicated and involves rules for handling a service request, preconditions to be met to be eligible for the service etc. Thus, we have to specify:

- The preconditions (in addition to the prerequisites); the formal and material requirements that have to be fulfilled before a service dialog can be initiated
- Who are the specific agents involved in each individual service
- What output is expected by the receiver of the service (e.g. citizens)
- What outcome is likely to be the effects for the completed service

The distinction between *output*, which we understand as the planned (automatic) result of the "service", while by "outcome" we understand the effect, as e.g. what a client (citizens or business) experiences from the service, e.g. a fulfilment of obligations as paying taxes, a permission as driver's license, a financial support, etc. Outcome may also include consequences for the provider, e.g. the update of a register, a reporting data from a business, the payment of a fine, etc. This is also in line with Jansen and Ølnes [35] in their distinction between service result and service effect.

6 Conclusions and Further Research

This paper has demonstrated that the various definitions of e-service are confusing and troublesome, as most often service or e-service are used without any further definition, especially in public documents where these concepts are crucial. We also find very different definitions both within and across research disciplines, not least within the e-Government domain.

Our Los case shows that lack of common definitions may create inconsistencies in our electronic systems. Consistent definitions are particularly important in the development of more semantically enhanced systems, and properly use of semantics is a prerequisite to increase levels of interoperability. There is thus a need to agree on key concepts and their definitions, as well as the relationship between them when building ontologies. The gap between plans and realities [28] shows us that this is not an easy task as little alignment, adoption, and adjustment has been done between the many vocabularies that exist in different organizations, sectors, and subject domains.

We are thus in line with Goldkuhl [3] who argues for more reflective studies on the service dimension in e-services and will argue that substantial parts of what is now called e-services are rather service descriptions, service interfaces, or service representations. There is an urgent need to properly define the key concepts of e-Government, and e-service is one of these, in order to make progression in the work with interoperability, and we believe our proposed model is a first step.

References

1. Lee, J.: 10 year retrospect on stage models of e-Government: a qualitative meta-synthesis. Gov. Inf. Q. **27**(3), 220–230 (2010)
2. Lindgren, I., Jansson, G.: Electronic services in the public sector: a conceptual framework. Gov. Inf. Q **30**(2), 163–172 (2013)
3. Goldkuhl, G.: What does it mean to serve the citizen in e-services? Int. J. Public Inf. Syst. **2007**, 3 (2007)
4. Alter, S.: Service system fundamentals: work system, value chain, and life cycle. IBM Syst. J. **47**(1), 71–85 (2008)
5. Baida, Z., Gordijn, J., Omelayenko, B.: A shared service terminology for online service provisioning. In: Sixth International Conference on Electronic Commerce ICEC 2004 (2004)
6. Papadomichelaki, X., Mentzas, G.: e-GovQual: a multiple-item scale for assessing e-government service quality. Gov. Inf. Q. **29**(1), 98–109 (2012)
7. Ogden, R.G., Richards, I.A.: The Meaning of Meaning. Routledge and Kenan Paul, London (1923)
8. Scholl, H.J.: eGovernment Reference Library (EGRL) version 10.5. University of Washington (2015)
9. Webster's, Webster's New Twentieth Century Dictionary Unabridged, 2nd ed. Simon and Schuster (1979)
10. Chesbrough, H., Spohrer, J.: A research manifesto for services science. Commun. ACM **49**(7), 35–40 (2006)
11. European Commission, Directive 2006/123/EC of the European Parliament and of the Council (2006)
12. European Commission, Consolidated versions of the Treaty on European Union and the Treaty on the Functioning of the European Union (2009)
13. Hill, T.P.: On goods and services. Rev. Income Wealth **23**(4), 314–319 (1977)
14. Maglio, P.P., Kieliszewski, C.A., Spohrer, J.C.: Handbook of Service Science. Springer, Berlin (2010)
15. Baida, Z.S.: Software-Aided Service Bundling: Intelligent Methods and Tools for Graphical Service Modeling. Vrije Universiteit, Amsterdam (2006)

16. Rust, R.T., Kannan, P.K.: E-Service: a new paradigm for business in the electronic environment. Commun. ACM **46**(6), 37–42 (2003)
17. Rowley, J.: An analysis of the e-service literature: towards a research agenda. Internet Res. **16**(3), 339–359 (2006)
18. O'Sullivan, J., Edmond, D., ter Hofstede, A.H.M.: What's in a service? Towards accurate description of non-functional service properties. DAPD **12**(2/3), 117–133 (2002)
19. Buckley, J.: E-service quality and the public sector. Managing Serv. Qual. **13**(6), 453–462 (2003)
20. Zeithaml, V.A., Parasuraman, A., Malhotra, A.: Service quality delivery through web sites: a critical review of extant knowledge. J. Acad. Mark. Sci. **30**(4), 362–375 (2002)
21. W3C: Web Services Glossary. W3C, W3C Working Group Note (2004)
22. OASIS: Reference Model for Service Oriented Architecture 1.0 (2006)
23. Wimmer, M.A.: Integrated service modelling for online one-stop government. Electron. Mark. **12**(3), 149–156 (2002)
24. W3C: W3C Semantic Web Frequently Asked Questions (2009)
25. Shadbolt, N., Hall, W., Berners-Lee, T.: The semantic web revisited. IEEE Intell. Syst. **21**(3), 96–101 (2006)
26. Gruber, T.R.: A translation approach to portable ontology specifications. Knowl. Acquisition **5**(2), 199–220 (1993)
27. Berners-Lee, T., Hendler, J., Lassila, O.: The semantic web. Sci. Am. **284**, 28–37 (2001)
28. Codagnone, C., Wimmer, M.A.: Roadmapping eGovernment research: visions and measures towards innovative governments in 2020. Guerinoni Marco (2007)
29. European Commission (IDABC): European Interoperability Framework 1.0. European Commission (2004)
30. European Commission: Towards interoperability for European public services - Annex II EIF 2. European Commission (2010)
31. Peristeras, V., Loutas, N., Goudos, S.K., Tarabanis, K.: A conceptual analysis of semantic conflicts in pan-European e-government services. J. Inf. Sci. **34**(6), 877–891 (2008)
32. Ølnes, S.: Interoperability in public sector: how use of a lightweight approach can reduce the gap between plans and reality. In: Wimmer, M.A., Chappelet, J.-L., Janssen, M., Scholl, H.J. (eds.) EGOV 2010. LNCS, vol. 6228, pp. 315–326. Springer, Heidelberg (2010)
33. ISO: ISO 2788:1986 Guide for the establishment and development of monolingual thesauri. ISO (1986)
34. Garshol, L.M.: Metadata? Thesauri? Taxonomies? Topic maps! Making sense of it all. J. Inf. Sci. **30**(4), 378–391 (2004)
35. Jansen, A., Ølnes, S.: The muddy waters of public e-services-the use and misuse of the concept and how to get out of the maze. Syst. Signs Actions **8**(1), 76–94 (2014)
36. European Commission: Core Public Service Vocabulary Specification v. 1.01. European Commission (ISA Programme). 29 March 2013

Removing the Blinkers: What a Process View Learns About G2G Information Systems in Flanders

Lies Van Cauter[1]([⊠]), Monique Snoeck[2], and Joep Crompvoets[1]

[1] Public Governance Insitute, KU Leuven, Leuven, Belgium
{Lies.VanCauter,Joep.Crompvoets}@soc.kuleuven.be
[2] Research Centre for Management Informatics, KU Leuven, Leuven, Belgium
Monique.Snoeck@kuleuven.be

Abstract. A major objective of government-to-government (G2G) e-government is information sharing and connecting different islands of information. Various barriers impede this connection. Factor research provides a partial explanation of why so many G2G information systems fail. In this paper we take a broader perspective by applying process research to study eight recurrent problems of Flemish G2G IS in their dynamic context. We test whether Sauer's needs and support-power analysis framework can provide additional management insights compared to factor based project management. Our results, based on interviews and focus groups, show that process management is better qualified for dealing with the dynamic context and interactions of Flemish G2G IS.

Keywords: IS failure · G2G · Process management · Needs and support power analysis

1   Introduction

Information necessary to provide better public services and to solve critical public problems is often not available within a single organisation [26, 34]. A major objective of e-government is information sharing and connecting different islands of information [31].

Information sharing at a government-to-government (G2G) level appears to be more complex and hence more prone to failure than in a single organisation [8]. Various barriers impede the connection of different islands of information. These barriers are not only of a technical nature but also of an economic, legal, political and management nature [23, 25].

The high degrees of G2G information systems (ISs) failure motivated practitioners as well as researchers to investigate the underlining problems [33]. Practitioners have conducted retrospectives such as project post-mortems, performance reviews, or lessons learned, while researchers have investigated the causes of failure, critical success/failure factors and approaches that contribute to project success. Despite intensive research in the last four decades, the degree of failure remains too high [7, 20]. Failure continues because of the tendency to let flops rest and go on [17] but also because of a too narrow focus on IS failure.

© IFIP International Federation for Information Processing 2015
E. Tambouris et al. (Eds.): EGOV 2015, LNCS 9248, pp. 209–221, 2015.
DOI: 10.1007/978-3-319-22479-4_16

For a long time positivistic factor-oriented research was the dominant focus when studying G2G IS failure. Researchers with this focus believe that G2G IS failure can be prevented if management can detect and eliminate the causal factors of failure [27]. Classical output of this research is a list of failure factors targeting IS managers. Eliminating failure factors does unfortunately not guarantee success because G2G IS projects are subject to dynamic interacting factors and stakeholders. Factor-oriented research however ignores the context and sees as such only a part of the IS failure puzzle. Because of this, no coherent explanation of the 'whys' and 'hows' can be obtained [30].

The narrow factor oriented focus has an influence on the way G2G IS projects are managed in practice. Project managers tend to focus on strict problem definitions, clear goals, tight time schedules and a predefined end product to minimize the risk of random events [10]. Output oriented models focus merely on the end product while ignoring the process [26]. Managers use lists of failure factors as a 'ready to use frame' to get grip on the situation. As explained above, this approach can never guarantee success because it is too simplistic to cope with the dynamic character of a G2G IS environment [5, 16]. Although attempts have already been undertaken to rethink project management, more research is still needed [10, 24, 32].

Last year [6] appealed for more research with a broader focus on local contingencies and a dynamic environment. In order to professionalise G2G IS managers should become aware of the dynamic interactions between different stakeholders and the environment [11]. To get this broader focus, two shifts are needed: firstly, a shift from factor-oriented research to process research, and secondly, a shift from project management to process management.

The process perspective sees IS as fundamentally social, grounded in a specific context and dependent on contingent processes [18]. Process managers focus on interests, intergovernmental consensus building in different arenas and on potential chances or barriers in an IS's environment [10]. As such a process research and management focus might help to see another part of the IS failure puzzle.

Process research has sought to get beyond the factor approach and advanced various frameworks including the interactionist (e.g. Davis), interpretivist (e.g. Myers, Young or Walsham) and exchange perspective (e.g. Sauer) [23]. None of these are widely accepted, and we might wonder whether this is rightly or not. The authors of this article elaborate further on Sauer's work. Sauer [22] believes that the first step to raise practitioners' awareness about the process perspective (such as context and dynamic interactions), could be achieved by conducting a needs analysis and support-power analysis. In this article we will conduct a needs and support analysis for 8 recurrent problems. These problems are distilled from experiences of Flemish (Belgium) G2G IS practitioners. Our research question is therefore:

RQ: Can the needs and support-power analysis of Sauer provide additional insights for G2G IS management in Flanders?

The remaining of the paper is organised as follows. Section 2 explains the theoretical framework. Section 3 elaborates on the applied methodology. The actual analysis is presented in Sect. 4 and the discussion of research results in Sect. 5. We conclude in Sect. 6.

2 Theoretical Framework

Sauer sees ISs as the product of a process which is open to flaws. The process by which a project organisation initiates, develops, implements and operates an IS is problematic. An IS process consists of both an innovation and a support management process. In the innovation process there are many uncertainties resulting from a variety of contextual sources. Support management aims for the project organisation to be able to sustain support to continuously pursue the innovation process. If the accumulation of problems results in too little support, this jeopardizes the continuation of the innovation process. If this happens the IS process fails entirely [22].

Sauer distinguishes a triangle of dependences: a system serves stakeholders, stakeholders support the project organisation and the project organisation innovates the system. The starting point to think about problems of the IS process, is this triangle of dependences. In order to analyse their situation, practitioners may start with a double analysis. (1) The needs analysis will define the problems to be solved, the context and the available problem solving mechanisms. This should be followed by (2) a support-power analysis to determine who has the power to provide the required support.

2.1 Needs Analysis

The project organisation's needs analysis will consist of two parts: (a) an analysis of problems and (b) an analysis of the required support to solve these problems:

(a)   Analysis of problems is twofold: it first maps what problems need to be solved and second a context scanning is done. Context helps to define problems but constraints originating in this context may make the innovation process problematic. The context is analysed along six dimensions: 1. human factors, 2. history, 3. technological process, 4. structure, 5. politics and 6. environment. Environment is further subdivided in: 6.1. customers, 6.2. suppliers, 6.3. competitors, 6.4. technology, 6.5. regulators, 6.6. interests and 6.7. culture.

(b)   The analysis of support looks at available problem-solving mechanisms [22].

Every G2G IS project is confronted with a series of problems. IS success/failure depends on how management tackles problems and on the effectiveness of collaboration. In the project organisation the idea champion takes up this important management task.

2.2 Support Power Analysis

Several questions pop up while doing a support power analysis: Who is able to provide the support identified in the needs analysis? What other relations are likely to affect stakeholders? Will there be competition for the support? [22].

Innovating G2G IS projects does not only involve the creation of new technical systems but also involves lots of other factors, such as a potential change in organisational structure, culture and power discourses. An example of such other factors is that costs and benefits may not be evenly divided: some stakeholders may win and some may lose during (un)intended trade-offs [10, 19]. Insight in power asymmetries also contributes to an improved understanding of IS projects [6]. Information and ICT are important resources which organisations use to protect their interests [3]. The idea champion therefore depends on other stakeholders, who may feel that their own objectives are not sufficiently reflected and will therefore frustrate or even sabotage the project planning. Only when these other stakeholders are involved in the project they may recognize their ideas in the problem solution and support the process. This illustrates the need for a process approach [5, 28].

This support-power analysis may be applied at any stage of a G2G IS project. Sauer [22] advices to regularly analyse changes in context and process.

3   Methodology

3.1   Data Collection

In 2012 we interviewed 20 experts of G2G IS projects in Flanders (Belgium). Two years later we conducted focus groups with 32 idea champions of G2G ISs. When the results of both studies are compared, recurrent problems for managing G2G ISs pop up. Considering this, we assume that these problems are rather structural and widespread for G2G IS projects in Flanders. We use Sauer's 'needs and support-power analysis'-framework as a basis for structuring our findings.

Our study mainly focuses on vertical G2G IS projects, meaning projects that span hierarchically related governance levels. Belgium is a state with a complex three layer structure. A top consisting of the federal state and the regions (Flanders, Wallonia and Brussels), a second layer consisting of the provinces and finally a third municipal layer. In this paper we focus on IS projects between the region Flanders and municipalities, possibly involving provinces as well. At regional level, different Flemish departments may be involved in these vertical G2G ISs. We further describe the purpose, sampling and data gathering technique of both data collection exercises.

Interviews 2012

In order to explore the state of affairs and possible problems, we interviewed 20 experts in 2012 who are known for their knowledge of the Flemish G2G IS field. For the sampling, interviewees were selected based on the snow ball method [1]. They worked for 14 different public organisations at all governmental levels (federal, Flemish, provincial and local). This selection was based on the fact that some organisations were known for successful G2G information sharing, others represented a subset of provincial and local governments, while a third group performed projects to optimise or evaluate G2G information sharing in practice. Data was collected by means of exploratory interviews in which we asked for the most important G2G ISs and to sketch the latest G2G IS trends and potential problems. The advantage of standardized open ended interviews is that these provide a richness of details, may give the researcher perspectives she did not consider before and reduce the risk that the respondent is led in a certain direction. All interviews lasted between 1–2 h and were fully transcribed.

Focus Groups 2014

To investigate whether additional problems of IS failure could be detected, data was collected from Flemish idea champions by means of Focus Groups (FG). FG represent a qualitative research method where participants are selected and brought together to discuss a specific topic [4, 14]. The last decade FGs are gaining acceptance in IS research [4]. This confirmatory research effort allowed for more structural data collection. IS failure is the result of a mesh of socio, technical and organisational complexities in a dynamic context. The FG method is effective in studying these as it defies to reduce a problem to few variables [2]. In 2012 we created an inventory of Flemish G2G IS as an overview was lacking. Out of this inventory, we selected 40 G2G idea champions. The selection was purposive: we chose for a mid-managerial level since this is high enough for capturing strategic aspects and motives, and low enough to identify specifics of implementation and outcomes [2].

We organised 5 FG sessions of 6 or 7 people in a building that was familiar to the participants. Five people did not show up. A group size of 6–8 people is optimal. [13]: small enough to let everybody talk, large enough to display diverse opinions. The participants formed a diverse but homogenous group. They all (had) managed a G2G IS project in Flanders. We combined managers of project on personal, geographic and 'business' data in order to cover a wide variety of situations.

To ensure the quality of the data gathering, a question route was developed to foster consistency [9]. The questions were pretested on two IS researchers and an IS layman. During a session of 2 h the moderator asked several open questions in an informal open atmosphere. Participants were asked to introduce themselves and got an ice breaking question. The moderator introduced the session schedule, explained how the respondents were selected and emphasized that no judgements would be made. We started with general questions and moved on to four key questions [13]: (1) When does an IS have added value? (2) What may stimulate or block an IS project? (3) Which characteristics of the public sector are judged to be different from the private sector? (4) What would you advise a future manager of a G2G IS? Dominant participants were asked to listen, silent ones to speak up [4, 9]. The moderator showed an encouraging body language. Before ending she asked for additional remarks. Finally the main points were summarised and people received a small gift.

One criticism on the FG method is that it is too dependent on the moderator's skills. The moderator was a PhD student, but the presence of a senior researcher with FG experience ensured a 'back-up'. This researcher took up the role of assistant moderator by taking notes, observing nonverbal behaviour, guarding time and summarising the session. All sessions were audio recorded. A student was present to manage the voice recording and transcribed these afterwards. Another criticism is that negative group dynamics might pop up. People tend to say what they feel is expected of them. To prevent this, a five minute write-down exercise on post-its was done for every key question. This forced participants to get involved [4]. We used a flip chart to organize the post-its but tried to limit the attention drawn to the moderator [13].

3.2   Data Analysis Method

The interview and FG questions were not based on a specific theoretical model so that the data could speak for itself (an inductive approach). A bottom up approach was used to discover a series of problems. A five-staged analysis framework was adopted to interpret the raw data [14]: (1) *Familiarisation*: Reading transcripts to get the whole picture, major themes emerge. (2) *Themes*: Concepts arise from text, categories are developed. Analysis happens via a questioning route. (3) *Indexing*: Sifting data, highlighting quotes, comparing within and between cases. (4) *Charting*: Re-arranging quotes under new codes. Comparing to reduce data. (5) *Mapping and interpretation*: making relationships quotes and links between the data.

We coded all data systematically in Nvivo, a qualitative data analysis software tool. In total, the collected data consisted of 287 pages of interview and FG transcripts. This data was analysed in two stages. During a first analysis the problems that came out of the interviews in 2012 were compared to those detected via the FG research in 2014. Several problems reoccurred, concerning political, technological, economic and juridical issues. During a second analysis the coded data was compared to Sauer's framework by applying the needs and support analysis framework.

4   Analysis

The data analysis revealed problems concerning political, technological, economic and juridical issues. Due to space limitations this article only presents 3 political and 5 technology related problems that seemed the most prominent in a Flemish G2G context. In the next paragraphs these eight recurrent problems will be discussed:

We will describe per problem, (a) what systematic problem solving needs to be undertaken (= problem description), (b) the context elements that have an influence on the needs (= context) as well as (c) the (potential) problem solving mechanisms or support (difficulties) of relevant stakeholders (= support). As several context elements are relevant per problem, these were numbered and we moreover indicate between brackets which context category is applicable. In the description of the support the numbers refer to the previous context elements in order to motivate which support element relates to which element of the context.

4.1   Political and Administrative Agreements

Problem 1: Skilled Idea Champion
Problem Description. Who should take the lead when you work in an intergovernmental project? A manager, called the 'idea champion' should act as project sponsor and leader for the G2G IS project.

Context. (1) The power of an idea champion partly depends on his hierarchical position and Flemish idea champions often appeared to work in the lower segment of the Flemish government (structure). (2) The respondents believe that an idea champion should have a sufficient skill level. As an example, in terms of IT-knowledge, the Flemish government outsourced most IT profiles during New Public Management reforms. As a result, there is a structural shortage of IT-knowledge (structure). (3) The respondents experience that another relevant skill for an idea champion is a spirit of realism. Managing a G2G IS is intense and several respondents suffered in the past from a burn out (human factors). (4) Creating trust is an essential skill for an idea champion (human factors). Stakeholders take past experiences into account, and it is therefore hard to restore damaged trust (history). One respondent remarked: *"We became the victim of our openness, the IS was developed to gather scientific data. After 4 years it was suddenly decided to tax us based on the data in the IS."*

Support. (1) The respondents believe politicians could make idea champions less vulnerable for sabotage by appointing top civil servants (2) Politicians try to solve the shortage of IT professionals by creating an IT pool via the 'Flanders Connect' initiative. (3) Politicians can support an idea champion by not pushing for unrealistic deadlines (4) A difficulty is that damaged trust hampers future support.

Problem 2: User Involvement

Problem Description. Many Flemish departments require data from local governments.

Context. (1) The Flemish government has a tradition of top down treatment of local users instead of considering them as equal partners (culture). (2) Local governments complain of an information asymmetry: they provide data to the Flemish government but get no feedback on what happens with it (culture). (3) The ability of a potential user to cooperate partly depends on the mandate from his own organisation (politics).

Support. (1) According to the respondents, involving local governments from the start might enlarge their willingness to support the system. While doing so the idea champion must guard the overall vision, as intense user involvement holds the risk of scope creep via (un)intended change requests. (2) According to claims in policy documents, Flemish politicians intend 'to treat municipalities less shabbily'. (3) Respondents insisted that municipal politicians should support G2G information sharing.

Problem 3: Top Management Support

Problem Description. Long term existence of an IS requires top management support, or, in case of G2G IS, top political support.

Context. (1) Politicians may make deficient IS ineradicable. Respondents notice that they have a stake in continuing the system or fear the opposition's criticism (politics). (2) The respondents experience that Flemish politicians often pay no attention to IT (politics). (3) Politicians could exercise a social pressure on Flemish stakeholders to cooperate, but they don't (human factors). (4) Currently an overall political vision is lacking, no party is responsible for G2G IS e-government. There is a lack of coordination between Flemish departments partly due to New Public Management reforms (politics). (5) Because of that the principle of 'gathering data only once' is often violated (environment), (6) which creates a local IS fatigue (history).

Support. (1) Some widely unsupported ISs are kept alive by top management. (2&3) To succeed, an idea champion needs to strive for support from the highest levels. Top management support helps to convince other stakeholders. Respondents notice that Flemish departments led by ministers of the same political party, support an IS more easily. (4) Recently Flemish ministers announced a fusion of several e-gov. divisions. (5&6) Local governments are tired of providing support to a whole bunch of Flemish G2G IS systems that request the same data over and over again.

4.2 Technological Agreements

Problem 4: Business Case Analysis

Problem Description. The initiation of ISs must be well-prepared, a business case needs to be made that describes the added value, challenges, strengths and weaknesses of an IS, reengineering possibilities and competitive systems in the environment.

Context. (1) The respondents claim that for a long time making a business case and reflection about the added value for local users was rather rare (culture). (2) Business process reengineering is sometimes skipped because of a lack of time or to prevent adaptions to complex legislation (regulators). Processes are digitized 'as is'.

Support. (1) The respondents believe that if you expect local users to share their data and provide support, they should gain some benefit in return. (2) A low effort expectancy would raise stakeholders' support for reengineering efforts.

Problem 5: IT Infrastructure

Problem Description. The IT infrastructure and processes of public organisations can be highly incompatible. These have to be aligned to share data.

Context. (1) In the past, local governments were regularly asked to re-enter data in Flemish ISs because of interoperability problems. Local governments now agree to use the 'Open Standard for Linked Governments', and the Flemish government can translate data to its own standards (technology). (2) Some interoperability problems remain as municipalities cooperate with 4 major vendors who fail to make their products interoperable. They are also path dependent to previous IT investments (history).

Support. (1&2) Stakeholders will more easily support a G2G IS if the effort to achieve interoperability is low. Stakeholder agreements about standards are hereby helpful.

Problem 6: Relationship with Developers

Problem Description. IS development requires developers, either in-house or external.

Context. (1) Because of the structural outsourcing of IT profiles, it is hard to knowledgeably audit public tenders. Sometimes a third party is hired to evaluate these tenders (history). (2) Development is often solely left to IT'ers because of a lack of the project manager's competence and a political disinterest (structure & politics).

Support. (1&2) The structural power imbalance between Flemish idea champions and developers needs to be restored. Currently, respondents have the feeling to buy a pig in a poke: *"If you are not a programmer, you cannot always estimate if a task really requires several days. You just have to believe what they say."*

Problem 7: Planning

Problem Description. Development by plans is advisable to prevent exceeding budget and time.

Context. (1) Flemish politicians want quick results and dare to set unrealistic deadlines (politics). (2) A project plan consists of design, implementation, testing and documenting. Respondents experience that testing is unpopular. But the agile approach, based on regular tests, gains importance with Flemish idea champions. Incremental modular steps are preferred in a G2G context. They believe that missing documents are a common problem. Money is rather spend on bug fixing (technological process).

Support. (1) Respondents believe it's better not to release an IS too soon, otherwise it will suffer from bugs and loose support. (2) The agile approach can be a means to involve stakeholders and make them reaffirm their support. But stakeholders do not always know what they want. Respondents think a visionary idea champion is required to prevent scope creep: *"The developer gets desperate. Do I have to break down what they asked me to build last month? Let stakeholders participate but make them realise that every question has a cost."*

Problem 8: Security

Problem Description. G2G ISs need to be secured from unauthorized access.

Context. (1) Security efforts are scattered; every local government has vulnerable servers (technological process). (2) Login procedures of Flemish IS are not aligned (technology).

Support. (1) The protection of a G2G IS is as strong as the weakest link. The respondents believe much could be gained if governmental stakeholders would combine efforts in a well-protected shared government cloud. (2) Flemish departments could agree upon login procedures (Table 1).

Table 1. Overview context constraints of Flemish G2G IS projects

Context	
Human factors	Technical process
• Idea champions suffer from a rather high burn out rate • Trust building skill important • Social pressure politicians/cabinet	• Agile development gaining ground vs unpopular testing • Missing documentation • Security efforts are scattered.
History	Structure
• Local fatigue about Flemish G2G IS • Hard to restore damaged trust • Path dependency on local vendors	• Structural shortage and outsourced IT profiles/hard to audit public tenders • Idea champion from lower segment of Flemish government hierarchy
Environment	Politics
• Culture: top down/no feedback on data usage/no business case/added value user forgotten • Customers: scope creep • Regulators: complex legislation • Technology: lack of interoperability standards/different login procedures	• No overall coordination G2G IS • Ineradicable deficient IS • Lack of coordination Flemish IS due to NPM reforms • Disinterest, development left to IT'ers • Unrealistic deadlines • Mandate organisation potential users

5 Discussion

Eight recurrent problems for Flemish G2G IS projects were uncovered: political-administrative agreements have to be made to prevent problems with (1) idea champion skills, (2) user involvement and (3) top management support. Agreements on technology and the technological process are required to prevent problems with (4) the business case analysis, (5) IT infrastructures, (6) developers, (7) planning and (8) security. Each problem on itself is not new, the factor research and project management literature list them too (for an overview see e.g. [15, 21]).

By conducting a needs and support-power analysis, it becomes clear that seemingly controllable problems have a much deeper roots, the resolution of which goes beyond project management. Even more, it seems that context and support elements of the different problems are interrelated:

Firstly, several elements point to a *tendency of Flemish idea champions to merely focus on Flemish interests*. In the past they forgot to look at the added value for local users. Local governments are just asked or legally obliged to provide data. They only experience the burden of gathering, importing or re-entering data but are not given the benefits. Due to a lack of feedback, it is not even clear to municipalities what the benefits for the Flemish government are. This contributes to a local G2G IS fatigue.

Secondly, several elements hint to a *lack of integration*. The principle of 'gathering data only once' is frequently violated as the actions of Flemish departments are not often aligned. No single party is responsible for G2G e-government and IS security efforts are scattered. The lack of business process reengineering or improvement efforts does not help integration of departmental actions any further.

Thirdly, several elements indicate a *political disinterest in information systems*. This results in outsourced IT skills, underestimated costs, unrealistic deadlines and the installation of indecisive idea champions. Success of Flemish idea champions depends to a significant extent on political choices. There appears to be a misfit between the agenda of Flemish politicians and interests of other G2G IS stakeholders.

Managers must tackle the recurrent problems at their roots, and it seems that mindsets are slowly changing:

Firstly more and more local governments refuse to share data even if this is legally obliged. The main reason is the lack of fulfilment of local self-interest which destroys support and always results in failure. A positive note is that a *new mind-set* comes to surface. Idea champions start to think and negotiate about potential win-wins and provide incentives to join an IS. We notice a shift from a rather top down project management style towards a more process management based style. Flemish idea champions become more aware that local governments are partners.

Secondly, two recent political decisions seem to point out *a rising awareness of politicians towards a lack of coordination*. Namely the introduction of an IT pool and the fusion of several e-government divisions. It is too soon to conclude whether these decisions will have the desired effect.

Thirdly the new Flemish government claimed the ambition in its coalition agreement to go 'radical digital' by 2020. It aims to do its transactions with local governments solely via digital channels. Whether this points to an *enlarged political interest in information systems*, has to be seen to be believed. Previous coalition agreements aimed digitization too, mostly without fulfilling the promises.

Our research focused on Flemish G2G IS projects but we notice that researchers in the Netherlands experience similar problems. The recent 'Elias-commission' study [29] on IS failure in the Netherlands also detects a lack of political ICT awareness, a poor estimation of IS costs, the problem of ineradicable insufficient ISs and that no single party seems responsible for G2G ISs (top management support). A lack of risk estimation, no business case nor attention for the added value of other stakeholders were mentioned too (business case analysis). The Dutch colleagues also experience a lack of IT experts in government (skilled idea champion). Like their Flemish colleagues, Dutch idea champions notice a power asymmetry with developers as well as a lack of documentation and the need to use standards (relationship with developers).

6 Conclusion and Future Research

In this paper we studied the roots of eight recurrent problems of Flemish G2G IS. We aimed to extend the body of knowledge by investigating how local contingencies and support-power relations affect the likelihood of failure of Flemish G2G IS projects. Based on our research we can confirm that the needs and support power analysis of Sauer provides additional insights for G2G IS management in Flanders. It adds a new piece to the complex IS failure puzzle by providing the insight that apparently controllable risks have deeper roots. A focus on Flemish interests by idea champions, political disinterest in technology and a lack of coordination discourage local stakeholders to support Flemish G2G IS projects. Like [10] we believe that future Flemish G2G IS idea champions should not only deal with potential problems but also pay attention to their context and support power interactions (process management).

By no means we attempted to map all context and support power issues. We targeted to enlarge the understanding of the eight Flemish reoccurring problems. It goes without saying that more context and support factors will be found when a specific G2G IS is studied on a micro level. Every IS innovation is slightly different, no two contexts can ever be exactly the same [12].

Future research might further explore similarities and differences in the G2G IS context of Flanders and the Netherlands and other countries or regions.

References

1. Arksey, H., Knight, P.: Interviewing for Social Scientists: An Introductory Resource with Examples. Sage Publications, London (1999)
2. Barzilai-Nahon, K., Scholl, H.J.: Siblings of a different kind: e-government and e-commerce. In: Wimmer, M.A., Chappelet, J.-L., Janssen, M., Scholl, H.J. (eds.) EGOV 2010. LNCS, vol. 6228, pp. 25–37. Springer, Heidelberg (2010)
3. Bekkers, V.: Flexible information infrastructures in Dutch e-government collaboration arrangements: experiences and policy implications. Gov. Inf. Q. **26**, 60–68 (2009)
4. Belanger, F., Tech, V.: Theorizing in information systems research: using focus groups. Australas. J. Inf. Syst. **17**(2), 109–135 (2012)

5. De Bruyn, H., ten Heuvelhof, E., in 't Veld, R.: Process Management. Why Project Management Fails in Complex Decision Making. Springer, Heidelberg (2010)
6. Dwivedi, Y.K., Wastell, D., Laumer, S., Zinner Henriksen, H., Myers, M.D., Bunker, D., Elbanna, A., Ravishankar, M.N., Srivastava S.C.: Research on IS failures and success: status update and future directions. In: Information System Frontiers. Springer, New York (2014)
7. Dwivedi, Y.K., Ravichandran, K., Williams, M.D., Miller, S., Lal, B., Antony, G.V., Kartik, M.: IS/IT project failures: a review of the extant literature for deriving a taxonomy of failure factors. In: Dwivedi, Y.K., Henriksen, H.Z., Wastell, D., De', R. (eds.) TDIT 2013. IFIP AICT, vol. 402, pp. 73–88. Springer, Heidelberg (2013)
8. Gil-Garcia, J.R., Pardo, T.A.: E-government success factors: mapping practical tools to theoretical foundations. Gov. Inf. Q. 22, 187–216 (2005)
9. Greenbaum, T.L.: Moderating Focus Groups, a Practical Guide for Group Facilitation, pp. 1–249. Sage Publications, London (2000)
10. Homburg, V., Bekkers, V.: Back-office of e-government, managing information domains as political economies. In: 35th Hawaii International Conference on System Sciences (2002)
11. Janssen, M., van der Voort, H., van Veenstra, A.F.: Failure of large transformation projects from the viewpoint of complex adaptive systems: management principles for dealing with project dynamics. Inf. Syst. Front. 17(1), 15–29 (2014)
12. Klein, H.K., Myers, M.D.: A set of principles for conducting and evaluating interpretive field studies in information studies. MIS Q. 23(1), 67–94 (1999)
13. Krueger, R., Casey, M.A.: Focus Groups, a Practical Guide for Applied Research. Sage Publications, London (2000)
14. Krueger, R.: Focus Groups: a Practical Guide for Applied Research. Sage Publications, London (1994)
15. McConnell, S.: Rapid Development. Taming Wild Software Schedules. Microsoft Press, USA (1996)
16. Munns, A.K., Bjeirmi, B.F.: The role of project management in achieving project success. Int. J. Project Manage. 14(2), 81–87 (1996)
17. Nelson, R.R.: Project retrospectives: evaluating project success, failure and everything in between. MIS Q. 4(3), 361–372 (2005)
18. Orlikowski, W.J.: The sociomateriality of organisational life: considering technology in management research. Camb. J. Econ. 34, 125–141 (2010)
19. Orlikowski, W.J., Robey, D.: Information technology and the structuring of organizations. Inf. Syst. Res. 2(2), 143–169 (1991)
20. Patanakul, P.: Managing large-scale IS/IT projects in the public sector: problems and causes leading to poor performance. J. High Technol. Manage. Res. 25(1), 21–35 (2014)
21. Petter, S., DeLone, W., McLean, E.R.: Information systems success: the quest for the independent variable. J. MIS 29(4), 7–61 (2013)
22. Sauer, C.: Why IS Fail: A Case Study Approach. Alfred Waller Publishers, Suffolk (1993)
23. Sauer, C., Southon, G., Dampney, C.N.G: Fit, failure and the house of horrors: toward a configuration theory of is project failure. In: Eighteenth International Conference on Information systems, pp. 349–366 (1997)
24. Sauer, C., Reich, B.H.: Rethinking IT project management: evidence of a new mindset and its implications. Int. J. Project Manage. 27, 182–193 (2009)
25. Scholl, H.J., Kubicek, H., Cimander, R., Klischewski, R.: Process integration, information sharing, and system interoperation in government: a comparative case analysis. Gov. Inf. Q. 29(3), 313–323 (2012)

26. Shah, S., Khan, A.Z., Khalil, M.S.: Project management practices in e-government projects: a case study of electronic government directorate (EGD) in Pakistan. Int. J. Bus. Soc. Sci. 2(7), 235–243 (2011)
27. Southon, G., Sauer, S., Dampney, K.: Lessons from a failed information systems initiative: issues for complex organisations. Int. J. Med. Inform. 55, 33–46 (1999)
28. Srivastava, S.C.: Is e-government providing the promised returns? A value framework for assessing e-government impact. Transforming Gov. People Process Policy 5(2), 107–113 (2011)
29. Tweede kamer der Staten Generaal: Parlementair onderzoek naar ICT-projecten bij de overheid, Eindrapport vergaderjaar 2014–2015, 33 326, nr. 5, pp. 1–219 (2014)
30. Volkoff, O., Strong, D.M.: Critical realism and affordances: theorizing it-associated organizational change process. MIS Q. 37(3), 819–834 (2013)
31. Weerakkody, V., Baire, S., Choudrie, J.: E-government: the need for effective process management in the public sector. In: 39th HICCS, pp. 1–10 (2006)
32. Winter, M., Smith, S., Morris, P., Cicmil, S.: Directions for future research in project management. Int. J. Project Manage. 24, 638–649 (2006)
33. Yeo, K.T.: Critical failure factors in information system projects. Int. J. Project Manage. 20, 241–246 (2002)
34. Zheng, L., Yang, T.M., Pardo, T., Yang, Y.: Understanding the "boundary" in information sharing and integration. In: 42nd HICCS, pp. 1–10 (2009)

Makers and Shapers or Users and Choosers Participatory Practices in Digitalization of Public Sector

Katarina L. Gidlund[✉]

Department of Information and Communication Systems,
Mid Sweden University, 85170 Sundsvall, Sweden
katarina.lindblad-gidlund@miun.se

Abstract. The idea that public e-services are better off being designed with the potential users' needs in focus is today an almost unquestioned truth (user centered design maybe being the most frequent methodological toolbox). The idea that they are even better off being designed with the potential users is an almost equally established understanding (where participatory design could be claimed to be the most prominent methodology). However, in this paper the overall claim is that by a combination of updated design thinking, and development and participatory studies from outside the digital design discipline, a deepened and more nuanced understanding of participatory practices is presented. This is shown by an exploratory study on the design process of a public e-service to make the city accessible for its citizens and visiting tourists.

Keywords: Public e-services · Critical design · Participatory practices · Exploratory study

1 Introduction

For long we have argued for user involvement in IT design, already in 1984 Ives and Olson [1] made a literature review touching upon user involvement and indicators of system success, and since then many others have followed [2–4], among others. This knowledge has spread and merged with knowledge on public administration development and different development strategies of enhanced service delivery for citizens. Moreover, areas such as eParticipation [5, 6] and demand driven development of public e-services surface and sometimes blurs the intersections between democratic participation, customer focus and IS design [7]. The idea of putting the user/citizen/customer in the center seems to be easily shared on a narrative level, however, what it might implicate in practice in the context of public sector (in terms of complexities and methods) is still often left out of the story [7]. What is repeated is the story of a positive correlation between user involvement and quality, such as for example in one of the central policy documents of digitalization of public sector in Europe; The European eGovernment Action Plan 2011–2015 [8]. In the Action plan it is stressed that the imperative of "involving users actively in design and production of eGovernment services" [8: 7] and throughout the document the importance of a user presence is repeated over and over again in different shapes: involvement, empowerment, collaboration, flexible and

© IFIP International Federation for Information Processing 2015
E. Tambouris et al. (Eds.): EGOV 2015, LNCS 9248, pp. 222–232, 2015.
DOI: 10.1007/978-3-319-22479-4_17

personalized, user satisfaction etc. From reasoning it is understood that user participation is perceived as fundamental. The line of thought is expressed as a strong need to "move towards a more open model of design, production and delivery of online services, taking advantage of the possibility offered by collaboration between citizens, entrepreneurs and civil society" [8: 3].

And of course, as this is in line with a lot of IT design research and practice it is both welcomed and appreciated by the community. However, as always when things seems to be going in what we perceive to be in the right direction and we easily can incorporate them in our established thinking there is an extra need for a nuanced and careful reflection; How come this happens now? Are there mechanisms that support this and what are then these mechanisms? And, is this only talk or is it supported in practice? With resources, methods, tools and deepened understanding of what is required in practice in order to not only let it be lip service?

All the questions above are in some way or another guiding the objective of this paper i.e. to dig deeper into the idea of participatory practices and do so with a critical approach. But the articulated aim is to challenge the established mechanisms of participatory approaches to design of public e-services, theoretically by an analytical framework, and in practice by an exploratory study.

The paper is structured as follows; first there is a section contextualizing participation in the design of public e-service by a brief analysis of how the idea is framed in six central policy documents on European and national level. Second, the theoretical framework of a combination of updated design thinking and development and participatory studies from outside the digital design discipline is put forward and argued for as missing pieces for understanding the intersections between democratic participatory ideals, market oriented target group ideals and user centered design orientations. Third, the set up of the exploratory study is presented in line with methodological reflections and the operationalization of the analytical framework. Next, the results of the study (performed in a Swedish municipality) is presented and discussed, followed by concluding remarks and thoughts of contributions.

2 Users, Citizens or Customers – Participatory Practices in Digitalization of Public Sector

As mentioned in the introduction the idea of an active participant in the development of information technology in general is far from new in the IS discipline [1–4] and the idea of an active participant in the development of public e-services is also rather well established in terms of research volume with for example a yearly international conference devoted especially to eParticipation issues and a vast amount of papers written with eParticipation as a key word [5, 6]. What is in focus here is therefore not to argue for, show evidence of, or analyze this area of research. Instead this section will be devoted to make a brief analysis of how this idea shows itself in crucial policy documents in Europe and the national case of Sweden, since the empirical case that will follow takes place in that context. The objective of this section is therefore to underpin and illustrate the statement that there is in fact an enhanced focus on user involvement in public sector digitalization, and also briefly show how it is framed.

Therefore, six texts are chosen, two on a European level and four Swedish policy documents (strategies and action plans) within eGovernment and digitalization of public sector. The texts included (see Table 1 below) are chosen because they are the 'active' policy documents at the time this paper is written and a very simple analysis is made in two steps. First, a search for instances of 'user' and 'citizen' in the document is made, secondly these instances are read through and a full sentence including either 'user' or 'citizen' is chosen to represent the kernel of how the document are arguing for participatory practices.

Table 1. Participation in eGovernment policy documents and digital agendas

Document	No. of instances	Bottom line
The European eGovernment Action Plan 2011-2015 SEC(2010) 1539 final, (Communication from the commission to the European Parliament, the council, the European economic and social committee and the committee of the regions)	Users (15) Citizens (35) Customers (0)	"Public services can gain in efficiency and users in satisfaction by meeting the expectations of users better and being designed around their needs and in collaboration with them whenever possible." (p. 16)
A Digital Agenda for Europe COM(2010)245 final, (Communication from the commission to the European Parliament, the council, the European economic and social committee and the committee of the regions)	Users (16) Citizens (31) Customers (6)	"European governments are committed to making user-centric, personalized, multi-platform eGovernment services a widespread reality by 2015." (p. 31)
A Strategy for public agencies' work on eGovernment (SOU 2009:86), Betänkande av E-delegationen, Stockholm 2009	Users (0) Citizens (52) Customers (2)	"In such a development citizens and entrepreneurs are not only seen as the "taxpayer" or "customers" but as competent citizens - in the same sense as employees or co-producers" (p. 37) "As such, the strategy lays the foundation for a demands-driven e-government." (p. 38)
As Easy as Possible for as Many as Possible / Så enkelt som möjligt för så många som möjligt(SOU 2010:62)	Users (94) Citizen (69) Customers (148)	E-governance will help to facilitate contact between government and citizens and to be characterized by accessibility and usability.
A Digital Agenda in the Service of Man / En digital agenda i människans tjänst (SOU 2014:13)	Users (28) Citizens (11) Customers (1)	The assessment of the Digital Agenda is that there are good conditions for authors, suppliers of services and materials and end users to take advantage of digitization.
With the citizen in the centre / Med medborgaren i centrum	Users (5) Citizens (20) Customers (1)	"We must put the citizen at the high seat, and together become better at meeting their needs based on the person's own circumstances. I [the IT-minister] want together with you to build a public service that puts the citizen's needs and desires at the center."

The above simple illustration has no intentions of being a deep and discursive analysis; it is only put forward to prove the case that the logic is repeated in similar ways in central documents. Still, it is possible to interpret the overall logic as: the citizens would use the e-services if they could be part of their creation and the underlying reason for the existence of e-services (and government IT spending on the creation of them) is articulated as "[public e-services] help the public sector develop innovative ways of delivering its services to citizens while unleashing efficiencies and driving down costs" [8, p. 3]. The solution is as such expressed as making the development of public e-services demand driven, based on the thought of ensuring the usage by letting the users-to-be to state what services they want, need and will use (even though these three elements not always corresponds). Moreover, it is stated that "eGovernment, which is intended to simplify contacts with citizens and companies, should always be conducted on the basis of user needs and benefits..." [23, p. 6]. The statement in the remit is regarded as one such instance (among many) where demand driven development is emphasized. Related to this is also a fear that citizens do not use the e-services enough; "the majority of EU citizens are reluctant to use them [the public e-services]" [8, p. 3]. Thus, that the expected savings will not be realized and it is supposed, that if the citizens are somehow involved in the development of these services, they will also be more inclined to use them. And the importance of a user presence is repeated over and over again in different shapes: involvement, empowerment, collaboration, flexible and personalized, user satisfaction etc. [8].

There is however little agreement on what this involvement in the development of public e-services is and on how it will come about (the logic as such leaves a lot of room for further interpretations in the social practices the documents are to be realized in). It seems as if it is wanted by all, but no one knows exactly what it is, there are very few (if any) conceptual analyses resting on a critical stance analyzing how this notion is translated in practical settings (leaving a gap in between for prac-titioners to solve) [9]. This is of course part of the nature of policy documents, to be enacted and translated in their contextual settings [10]. Nevertheless, a number of actors, such as director generals, systems designers and various employees in public sector organizations, are about to realize the thought on different levels and the field of eGovernment research could contribute to their practices by deconstructing the idea and link it to practical undertakings.

As Gidlund [7] and Sefyrin et al. [11] have shown the question of who participates in participatory practices such as demands driven development, and on what grounds, determines much of the legitimacy for these projects in the wider democratic system. In the Swedish guidelines for demands driven development [12], it is stated that "A difficult question is how to find users who are representative for a target group and whose demands and wishes covers the demands of the whole target group. Additionally asking everybody is too costly. The point of departure should be that it is always better to have asked 'some' than not to have asked at all. One does not get a comprehensive image of the demands, but at least some general demands can be found" [12: 20]. Statements as the ones above shows that there is a need for further analysis on in what way the partic-ipation takes place and in the next section a combination of updated design knowledge and development and participatory studies is put forward as a rewarding analytical framework to address what is done today and what could be done tomorrow. Some things we are doing today are of course important to keep, while others are equally important to question and further develop if taking the idea of participation seriously.

3   Analytical Toolkit – Prepositions and Roles

In a recent article Sanders and Stappers [13] draws a picture of the design discipline from 1984 to 2044 (including user-centered design, participatory design, co-creation and several others), addressing both the what-question (results of designing), the who-question (the roles and professions), and the why-question (the values that guide design decisions). According to Sanders and Stappers all three questions could be illustrated by three phases. In 1984 we designed products (what), for consumers (who) guided by sales in marketplace (why). In 2014 we design interaction person-product (what), with users (who) to create sales and long-term relations (why). Their forecast is that in 2044 we will design multiple relations between people, products, services and infrastructures (what), by people (who) for multiple values not reducible to a single dimension (why). This of course raises questions on design thinking and design knowledge and the need for a new set of skills for digital designers. In this paper their use of three different prepositions (for, with and by) are used to shed some light on the ideas of participatory practices in the digitalization of public sector; where one dimension is their use of consumer, user and people (in relation to the use of citizen, consumer and user in the policy texts listed above) and the other dimension is the power position implied by the different terminology. A consumer chooses a certain product among other products, a user is involved in a certain degree in the design of the product whereas design by people implies that it is them themselves that makes and shapes the result of designing.

A similar discussion is put forward in a quite different setting, that of development and participatory studies, by Cornwall and Gaventa [14] and Cornwall [15] talking about "from users and choosers to makers and shapers". Even though development and partic-ipatory studies are not especially focused on digital de-sign but on societal development in general and in most often in development region and countries [16] it holds several interesting reflections due to a longer time span of reflection. In the beginning, around 1940's and 1950s development theory was mostly influence by colonial efforts and participation was seen as an obligation of citizenship, in 1960s and 1970s it changed into post-colonial and emancipator efforts stressing participation as both a right and obligation, whereas in the 1980s a focus on more populist efforts where the idea of participation had a more project-oriented logic (development professionals and agencies and some local participants), and finally, late 1990s to present a focus on participatory governance giving that participation is primarily seen as a right (for a more thorough description see Hickey and Mohan [16]). What Cornwall and Gaventa [14] then address is what they talk about as a more actor-oriented approach, going beyond "users and choosers" and instead introduce the idea of "makers and shapers". Makers and shapers are not only practicing their rights but also social responsibilities exercised through self-action [14]. By repositioning participation "to encompass the multiple dimensions of citizenship – including a focus on agency based on self-action and self-identity, as well as demands for accountability amongst actors" [14: 59]. According to Cornwall and Gaventa, the role and capacity of civil society is growing resulting in an increasing pressure for democratization and new forms of citizen-state interaction.

Cornwall presents four different modes of participation; (1) functional, (2) instrumental, (3) consultative and (4) transformative giving that participants are viewed as; (1) objects, (2) instruments, (3) actors and (4) agents. These different modes of participation hold different motives for inviting and involving participants; (1) to secure compliance, minimize dissent and lend legitimacy, (2) to make projects or interventions run more efficiently, by enlisting contributions and delegating responsibilities, (3) to get in tune with public views and values, to garner good ideas, to diffuse opposition, to enhance responsiveness, and (4) to build political capabilities, critical consciousness and confidence, to enable to demand rights, to enhance accountability.

In this paper it is claimed that these two different disciplines have touched up-on a similar trend that is very topical for the area of participatory practices in digitalization of public sector; the difference between for/with/by and choose and use/make and shape i.e. the difference in between active claims-making critical agents and rather passive customers choosing in between different off-shelf products. The overall claim here is that a similar updating is needed in the realm of participatory practices in eGovernment, not only in practice but conceptually and theoretically. And the above will serve as a lens in order to analyze this with the help of an explorative case. The shift in prepositions (for, with and by) is supported by the shift of roles (users and chooser or makers and shapers) and it also informs design actions in practice. To open up the design space (from functional to transformative) implies that it is important to not narrow the "what" before or without, the "who". The values that guide design decisions are not to be decided by anyone else than the people who will use what will be designed. In order to touch upon these issues the explorative case is presented together with some critical design notions that have been guiding the performance.

4   The Explorative Case – Methodological Reflections

In recapitulating the dimensions of the explorative study the first one is based on the analytical toolkit above which guided the objective and purpose of the study. But yet another dimension is added, not as a theoretical or analytical tool, but as a practical influence in order to open up the design space in the specific situation of the explorative work shop i.e. critical design. Before describing some of the underpinnings of critical design it is then possible to say that they explorative study, based on the analytical reasoning above, tried to challenge:

- the what
- the who
- the why

However, according to the idea of critical design put forward by Dunne [18] it is crucial to address the ideological and norm reproducing elements of what, who and why which could be described as "the how". To be able to touch upon how the ideological and norm reproducing elements work Dunne claims that designing starts when the technological artifacts are linked to a certain discourse (guiding values). This gives that the ideological nature of how our everyday social and cultural experiences are mediated by digital artifacts are in focus. This in order to deconstruct or dematerialize what is proposed, but also to increase the possible interpretations in order to give room for creativity and new approaches, i.e. not delaying the possibility of new translations. If not, we might be "superimposing the known and comfortable into the new and alien" [18: 17].

It is therefore essential to create opportunities for 'defamiliarizing' and 'making strange' what is linked to the "ideological dimension of everyday technologies" [18: 2]. To defamiliarize is to provoke, making ambiguous, and making strange in order to discuss hidden social meanings. Defamiliarizing could then be used as a methodology to break free of structures, in line with rethinking the assumptions that underlie technology [19, 20]. Making the constructs (discourses) strange provides the opportunity to actively reflect on existing politics and culture, and develop new alternatives for design [21] i.e. to remove objects from the automatism of perception; "it seeks to explore the ways in which our categories of thought reduce our freedom by occluding recognition of what could be" [22: xviii]. Questioning the naturalized assumptions inherent in the design opens up design spaces, and is a critical endeavor for two reasons: it (i) questions the taken for grantedness and (ii) reveals possibilities for transformative redefinition. And to make the familiar strange Dunne proposes the idea of gentle provocation [18], i.e. a way of provoking complex and meaningful reflection. To gently provoke, disturb and make uneasy means to gently make the line of thought more reflective, to struggle with uneasiness. Therefore, what is challenged by the explorative case study is also:

- the how

The four challenges (what, who, why, how) are then used to intentionally provoke and create a situation where these four issues could be addressed in an alternative manner. The results of the intervention are then discussed as a back-drop to gain a deeper understanding of, and challenge the existing mechanisms of, participatory practices in the digitalization of public sector.

4.1 A Collaborative Workshop on Making the Digital Story of a Town

The empirical material is multi-facetted and rich and is based on a series of explorative initiatives related to making the digital story of a town. The back-ground is digitalization in general and accessibility in specific and concerns a medium-sized town in Sweden trying to develop a digitally interactive story targeted both to the town's inhabitants and tourists. When trying to complement printed information and marketing material with what they perceive as modern tools, a discussion on digitalization surfaced. During that discussion a contact with the regional university were established and started as an open-ended discussion between a representative from the municipality and two representatives from the university. The municipal representative was the secretary of cultural affairs at the municipal cultural center (called Kulturmagasinet) and the representatives from the university were two researchers, one from sociology and one from informatics, working within a research group of critical studies of digital technology and societal change.

The project name became 'Technology in becoming' and the point of departure were a shared apprehension that digitalization could be more than just making the existing databases, the established and already at hand stories of the town, accessible in digital form. The aim of the co-work was formulated as; - the digital stories could be more than only doing what is already done. In the town there were already stories made, a lot of material (exhibitions, city walks, interactive performances during open city days and traditional marketing and information material) existed based on established and well known stories of the town. Famous historical inhabitants, well known historical events and historical information about buildings etc. were all part of that. The objective then became to challenge, provoke and co-construct new stories.

The above then led to several steps, the first meeting (attended by the secretary of cultural affairs and the two researchers) circled around if, and if so, how, it was possible to re-create the established stories, and be more inclusive to other stories than the established ones, during the digitalization. And as a result of that discussion the secretary of cultural affairs invited two artists to the discussions as experts on friction and change of perspectives, and also managed to attract internal funding for paying for their participation.

The next step was then to continue the discussion of 'technology in becoming' in the larger group (the initial three participants and the added two artists) and develop a work form in order to, in a more inclusive and alternative way, create the stories that were to be digitalized. After presenting the ideas in the larger groups the two artists continued the discussion separately from an artistic point of view and developed a first suggestion of a work form. There after the larger group met again and discussed the artists' suggestions and collectively decided upon a work flow.

The final idea was to make a fully open event in the cultural center; it was to be both announced in the local newspaper and spread through several mail lists and held in a very architecturally creative studio at the cultural center. The day was chosen to create the opportunity for as many as possible to be able to participate and was therefore decided to be on a Sunday between 14 and 16 pm. In the studio there was a table with a printed three by three meters large map of the town in color and a lot of adhesive dots and stars in a multitude of colors (see picture 1 below) related to the questions the artists were to ask the participants.

The two hours were structured as below:

- 5 min very short introduction (important to not become too long and steer the associations)/by the research leader
- 5 min equally short introduction of some of the work done by the university on mobile applications and visualization (in the same way important not to become too long and give the workshop a technology centered focus)/an invited researcher in computer science
- 5 min short introduction of the project team
- Straight after the above the workshop started with the first quick introductory exercise. The artists asked the participants (also the researchers, the secretary of the cultural affair, and the artists participated) to mark eight places on the map (a place in town that I would show children/show friends from another country/show the prime minister/a forbidden place for children/a place where I get ideas/a very ugly place/a place I avoid/a place dogs like) (20 min)
- A short break and a cup of coffee

– The second exercise. The artists asked the participants to mark four places (the most beautiful place in town, the darkest place in town, the most equal place in town, the hottest place in town). Important to note is that the questions were deliberately a bit fuzzy (20 min)
– The third exercise. The artists asked the participants to mark "the most memorable place in town" (15 min)
– Discussion and reflections

The above exercise gave a map (for one fraction of the map see picture 2 below) with a lot of different dots and stars on the giant map in the center of the studio which the participants could reflect upon, ask each other about, try to understand and also discuss as they were easily accessible and very illustrative. The tangibility of the map in the room with all the markings and the participants moving around in the room bumping in to each other, trying to both put their dots on the map and see where others put their dots, created a movement and atmosphere in the room that encouraged discussion.

5   Results and Analysis – Disrupting Established Stories

There are several interesting reflections made during the six months long project and the final workshop. First of all, it is hard to get funding for these kind of risk taking, nonprofit work with a norm critical approach which needs actors that holds a strong belief that it is important to address these issues even though they are not instantly linked to the step of becoming a realized product. They also need to be very creative to find the small resources that are available. Second, this gives that the project group had to be organically formed, and not to be decided upon from the beginning. The adding of the two artists was central to the final results and that was not at all the initial understanding in the first discussions. But during the discussion the need for competence in disruptive practices surfaced as highly important. Third, the inclusive and open invitation to the de-sign activity (regarding place and time) were crucial. The place is a very well-known place and has also been ranked as "the most open and inclusive place" for a multitude of citizens. The choice of time, a day of week and a time at day when most people could participate without losing income, also showed to be important in order to get a diverse group of participants. Finally, the disruptive stories created by the artists showed to be very useful in order to create provocation, reflection and discussion and get hold of stories outside of the established stories of importance in the already existing archival artifacts.

All the above created could be linked to the four challenges the analytical framework touch upon: the what, the who, the why and the how. In participatory practices 'the what' is very often already decided upon, in this exploratory case it was important to keep 'the what' an as open question as possible, throughout the initial project meetings and to the end with the final workshop. And 'the who' is maybe one of the most interesting questions during this project, to be able to stay in ignorance of who will attend is challenging for several reasons. To stand there at the day of the workshop without any knowledge about who the participants will be was demanding. The project team was a bit nervous and tried to comfort each other that morning and it was important to have the ability to share the responsibility in between the professions and competencies (IS-researcher, researcher in sociology, secretary of cultural affairs, and artistic skills). This also influenced 'the why', it was discussed together with the different participants and there were room for translations and re-translations regarding why it could be of importance to open up a discussion of what story that should be told about the town. Finally, concerning 'the how', as shown by the discussion above, to choose these kinds of work forms requires courage and nerves to deal with insecurities- which also proves why we often chose not to. To be as iterative and open as possible while also consciously adding provocations forces us to challenge our own professional positions and legitimacy. The fact that, as researchers and project leaders to some extent, attend the exploratory workshop with on equal terms and use private and personal experiences while trying to add to the co-constructed map and story really brought us out of our comfort zone.

6   Conclusions and Contributions

The overall conclusion of the case discussed in this paper is that the idea of participatory practices in the digitalization of public sector is still an open question from many perspectives. The four challenges used in this paper highlight some of these and especially the perception of 'participation'. To use development and participatory studies in combination with up-dated design thinking provided tools to analyze 'participation' in more detail and also repositioned the idea of participatory subjects. Throughout the empirical case the framework provided a sensibility to the boundaries and legitimacy of who were to make and shape and who were to use and choose and what it actually means to transmit that power to an unknown crowd of participants. The four questions, the what, the who, the why and the how, proved to be practical and useful and it is argued here that they could be part of a new era of design of public e-services. However demanding, they, used to the fullest or not, address aspects of participation that needs to be addressed to avoid empty and almost dishonest promises of participation that in the end fosters frustration and disappointment that could backfire on very well intended digitalization processes. The argument here is not that every digitalization project should be designed as the one above, rather than an awareness of these aspects creates a better take-off in communicating the initiatives in a more truthful manner.

References

1. Ives, B., Olson, M.: H.: User involvement and MIS success: a review of research. Manage. Sci. **30**(5), 585–603 (1984)
2. Kappelman, L.A., McLean, E.R.: The respective roles of user participation and user involvement in information system implementation success. In: Proceedings, Twelfth International Conference on Information Systems, New York, pp. 339–349 (1991)
3. Hartwick, J., Barki, H.: Explaining the role of user participation in information system use. Manage. Sci. **40**(4), 440–465 (1994)
4. Iivari, J., Igbaria, M.: Determinants of user participation: a finnish survey. Behav. Inf. Technol. **16**(2), 111–121 (1997)

5. Sæbø, Ø., Rose, J., Flak, L.S.: The shape of eParticipation: characterizing an emerging research area. Gov. Inf. Q. **25**(3), 400–428 (2008)
6. Sanford, C., Rose, J.: Characterizing eParticipation. Int. J. Inf. Manage. **27**(6), 406–421 (2007)
7. Gidlund, K.L.: 'Demand driven development of public e-services'. In: Scholl, H.J., Janssen, M., Wimmer, M.A., Moe, C.E., Flak, L.S. (eds.) EGOV 2012. LNCS, vol. 7443, pp. 66–77. Springer, Heidelberg (2012)
8. The European eGovernment Action Plan 2011–2015, Harnessing ICT to promote smart, sustainable and innovative Government, SEC(2010) 1539 final, Brussels, 15.12.2010, COM(2010) 743 final
9. Gidlund, K.L.: One for all, all for one – performing citizen driven development of public e-services. In: Tambouris, E., Macintosh, A., de Bruijn, H. (eds.) ePart 2011. LNCS, vol. 6847, pp. 240–251. Springer, Heidelberg (2011)
10. Giritli-Nygren, K., Lindblad-Gidlund, K.: Leaders as mediators of global megatrends: a diagnostic framework. Int. J. Electron. Gov. Res. (IJEGR) **5**(4), 28–42 (2009)
11. Sefyrin, J., Gidlund, K.L., Öberg, K.D., Ekelin, A.: Representational practices in demands driven development of public sector. In: Wimmer, M.A., Janssen, M., Scholl, H.J. (eds.) EGOV 2013. LNCS, vol. 8074, pp. 200–211. Springer, Heidelberg (2013)
12. Vägledning för behovsdriven Utveckling, Vägledning från E-delegationen, version 1.0
13. Sanders, E.B.N., Stappers, P.J.: Co-creation and the new landscapes of design. Co-design **4**(1), 5–18 (2008)
14. Cornwall, A., Gaventa, J.: From user and chooser to maker and shaper: repositioning participation in social policy. IDS working paper, no. 127, 34 p. Institute of Development Studies, Brighton (2001)
15. Cornwall, A.: Whose voices? Whose choices? Reflections on gender and participatory development. World Dev. **31**(8), 1325–1342 (2003)
16. Hickey, S., Mohan, G. (eds.): Participation-From Tyranny to Transformation? Exploring New Approaches to Participation in Development. Zed books, London (2004)
17. Akrich, M.: The description of technical objects. In: Shaping Technology/Building Society, pp. 205–224. MIT Press, Cambridge (1992)
18. Dunne, A.: Hertzian Tales: Electronic Products, Aesthetic Experience, and Critical Design. MIT press, Cambridge (2005)
19. Agre, P.: Toward a critical technical practice: lessons learned in trying to reform AI. In: Bridging the Great Divide: Social Science, Technical Systems, and Cooperative Work, pp. 131–157. Erlbaum, Mahwah (1997)
20. Dunne, A., Raby, F.: Design Noir: The Secret Life of Electronic Objects. Springer, London (2001)
21. Bell, G., Blythe, M., Sengers, P.: Making by making strange: defamiliarition and the design of domestic technologies. ACM Trans. Comput. Hum. Interact. (TOCHI) **12**(2), 149–173 (2005)
22. Calhoun, C.: Critical Social Theory: Culture, History, and the Challenge of Difference. Wiley, New York (1995)
23. Strategy for the government agencies work on eGovernment, Summary of SOU, p. 86 (2009)

Why Realization Mismatches Expectations of e-Government Project Benefits? Towards Benefit Realization Planning

Dian Balta[1(✉)], Vanessa Greger[2], Petra Wolf[1], and Helmut Krcmar[2]

[1] Fortiss – An-Institut der TU München, Munich, Germany
{balta,wolf}@fortiss.org
[2] TU München, Munich, Germany
{vanessa.greger,helmut.krcmar}@tum.de

Abstract. The effective management of stakeholders' benefits is crucial for the success of e-government projects. This success can be expressed as the match between realized project benefits and their anticipation by stakeholders according to their expectations. Unfortunately, recent studies report that there is often a mismatch between realized and expected benefits. Hence, understanding the reason for this mismatch would be of value for theory and practice. Guided by stakeholder and resource dependency theory, we aim at explaining this mismatch. Therefore, benefit aspects to be considered during realization planning are derived from literature. Based on these aspects, we interpret four types of benefits in a study of an e-government project in a German public administration: project guiding, endangered, questioned and out-of-focus benefits. We suggest that a mismatch between realized and expected benefits results from issues concerning particular benefit types and provide conjectures for effective management in practice.

Keywords: Benefits management · Benefit realization planning · Benefit realization typology · Stakeholder management

1 Introduction

In order to achieve project success, management traditionally focuses on reaching the project goals by deciding upon the aspects time, budget and quality. However, past research has recognized a number of limitations of this decision approach [1], since the realization of project benefits is often neglected [2, 3]. This is especially the case in the context of information systems (IS), as - irrespective of the perceived project success according to the level reached of each of the three aspects - many IS projects fail to realize expected benefits [4, 5]. Particularly in the e-government domain, this is an important issue, since perceived project success depends upon the involvement of numerous stakeholders [6] who anticipate divergent benefits.

© IFIP International Federation for Information Processing 2015
E. Tambouris et al. (Eds.): EGOV 2015, LNCS 9248, pp. 233–245, 2015.
DOI: 10.1007/978-3-319-22479-4_18

Benefits management offers a number of methods for achieving anticipated project benefits [7]. A benefit is understood as "an advantage on behalf of a particular stakeholder or group of stakeholders" and its management as "(t)he process of organizing and managing such that the potential benefits arising from the use of IS/IT are actually realized" [5]. Especially the focus on stakeholders can be considered superior to traditional approaches to project management, as examples of benefits management show in the e-government practice [8–10].

Despite the intensive development of benefits management in both academia and practice[1] [8, 9, 11–13], planning the realization of benefits expected by project stakeholders is still an existing research gap [14]. This research gap can be described as a missing link between the identification of stakeholders' benefits and the corresponding benefit realization planning towards successful projects [5, 12, 15]. For example regarding an e-government project, project sponsors (e.g. a governance board) define and prioritize a set of rather generic benefits that have to be planned and realized by a project management team, taking inadequately the perspective of stakeholders (e.g. different groups of citizens and private organizations) and their expectations into account. Consequently, they consider only to a rather limited extent the perspective of these stakeholders in terms of benefit's importance.

In order to close this research gap, we derive a set of aspects for categorizing benefits and synthesize a benefit typology for realization planning. Therefore, we take into account (i) the **perspective of stakeholders** who anticipate project benefits and serve as a basis for identification of **expected benefits** and (ii) the **perspective of the project team** (sponsors, management, developers) responsible for the **realized benefits**. In consideration of both perspectives, we derive aspects from literature and interpret different types of benefits based on a case study of an e-government project in a German public administration. Based on the overall objective to provide an answer for the mismatch between realized and expected benefits of e-government projects, we address the following research questions (RQ):

- RQ1: What aspects should be considered as a basis of the realization planning of e-government project benefits?
- RQ2: What are managerial implications for benefit realization planning in e-government projects?

The remainder of this paper is structured as follows. First, a theoretical framework for the analysis of aspects is derived from literature. Next, findings of the case study are presented. Based on these findings, we synthesize a benefit typology for realization planning and discuss this typology. Finally, the paper concludes with implications to theory and practice and an outline of future research.

---

[1] E.g. in practice present in project management methodologies such as PMBoK, PRINCE2, etc.

2 Theoretical Framework

2.1 Perspective of the Stakeholders of an e-Government Project

An approach to tackle the value of an e-government project is to study the distribution of its benefits, i.e. to observe the stakeholder-based value distribution [16]. Therefore, stakeholders need to be managed [17]. Stakeholders are defined as "any group or individual who can affect or is affected by the achievement of the organization's objectives" [17]. Stakeholder activities need to be considered [17] and the relationships between stakeholders need to be understood by managers [18]. Consequently, stakeholder theory develops an understanding of the types of stakeholder influence and corresponding organization's responses towards project success, since stakeholders have **expectations** regarding the benefits of an e-government project.

We focus on the concept of stakeholder salience [19]. This concept combines the stakeholder definition with the relevance of the involved stakeholders based on the attributes power, legitimacy and urgency. The aim is explaining stakeholder salience, i.e. who and what should count and managers should pay attention to [19]. Consequently, project managers should focus on benefits perceived by stakeholders in conjunction with their salience. Thus, the concept of stakeholder salience is of high importance for the determination of benefits.

Besides, stakeholders can influence each other through various interactions. These interactions are based on the exchange of resources like budget or information. In order to obtain a deeper understanding of this stakeholder influence and corresponding organization's actions, we recognize the importance of resource dependencies [20]. A resource dependency is defined as "the product of the importance of a given input or output to the organization and the extent to which it is controlled by [...]" stakeholders. It measures the degree to which stakeholders need to be considered due to their perceived importance for project success [20]. For example, in the context of an e-government project, the project team within the public administration interacts with multiple (internal and external) stakeholders and creates a number of dependencies. As a consequence, the public administration influences its stakeholders and vice versa. Moreover, dependencies might exist between stakeholders. This leads to a network of dependencies, which should be considered when studying the distribution of stakeholder value [21].

Frooman [23] argues that stakeholders can influence an organization through their resource relationships with it. Thus, their influence results not only from their attributes, but also from power as attribute of their dependencies, i.e. a dependency results from the control over a resource [20]. Consequently, stakeholder salience and resource dependencies are aspects of the **stakeholder influence** on an e-government project. Moreover, stakeholders have a particular interest in a benefit according to their expectations. Thus, their interest should be considered as well when analyzing stakeholder influence regarding a particular benefit (cf. Table 1).

Table 1. The concept of stakeholder influence and its dimensions

Concept	Dimensions (with examples and corresponding sources)
Stake-holder influence	• Interest (e.g. claim, concern, objective, issue, problem, expectation, attitude, impact of interest, perceived importance, threat potential) [22–29] • Resource dependency (e.g. resource availability, coalition, power in relationship, network position, action in a particular process) [23, 30–32] • Salience (e.g. power, urgency, manager/stakeholder perspective) [19, 26, 33]

2.2 Perspective of the Project Team of an e-Government Project

From a project team perspective, the distribution of benefits among stakeholders considers the management of these benefits, i.e. the organizing and guiding of benefits towards their effective **realization**. In particular, benefits management involves a five step cyclic process [4, 5]: (i) benefit identification and classification (with intense stakeholder involvement), (ii) benefit realization planning, (iii) execution of the benefit realization plan, (iv) benefit realization evaluation and (v) identification of further benefits.

Although our focus is put on the first two steps, we acknowledge that benefit realization depends upon the availability of resources assigned to a project. Hence resource dependencies have to be considered [12]. Building upon the concept of resource dependencies [20], the resource-based view develops an understanding of organizations' key resources upon which the realization of the organizational strategy depends [34]. In the case of benefits management in an e-government project, the resource-based view allows to focus on a set of decisive resources for the realization of the expected project benefits.

Building upon the existing understanding of benefits management in theory and practice (cf. Table 2), the concept of **benefit realization capability** is defined as "an organizational capability that has the express purpose of ensuring that investments made in IT consistently generate value, through the enactment of a number of distinct, yet complementary, competences" [12]. For an organization, there are a number of under-pinnings (e.g. knowledge, skills, experience and behaviors) of the practices that define specific competencies for benefit realization, while the latter enact the benefit realization capability [12].

2.3 Integration of Perspectives and Concepts

This section integrates the concept of stakeholder influence and benefit realization capability as follows. First, as suggested by the definition of a benefit [5], stakeholders advance from and influence the outcomes of an e-government project. Consequently, their perspective should be considered during benefit identification, prioritization and

Table 2. The concept of benefit realization capability and its dimensions

Concept	Dimensions (with examples and corresponding sources)
Benefit realization capability	• Competence (e.g. planning, delivery, review, exploitation) [12, 35, 36] • Organization (e.g. culture, readiness, link to business strategies, strategic governance, ownership/accountability) [37–39] • Practice (e.g. ways of doing things, timing) [12, 36, 38] • Resource availability (e.g. knowledge, skills, experience, behaviors, budget, top management support) [12, 36–39]

realization planning [12, 23]. Second, the project team (e.g. project sponsors and management team) should be considered, since they decide upon project outcomes and build the capability required for benefit realization [12, 13]. Third, the interactions of both perspectives should be considered, i.e. the overlapping of benefits considered important by stakeholders including their corresponding means to influence the project as well as the response by the project management to this influence. As a result, we recognize a theoretical framework for aspects of benefit realization planning that is built upon concepts found in literature (cf. Figure 1).

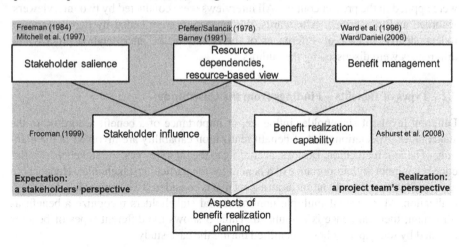

Fig. 1. Theoretical framework for analysis based on aspects of benefit realization planning

3 Case Study

3.1 Research Approach and Case Background

Since we do not construct our research based on a predefined theory but apply theory "as an initial guide to design and data collection" [40], we conduct an interpretative research of the phenomena of interest [41] based on a case study [42]. Hence, we apply an initial theoretical framework – that we derived from literature – for analysis in the iterative research process. We choose both aspects of benefit realization planning as a basis for primary data sampling in a case study of an e-government project in German public administration. Consequently, we interpret a possible explanation of the mismatch between realized and expected benefits in the project under study.

The project under study aims at developing a pre-filed tax system called VaSt by upgrading the existing system. The project has heterogeneous target groups (cf. [43]) and is built with the aid of third parties (e.g. companies, consultants). Hence, it is characterized by a huge number of stakeholders with different expectations and benefits. The first version of the VaSt system was deployed in January 2014. Hence, the project management team was able to recall benefit identification and realization.

We organized a workshop for the project management team in February 2015 in order to present the theoretical framework for analysis and to report a set of benefits expected by stakeholders that were identified in previous studies in the project VaSt. Moreover, we conducted semi-structured interviews with each of the six participants after the workshop. The participants have the following roles in the project: project manager (I1), deputy project manager (I2), multi project manager (I3), program manager (I4), a system deputy (I5) and developer (I6). The interviews took 28 min in average. Topics of the interviews were the aspects of benefit realization planning and how they were applied in the project context. All interviews were conducted by two interviewers, recorded and transcribed. Afterwards, the interviews were coded by two researchers independently. In case of differences of the results of the interpretation process, the differences were discussed by the authors.

3.2   Types of Benefits – Findings from the Case Study

Different levels of stakeholder influence, of importance of a benefit according to the stakeholder expectations and of benefit realization capability are involved in the planning of benefit realization. Besides, according to the interviewees, the stakeholder influence is conjunct with importance of a benefit for the particular stakeholder. Hence, both are considered in a combination as an aspect that is considered when planning the benefit realization. Moreover, if multiple non-influential stakeholders recognize a benefit as important, their influence is cumulated. Table 3 shows the different types of benefits (labeled by the paper authors) identified during the case study.

Project Guiding Benefits Are associated with a high level of stakeholder influence and a high realization capability. An example for such a benefit from the case study is the "*reduction of overhead*" (e.g. I1, I3). All stakeholders mentioned this benefit as important and the required realization capability is given, since this benefit is one of the main project goals. Hence, this benefit is realized during the project.

Table 3. Types of benefits

Label	Stakeholders' perspective	Project team's perspective
Project guiding benefits	**Benefits** of influential stakeholders or benefits with high importance for multiple stakeholders	**Realizable** by the project team since defined in the scope of project goals
Endangered benefits	**Benefits** of influential stakeholders or benefits with high importance for multiple non-influential stakeholders	**Not realizable** by the project team due to insufficient capabilities
Questioned benefits	**Benefits** of non-influential stakeholders or benefits with a low importance for stakeholders or benefits which are not anticipated	**Perceived** and realizable by the project as an innovation towards future stakeholder expectations
Out-of-focus benefits	**Benefits** of non-influential stakeholders or benefits with a low importance for influential stakeholders	**Not realizable** by the project team due to insufficient capabilities

Endangered Benefits Are associated with a high level of stakeholder influence, while the level of realization capability is low. An example for such a benefit mentioned by the interviewees is *"simplification through data completeness"* (e.g. I5) as well as *"simplification through an authorization database"* (e.g. I6). Stakeholders with a strong lobby and high influence on the project recognized these benefits as important or multiple non-influential stakeholders recognize these benefits and thus their influence is cumulated. However, the project team is not able to realize them, since the data providers could not be integrated as required (in the case of *"simplification through data completeness"*) and since resources were missing (in the case of *"simplification through an authorization database"*).

Questioned Benefits Are associated with a low level of stakeholder influence, while the level of the corresponding realization capability is high. The interviewees mentioned the *"flexibility through mobile device interface"* (e.g. I3) and the *"flexibility through guaranteed 24 h availability"* (e.g. I1, I4) as examples for this type of benefits. These benefits were not seen as important by stakeholders. However, the project team suggests that the benefits would be expected by stakeholders in the future.

Finally, the interviewees mentioned that benefits could be associated with a low level of stakeholder influence and realization capability. These benefits can be seen as rather unimportant for (influential) stakeholders. Thus, we apply the label **out-of-focus benefits**. An example for such a benefit is *"unified authentication"* (e.g. I5).

4 Benefit Typology for Realization Planning – a Synthesis

Referring to the work by Doty and Glick [44] on typologies, we interpret the existence of four ideal types of benefits (cf. Figure 2). Each benefit can be assigned to one of the four ideal types according to the value levels of its realization planning aspects, since the types are mutually exclusive and collectively exhaustive. We further interpret the aspects to be considered in planning benefit realization as answers by the project team to the following questions: (i) What is the level of stakeholder influence conjunct with the stakeholders' perceived importance of an expected benefit? (ii) What is the level of the capability required by the project team to realize the benefit?

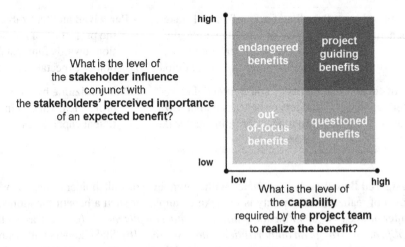

Fig. 2. A benefit typology for realization planning

The two aspects stakeholder influence and perceived importance of an expected benefit are combined above, as they both represent integral parts of the stakeholders' perspective. Hence, benefits can be allocated by considering the stakeholders' perspective on a benefit (by answering the first question, i.e. the y axis) and the perspective of the project team (by answering the second question, i.e. the x axis). The level of each aspect can be set to low or high. Those levels can be determined directly (by e.g. interviewing and analyzing the stakeholder perception) or estimated based on the perception of the project management.

5 Discussion

An explanation of the mismatch between realized and expected benefits is derived based on the aspects of benefit realization planning. Therefore, we discuss the two research questions by interpreting the aspects and the benefit typology towards implications for management of e-government projects.

Regarding RQ1, the first aspect sets the level of **stakeholder influence** conjunct with the perceived **importance of a benefit** by a stakeholder (cf. Figure 2, y axis). Hence, it presents the perspective of a stakeholder on the e-government project by shedding light on the stakeholder's expectations. However, both the influence of a stakeholder and the importance of a benefit for a particular stakeholder can change over time [45], e.g. urgency can augment due to an external event. Consequently, the determination of the level on the y axis is not static, but depends on the point in time of determination. Besides, the determination of stakeholder influence is conjunct with the subjective perception of the project team. If stakeholder influence is estimated based e.g. on the attributes power, legitimacy and urgency [19], the project team prioritizes the stakeholders by determining the level of stakeholder influence. In order to achieve a rather objective determination of stakeholder influence, we suggest that the determination should be done by several project members independently or by a third party through interviews with stakeholder representatives.

The second aspect sets the level of the benefit realization capability required by the project team (cf. Figure 2, x axis). This level of capability is influenced by the availability of resources (e.g. time, budget and staff), the teams' competence or the current practice in the organization. If the level of the benefit realization capability is low, the project team can try to acquire missing resources. This requires an intense coordination with the project sponsor, so that the e-government project is not only successful in meeting the stakeholders' expectations, but also in finishing the project in time, in budget and in quality.

Regarding RQ2, we derive two managerial implications for benefit realization planning in e-government projects based on the benefit typology. First, **project guiding benefits** are linked with the project goals. Thus, they need to be realized. These benefits are commonly listed in the project specification. In order to meet the project goals, the project team, project sponsor and further stakeholders should agree upon them. **Out-of-focus benefits** can be seen as contrasting to the project guiding benefits. They are not important for stakeholders and not linked to the project goals. However, the relevance of these benefits can be increased due to a change in the importance of stakeholders. Hence, these benefits should not be ignored. Instead, the observation of these benefits should be integrated in the project management.

Second, endangered as well as questioned benefits should be paid attention to by e-government project managers. The existence of **endangered benefits** indicates that an e-government project might be perceived as less successful. Even more, a project can be perceived as a failure when a greater number of endangered benefits are not realized – even if the project is finished in time, in budget and in quality. Since the project success is linked to the stakeholders' expectations, the threshold between success and failure in terms of endangered benefits should be actively managed. **Questioned benefits** are innovative benefits according to the project team. However, stakeholders do not follow this perception of the project team. They perceive these benefits as unimpressive or do not address them as benefits at all. Hence, in order to make these benefits valuable for the stakeholders, communication between the potential stakeholders and the project team needs to take place. Through communication (e.g. marketing), these benefits can be perceived by stakeholders and their interest can be adjusted.

Based on the aspects and managerial implications, we derive the following explanation of the **mismatch between realized and expected benefits** in e-government projects. Project guiding benefits are the project goals which need to be achieved during the project. The achievement of these benefits is the basis for project success. Thus, their realization should be monitored, otherwise a mismatch would emerge. Endangered and questioned benefits should be in the focus of the benefit realization management by the project team, since benefits of these types bear a higher risk potential and need to be negotiated or communicated. If a finished project still has a number of endangered benefits, there will be much likely a great mismatch between realized and expected benefits. If a number of questioned benefits exist, the project team might be obliged to account for a perceived waste of resources that could be used instead in realizing benefits important for stakeholders.

Since the importance of a benefit for a stakeholder could be estimated wrong (e.g. the benefit is classified as out-of-focus or questioned benefit – instead of an endangered or project guiding benefit), we conjecture the following regarding benefit realization planning towards project success, i.e. towards managing the match between realized and expected benefits in e-government projects:

- **conjecture 1:** the typology presented should be applied at the very beginning or even before the project has started. In that case, project sponsors would be able to prioritize a set of benefits and to allow for the development of the required realization capability by the project team.
- **conjecture 2:** benefits should be discussed with influential stakeholders at the beginning of an e-government project. This could help to avoid wrong expectations and to diminish possible conflicts.
- **conjecture 3:** the benefits assigned to each ideal type should be reviewed on a regular basis, since the levels of each benefit along the both axes could change.
- **conjecture 4:** the project management should try to negotiate with the stakeholders about endangered benefits and communicate the criticality before the project or as soon as possible during each project phase.

6   Conclusion

Whereas literature analyzes the identification and classification of stakeholders and their benefits regarding e-government projects in detail, the planning of benefit realization is an under-researched field. In order to close this research gap, we apply a theory-based analytical framework of aspects of benefit realization planning to a case study in a German public administration. We identify aspects for benefit realization as follows: (i) the stakeholder influence conjunct with the stakeholders' perception of a benefit's importance as well as (ii) the capability of the project team to realize a benefit. Based on these aspects, we present a benefit realization typology which allows for classifying benefits. The typology serves as a basis for effective benefits management and provides an explanation of the mismatch between realized and expected benefits.

Future research includes the application of the benefits typology along the complete lifecycle of an e-government project, since stakeholders salience could change with time passing [45]. Moreover, the typology should be applied in a number of case studies in order to reflect and validate the variability of benefit types.

Acknowledgments. We are grateful for the support provided by ISPRAT e.V. in terms of funding our research project. We also thank all reviewers, project participants and interviewees, especially the project staff, for their most helpful input and feedback.

References

1. Shenhar, A.J., Dvir, D.: Reinventing project management: the diamond approach to successful growth and innovation. Harvard Business Review Press, Boston (2007)
2. Samset, K.: Projects, their quality at entry and challenges in the front-end phase. In: Williams, T., Samset, K., Sunnevåg, K. (eds.) Making Essential Choices with Scant Information, pp. 18–35. Palgrave Macmillan, Basingstoke (2009)
3. Zwikael, O., Smyrk, J.: A general framework for gauging the performance of initiatives to enhance organizational value. Br. J. Manag. **23**, S6–S22 (2012)
4. Ward, J., Taylor, P., Bond, P.: Evaluation and realisation of IS/IT benefits: an empirical study of current practice. Eur. J. Inf. Syst. **4**, 214–225 (1996)
5. Ward, J., Daniel, E.: Benefits Management: Delivering Value from IS and IT Investments. Wiley, Chichester (2006)
6. Lindgren, I.: Towards a conceptual framework for identifying public e-service stakeholders: on where to start looking. In: Proceedings of Ongoing Research and Projects of IFIP EGOV and IFIP ePart 2012, pp. 175–183 (2012)
7. Eckartz, S., Katsma, C., Maatman, R.O.: A design proposal for a benefits management method for enterprise system implementations. In: 2012 45th Hawaii International Conference on System Science (HICSS), pp. 4642–4651 (2012)
8. Flak, L.S., Solli-Saether, H.: Benefits realization in eGovernment: institutional entrepreneurship or just hype? In: Proceedings of the 46th HICSS, pp. 2062–2071 (2013)
9. Hellang, Ø., Flak, L.S., Päivärinta, T.: Diverging approaches to benefits realization from public ICT investments: a study of benefits realization methods in Norway. Transforming Gov. People, Process Policy **7**, 93–108 (2013)
10. Flak, L.S., Eikebrokk, T.R., Dertz, W.: An exploratory approach for benefits management in e-government: insights from 48 Norwegian Government funded projects. In: Proceedings of the 41st HICSS (2008)
11. Ashurst, C., Doherty, N.F.: Towards the formulation of 'a best practice' framework for benefits realisation in IT projects. Electron. J. Inf. Syst. Eval. **6**, 1–10 (2003)
12. Ashurst, C., Doherty, N.F., Peppard, J.: Improving the impact of IT development projects: the benefits realization capability model. Eur. J. Inf. Syst. **17**, 352–370 (2008)
13. Doherty, N.F., Ashurst, C., Peppard, J.: Factors affecting the successful realisation of benefits from systems development projects: findings from three case studies. J. Inf. Technol. **27**, 1–16 (2012)
14. Braun, J., Ahlemann, F., Riempp, G.: Benefits management-a literature review and elements of a research agenda. Wirtschaftsinformatik, pp. 555–566 (2009)
15. Irani, Z., Love, P.: Evaluating Information Systems: public and private sector. Routledge, London (2008)
16. Jurison, J.: Toward more effective management of information technology benefits. J. Strateg. Inf. Syst. **5**, 263–274 (1996)
17. Freeman, R.E.: Strategic management: A Stakeholder Approach. Pitman, Boston (1984)
18. Mishra, A., Mishra, D.: Applications of stakeholder theory in information systems and technology. Eng. Econ. **24**, 254–266 (2013)

19. Mitchell, R.K., Agle, B.R., Wood, D.J.: Toward a theory of stakeholder identification and salience: aefining the principle of who and what really counts. Acad. Manage. Rev. **22**, 853–886 (1997)
20. Pfeffer, J., Salancik, G.R.: The external control of organizations: a resource dependence perspective. Harper and Row, New York (1978)
21. Balta, D., Greger, V., Wolf, P., Krcmar, H.: E-government stakeholder analysis and management based on stakeholder interactions and resource dependencies. In: Proceedings of the 48th HICSS, pp. 2456–2465 (2015)
22. Savage, G.T., Nix, T.W., Whitehead, C.J., Blair, J.D.: Strategies for assessing and managing organizational stakeholders. Executive (19389779) **5**, 61–75 (1991)
23. Frooman, J.: Stakeholder influence strategies. Acad. Manag. Rev. **24**, 191–205 (1999)
24. Carolan, M.: Stepping into the light: stakeholder impact on competitive adaptation. J. Organ. Change Manage. **15**, 255–272 (2002)
25. Olander, S., Landin, A.: Evaluation of stakeholder influence in the implementation of construction projects. Int. J. Project Manage. **23**, 321–328 (2005)
26. Bendahan, S., Camponovo, G., Monzani, J.-S., Pigneur, Y.: Negotiation in technology landscapes: an actor-issue analysis. J. Manage. Inf. Syst. **21**, 137–172 (2005)
27. King, B.: A social movement perspective of stakeholder collective action and influence. Bus. Soc. **47**, 21–49 (2008)
28. Walker, D.H.T., Bourne, L.M., Shelley, A.: Influence, stakeholder mapping and visualization. Constr. Manage. Econ. **26**, 645–658 (2008)
29. Hester, P.T., Adams, K.M.: Determining stakeholder influence using input-output modeling. Procedia Comput. Sci. **20**, 337–341 (2013)
30. Álvarez-Gil, M.J., Berrone, P., Husillos, F.J., Lado, N.: Reverse logistics, stakeholders' influence, organizational slack, and managers' posture. J. Bus. Res. **60**, 463–473 (2007)
31. Balzarova, M.A., Castka, P.: Stakeholders' influence and contribution to social standards development: the case of multiple stakeholder approach to ISO 26000 development. J. Bus. Ethics **111**, 265–279 (2012)
32. Hemanta, D.: Assessing stakeholders' influence on social performance of infrastructure projects. Facilities **30**, 531–550 (2012)
33. Aaltonen, K., Kujala, J.: A project lifecycle perspective on stakeholder influence strategies in global projects. Scand. J. Manag. **26**, 381–397 (2010)
34. Barney, J.: Firm resources and sustained competitive advantage. J. Manag. **17**, 99–120 (1991)
35. May, D., Sapountzis, S., Yates, K., Kagioglou, M., Aouad, G.: Realising benefits in primary healthcare infrastructures. Facilities **27**, 74–87 (2009)
36. Love, P.E.D., Matthews, J., Simpson, I., Hill, A., Olatunji, O.A.: A benefits realization management building information modeling framework for asset owners. Autom. Constr. **37**, 1–10 (2014)
37. Lin, K., Lin, C., Tsao, H.: IS/IT investment evaluation and benefit realization practices in Taiwanese SMEs. J. Inf. Sci. Technol. **2**, 44–71 (2005)
38. Breese, R.: Benefits realisation management: panacea or false dawn? Int. J. Project Manage. **30**, 341–351 (2012)
39. Serra, C.E.M., Kunc, M.: Benefits realisation management and its influence on project success and on the execution of business strategies. Int. J. Project Manage. **33**, 53–66 (2015)
40. Walsham, G.: Interpretive case studies in IS research: nature and method. Eur. J. Inf. Syst. **4**, 74–81 (1995)
41. Klein, H.K., Myers, M.D.: A set of principles for conducting and evaluating interpretive field studies in information systems. MIS Q. **23**, 67–93 (1999)
42. Yin, R.K.: Case Study Research: Design and Methods. Sage, London (2009)

43. Greger, V., Balta, D., Wolf, P., Krcmar, H.: Analyzing stakeholders in complex E-government projects: towards a stakeholder interaction model. In: Janssen, M., Scholl, H.J., Wimmer, M.A., Bannister, F. (eds.) EGOV 2014. LNCS, vol. 8653, pp. 194–205. Springer, Heidelberg (2014)

44. Doty, D.H., Glick, W.H.: Typologies as a unique form of theory building: toward improved understanding and modeling. Acad. Manag. Rev. **19**, 230–251 (1994)

45. Jawahar, I.M., McLaughlin, G.L.: Toward a descriptive stakeholder theory: an organizational life cycle approach. Acad. Manag. Rev. **26**, 397–414 (2001)

Electronic Data Safes as an Infrastructure
for Transformational Government? A Case Study

Joachim Pfister[✉] and Gerhard Schwabe

Department of Informatics, University of Zurich, Zurich, Switzerland
{pfister,schwabe}@ifi.uzh.ch

Abstract. This article introduces and explores the potential of an active electronic data safe (AEDS) serving as an infrastructure to achieve transformational
government. An AEDS connects individuals and organizations from the private
and the public sector to exchange information items related to business processes
following the user-managed access paradigm. To realize the transformational
government's vision of user-centricity, fundamental changes in the service provision and collaboration of public and private sector organizations are needed.
Findings of a user study with a prototype of an AEDS are used to identify four
barriers for the adoption of an AEDS in the light of transformational government:
(1) offering citizens unfamiliar services having the character of experience-goods;
(2) failing to fulfil common service expectations of the customers; (3) failing to
establish contextual integrity for data sharing, and, (4) failing to establish and run
an AEDS as a multi-sided platform providing an attractive business model.

Keywords: Electronic data safes · Transformational government · User-
managed access · Case study · Barriers

1 Introduction

In many countries, electronic government (e-government) initiatives have been
introduced that are progressing from the stage of information provisioning and
simple transactions to more customer-centric stages of integrated service delivery
[1]. Several e-government maturity models and e-government definitions have been
proposed [2] but, actually, many e-government initiatives resulted in digitizing
existing practices and were not able to reach more mature stages. In recent years, the
idea of "transformational government" (t-government) gained momentum which is
defined as "[…] the ICT-enabled operations, internal and external processes and
structures to enable the realization of services that meet public-sector objectives such
as efficiency, transparency, accountability and citizen centricity." [3] The realization of t-government entails fundamental changes in the public service sector's practices and structures, for instance organizations need to cooperate and integrate their
activities [4]. This means to overcome data silos, take a holistic view on the relationships between the public sector and citizens or private sector stakeholders and
to empower the citizens [5]. This results in a more efficient service delivery and a
more transparent and responsive government [1].

© IFIP International Federation for Information Processing 2015
E. Tambouris et al. (Eds.): EGOV 2015, LNCS 9248, pp. 246–257, 2015.
DOI: 10.1007/978-3-319-22479-4_19

In this paper, the concept of active electronic data safes (AEDS) as an infrastructure to support t-government is introduced and will be explored empirically. These AEDS are based on the paradigm of user-managed access, i.e. that an individual decides which information items are shared with an organization. Using the genre of a case study, a prototypical implementation of an AEDS connecting citizens, the public administration and private sector companies will be analyzed. This concept of user-managed access put into practice will be used to identify challenges with respect to t-government. Therefore, the research questions is: What are the challenges with respect to t-government when the concept of user-managed access with an AEDS is put into practice?

The contribution of this article is to identify challenges for solutions supporting t-government that follow the paradigm of user-managed access based on a user study with ordinary citizens. Such an approach helps to complement existing literature-based approaches. For electronic data safes, to the best of our knowledge, no evaluation exists helping to identify this new class of tool's implementation challenges. Heath et al. [6] describe evaluation results from an AEDS-like tool but not with a focus on user perceptions. And research concerning the adoption of an electronic postal service, which also goes into the direction of an AEDS, has been carried out by Berger and Hertzum [7], but they are focusing more on the challenges of the organizational introduction.

Existing research on the adoption of t-government and the identification of potential barriers to t-government is performed on a very high level such as analyzing the policies of national governments to assess their t-government readiness [27]. Other research contributions use case studies in which they interview experts that are responsible for designing and running e-government services [1, 4]. Moreover, technological solutions that support t-government's service delivery are also researched: For example a platform-based approach [16, 28] to exchange data is discussed but only from a G2B perspective and with a focus on platform governance and information infrastructure. Hence, in existing research with respect to t-government, the individual as a citizen is rather put aside although user-centricity is a widely heralded tenet of t-government. We argue that a thorough understanding of the socio-technological issues is needed before services are designed. A deeper understanding of the citizens' needs and preferences contributes to successful service design which will entail adoption by the citizens. This point of view has been recognized in IS research [29] and needs to be embraced in the t-government context, too. To achieve this, early testing and gaining feedback from potential end-users of t-government services is needed to uncover yet unknown barriers that may surmount existing categories such as organizational and managerial or technical. This is done in exploratory research that will navigate through the problem domain, discover unknown phenomena and suggest hypotheses or propositions – an approach we have chosen to follow in this article.

Therefore, this article closes the gap of having a lack of understanding in the context of t-government what potential end users think of tools following the user-managed access paradigm. T-Government practitioners and policy makers can use the newly identified challenges to address them in the service design of solutions, for example an AEDS, that are needed to realize the vision of t-government.

2 Background

This section provides background information on the concept of an AEDS. We suggest that an AEDS can serve as an infrastructure component to support t-government. Existing barriers identified in the literature to achieve t-government will be presented, too.

2.1 Active Electronic Data Safes

In the domain of e-government, electronic data safes have been proposed as a cloud-based service to securely store documents and data [8, 9]. These services are evolving from portals [10] and plain document storage solutions to an infrastructure component for user-managed information and process management [11, 12]. The user-managed access paradigm is the central design principle of an electronic data safe which means that the safe owners decide with whom and with which e-business or e-government processes they share their information items. This article uses the term "active electronic data safe" in order to emphasize the process support capabilities that transcend mailbox-like document reception and storage. Thus, an AEDS serves as an "one-stop-shop" [13, 14], i.e. an individual's single contact and interaction point for information items and processes related to organizations from the public and the private sector.

Active electronic data safes act as an intermediary replacing many point-to-point-connections and they serve as a multi-sided platform (MSP) to connect individuals and organizations – both, from the private and the public sector [15] (see Fig. 1). Connecting the public and private context via a MSP in the e-government context was diagnosed as an embryonic research area [16]. The simultaneous use of an infrastructure component, such as an AEDS, by the private and public sector makes sense because one organization alone often has too few customer contacts in order to justify the development and maintenance of such an infrastructure. For example, a German citizen is said to have one to two contacts with the public administration per year [17]. AEDS are a network good: The more organizations offer services on an AEDS' platform, the more attractive it will become for customers – and vice versa. Postal services or telecommunication providers who consider themselves as established and natural intermediaries are complementing their portfolio of electronic document delivery solutions, for example, by providing electronic payment, authentication or secure storage for individuals and organizations [18], thus, also moving into the direction of AEDS. Nevertheless, these classic intermediaries often stick to a document-centric "mailbox" metaphor which is extended in the AEDS' vision by process support capabilities or value-added services to assist in personal information management [12] tasks.

Fig. 1. Active electronic data safe as an intermediary.

2.2   AEDS as an Infrastructure for t-Government

With an AEDS, individuals benefit from a reduction in information fragmentation [19], something that happens, for example, when electronic bills are distributed over several provider-specific online portals. Now, customers are equipped with a tool for exerting informational self-determination in the sense of "vendor relationship management" [20] which is an inverse of the provider-centric idea of customer relationship management (CRM). An AEDS as an intermediary (a) reduces transaction costs and increases the entire transaction value for all participants [21] and (b) overcomes the problems of information silos [22]. Using an AEDS, service provider-specific information silos are replaced by a collaboration of autonomous organizations forming a value chain network [1] glued together by the individual's decision for sharing. This also supports t-government's aims of citizen empowerment: With an AEDS, individuals have the power to decide with whom they will share information items while, at the same time, they still will have an overview which organizations stores what about them. Moreover, this will also contribute to realize the t-government's aims to benefit from fully (horizontally and vertically) integrated government services and citizens having only one contact point for interacting with the public or private sector. To achieve this, all the stakeholders are required to undergo considerable changes – something that needs to be sparked by the introduction of citizen-centric services [3]. Following this line of argumentation, an AEDS will serve as a tool to surmount "the wall" placed in between a government-centric CRM view and the vision of a citizen-centric, co-production oriented, empowered and engaged citizen [cf. 23].

Related work that employs the user-managed access paradigm can be found in the domain of electronic health [24]. Therein, collaboration between different stakeholders (patients, health care providers, insurance companies) is needed but information silos prevail. To overcome this situation, personal health records (PHR) have been suggested. They contain the lifelong medical information of a patient and are maintained and shared by the patients themselves – in analogy to an AEDS. These PHRs can be stored with private sector based intermediaries such as Google Health or Microsoft HealthVault, also supporting the user-managed access paradigm. Research in the e-health domain [25] has shown that the acceptance of such PHR systems suffers from issues related to privacy, autonomy, and accessibility.

2.3   Barriers to t-Government

Veenstra et al. [1] developed a literature-based categorization of impediments to achieve the stage of t-government and added empirically derived impediments on the basis of three case studies which involved interviewing three key people from line management and ICT staff. In total, they identified 23 impediments which were grouped into three main categories: governance (7 impediments), organizational and managerial (9 impediments), and technical (7 impediments). Veenstra et al. could confirm twelve literature-based impediments and identify eleven new ones. On the governance level, the main barriers were identified as a lack of a government-wide strategy and vision enabling collaboration in forms of networks and value chains. On the organizational and managerial level, huge and joint efforts of stakeholders embedded in complex relationships are needed which creates many barriers. In addition, on the technological level, the lack of knowledge to achieve innovations, for instance due to an organization's dependency upon legacy systems, has been diagnosed. Moreover, Weerakkody et al. [26] identified challenges and issues for achieving t-government. They carried out a case study to empirically identify challenges that added to the literature-based ones. Therefore, they interviewed e-government practitioners on their experiences but no citizens. 48 change barriers have been identified which were grouped into four categories (in brackets: number of identified change barriers): organizational challenges (19), process change challenges (11), IS/IT integration challenges (8), and cultural and social challenges (10; such as fear of information technology or organizational resistance).

3   Research Design

As presented in the previous sections, current research on t-government seems to neglect the individual as a citizen who interacts with t-government services. To overcome this weakness, we will carry out an exploratory user study involving twelve citizens and three representatives of public and private sector organizations which will serve as this case study's empirical foundation. In order to enable an in-depth and hands-on experience with the concept of an AEDS, the user study participants (six male and six female; average age 27.6 years) worked in a lab-based setting with a prototype. The three tasks they worked upon were designed to realistically mirror exceptional, but nevertheless, common business transactions with a sufficient degree of complexity: (a) to report a theft to the Police, (b) to file a claim with an insurance company and (c) to get a quote from a security company based on some fictitious vulnerabilities of the home such as a weak door. Three representatives of organizations (Police, insurance and a security company) were involved to interact with the study participants through the AEDS prototype (answering/asking questions through a messaging component) and to evaluate the usefulness of the exchanged information items that have been captured by the study participants (taking photos of valuables and electronically attaching receipts to build an inventory list). After the tasks have been carried out, all the participants completed a questionnaire with respect to technology acceptance which also contained additional items to ask about the participant's attitude towards a possible future adoption of an AEDS. Finally, a semi-structured interview was carried out and audio recorded. The interviews were transcribed and qualitative content analysis was performed using the method of a thematic analysis [30] which has proven to be successful in the field of HCI [31]. Following the transcription, initial codes were assigned using the software MAXQDA. After iteratively reading and refining the coding, themes were assigned in a "data-driven" manner. Writing internal project reports served to review the emerging themes and to discuss them with fellow researcher before defining, naming and compiling them in a final report.

4   Barriers to t-Government in the Context of an AEDS

Based on the empirical data elaborated in the user study and applying the thematic analysis as a method, four barriers to achieve the stage of t-government using an AEDS were identified. We acknowledge that other factors originating from other components that contribute to t-government might lead to further barriers. However, we argue that due to our research design the identified barriers are related predominately to the AEDS. The participants were primed by the quasi-realistic tasks in the user study that enabled them afterwards to thoroughly reflect upon the experienced and future suitability of the user-managed-access paradigm. Quotations are added in order to illustrate the identified themes based on the interpreted data, an approach that is common in qualitative analysis [30]. They have been translated into English by an author of this article.

4.1   Offering Unfamiliar Services Having the Character of Experience-Goods

The results from the user study show that the study participants preferred clearly structured processes like filing a claim with an insurance company. The study participants were asked to rate which future business transactions they would like to carry out with an AEDS (Likert-scale ranging from 1 = no, never; 4 = undecided; 7 = yes, absolutely), which resulted in the following ranking: Obtain a quote from a security company (3.36); Manage personal information items in an AEDS (4.55); Report a theft to the Police (5.00); Inventory important objects or documents (5.00); File a claim with an insurance company (5.45). Citizens and service-providers disliked openly structured or largely unknown business processes which lack prior experience or that require a highly individualized configuration. This has been observable with the task of obtaining a quote from a security company. Looking at the interview data, an explanation for this observation can be given: In such open and unknown business processes, the study participants feared to receive the wrong product or the wrong service. Under such circumstances, participants emphasized the need for having a human providing trust and guidance, something which is not necessary in well-known and already experienced form-based business processes such as filing a claim with an insurance company. *"Especially the security company, I would like to have personal contact with. With bureaucratic processes, like in an insurance company, I would more readily accept guidance by a program."* (P11) Furthermore, obtaining a quote from a security company can be regarded as a service that needs substantial explanatory support for which not every necessary detail can be transmitted via online channels to achieve satisfying results. Thus, such a kind of service falls into the category of delivering experience goods [32]. It seems unlikely that experience good-like services can be fully supported via intermediaries such as an AEDS; a partial support in less critical transaction phases such as billing might be possible. Because citizens seem to prefer known business process transaction schemes, an AEDS should first provide transactional processes that support self-services which will help to familiarize with an AEDS. Complex services transaction schemes with a higher degree of individualization should be provided later. Summing up, we conclude in **barrier 1:** Offering unfamiliar services that have a character of experience-goods will be a barrier to an AEDS' adoption.

4.2   Failing to Fulfil Common Service Expectations of the Customers

The participants in the user study complained about having too little information about the current status of a business process they had started because the prototype did not implement such a functionality. The different philosophies for delivering an effective and efficient service can be identified quite prototypically following a traditional private/public sector distinction. *"The claimants want something from us [the Police] – therefore it is their duty to provide correct information."* (Police representative) Private sector organizations, such as an insurance company, aim at customer satisfaction: *"Customers should always know about the current status of their case."* (insurance company representative) Therefore, providing status updates comes natural to them. In contrast, the Police as a public sector organization neglects providing such established success factors in e-business [33] because yet, they did not need to embrace a customer-centric view. This is due to various reasons (resources, strategy etc.). Therefore, we conclude in **barrier 2:** Not fulfilling common service expectations of the customers will result in a barrier to an AEDS's adoption.

4.3   Failing to Establish Contextual Integrity for Data Sharing

In the user study, the participants raised privacy and security concerns. They wanted to know what happens with their shared data: where is it stored and who can access it? Using a cloud-based service, such as an AEDS, for storing personal information items was criticized and rationalized at the same time. Some participants (five out of twelve) felt generally unsafe having stored personal data in the cloud. One participant framed this feeling of insecurity as follows: *"I would like to control my documents. I would like to know who has access to it. Nobody can guarantee this if I am using Dropbox or Skydrive. And if it rains, then 'the cloud' has gone. I do not trust them. I use cloud services, but only for insignificant stuff."* (P02) If an end-to-end encryption exists, as stated by a tech-savvy participant (P12), he would not have any concerns. The service's geographic location was the decisive factor for another participant: *"Probably, I would inform myself before I would use such a service. I would prefer such a service being located in Germany, Switzerland or the European Union."* (P08) Thoughts about security influenced their decision what should be stored in an AEDS and what not. The same participant (and three more of twelve) explained his preference for having a public sector organization to run an AEDS instead of a private sector company or a start-up company: *"I consider a public authority to be more qualified than a private sector company. With a private company, I feel afraid that they might abuse my data for advertisement or their own purposes because they want to exploit them commercially. That seems less probable with public sector organizations."* (P08) We conclude therefore that creating transparency for information storage and use is an essential design principle for information systems following the user-managed access paradigm. To meet this expectations, already established knowledge of privacy enhancing technologies [34] must be combined with the process-oriented transaction support in an AEDS. The participants in the user study had concerns where and by whom a service is provided. This observation can be attributed to an individual's aim for keeping "contextual integrity", a concept developed by Nissenbaum [35]. Therein, information items can be shared guided by norms of appropriation and distribution tied to a certain context. The context is formed by the source, destination and the appropriateness of the content. By exerting control and having transparency, people are able to maintain contextual integrity. This point of view also gains momentum in other areas of research, such as HCI [36]. We, therefore, conclude in **barrier 3**: Failing to establish contextual integrity will cause a barrier to the adoption of an AEDS.

4.4   Failing to Establish and Run a Multi-sided Platform

Taking the customer perspective, the study participants generally recognized the advantages of creating and receiving information items digitally and their re-use in digital business processes. Having everything at one place and being able to forward information items was judged by nearly all (nine out of twelve) participants as something positive and beneficial: *"Forwarding things, for instance to the Police or to an insurance company, would not have been possible with my system [Dropbox]."* (P09) Another participant stated, that if he had all his digital belongings and documents organized neatly in an AEDS, he would not like to suffer from a vendor lock-in. The information items as well as all the effort to organize them should not be lost when, due to some reason, a change of the AEDS provider is necessary. Looking at the service-providers, a mixed picture arises: In general, the Police representative was critical about the current prototype. Without a deep integration into the Police's back-end systems (which has not been done in the prototype), he concluded that the AEDS prototype only brings advantages to the citizen and not to him. The insurance company representative was convinced by the concept of an AEDS and its prototypical implementation but wondered about the need for critical mass: *"If the usage numbers are big enough, such a concept would be beneficial to us. The problem is to motivate a substantial number of our customers to use such a tool to achieve enough usage."* (insurance representative)

To summarize, an AEDS as a multi-sided platform faces challenges to find a suitable business model that satisfies all relevant stakeholder: (a) the AEDS platform provider, (b) the service-providers from the private and public sector that offer services using the AEDS platform, and (c) the customers willing to engage in business transactions and/or store personal information items. Attracting a sufficient number of customers and service-providers, which is vital for a network good, resembles the well know chicken-and-egg problem. In an free market, where many AEDS platform providers compete for customers, they need to differentiate by offering "value-added" services going beyond the simple storage of information items [12]. For example, individuals can be supported in their personal information management by breaking down larger information organizing tasks into smaller tasks that can be worked upon using different devices at different locations, for instance, tagging photos and grouping them into galleries. This strategy is called "Selfsourcing" [37]. It could be complemented for specific tasks with the concept of crowd sourcing which served as the original inspiration for the selfsourcing concept. We summarize these challenges in **barrier 4**: Failing to establish and run an AEDS as a multi-sided platform with an attractive business model will be a barrier for the adoption amongst all stakeholders.

5 Discussion

In order to categorize the four barriers that have been elaborated in the previous section we argue for the creation of a new, "citizen-oriented service design" category. The four newly discovered barriers do neither resemble impediments on the governance, organizational or managerial or technological level as categorized by Veenstra et al. [1]. Nor, they can be understood as "organizational and social" challenges within an organization, a category used by Weerakkody et al. [26]. The character the four impediments share is related to the citizens, their service expectations, needs or fears. Therefore, we suggest to summarize these four barriers under the new category "citizen-oriented service design". Reflecting upon the newly discovered barriers contributes to the design of AEDS and to t-government at the same time which will be discussed in the following.

Electronic data safes have the potential to help citizens in overcoming the problem of information fragmentation. The ability to interact with business processes transforms electronic data safes into active electronic data safes. Certainly, these tools provide more capabilities for information sharing under the user-managed access paradigm than ordinary portals or electronic data safes. Nevertheless, they will face challenges related to the governance, organizational or managerial, technological or social level. But our results also indicate that the service design needs to pay attention to the individuals as users or customers of an AEDS. Using the perspective of a "citizen-oriented service design", we interpret our findings as a call for action to come up with research to identify further barriers that are related to the citizen who makes use of new technologies and services. In doing so, the following question can be answered to shape new services before they are rolled out: With respect to a new service delivery paradigm, such as an AEDS, which character of services do citizens favor under which conditions?

T-government can benefit from integrating the citizen-oriented service design perspective, too, in order to develop solutions that are truly citizen-centric. As our example with an exploratory study of an AEDS has shown, innovations or new technologies to support t-government need to bring utility not only to the organization but also, and foremost, to the citizen as service users. Thus, they need to have a satisfying degree of maturity. Therefore, we conclude that an assessment of t-government readiness from a user-perspective needs to be integrated in the discussion of future barriers. Instead of just looking back on what went wrong after new services and technologies have been launched, t-government research should take an active stance to identify unknown barriers ahead. User studies in a quasi-realistic setting seem promising to achieve this.

6 Limitations

As a limitation to this study, the participants in the user study do not reflect a representative part of the population, and the number of service providers might seem too limited and narrow to come up with results having a high internal validity and, thus, not being fruitful for generalization. Nevertheless, (single) case studies produce rich observations and propositions can be derived from all observations helping to guide further theory development, for example, by pointing to new research challenges that arise and would not have been found otherwise. This argument reflects this article's exploratory approach to identify future challenges and impediments of an emerging class of tools following the user-managed access paradigm, such as an AEDS. Furthermore, the tasks in the user study were purposefully chosen to cover realistic problems and that the participants could work in a nearly realistic setting (mock home-office).

7   Conclusion

In this article, we identified four new impediments or challenges related to an AEDS when such a tool is used to support t-government by offering a technical solution to put the paradigm of user-managed access into practice in order to overcome data silos: 1.) offering citizens unfamiliar services having the character of experience-goods; 2.) failing to fulfil common service expectations of the customers; 3.) failing to establish contextual integrity for data sharing; 4.) failing to establish and run a multi-sided platform. Without our exploratory approach involving a user study with a prototype, those impediments would have been not identified. Therefore, we argue that t-government projects benefit from early prototyping and evaluation with all relevant stakeholders in order to avoid misconceptions leading to unusable and not accepted solutions. User-centered design methods and design science research [38] help to uncover "hidden" assumptions or problematic areas which need to be addressed. Applying such methods and paradigms helps to understand better specific contexts but they may also generate transferable knowledge for other contexts or domains. The study participants welcomed the concept of an AEDS helping them in organizing their administrative burdens. This gives confidence that the concept of an AEDS and its user-managed access approach will fall on fertile grounds. Nevertheless, further research is needed to come up with solutions that tackle the newly identified and existing impediments to t-government.

References

1. Veenstra, A.F.V., Klievink, B., Janssen, M.: Barriers and impediments to transformational government: insights from literature and practice. Int. J. Electron. Gov. **8**, 226 (2011)
2. Yildiz, M.: E-government research: reviewing the literature, limitations, and ways forward. Gov. Inf. Q. **24**, 646–665 (2007)
3. Weerakkody, V., Janssen, M., Dwivedi, Y.K.: Transformational change and business process reengineering (BPR): lessons from the British and Dutch public sector. Gov. Inf. Q. **28**, 320–328 (2011)
4. Dhillon, G.S., Weerakkody, V., Dwivedi, Y.K.: Realising transformational stage e-government: a UK local authority perspective. Int. J. Electron. Gov. **5**, 162–180 (2008)
5. Citizen Service Transformation: A manifesto for change in the delivery of public services. http://www.cstransform.com/resources/white_papers/CitizenServiceTransformationV1.pdf. Accessed 12 Feburary 2010

6. Heath, W., Alexander, D., Booth, P.: Digital Enlightenment, Mydex, and restoring control over personal data to the individual. In: Hildebrandt, M., O'Hara, K., Waidner, M. (eds.) Digital Enlightenment Yearbook 2013: The Value of Personal Data, pp. 253–269. IOS Press, Amsterdam (2013)

7. Berger, J.B., Hertzum, M.: Adoption patterns for the digital post system by Danish Municipalities and citizens. In: Proceedings of the European Conference on Information Systems (ECIS) 2014, Tel Aviv, Israel (2014)

8. Breitenstrom, C., Brunzel, M., Klessmann, J.: Elektronische Safes für Daten und Dokumente. Fraunhofer Institut für Offene Kommunikationssysteme (FOKUS), Berlin (2008)

9. Schulz, S., Hoffmann, C., Klessmann, J., Penski, A., Warnecke, T.: Dienste auf Basis elektronischer Safes für Daten und Dokumente. Lorenz-von-Stein-Institut, Fraunhofer FOKUS (2010)

10. von Lucke, J.: Portals for the public sector. In: Anttiroiko, A.-V., Malkia, M. (eds.) Encyclopedia of Digital Government. pp. 1328–1333. IGI Global (2007)

11. Kuppinger, M., Kearns, D.: Life management platforms: control and privacy for personal data. In: Hildebrandt, M., O'Hara, K., Waidner, M. (eds.) Digital Enlightenment Yearbook 2013: The Value of Personal Data, pp. 243–252. IOS Press, Amsterdam (2013)

12. Pfister, J., Schwabe, G.: The landscape of electronic data safes and their adoption in E-Government and E-Business. In: 46th Hawaii International Conference on System Sciences (HICSS), pp. 1963–1972 (2013)

13. Kohlborn, T., Korthaus, A., Peters, C., Fielt, E.: A Comparative study of governmental one-stop portals for public service delivery. Int. J. Intell. Inf. Technol. 9, 1–19 (2013)

14. Wimmer, M.A.: Integrated service modelling for online one-stop government. Electron. Markets 12, 149–156 (2002)

15. Brunzel, M.: Intermediäre Geschäftsmodelle an den Schnittstellen zur öffentlichen Verwaltung. In: Brüggemeier, M., Lenk, K. (eds.) Bürokratieabbau im Verwaltungsvollzug: Better Regulation zwischen Go-Government und No-Government, pp. 125–134. Edition Sigma, Berlin (2011)

16. Bharosa, N., Janssen, M., Klievink, B., Tan, Y.: Developing multi-sided platforms for public-private information sharing: design observations from two case studies. In: Proceedings of the 14th Annual International Conference on Digital Government Research, pp. 146–155. ACM (2013)

17. Lenz, T.: E-Government und E-Nonprofit. Management von Internetprojekten in Verwaltung und Nonprofit-Organisationen. Schäffer-Poeschel (2001)

18. Finger, M., Bukovc, B., Burhan, M. (eds.): Postal Services in the Digital Age. IOS Press, Amsterdam (2014)

19. Tungare, M.: Mental workload at transitions between multiple devices in personal information management (2009). http://pimworkshop.org/2009/papers/tungare-pim2009.pdf

20. Project VRM: Main page - project VRM. http://cyber.law.harvard.edu/projectvrm/Main_Page

21. King, R.C., Sen, R., D'Aubeterre, F., Sethi, V.: A trade value perspective on ecommerce research: an integration of transaction value and transaction cost theories. Int. J. E-Bus. Res. 6, 59–77 (2010)

22. Bannister, F.: Dismantling the silos: extracting new value from IT investments in public administration. Inf. Syst. J. 11, 65–84 (2001)

23. King, S., Cotterill, S.: Transformational government? The role of information technology in delivering citizen-centric local public services. Local Gov. Stud. 33, 333–354 (2007)

24. Duennebeil, S., Sunyaev, A., Leimeister, J.M., Krcmar, H.: Strategies for development and adoption of EHR in German ambulatory care. In: 2010 4th International Conference on Pervasive Computing Technologies for Healthcare, pp. 1–8 (2010)

25. Weitzman, E.R., Kaci, L., Mandl, K.D.: Acceptability of a personally controlled health record in a community-based setting: implications for policy and design. J. Med. Internet Res. **11**(2), Article ID e14 (2009). doi:10.2196/jmir.1187

26. Weerakkody, V., Dhillon, G., Dwivedi, Y., Currie, W.: Realising transformational stage e-government: challenges, issues and complexities. In: AMCIS 2008 Proceedings, p. 181 (2008)

27. Parisopoulos, K., Tambouris, E., Tarabanis, K.: An investigation of national policies on transformational government (t-Gov) in Europe. Int. J. Inf. Technol. Manage. **13**, 305–323 (2014)

28. Janssen, M., Estevez, E.: Lean government and platform-based governance - Doing more with less. Gov. Inf. Q. **30**(Supplement 1), S1–S8 (2013)

29. Brenner, W., Karagiannis, D., Kolbe, L., Krüger, J., Leifer, L., Lamberti, H.-J., Leimeister, J.M., Österle, H., Petrie, C., Plattner, H., Schwabe, G., Uebernickel, F., Winter, R., Zarnekow, R.: User, use & utility research: the digital user as new design perspective in business and information systems engineering. Bus. Inf. Syst. Eng. **6**, 55–61 (2014)

30. Braun, V., Clarke, V.: Using thematic analysis in psychology. Qual. Res. Psychol. **3**, 77–101 (2006)

31. Fitzgerald, C.A., Flood, P.C., O'Regan, P., Ramamoorthy, N.: Governance structures and innovation in the Irish Software Industry. J. High Technol. Manage. Res. **19**, 36–44 (2008)

32. Girard, T., Korgaonkar, P., Silverblatt, R.: Relationship of type of product, shopping orientations, and demographics with preference for shopping on the internet. J. Bus. Psychol. **18**, 101–120 (2003)

33. Liu, C., Arnett, K.P.: Exploring the factors associated with web site success in the context of electronic commerce. Inf. Manage. **38**, 23–33 (2000)

34. Camenisch, J., Fischer-Hübner, S., Rannenberg, K. (eds.): Privacy and Identity Management for Life. Springer, Berlin (2011)

35. Nissenbaum, H.F.: Privacy in Context: Technology, Policy, and the Integrity of Social Life. Stanford Law Books, Stanford (2010)

36. Barkhuus, L.: The mismeasurement of privacy: using contextual integrity to reconsider privacy in HCI. In: Proceedings of the SIGCHI Conference on Human Factors in Computing Systems, pp. 367–376. ACM, New York, NY, USA (2012)

37. Teevan, J., Liebling, D.J., Lasecki, W.S.: Selfsourcing personal tasks. Presented at the CHI 2014, Toronto, Ontario, Canada (2014)

38. Hevner, A.R., March, S.T., Park, J., Ram, S.: Design science in information systems research. MIS Q. **28**(1), 75–105 (2004)

An Ontology of eGovernment

Arkalgud Ramaprasad[1], Aurora Sánchez-Ortiz[2], and Thant Syn[3(✉)]

[1] University of Illinois at Chicago, Chicago, IL, USA
prasad@uic.edu
[2] Universidad Católica del Norte, Antofagasta, Chile
asanchez@ucn.cl
[3] Texas A and M International University, Laredo, TX, USA
thant.syn@tamiu.edu

Abstract. Amidst this rapid explosion of interest in eGovernment there is absent a clear definition of the concept and its domain. We review the extant definitions of the term and present an ontology of eGovernment to articulate its combinatorial complexity. The ontology parsimoniously encapsulates the logic of eGovernment. It moves away from technology-based conceptualizations to a systemic one. It makes the 'elephant' visible. It can be used to articulate the components and fragments which constitute eGovernment using structured natural English sentences and phrases. It serves as a multi-disciplinary lens to study the topic drawing upon concepts from information systems, knowledge management, public administration, and information technology. The ontology can be used to systematically map the state-of-the-research and the state-of-the-practice in eGovernment, discover the gaps in research and between research and practice, and formulate a strategy to bridge the gaps.

Keywords: eGovernment · Ontology · Gap analysis · Roadmap

1 Introduction

Advancements in information technology over the past twenty years have motivated many governments around the world to use it to improve their services. This initiative by the governments to electronify their services has been termed eGovernment or e-Government. The use of the term eGovernment has become common among researchers in the field; at least twenty three journals publish research on eGovernment [1].

Despite the widespread use of the term and an intuitive understanding of the same, there is a lack of agreement among researchers on the connotation of eGovernment. Yildiz [2] named this difficulty "definitional vagueness" of the eGovernment concept. The difficulties are associated with the complexity of the construct, not only because it is multidimensional but also because the dimensions are highly interconnected. Its complexity is combinatorial.

The focus of the literature to date has been mostly on the type of electronic medium used, the type of government for whom it functions, the target of its services, the types of services provided, and the overall purpose of its existence [2–4]. eGovernment

© IFIP International Federation for Information Processing 2015
E. Tambouris et al. (Eds.): EGOV 2015, LNCS 9248, pp. 258–269, 2015.
DOI: 10.1007/978-3-319-22479-4_20

perspectives in the literature can be divided into those related to its availability (infrastructure and policies) and to its use (citizens, businesses, NGOs, government employees) [5]. Additional elements pointed out by Ndou [3] are the components of eGovernment which include the use of information technology to transform government in three critical areas (internal, external, and relational applications), the targets of the government actions (citizens, businesses, government organizations, and employees), and the domains of their applications (e-services, e-democracy, and e-administration).

Researchers and practitioners have focused selectively on different parts of the whole, neglecting the "big picture" – a theme analogous to the story of the five blind men and the elephant [6, 7]. This selectivity results in fragmentation of the research and development agenda; the sum of the parts simply falls short of making the whole. There is a need to articulate and make the combinatorial complexity of eGovernment visible to facilitate both the effective design and evaluation of eGovernment systems [8].

The eGovernment concept is a challenge many researchers have tried to tackle; but there are significant gaps in the research due to their selective focus. To discover and address these gaps systematically and systemically we propose an ontology. The main goal of this ontology is to provide a synoptic perspective to assess and guide eGovernment research and practice.

We will first review some of the key definitions of eGovernment and then logically deconstruct the concept using an ontology. We will then describe how the ontology can be used to define the domain of eGovernment, and how it can be extended, reduced, refined, and coarsened to adapt to the evolving technology and environment for eGovernment. Last, we will delineate how the ontology can be used to map the state-of-the-research and the state-of-the-practice in eGovernment, discover the gaps in research and between research and practice, and formulate a strategy to bridge those gaps and generate synergy – all with the goal of making the whole greater than the sum of its parts.

The problem with the definition of eGovernment arises from the "vagueness of the e-government concept" and the concept is limited for many reasons [2]. First, the eGovernment concept is guided by the objective of the activity instead of the technology used. Second, each definition emphasizes a particular set of pet issues of government, for example: accountability, transparency, interactivity, participation, and cost-effectiveness. Third, the term eGovernment has something of a hype and promotion in it. Fourth, the level of change needed for an eGovernment project is ambiguous. Although many researchers attempt to define eGovernment in an all-encompassing manner, there is still a need for a more complete understanding of it [1].

2   Definitions of eGovernment

The initial work on the use of information technology (IT) in public administration can be found in Garson [9]. It proposes four frameworks to conceptualize the relationship among public concern, policy development, and the potential of IT. These frameworks conceptualize: (a) eGovernment as the potential of IT in decentralization and democratization, (b) limitations and contradictions of technology, (c) interaction between the technology and organizational-institutional environment, and (d) position of eGovernment within of global integration theories. The term eGovernment as such can be traced back to a model proposed by Layne and Lee [10] to assess the stages of eGovernment development. Their view of eGovernment focuses on the importance of the interaction between citizens, businesses, and government, and the need to assess the level of eGovernment development to identify the current state of development and to understand how to work towards the implementation of a more efficient government.

2.1 Frameworks and Models of eGovernment Development

The development of eGovernment research lags that of practice. This gap gives rise to many frameworks and models that assess the states of eGovernment research and practice from varying perspectives. On the one hand, the initial frameworks proposed by Layne and Lee [10] are based on advances in practice. On the other hand, there are many conceptual models and frameworks that assess the advances in research.

Models that assess the development of eGovernment in practice vary in the number of stages and the description of each one of them. Most of the stages contain different levels of technological sophistication, administrative integration, and citizen orientation [11].

The Gartner 2000 model [12] segregates the development of eGovernment into four stages: web presence, interaction, transaction, and transformation. Many of the subsequent models preserve the essence of those stages with semantic variations [10, 13–19]. Some models incorporate a fifth stage, usually called e-democracy, which refers to the involvement of citizens in online political processes [15, 16, 18, 20]. This fifth stage is necessary because it is used by governments to increase political participation, citizen involvement, and politics transparencies using online services such as online voting, polling, and surveys [18]. Most models locate the e-democracy as a fifth stage though some researchers [21] consider it an integral part of the earlier interaction stages instead of a standalone process.

Many researchers have proposed frameworks to assess the development of eGovernment research in the literature. Snead and Wright [22] analyzed 100 journals articles between 2007 and 2011 and proposed a framework that includes the government level (federal, state, local, tribal, and multiple levels), four research perspective categories (policy, governance, technology, and websites), and ten governance topics and subtopics. They characterized the methodology of the papers based on research orientation (outputs, outcomes, processes, models, and theory), research purpose (exploratory, descriptive, and explanatory), data sources (primary and secondary), and research methods [22]. Results obtained using this framework, with the sample of journal articles, revealed various gaps in research efforts not only on important areas but also throughout different levels of government. The authors found that eGovernment research occurred at federal level (37 %), state level (19 %), local level (28 %), multiple levels (15 %), and tribal level (1 %). They also found that most attention were devoted to output studies (58 %) and outcomes studies (24 %). However, very little attention was given to the process as a research orientation, only 6 % of the sample.

Almarabeh and AbuAli [23] also proposed an eGovernment framework by answering three main questions, "What, Why and How E-government?" They also addressed the ten question proposed by the Working Group on eGovernment in the Developing World [24]. "Why are we pursuing E-government? Do we have a clear vision and priorities for E-government? What kind of E-government are we ready for? Is there enough political will to lead the E-government effort? Are we selecting E-government projects in the best way? How should we plan and manage E-government projects? How will we overcome resistance from within the government? How will we measure and communicate progress? How will we know if we are failing? What should our relationship be with the private sector? How can E-government improve citizen participation in public affairs?" [24, p. 8]. Finally, through the answers to these questions these researchers proposed some definitions and assessed the maturity of eGovernment addressing the challenges and opportunities for developing a successful eGovernment.

Many frameworks and models in eGovernment can be found in the literature. However their focus varies based on the researchers' perspective. The main perspectives of analysis in eGovernment frameworks are the assessment of the advancement of a particular government – at local, provincial, central levels, the level of the technology used, the target and type of the eGovernment services, and the overall purpose of its existence. The other group of eGovernment frameworks is focused on the assessment of the research and scholarly literature that has been published on the topic. Among these the focus is divided between the availability of eGovernment (infrastructure and policies) and its use (citizens, businesses, NGOs, government employees) [2–5]. Additional elements are presented by Ndou [3] as mentioned earlier.

3 An Ontology of eGovernment

In this section we present a simple ontology of eGovernment as a systemic framework to systematically study the topic. More than a decade ago Kaylor et al. [25] bemoaned the lack of research "into the specific functions and services as they emerge on municipality websites." [p. 293] To correct the situation they proposed a very broad definition of eGovernment as "the ability for anyone visiting the city website to communicate and/ or interact with the city via the Internet in any way more sophisticated than a simple email letter to the generic city (or webmaster) email address provided at the site." [25] They wanted to draw attention to the functions of an eGovernment articulated through the government's website.

While local eGovernment research and implementation continue to be popular and important, there has not emerged a systemic framework to conceptualize it. Researchers and practitioners focus on different parts of the whole but not on the whole – analogous to the story of the five blind men and the elephant [6, 7]. There is a need to make the combinatorial complexity of eGovernment visible to facilitate their effective design and evaluation [8]. We use an ontology to represent the complexity of eGovernment and make it visible.

An ontology represents the conceptualization of a domain [26]; it organizes the terminologies and taxonomies of the domain. It is an "explicit specification of a conceptualization," [27, p. 908] and can be used to systematize the description of a complex system [28]. "Our acceptance of an ontology is... similar in principle to our acceptance of a scientific theory, say a system of physics; we adopt, at least insofar as we are reasonable, the simplest conceptual scheme into which the disordered fragments of raw experience can be fitted and arranged." [29, p. 16].

We deconstruct eGovernment into four dimensions, each represented by a taxonomy (Fig. 1). They are, from left to right, Medium, Entity, Service, and Outcome. The dimensions and elements of the taxonomies are defined in the glossary below the ontology and described below. Four illustrative components of eGovernment derived from the ontology are listed below the ontology with examples. The ontology is applicable to eGovernments in general; however, we will focus on local/municipal eGovernments' perspective only in this paper. The method can be generalized to the study of other eGovernments.

3.1 Medium

The 'e' in eGovernment indicates a fundamental shift in the media used by a government in its operation due to the revolution in information technology. The historical media for government operations were first people and then paper. The new medium is electronic. In the early stages of the information technology revolution personal computers were emblematic of the 'e', now in addition there are the smart phones and social media.

The government portals such as FirstGov.gov are an important step toward the use of electronic medium at the government level and the implementation of some critical legislation regarding the government's use of IT – for example, Paperwork Reduction Act (PRA), Electronic Freedom of Information Act (EFOIA), Personal Responsibility and Work Opportunity Reconciliation Act (PRWORA), the Information Technology Management Reform Act (the Clinger–Cohen Act), and the E-government act. They also support the increased use of electronic means in government [2]. "Until the introduction of the Internet and widespread use of personal computers, the main objectives of technology use in government were enhancing the managerial effectiveness of public administrators while increasing government productivity. Until then, the main use of technology in government organizations was the automation of mass transactions such as financial transactions using mainframe computers" [30, p. 121]. Norris and Reddick [31] analyzed the level of eGovernment development and found that at least two thirds of the municipalities in their sample (1,326) had adopted at least one social medium.

The induction of new media – first paper and then electronic – has not eliminated the use of old media, but simply changed their role. People and paper continue to be important in the operation of even the most advanced eGovernment. The importance of people, for example, is illustrated by the emergence of contact centers [32] for providing service. Similarly, paper will continue to play a role in managing the long-term continuity of records from the past to the future [33].

Thus, we articulate the Medium dimension as a two-level taxonomy. At the first level are People, Paper and Electronics; and at the second level there are three subcategories of Electronics, namely: PC/Web, Smart phone, and Social media. (Note: Words which refer to the dimensions, categories, and subcategories in the ontology are capitalized to distinguish them from common usage of the same).

Medium		Entity		Service		Outcomes	
People	[based system for]	Governments	[to provide/obtain]	Information	[services for]	eGovernment	[functions]
Paper		Local/Municipal		Transaction		eGovernance	
Electronics (E-)		Provincial/State		Interaction		eDemocracy	
PC/Web		Central/Federal					
Smart phone		Intermediaries					
Social media		Citizens					
		Businesses					
		NGOs					

Illustrative Components:

1. People based system for governments to provide/obtain information services for eGovernment functions.
For example, visiting the municipal office to obtain information on parking zones and restrictions from the clerk.

2. Paper based system for citizens to provide/obtain transaction services for eDemocracy functions.
For example, voting with paper ballot.

3. Electronics based system for businesses to provide/obtain interaction services for eGovernance functions.
For example, online discussion on new city tax policies.

4. Electronics $_{social\ media}$ based systems for citizens to provide/obtain information services for eGovernment services.
For example, posting city office closure messages on Facebook. (A subcategory is shown as a subscript.)

Glossary:

Medium: The medium for providing government services
  People: People based services
  Paper: Paper forms, document services
  Electronics (E-): Information technology based services
    PC/Web: Personal computer, worldwide web, internet based services
    Smart phone: iPhone, Android, and other smart phone based services
    Social media: Facebook, Twitter, Yelp, and other social media based services
Entity: The entity providing or receiving the government services
  Governments The different levels of government
    Local/Municipal: The lowest level of government
    Provincial/State: The government of a province or state, above the local/municipal government
    Central/Federal: The government of the country
  Intermediaries: Organizations aiding the relationship with the government
  Citizens: The citizens of the community governed by the local government
  Businesses: Businesses within the community and having relationship with it at its government
  NGOs: Non Government Organizations working with the community
Service: The types of services provided and received by the entities
  Information: Providing and receiving information
  Transaction: Exchange of funds, material, services, and information
  Interaction: Continuing exchange of funds, material, services, and information
Outcomes: The outcome of government
  eGovernment: Electronification of administrative functions
  eGovernance: Electronification of government decision and policy making
  eDemocracy: Electronification of political participation

Fig. 1. Ontology of eGovernment

3.2 Entity

Entities are the stakeholders in the eGovernment. The municipal/local government and the citizens are the central entities by definition in a democracy – the government is of the citizens, by the citizens, and for the citizens. Any local government has to operate in cooperation and collaboration with other local governments, the provincial or state government, and the central or federal government. These other government entities can play a significant role in the effectiveness of the eGovernment.

Between the local government and citizens there may be intermediaries. On the one hand, eGovernment is intended to eliminate many traditional intermediaries (middlemen) to increase transparency in services like issuing licenses and permits [34]. On the other hand, there appears to be emerging a new type of intermediary such as a contact center [32] to help citizens with the new technology and processes. In the same vein public libraries too could be intermediaries [31].

Businesses drive the local economy and are driven by it. In addition, local and external businesses supply products and services to the local government and the local businesses. In performing their activities the businesses may need to interact with the local government to obtain information, provide information, obtain licenses, pay taxes, bid on contracts, etc. eGovernments are intended to make these interactions more efficient and effective. Thus, Businesses are an important entity.

Non-Government Organizations (NGOs), are usually non-profit entities which are neither businesses nor part of the government but provide important services in the locality. It may be a charity, a shelter for the homeless, or a free medical care facility. They play a significant role in many localities and constitute an important entity of the eGovernment.

Thus the taxonomy of Entities includes the Governments, Intermediaries, Citizens, Businesses, and NGOs. The three subcategories of Governments are: Local/Municipal, Provincial/State, and Central/Federal. The eGovernment Media have to support the functioning of the Local/Municipal government as well as its interactions with the other Entities, and perhaps among the entities at a later stage.

3.3 Service

The taxonomy of services reflects their typical evolution – for providing/obtaining information, to supporting transactions, and then to supporting interactions [31]. This is similar to Fan and Luo [35] scale of Cataloging, Interaction, and Transaction, and to providing Content, Services, and Engagement [36].

Information services are the most rudimentary. The eGovernment website may provide information about parking permits, snow removal, etc. It may also allow Citizens to input information about potholes, complaints, and community actions.

Transaction services can be a little more complex. They may include paying real estate taxes, water bills, traffic tickets, etc. They often require real-time exchange of information with privacy, validation, security, and other features.

Interaction services are the most complex. In contrast to transaction services where the volume of information exchanged may be small and the type of information simple, in interaction services the volume may be large and the information complex. An example would be eProcurement services [36, 37].

Research regarding the acquisition, management, storage, retrieval and use of information and data are very limited. Gil-García and Pardo [38] suggest that inconsistent data structures, semantic issues, and incomplete data can have an impact on the success of the eGovernment initiatives, and also the integration of the information and data at different levels of governments need to be explored. Bhattacharya et al. [11] claim that most of the literature on government e-services are theoretical and based on theories of management. They also analyze the quality of the e-services throughout the government portals in India and argue that since they are designed and implemented only by the IT professionals, they fail to provide the services needed by the citizens [11]. They highlight the problems with multi-language, interface design, services, interoperability, and communication. Norris and Reddick [31] analyze the trajectory of local government in the United States through the survey of 1,326 municipalities. They found the development of services has not been as good as predicted and most of those services have been mainly about delivering information and services online but there are few transactions and limited interactivity. They show that in the USA, local governments offering information and communication applications through the web grew considerably between 2004 and 2011; however, transaction-based services have not been growing at the same pace because of the difficulty in their implementation on the web and their cost.

From Information to Transaction to Interaction, there is an increase in the complexity, cost, and difficulty of providing the services. The technology is capable of providing the services at all three levels. Moreover, the availability of similar services in other domains, for example – online purchasing, may increase the pressure on Local/Municipal eGovernments to provide similar services. An eGovernment has to provide all the three types of Services, using all the three Media, for all the Stakeholders. The Medium x Service mix may vary by the stage of development. At an early stage of development the Information Services may be Electronic and the Interaction Services People-based; at a later stage all but the most complex services may be Electronic.

3.4 Outcome

The taxonomy of outcomes is based on the posited stages of evolution of eGovernment into eGovernance to eDemocracy. We draw upon Moreno-Jiménez, Pérez-Espés and Velázquez [39] to distinguish between them as follows. eGovernment is what Moreno-Jiménez, Pérez-Espés and Velázquez [39] call "e-Administration, oriented towards the improvement of public services offered to the citizens" [and other Entities] by the local/municipal government. eGovernance is the "processes that are based on the intervention of the citizens and their representatives in public decisions relative to the government of society..." [p. 186] for example, policy making. eDemocracy extends the Services to some of the core functions of the democracy such as political participation [35] through e-Voting [39] and similar mechanisms.

Linders [40] analyzed the role of citizens in the coproduction or what has been labeled as "Citizen sourcing" for shaping policies at local level in areas as budget and mass collaboration. The author discusses the potential implications of electronic citizen coproduction for public administration, presents the limitations of this concept, and raises social concerns about the role and power of public citizens in government. Nam [41] suggests that citizen sourcing has also been studied as a source of collective decision-making and an input for policymaking, and calls for assessments of the impact of citizen sourcing in order to reveal if this is mainly a rhetorical issue or it is really significant for society.

3.5   Components of eGovernment

The four dimensions of the ontology are arranged left to right with connecting word/ phrases to enumerate all the components of eGovernment in natural English. A component can be concatenated by combining a word/phrase from each dimension (column) and combining it with the interleaved word/phrases. Four illustrative components of eGovernment with examples are listed below the ontology (Fig. 1).

The ontology has $5*7*3*3 = 315$ components encapsulated in it. It can be argued that these components constitute the domain of eGovernment systematically and systemically. In any government it is likely that only some of these components will be instantiated. Moreover, some components may be instantiated frequently and some infrequently. We will call the frequently instantiated components the 'bright' spots; the infrequently instantiated ones the 'light' spots; and the uninstantiated ones the 'blind/blank' spots [42]. A component may be 'bright' because it is important, or because it is easy to implement. By the same token, a 'light' component may be unimportant, or difficult to implement. Last, a component may have been overlooked and hence 'blind', or infeasible and hence 'blank'.

4   Discussion – Ontology of eGovernment as a Lens

The ontology of eGovernment presented in this paper makes visible the combinatorial complexity of a growing topic in public administration. Our attempt seeks to include, refine, and extend previous definitions and conceptualizations.

The ontology is logically constructed but grounded in the theory and practice of the domain. The dimensions are logically specified and not empirically generated. They are deduced from the definition of the domain.

The logical construction of the ontology minimizes the errors of omission and commission. For example, the inclusion of all the three basic Media compels the researcher to explicitly consider their roles individually and in interaction with each other. Without consideration of Paper (error of omission), for example, the researcher is likely to overlook the continued importance of a medium (especially in the government to fulfil legal requirements) despite the highest level of electronification. Further, within Electronics, the ontology can help specify the individual media for combination of them, instead of specifying it generally (error of commission).

The ontology can be extended and refined to adapt to technological changes over time and contextual differences (say between countries). But the core of the ontology and its logic are constant. The differences between contexts and countries will be revealed in the different 'bright', 'light', and 'blind/blank' spots. In fact, to study the differences, the ontology/lens has to be held constant.

Last, the ontology is a multi-disciplinary lens. The Medium and Service dimensions are drawn from the information systems literature and refined for eGovernment; the Entity and Outcomes dimensions are drawn from the public administration literature. The ontology compels the user to analyze the eGovernment problem and synthesize solutions by drawing upon these disciplines.

5   Conclusion

There is a need to address the issue of eGovernment holistically, instead of doing so fragmentarily. There is also a need to map the research, policies, and practice of eGovernment systematically and systemically to understand the gaps within each, and between them. Understanding and bridging the two sets of gaps will be critical to the translation of research to policy to practice.

The proposed ontology of eGovernment can advance the state-of-the-research, state-of-the-policy, and the state-of-the-practice in the domain. It can be used to systematically identify the 'bright', 'light', and 'blind/blank' spots in the three states and between the two states. Such mapping will reveal opportunities for research, policy, and implementation. It can be used to develop a roadmap for eGovernment.

For a domain without a standard definition, the ontology can serve as the nucleus of a standardized definition. The ability to extend and refine the ontology makes it suitable to study the phenomenon at different levels of granularity in different contexts. The present ontology encapsulates most of the present definitions; it also highlights the gaps in them. It can be a starting point for the systematization of the domain, its knowledge, and application.

References

1. Madsen, C.Ø., Berger, J.B., Phythian, M.: The development in leading e-Government articles 2001-2010: definitions, perspectives, scope, research philosophies, methods and recommendations: an update of heeks and bailur. In: Janssen, M., Scholl, H.J., Wimmer, M.A., Bannister, F. (eds.) EGOV 2014. LNCS, vol. 8653, pp. 17–34. Springer, Heidelberg (2014)
2. Yildiz, M.: E-government research: reviewing the literature, limitations, and ways forward. Gov. Inf. Q. **24**, 646–665 (2007)
3. Ndou, V.: E-government for developing countries: opportunities and challenges. Electron. J. Inf. Syst. Dev. Countries **18** (2004)
4. Baltra, D., Wolf, P., Krcmar, H.: The public-private partnership concept: a systematic review of e-government related literature. In: Proceedings of EGPA Annual Conference 2014, Speyer, Germany (2014)
5. Ovais Ahmad, M., Markkula, J., Oivo, M.: Factors affecting e-Government adoption in Pakistan: a citizen's perspective. Transform. Gov. People Process Policy **7**, 225–239 (2013)
6. Ramaprasad, A., Papagari, S.S.: Ontological design. In: Proceedings of DESRIST 2009, Malvern, PA (2009)
7. Börner, K., Chen, C., Boyack, K.W.: Visualizing knowledge domains. Ann. Rev. Inf. Sci. Technol. **37**, 179–255 (2003)
8. Ramaprasad, A., Syn, T.: Design thinking and evaluation using an ontology. In: Helfert, M., Donnellan, B., Kenneally, J. (eds.) EDSS 2013. CCIS, vol. 447, pp. 63–74. Springer, Heidelberg (2014)
9. Garson, G.D.: Information systems, politics, and government: leading theoretical perspectives. In: Garson, G.D. (ed.) Handbook of Public Information Systems, pp. 591–605. CRC Press, New York (1999)
10. Layne, K., Lee, J.: Developing fully functional E-government: a four stage model. Gov. Inf. Q. **18**, 122–136 (2001)

11. Bhattacharya, D., Gulla, U., Gupta, M.: E-service quality model for Indian government portals: citizens' perspective. J. Enterp. Inf. Manage. **25**, 246–271 (2012)
12. Baum, C., Di Maio, A.: Gartner's four phases of e-government model. Gartner Group (2000)
13. Affisco, J.F., Soliman, K.S.: E-government: a strategic operations management framework for service delivery. Bus. Process Manage. J. **12**, 13–21 (2006)
14. Al-Adawi, Z., Yousafzai, S., Pallister, J.: Conceptual model of citizen adoption of e-government. In: The Second International Conference on Innovations in Information Technology (IIT 2005), pp. 1–10 (2005)
15. Esteves, J., Bohórquez, V.: Analyzing the development of municipal e-Government in Peruvian cities. In: Proceedings of the 9th International Conference on Social Implications of Computers in Developing Countries, São Paulo, Brazil (2007)
16. Hiller, J.S., Belanger, F.: Privacy strategies for electronic government. E-government **200**, 162–198 (2001)
17. Moon, M.J.: The evolution of e-government among municipalities: rhetoric or reality? Public Adm. Rev. **62**, 424–433 (2002)
18. Siau, K., Long, Y.: Synthesizing e-government stage models-a meta-synthesis based on meta-ethnography approach. Ind. Manage. Data Syst. **105**, 443–458 (2005)
19. West, D.M.: E-government and the transformation of service delivery and citizen attitudes. Public Adm. Rev. **64**, 15–27 (2004)
20. Wescott, C.G.: E-Government in the Asia-pacific region. Asian J. Polit. Sci. **9**, 1–24 (2001)
21. Lee, J.: 10 year retrospect on stage models of e-Government: a qualitative meta-synthesis. Gov. Inf. Q. **27**, 220–230 (2010)
22. Snead, J.T., Wright, E.: E-government research in the United States. Gov. Inf. Q. **31**, 129–136 (2014)
23. Almarabeh, T., AbuAli, A.: A general framework for e-government: definition maturity challenges, opportunities, and success. Eur. J. Sci. Res. **39**, 29–42 (2010)
24. http://www.itu.int/wsis/docs/background/themes/egov/pacific_council.pdf
25. Kaylor, C., Deshazo, R., Van Eck, D.: Gauging e-government: a report on implementing services among American cities. Gov. Inf. Q. **18**, 293–307 (2001)
26. Gruber, T.R.: Ontology. In: Liu, L., Ozsu, M.T. (eds.) Encyclopedia of Database Systems. Springer, Berlin (2008)
27. Gruber, T.R.: Toward principles for the design of ontologies used for knowledge sharing. Int. J. Hum Comput Stud. **43**, 907–928 (1995)
28. Cimino, J.J.: In defense of the desiderata. J. Biomed. Inf. **39**, 299–306 (2006)
29. Quine, W.V.O.: From a Logical Point of View. Harvard University Press, Boston (1961)
30. Schelin, S.H.: E-government: an overview. In: Public Information Technology, pp. 120–137. IGI Publishing, Hershey (2003)
31. Norris, D.F., Reddick, C.G.: Local E-government in the United States: transformation or incremental change? Public Adm. Rev. **73**, 165–175 (2013)
32. Kallberg, M.: Issues with contact centres - as a new interface between public organisations and citizens. Rec. Manage. J. **23**, 90–103 (2013)
33. Svärd, P.: Enterprise content management and the records continuum model as strategies for long-term preservation of digital information. Rec. Manage. J. **23**, 159–176 (2013)
34. Ganapati, S., Reddick, C.G.: The use of ICT for open government in U.S. municipalities: Perceptions of chief administrative officers. Public Perform. Manage. Rev. **37**, 365–387 (2014)
35. Fan, B., Luo, J.: Benchmarking scale of e-government stage in Chinese municipalities from government chief information officers' perspective. Inf. Syst. e-Bus. Manage. 1–26 (2013)

36. Holzer, M., Zheng, Y., Manoharan, A., Shark, A.: Digital Governance in Municipalities Worldwide (2013-14). E-Governance Institute (2014)
37. Doherty, N.F., McConnell, D.J., Ellis-Chadwick, F.: Institutional responses to electronic procurement in the public sector. Int. J. Public Sect. Manage. **26**, 495–515 (2013)
38. Gil-García, J.R., Pardo, T.A.: E-government success factors: mapping practical tools to theoretical foundations. Gov. Inf. Q. **22**, 187–216 (2005)
39. Moreno-Jiménez, J.M., Pérez-Espés, C., Velázquez, M.: E-cognocracy and the design of public policies. Gov. Inf. Q. **31**, 185–194 (2014)
40. Linders, D.: From e-government to we-government: defining a typology for citizen coproduction in the age of social media. Gov. Inf. Q. **29**, 446–454 (2012)
41. Nam, T.: Suggesting frameworks of citizen-sourcing via government 2.0. Gov. Inf. Q. **29**, 12–20 (2012)
42. Ramaprasad, A., Syn, T.: Ontological meta-analysis and synthesis. In: Proceedings of the Nineteenth Americas Conference on Information Systems Chicago, IL, USA (2013)

Application Areas and Evaluation

Privacy in Digital Identity Systems: Models, Assessment, and User Adoption

Armen Khatchatourov[1,4(✉)], Maryline Laurent[2,4],
and Claire Levallois-Barth[3,4]

[1] Télécom Ecole de Management, Évry, France
armen.khatchatourov@telecom-em.eu
[2] Télécom SudParis, Évry, France
[3] Télécom ParisTech, Paris, France
[4] Chair Values and Policies of Personal Information,
Institut Mines-Télécom, Paris, France

Abstract. The use of privacy protection measures is of particular importance for existing and upcoming users' digital identities. Thus, the recently adopted EU Regulation on Electronic identification and trust services (eIDAS) explicitly allows the use of pseudonyms in the context of eID systems, without specifying how they should be implemented. The paper contributes to the discussion on pseudonyms and multiple identities, by (1) providing an original analysis grid that can be applied for privacy evaluation in any eID architecture, and (2) introducing the concept of *eID deployer* allowing virtually any case of the relationship between the user, the eID implementation and the user's digital identities to be modelled. Based on these inputs, a comparative analysis of four exemplary eID architectures deployed in European countries is conducted. The paper also discusses how sensitive citizens of these countries are to the privacy argument while adopting these systems, and presents the "privacy adoption paradox".

Keywords: eID · eID deployer · Pseudonymous authentication · Privacy · Multiple/partial identities · Technology adoption · Selective disclosure · Privacy adoption paradox · Digital identity · Privacy by design · Personal data · Privacy impact assessment · eIDAS · e-Government

1 Introduction

The use of digital or electronic identity (eID) systems is a growing trend in on-line environments, both in public and private sectors. In the public sector, the eID eco-system is believed to be a driver for stronger e-Government adoption by citizens, while the private sector (banks, travel companies, etc.) may also be interested in secured solutions strongly linked to the civil identity. In the European Union, a long term strategy has been in place for the last few years, and has resulted in a recent adoption (in 2014) of the Regulation on Electronic identification and trust services (eIDAS) [1]. This text establishes the main principles that will guide implementation and use of digital identities in the Member States in the near future. While the scope of the

© IFIP International Federation for Information Processing 2015
E. Tambouris et al. (Eds.): EGOV 2015, LNCS 9248, pp. 273–290, 2015.
DOI: 10.1007/978-3-319-22479-4_21

Regulation concerns public e-services only, the goal is clearly to set a global policy framework to boost the adoption of eID in both public and private sectors.[1]

Basically, an *electronic identity management system* (eIDMS) allows user identification and authentication to on-line services through the use of various authentication means (from login/password to smartcards). Once authenticated, the user is linked to a set of attributes (civil identity, date of birth, address, etc.) and is able to use the service. Today's eIDMSs use various approaches defining technical and organizational architectures to establish trust relationships between the following entities: users, the Identity Provider (IDP) which is a trusted third party in charge of managing the eID of users, and Service Providers (SPs) which deliver a service to the user [2]. As the cornerstone of that architecture, the IDP has an influential role in privacy handling: it belongs to a continuum where at one extremum the IDP only manages issuance and revocation (e.g. when the eID is declared stolen) and, at the other extremum, it knows all about the users' transactions as it is asked each time to assert user attributes.

In these architectures, different stakeholders (SPs, IDP) manage users' attributes, which are personal data in the sense of the Data Protection Directive 95/46/EC [3]. Consequently, the use of eIDMS raises several privacy concerns. It must be emphasized here that the EU legislation deals with the notion of personal data, which is clearly distinguished from the notion of privacy [4]. However, for the sake of simplicity, this paper uses both notions without distinction.

The main privacy concerns are disproportionate data disclosure and user linkability across service providers, which may lead to the knowledge of a user's behaviour by third parties, and thus to unwanted behaviour profiling [5]. If the user has to prove to be over 18 years old to access a service, there should be no disproportionate data disclosure of an exact age and/or civil identity for that purpose. If the user accesses an e-health service and a bank service, in principle there should be no possible linking of the two actions, neither by both SPs nor by IDP.

A possible way to cope with such privacy threats is to implement two measures. The first one is pseudonymous authentication which basically refers to the use of one or many pseudonyms, not unequivocally associated to the civil identity, for identification and authentication to on-line services. Only the issuing authority (IDP) has the knowledge of this association and may reveal it for legal reasons (e.g. fraud). The second one is user-controlled selective attributes disclosure, which is usually implemented as a checkbox allowing the user to select which attributes are disclosed to a particular SP. Both the effectiveness and the user's perception of privacy protection may be quite different depending on design choices about how the pseudonymous authentication and the data flows between the different stakeholders are designed.

These privacy protection principles are recalled in the aforementioned eIDAS Regulation under Art. 5 which states that (1) processing of personal data shall be carried out in accordance with Directive 95/46/EC (that is respecting among other principles that the data disclosed are "adequate, relevant and not excessive in relation to

---

[1] We use the term *digital identity* in a broad sense relevant for all on-line transactions, and the term *eID* when the context is particularly relevant to the eIDAS Regulation. The findings of this paper are relevant for both cases.

the purposes for which the data are collected and/or further processed") and that (2) "the use of pseudonyms in electronic transactions shall not be prohibited". The Regulation however does not specify how these principles should be implemented, nor does it take into account the eIDMS already deployed in several Member States. However, according to the design choices made by Member States, these eIDMS lead to different privacy protection levels.

The goal of this paper is to provide a comprehensive analysis of eIDMS architectures with regard to the data protection criteria, and to generalize into an analysis grid for privacy evaluation of any existing or future eIDMS. The paper is organized as follows. Section 2 highlights the methodology of the comparative analysis and introduces the analysis grid. Section 3 motivates the selection of four European States and provides a brief description of their eIDMS. Section 4 introduces the models of the relationship between the user, the eID implementation and user's digital identities, develops the analysis grid and applies it to four countries to describe the efficiency of privacy protection. Finally, Sect. 5 addresses two open questions. First, as the privacy concerns seem to grow among the population, it could be expected that more privacy preserving eIDMS would get larger user adoption. However, we underline that, as of today, there is no strong evidence of such a correlation. Second, we identify some of the key factors (namely the number of services available for the user and the perceived privacy) that may influence the user adoption of eIDMS.

2 Methodology

To conduct the comparative analysis, we adopt a particular methodology, articulated around three points.

First, the paper aims to propose a relevant level of description of privacy protection measures, mainly related to pseudonymity. The literature often provides either a too high-level description in terms of models of trust [6, 7], or a too detailed technical description in terms of data flows. While both are necessary in their own contexts, we are looking for an approach which is able to catch at the same time the functional relations between parties, and the relevant aspects of actual, existing systems, while not being lost with low-level details. We believe that such a "big picture" can benefit the discussion in the context where people from different viewpoints (engineers, policy makers, service providers, lawyers, civil society) are brought together to discuss these important issues.

Second, our analysis considers only already deployed architectures, and not well-known theoretical models (such as central, federated or user-centric), nor EU research and development projects. Indeed, existing systems are known to exhibit notable differences from theoretical models. For example, the Austrian eID architecture is a complex mixture of central, federated and user-centric models [8]. Similarly, the German eID does not fit any of existing theoretical models or "pure" architectures such as SAML, OAuth, etc., or their privacy characteristics as described in [9]. We wish our analysis to be very practical and realistic.

Third, we identify three inter-related design axes (illustrated Fig. 1) that help evaluate the privacy protection level in a real system. Axis 1 concerns the relationship between eID carriers, *eID deployers* (the concept we introduce on this occasion, see Sect. 4 for details) and multiple pseudonyms; we also mention public policy on multiple pseudonyms and user initiatives related to the presence of pseudonymous authentication. Axis 2 deals with the management of user attributes. Axis 3 concerns the way the authentication scheme and the functional relations between parties are implemented. The 3 axes are inter-related from the privacy protection point of view, and the inter-axis analysis is provided in Subsect. 4.4, leading to a full analysis grid applicable to any country.

Axis 1. Pseudonymous authentication
- **Three models of *eID deployer***
  - No pseudonym: one identifier for multiple carriers
  - One pseudonym from multiple carriers
  - Multiple pseudonyms from one (or multiple) carrier(s)
- **Public policies on multiple pseudonyms**
- **User's or Service Provider's control over pseudonymous authentication**

Axis 2. Attributes location
  - Local
  - Distributed
  - Centralized

Axis 3. Authentication schemes
- **Privacy against Identity Provider**
- **Privacy against Service Providers**
- **User controlled selective attributes disclosure**

Fig. 1. Analysis grid. Bullet items are sub-axes, dash items are design options (if relevant).

3   Choice of Countries

For the purposes of our analysis, we identified four countries. While small, this sample is quite representative of the diversity of solutions: from a basic non-pseudonymized solution to complex privacy protection oriented ones. All the systems offer electronic authentication and electronic signature (this feature is not directly addressed here). The available service providers cover a large range of public (e-Government, social security) and private (banking, insurance, travel) services.

Estonian eID. Launched as early as 2002 and often described as a success story, the Estonian eID can be supported by various carriers (smartcard, mobile) and allows the user to be authenticated by on-line services. The main compulsory eID card serves also as National ID document in off-line identification. The user is identified by a unique Personal Identification Code, considered as non-confidential in Estonia and based on the Population Register. The main privacy protection mechanism is related to the management of a user's attributes [10, 11].

Austrian Citizen Card (CC). Massively rolled-out by 2006, the Austrian eID is a flexible approach based on a particular technology called the Citizen Card concept (CC). The eID can be supported by various carriers such as mobile phones or chip cards (e.g. Social Security e-card). The CC and its carriers are not National ID documents, but are the official eID. As in Estonia, there is a central database called the Central Residents Register. However, the Austrian legislation prohibits the use of these identifiers by service providers. The main privacy protecting mechanism is the use of sector-specific pseudonymous authentication [12, 13].

German eID. Launched in 2010, the German credit-card format carrier fulfils two functions: eID, machine-readable travel document and National Identity card (or "nPA" which stands for "neue Personalausweis", i.e. new passport). Here, national legislation does not allow a central database of identifiers. The main privacy preserving mechanisms are: pseudonymous authentication, user controlled disclosure of attributes, no knowledge of users' activities by IDP, and mutual authentication between the user and the SP (the SP's validity is systematically verified) [14–16].

SuisseID. Launched in 2010 as a mostly private-sector initiative, SuisseID is used only for on-line authentication, and is not an ID document. Different form-factors (smartcards, usb-sticks and mobiles) are available. The privacy protection mechanisms are optional pseudonymous authentication and selective disclosure [17, 18].

4   Analysis Grid and Its Application to eID Management Systems

In this section, several design choices for privacy protection in the four countries selected are described following the analysis grid illustrated in Fig. 1. In the following, we use the terms identifier (when unequivocally linked to civil identity) and pseudonym (when not) to refer to the way a Service Provider (SP) identifies the user. The same user may be represented by different pseudonyms for different SPs.

4.1   The *eID Deployer* Concept

To model virtually any case of the relationship between the user, the eID implementation and the user's digital identities (pseudonymized or not), here we introduce the concept of the *eID deployer*. The digital identities are deployed by the *eID deployer* which is an abstract functionality to establish the link between the physical form-factor of an authentication mean (called *carrier*) and the identifier or pseudonym. Several *carriers* may instantiate the same *eID deployer* if they fulfil the same function and disclose the same identifier/pseudonym and/or attributes. For example, two *carriers* belonging to the same user (e.g. a smartcard and a smartphone) may deploy the same *pseudonym* or a set of *pseudonyms* representing this user. Alternatively, the user can possess several carriers, each of which deploys its own eID, i.e. its own identifier or pseudonym. That is, multiple pseudonyms can be achieved in two manners: either by generating one pseudonym by the *eID deployer* and providing the user with many *eID deployers*, or by generating multiple pseudonyms from one *eID deployer*. From the user's point of view, this mechanism allows partial [19, 20] digital identities to be managed in the sense that a user's actions in one usage context are not known in the other one (the user is cross-domain unlinkable).

In the rest of this section, we analyze the level of privacy protection according to 3 design axis: pseudonymous authentication, attributes' location and authentication schemes.

4.2   Pseudonymous Authentication

Three Models of eID deployer. This sub-section describes the three models relative to the *eID deployer* implementation.

No Pseudonym: One Identifier from Multiple Carriers. There can be no pseudonymity, in which case the user is always identified with a unique identifier unequivocally linked to the civil identity (typically, the unique citizen identification number from the population register). It must be noted that in this case, because of the static nature of the link between unique identifier and civil identity, the latter can be regarded as a part of the former, and not as a distinct attribute. The *eID deployer*'s function is simply to disclose the same identifier to different SPs. This is the case in Estonian eID where civil identity (i.e. name and date of birth) and unique identifier are stored directly in the electronic certificate and disclosed at each authentication session. In Estonia, the *eID deployer* is implemented on several carriers: mandatory National ID with eID based on a smartcard, optional DigiID based on a smartcard and which allows the same actions as the main eID without being a National ID document, and optional smartphone based Mobile-ID. In digital environments, all theses *carriers* act in the same manner and fulfil the same function to uniquely represent the user.

One Pseudonym from Multiple Carriers. The simplest way to implement pseudonymity is to envisage an *eID deployer* which discloses one pseudonym instead of civil identity. In this case, the civil identity is known only by the eID issuing authority (IDP). The SP knows the user only as the pseudonym, and if the civil identity is disclosed to the SP, it is an attribute of the pseudonym. Again, there can be multiple carriers on which the same *eID deployer* is implemented, disclosing the same pseudonym. This approach is implemented in SuisseID, where the user can purchase a smartcard-based or usb-stick based carrier, and can opt for a complementary mobile phone-based carrier, all deploying the same eID. With this solution, if the user wishes to use multiple pseudonyms, he has to purchase as many carriers with corresponding *eID deployers* as the number of pseudonyms he wishes. Typically, one may want to have a non-pseudonymized eID and one or several pseudonymized eID for different usage contexts (see below the sub-section *User's or Service Provider's control on pseudonymous authentication* for details).

Multiple Pseudonyms from One (or Multiple) Carrier(s). A more sophisticated mechanism is used in Austria and Germany. The *eID deployer* can generate software defined sector-specific pseudonyms, each of which is used in the corresponding sector.

In Austria for example, there are 26 distinct sectors, from social security to banking. It seems that there is no technical difficulty to increase the granularity from sector- to service-specific pseudonyms. The SP identifies the user only as the pseudonym specific to the sector so that no cross-sector linkability is possible. In this approach, there is no "root" pseudonym or identifier. Indeed, German legislation prohibits central registry of citizens and unique identification numbers in general. The Austrian eID system does rely on the Central Registry of Residents (CRR), but there are additional one-way hash mechanisms implemented at two stages: first, to prevent the tracking back from a sector-specific pseudonym to the sourcePIN stored in a separate container on the eID carrier, and second, to prevent tracking further back from the sourcePIN to the CRR. Here also, all the *carriers* (social security smartcard, bank smartcard, mobile phone, etc.) represent the same *eID deployer*, because all *carriers* fulfill the same functional role to generate sector-specific pseudonyms in the same manner. In Austria, it is not possible to hold more than one *eID deployer*: whatever the carrier is, the same user will be represented by the same pseudonym in the same sector. In Germany, only one carrier and thus one *eID deployer* is allowed for the moment which is a smartcard combining eID, national ID and a machine readable travel document. There are however plans to implement mobile *carriers* as well, as in Austria. The three models are depicted Fig. 2.

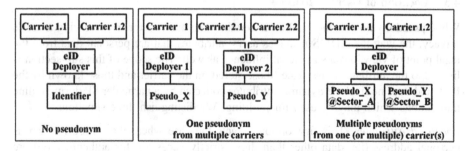

Fig. 2. Three models of *eID deployer*, implemented in Estonian eID; SuisseID; Austrian Citizen Card and German eID respectively (from left to right).

Public Policies on Multiple Pseudonyms. Different states present different public policies with regard to the use of multiple pseudonyms and to the enrolment procedure. It is interesting to note that the strength of enrolment is not directly related to the presence of pseudonymity. Estonia and Germany exhibit rather strict procedures involving the Ministry of Interior, while they do have opposite policies as to the use of pseudonyms. Austria and especially Switzerland have lighter procedures, with possibly remote activation, via Internet or post.

This can be explained by the fact that policy strategies are based not on the presence of pseudonyms per se, but on the articulation between the national ID document and the *eID deployer*. Indeed, in countries with the strictest enrolment procedures where at least one of the carriers fulfils the traditional physical identity card purpose, only one *eID deployer* is allowed. In countries with the lightest enrolment procedure where there is no direct link with the traditional ID purpose (SuisseID), there are no restrictions on the number of *eID deployers*. Austria falls in between: while not being a National ID, the eID is official for on-line transactions; thus, multiple *eID deployers* are not allowed.

User's or Service Provider's Control over Pseudonymous Authentication. When pseudonymity is implemented, the user may be granted or not the initiative of its use. The pseudonymity can be called automatic when all authentications make use of a pseudonym, as in Germany and Austria, and user-defined when the user has the initiative to use the pseudonym or not, as with SuisseID. In the particular case of SuisseID however, for unknown reasons, it is not possible to have both a pseudonym and a real name in the same *eID deployer* so that the user's choice at issuance is definitive.

It has to be noted however that whatever the design choice, a specific SP such as the tax office may require civil identity to be disclosed. In automatic pseudonymisation this situation may be handled by the eID deployer and does not prevent the use of the service. In user-defined pseudonymisation, at least in the particular case of SuisseID, this may prevent the use of a service if the pseudonymisation was chosen at issuance. In other words, the SP may have the last word on the use of pseudonyms, possibly by preventing the use of the service.

4.3   Location of User's Attributes

While pseudonymous authentication is certainly the main factor in preserving a user's privacy, the way the eIDMS manages users' attributes that are personal data from the legal point of view, has a significant influence as well. The scope of this sub-section is limited to the attributes at issuance (those stored on the carrier and those known by the IDP) and does not include dynamic attributes collected by a particular SP during online transactions which may be used for profiling. We distinguish three situations.

Localized Attributes. This first option depicts the case where the attributes such as personal address (i.e. data other than those strictly necessary for authentication) are stored locally on the carrier, and are not continuously stored by the IDP or SP, thus reducing the degree to which personal data can be accessed by third parties. This scheme is implemented in the German eID where the carrier bears attributes such as family and given names; artistic name and doctoral degree; date and place of birth; address and community ID; expiration date and optional fingerprints.

Distributed Attributes. The opposite option is to store only minimum attributes on the carrier itself (e.g. name, date of birth and nationality). In this case, the different SPs manage the attributes relative to their services, such as the personal address, for example. This option has certain advantages: the IDP does not have any additional information about a user's attributes, and a given SP normally cannot access attributes stored by other SPs. This option is implemented in the Estonian eID. Here however, these advantages are enforced by legal requirements only, as the use of a unique personal identifier across public and private SPs makes the cross-service correlation of attributes technically possible. In the Austrian Citizen Card, few attributes are present in the eID deployer (name and date of birth).

Centralized Attributes. In this intermediate option, the *eID deployer* itself contains fewer personal data than the set managed by the issuing IDP. The role of the IDP is complex as it deals both with the knowledge of attributes themselves, and with their assertion and disclosure to the SP: in some cases, the IDP could disclose all attributes that it stores, while in other cases only a sub-set of attributes. The centralized design option is implemented in the SuisseID, where the only mandatory attributes on the carrier are the SuisseID number and the name or the pseudonym. However, despite this minimal mandatory design, the SuisseID carrier can also carry optional attributes, such as affiliation, e-mail, etc., if the user decides so. In addition, the SuisseID introduces "auxiliary identity providers" distinct from the IDP involved in the issuing of the SuisseID. They are similar to what is classically called Attribute Providers: while the main IDP manages only basic personal data, these providers manage extended attributes (e.g. professional data, such as lawyer, representative of a moral person, etc.). There can be an arbitrary number of Attribute Providers, allowing further development of the usages. The design decisions implemented in the SuisseID confer a central role to the IDP and to Attribute Providers and require a great amount of trust in them.[2]

4.4 Authentication Schemes

The authentication scheme determines the roles of IDP and SPs, and the flow of attributes between them during the authentication. Also, in relation to the scheme, an eventual user controlled selective attributes disclosure can be implemented, which is typically done via a dashboard or a checkbox. In the following, we describe 4 schemes of high-level functional relations (and not the low-level data flow) between the parties.

Offline Scheme (A). In this scheme, illustrated in Fig. 3, the IDP is normally not aware of the flow of user attributes which are managed directly by SPs. After the enrolment, IDP manages only revocation lists and verification of a card's status by SPs. Along with distributed attributes management described above, this scheme is intended to prevent the establishment of a central data holder. However, when implemented together with a unique identifier, it does not prevent cross-SP linkability.

In the particular case of Estonia, where this scheme is implemented, the user has no *a priori* control on attribute management. This lack is partially compensated by *a posteriori* user access, as there are legal dispositions allowing the user to monitor which attributes are accessed or stored by each SP. However, it is unclear to what

---

[2] Note that the 4 countries studied here have actually limited differences on *location* criterion: the most localized solutions add only address, age, doctoral degree and optional fingerprints (Germany) to the basic set present on the most distributed ones. However, other countries or future eIDMS could give a different picture, by including attributes such as tax number or profession. This is why we think it is important to include this criterion in the discussion.

Fig. 3. Off-line (A)

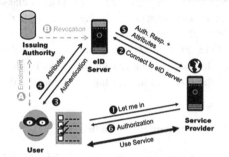

Fig. 4. Federation without user control (B)

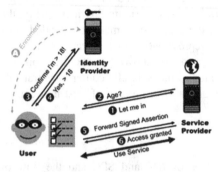

Fig. 5. Federation with user control (C)

Fig. 6. Mediation with user control (D)

extent this obligation is respected, and several reports[3] [21] and users' comments [22] seem to doubt about the system's transparency.

Federation Without User Control (B). In the scheme illustrated in Fig. 4, implemented in the Austrian Citizen Card, the federal IDP plays a central role. This scheme requires that the SP send an authentication request to the IDP in a systematic manner.

As already mentioned, the privacy against SPs is guaranteed by the use of sector specific pseudonyms generated by the IDP. There is no selective disclosure, and it seems that the personal data transmitted to SPs may on some occasions contain more than that strictly needed for the authentication (e.g. the name and the date of birth) [23]. The privacy against the IDP is not ensured as the IDP knows all the services accessed by the user. Overall, this scheme requires a high level of trust in the IDP.

Federation with User Control (C). The scheme illustrated in Fig. 5 is implemented in the SuisseID. This scheme is guided mainly by the wish to allow more user control.

---

[3] The Estonian Data Protection Inspectorate Annual Report 2012 mentions that (i) misuse of the Population Register is the most common reason for misdemeanor proceedings (30 of 43 completed proceedings); (ii) only 2 of 66 companies monitored published private debt data on their websites in full compliance with the Estonian Personal Data Protection Act.

To enable this, all authentication requests are redirected to the user who controls, via a checkbox-style interface, which attributes he agrees to disclose to the SP.

To guarantee the privacy against SPs, both basic and extended attributes follow this selective disclosure procedure. As multiple *eID deployers* are allowed, when the same user has several (pseudonymized) SuisseIDs, the linking across SPs is more difficult. As for the privacy against the IDP, the IDP still holds a central role and is able to link the identifier and pseudonyms across different SPs that the user access to.

Mediation with User Control (D). The last scheme illustrated in Fig. 6, implemented in Germany, is guided by extended security and privacy requirements. Mutual authentication between the user and the SP is used to provide access control, so that only authorized, white-listed SPs can access the user attributes. To this end, an additional element called the eID Server is implemented at the SP side to support communications with the eID client. The eID Server regularly receives, from the authorization certificates authority, updated authorization certificates for the SPs and revocation lists for eID cards. The role of the eID Server is quite different from the IDP's in its classical acceptance, as it is not a centralized federation operator. The SP can develop its own eID Server according to publicly available specification. Alternatively, 4 eID servers are certified by the German Federal Office for Information Security and made available for SPs to establish connection to.

Once the connection between the eID deployer and the SP is established through the eID Server, the attribute disclosure is controlled by the user via a checkbox.

To avoid that SPs uniquely identifies the user, an additional mechanism is implemented. The same authentication key is placed on a batch of carriers belonging to different users. Thus, the SP knows only that it is communicating to an authentic *eID deployer* but does not know to which one in the batch.

4.5   Interdependencies Between Design Axes

We can now draw conclusions on the design inter-dependencies between the 3 design axes we are interested in, which are pseudonymity, attributes location and authentication schemes. Three main aspects are addressed here: privacy against IDP (knowledge of user's actions and attributes), privacy against SPs (cross-SP linkability of the identifier or pseudonym, and cross-SP linkability of attributes) and selective attributes disclosure to SPs.

In both cases of *No pseudonym* and *One pseudonym*, there is no *a priori* necessity to grant a central role to the IDP.

In the *No pseudonym* design option, most of the time, the IDP is not informed about a user's transactions and attributes. The IDP is informed only when the SP needs to check the revocation state of a certificate, as can be seen in the authentication scheme (A). Distributed attributes is a possible way to achieve some privacy protection against cross-SP attributes linkability, even if cross-SP identifier linkability is not addressed, as in the Estonian eID. As few attributes are present on the *eID deployer*, there is little interest in implementing a selective disclosure of attributes, although it could be technically possible.

In the *One pseudonym* approach, such a global scheme could also be implemented. However, if additional Attribute Providers are envisaged, the IDP and Attribute Providers are playing a more central role, both in terms of the knowledge of centralized attributes and their assertion to SPs. To partially prevent excessive knowledge of attributes by SPs and thus cross-SP attributes linkability, the selective disclosure can be implemented. The simplest and most "natural" way is to handle it at the level of the IDP which asserts user attributes at each transaction, as illustrated by the authentication scheme (C). These measures, implemented in the SuisseID, do not address cross-SP linkability of the pseudonym (unless the user has many *eID deployers*), or the knowledge of the user's actions by the IDP.

In *Multiple pseudonyms*, the main gain is the absence of cross-sector or cross-SP linkability. The simplest way to achieve this is to involve the IDP as the trusted third party in pseudonym generation and confirmation to SPs, as illustrated by authentication scheme (B). The obvious drawback is that the IDP may gain a central role. Intrinsically, the IDP's knowledge of services visited by the user is difficult to avoid in this authentication scheme. To limit at least the knowledge of users' attributes by the IDP, a *distributed* approach to attribute management can be implemented as a complementary measure, as in the Austrian eID.

To mitigate these issues and to preserve privacy against both the IDP and SPs simultaneously, a much more complex global scheme is needed. Along with already discussed selective disclosure, two additional steps can be performed: the batching of authentication keys, so that the SP cannot attribute a unique identifier to or even track the user, and a direct connection between the user and the SP, so that no central IDP knows which service is visited by the user. Altogether, these design decisions implemented in the German eID, give more technical complexity (in terms of interconnections) but allow strong privacy protection.

To conclude, from a strictly technical point of view, the German eID solution offers the best level of privacy protection, at the price of a relatively complex and expensive architecture. SuisseID offers an elegant and flexible solution with reasonable technical complexity and cost, but does not address the IDP knowledge of a user's activities.

5 Do Privacy Protection Measures Influence the Adoption Rate?

One could suppose that better privacy protecting solutions will get larger adoption by the public. In the present section, we put the levels of privacy protection described above into correspondence with the effective use of the eID systems by target populations, and analyze some of the factors that may influence the adoption rate.

5.1 Privacy Adoption Paradox

To assess the extent of usage, different parameters can be taken into account: the number of services available to eID authentication, the roll-out, and the usage rate (i.e. percentage of population which effectively use the eID services). We believe that only the last parameter is suitable to assess the real adoption rate. Indeed, the roll-out rate and to a lesser extent the number of available services may result from a voluntaristic policy without triggering the real usage by the population.

One methodological problem is that it is difficult to compare different eID solutions at a given point of time because they have different ages. To compensate for this, we will compare the usage rate with respect to the number of years of existence. The fact that the social and technical context pushes users to adopt digital solutions in 2013 faster than in 2002 cannot be taken into account with the publically available data. Another limitation is that data sources use different procedures: for Germany and Austria the evaluation is based on a representative sample, for Estonia on estimation by involved actors, for Switzerland on sales and estimations (see the Table 1 below). Finally, it should be emphasized that extensive, correct and yearly updated data on the subject is extremely difficult to find, probably because of their sensitive political nature.

Table 1 shows the roll-out and usage rates (as of 2013 for Estonia and Switzerland, as of 2014 for Germany and Austria). Figure 7 shows a graphical representation by country and outlines the rate of adoption which is the relative speed with which the innovation is adopted. More complete data sets could determine if indeed all the countries follow the same logistic s-curve [24, 25] which is classically used to study the rate of adoption.

Table 1. Roll-out and usage rate

	No. years old	Roll-out	Usage rate
Estonia [26, 27][a]	11	98 % (compulsory)	37 %
Austria [28, 29]	8	21 % (opt- in)	21 %
Germany [29]	4	10,5 % (opt-in)	10,5 %
Switzerland [30, 31][b]	3	5,2 % (opt-in)	5,2 %

[a][26] estimates the usage rate at 40 %, and [27] at 37 % (at least once usage occurrence in last 12 months). The middle point at year 6 is from an official presentation of Estonian executives at that time.
[b]In 2010, the number of SuisseID sold was equal to 4.2 % of Switzerland's active population. There is no reliable data on the 2nd and 3rd years but +0.5 % per year seems a reasonably conservative estimation. Besides, in 2013, 6 % of business representatives used the SuisseID for professional purposes, and 3 % of them used it for personal purposes as well. These figures indicate that SuisseID usage is driven by the professional context.

As the data suggest, we can see what could be called a "privacy adoption paradox": there is no evidence that a higher level of privacy protection leads to a higher rate of adoption. It can then be hypothesized that the advantages offered by extended privacy protection solutions do not trigger an *a priori* increase in the rate of adoption, or are counterbalanced by other factors. The fact that the eID functionality follows an opt-out strategy (in Estonia, all the compulsory eID cards are delivered as active) or an opt-in strategy (in the other countries, the holder has to activate the eID functionality) does not seem to have a decisive influence on the adoption rate. These questions are discussed in the next sub-section.

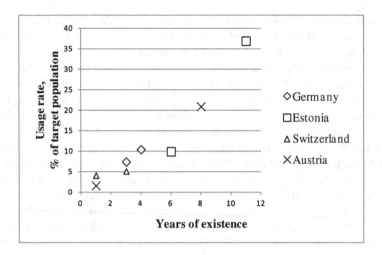

Fig. 7. Rate of adoption in 4 countries

5.2   Factors of Low Adoption Rate

A large number of factors influence the adoption of eID solutions; for example, [32] identifies no fewer than 20 of them. We will limit the discussion to two factors in the context of the most privacy protecting solution identified in the previous sections, the German eID. What may limit the adoption in the case where the eIDMS objectively offers a good level of privacy protection?

Lack of Applications. One factor could be the lack of useful applications limiting the adoption by users. This issue is usually presented as a classic chicken-and-egg problem [15]. The take-off can only be envisaged if a sufficient number of services are offered to the user. On the side of SPs, the incentives to offer such services are however limited by the lack of users and thus by the lack of return on investment. No magic solution seems to be present in the countries studied here as well as in others.

Let's analyze the German example in this light. On one hand, the available figures show that, as of 2013, there were 147 (40 % public and 60 % private) services supporting eID authentication [33], which could cover a large range of everyday usages; thus the lack of applications does not seem to be the main limiting factor.

On the other hand, there is indeed a certain general reluctance of private SPs to develop such eID-supporting services, especially when existing solutions (e.g. bank authentications) already fulfil their purpose [33]. Moreover, as of 2012, only 7 % of service providers did offer privacy-preserving functionality or intended to. The remaining 93 % did require full and true civil identity, while many of them did not belong to sectors where civil identity was required (e.g. banks) [34]. This reflects the specific reluctance of private SPs to offer privacy-preserving functionality.

While this specific reluctance should be addressed at the level of SPs, it is not sure that the usage rate is solely limited by this issue, in particular because users' awareness on pseudonymisation is quite low, as will be shown below. We think that a broader question here is the way the articulation between e-Government and the private sector is thought of. Usually, and this seems to be the rationale behind the eIDAS Regulation, the eID-supporting public services are considered as a trigger for wider user adoption of private SPs. The underlying hypothesis is that the same eID, possibly pseudony-mized, will be used across all the sectors and services. The question is however, does the user want to use the same eID in such different contexts? To take a historic parallel in the pre-digital age, does the user want to use the same key to gain access to his home, to his car and to his workplace? The answer is not as obvious as it may seem, and brings us to the user perception which may limit the eID adoption.

Perceived Privacy. The notion of perceived privacy refers to the way the users foresee the outcome of their actions, and encompasses different factors, such as trust in the technical system and organizations, reluctance to personal data disclosure, etc. A growing body of literature addresses several counter-intuitive aspects such as the "control paradox" (more control over the publication of one's own personal data increases an individual's willingness to publish it and decreases privacy concerns) [35] and "reverse privacy paradox" (lower privacy concerns are combined with a greater use of protection strategies) [36]. These empirical results are always different across countries and age-groups [37].

The point here is that the perceived privacy has little to do with objective char-acteristics of an eIDMS. For example, [34] reports that in Germany there is a clear influence of the official nature (Identity Card) of the eID on the usage rate. Participants in this study have doubts about using an official and highly personal document to play around on the Internet, and see a "possible contradiction between being pseudony-mously authenticated while using an ID card with their photo on it." Moreover, when the pseudonymous authentication mechanisms are explained, they are quickly forgotten or judged not usable enough in the light of the above-mentioned issues.

That is, the usage rate of German eID depends not only on the presence of pseu-donymity as an available feature, but also on the user's perception of the system and reluctance to use the same *eID deployer* in different contexts. While people make little use of systems with poor privacy protection, the systems with good privacy protection, even when explained to citizens, does not necessarily trigger a significantly higher adoption rate if perceived privacy is low.

In this respect, an approach based on separate *eID deployers*, with distinct enrol-ments for each type of use (e.g. for e-Government and for e-Commerce), could be an interesting solution, allowing usage contexts to be dissociated, from the user's point of view. Such could be the case if multiple *eID deployers* were allowed as with SuisseID. For example, there may be a way to authorize multiple *eID deployers* in the German eID infrastructure, if accompanied by appropriate legal provisions for lighter enrolment depending on usage contexts. This last consideration brings us to the state's global policy guiding the degree to which the civil identity is linked to electronic authenti-cation means. This question should be taken into account in future research.

6 Conclusion

In this paper, we developed the methodology and the grid of analysis of privacy protection in existing eIDMS, allowing past and future design decisions to be analyzed. We introduced the concept of the *eID deployer* and provided models for multiple digital identities.

The important structural differences in privacy protection can influence users' predisposition to adopt better solutions in everyday usages. To verify if this is the case, we compared the rate of adoption in four European countries. Paradoxically, there is no evidence for significant influence of privacy preserving characteristics on the rate of adoption of eIDMS. We discussed then the factors that may counterbalance an eventual advantage of privacy protecting solutions and limit the rate of adoption. Among those factors, perceived privacy seems of particular importance.

This analysis is of particular interest in the recent context where national legislations reinforce personal data protection measures, both at the European (with the forthcoming General Data Protection Regulation [38]) and at the international level.

Acknowledgement of Funding. This research was partially financed under the sponsorship program *Chair Values and Policies of Personal Information, Institut Mines-Télécom, France* (www.informations-personnelles.org). The views expressed herein are those of the authors and are not necessarily those of the Funders.

References

1. Regulation (EU) No 910/2014 of the European Parliament and of the Council of 23 July 2014 on electronic identification and trust services for electronic transactions in the internal market and repealing Directive 1999/93/EC. Official Journal L 257 **57**, 73–115, Aug 28 2014
2. Laurent, M., Bouzefrane, S. (eds.): Digital Identity Management. ISTE Press, London (2015)
3. Directive 95/46/EC of the European Parliament and of the Council of 24 October 1995 on the protection of individuals with regard to the processing of personal data and on the free movement of such data. Official Journal L **281**, 0031–0050. Nov 23 1995
4. Levallois-Barth, C.: Legal challenges facing global privacy governance. In: Dartiguepeyrou, C. (ed.) The Futures of Privacy. Fondation Télécom, Paris (2014). ISBN 978-2-915618-25-9
5. Opinion of the European Data Protection Supervisor on the Commission proposal for a Regulation of the European Parliament and of the Council on trust and confidence in electronic transactions in the internal market (2012). https://secure.edps.europa.eu/EDPSWEB/webdav/shared/Documents/Consultation/Opinions/2012/12-09-27_Electronic_Trust_Services_EN.pdf
6. Jøsang, A. Fabre, J., Hay, B., Dalziel J., Pope, S.: Trust requirements in identity management. In: Proceedings of the Australasian Information Security Workshop (AISW 2005), Newcastle, Australia (2005)
7. Benantar, M. (ed.): Access Control Systems: Security, Identity Management and Trust Models. Springer, Berlin (2006)

8. Strauß, S., Aichholzer, G.: National electronic identity management: the challenge of a citizen-centric approach beyond technical design. Int. J. Adv. Intell. Syst. **3**(1&2), 2010 (2010)
9. Corella, F., Lewison, K.: Privacy postures of authentication technologies. In: The Internet Identity Workshop (IIW), Mountain View, CA (2013)
10. Martens, T.: Electronic identity management in Estonia between market and state governance. Identity Inf. Soc. **3**(1), 213–233 (2010). (Springer)
11. AS Sertifitseerimiskeskus: The estonian ID card and digital signature concept. http://www.id.ee/public/The_Estonian_ID_Card_and_Digital_Signature_Concept.pdf. Accessed Oct 2014
12. Leitold, H., Hollosi, A., Posch, R.: Security architecture of the Austrian citizen card concept. In: Proceedings of ACSAC 2002, pp. 391–400 (2000). ISBN 0-7695-1828-1
13. Federal Act on Electronic Signatures 2001 (Signature law). Austrian Federal Law Gazette, part I, Nr. 190/1999, 137/2000, 32/2001
14. BSI: Technical guidelines eID-server. part 1: functional specification, BSI (2014). https://www.bsi.bund.de/SharedDocs/Downloads/DE/BSI/Publikationen/TechnischeRichtlinien/TR03130/TR-03130_TR-eID-Server_Part1_pdf.pdf?_blob=publicationFile
15. Poller, A., Waldmann, U., Vowe, S., Turpe, S.: Electronic identity cards for user authentication - promise and practice. IEEE Secur. Priv. **10**(1), 46–54 (2012). doi:10.1109/MSP.2011.148
16. BSI: Innovations for an eID architecture in Germany (2010). http://www.personalausweisportal.de/SharedDocs/Downloads/EN/Flyers-and-Brochures/Broschuere_BSI_innovations_eID_archi tecture.pdf?_blob=publicationFile. Accessed Oct 2014
17. Hemmer, P.: La SuisseID, qu'est-ce que c'est? (2010). http://www.ari-web.ch/docs/ARI_2010_06_18_SUISSE_ID_020_PROJET_EXPOSE.pdf. Accessed Oct 2014
18. Doujak, M. (ed.): SuisseID specification, eCH-0113 (2011). http://www.suisseid.ch/endkunden/suisseid/news/update_spezifikationen/
19. Pfitzmann, A., Hansen M.: A terminology for talking about privacy by data minimization: anonymity, unlinkability, undetectability, unobservability, pseudonymity, and identity management. TU Dresden (2010). http://dud.inf.tu-dresden.de/Anon_Terminology.shtml
20. International Standard: Information technology - Security techniques - Privacy framework, ISO/IEC29100, 1st edn., Dec 2011
21. The Estonian Data Protection Inspectorate Annual report (2012)
22. Marvet, P. (Reteep Tevram @petskratt) 2013, Comment to *Government as a data model.* https://gds.blog.gov.uk/2013/10/31/government-as-a-data-model-what-i-learned-in-estonia/#comment-3776. Accessed Oct 2014
23. Slamanig, D., Stranacher, K., Zwattendorfer, B.: User-centric identity as a service-architecture for eIDs with selective attribute disclosure. In: Proceedings of the 19th ACM Symposium on Access Control Models and Technologies SACMAT 2014. ACM (2014)
24. Rogers, E.: Diffusion of Innovations. Simon & Schuster, New York (2003)
25. Hühnlein, D., Roßnagel, H., Zibuschka, J.: Diffusion of federated identity management. In: Freiling, F.C. (ed.) Sicherheit, pp. 25–36. Köllen Druck + Verlag GmbH, Bonn (2010)
26. GSMA: Estonia's mobile-ID: driving today's e-services economy (2013). http://www.gsma.com/personaldata/wp-content/uploads/2013/07/GSMA-Mobile-Identity_Estonia_Case_Study_June-2013.pdf. Accessed Oct 2014
27. Estonian Ministry of Economic Affairs and Communications: Digital agenda 2020 for Estonia (Source: AS Sertifitseerimiskeskus) (2014). http://e-estonia.com/wp-content/uploads/2014/04/Digital-Agenda-2020_Estonia_ENG.pdf. Accessed Oct 2014
28. eID Interoperability for PEGS: Austrian country profile: IDABC - European e-Government Services (2009). http://ec.europa.eu/idabc/en/document/6484.html. Accessed Oct 2014

29. Institute for Public Information Management: eGovernment Monitor 2014 (2014). http://www.initiatived21.de/wp-content/uploads/2014/09/eGovMon2014_web.pdf
30. Newsletter E-Government Suisse (2011). http://www.egovernment.ch/dokumente/newsletter/Newsletter-E-Gov-02-2011-f.htm Accessed Oct 2014
31. ATS: Les entreprises suisses satisfaites des prestations internet des administrations (source ATS) (2013). http://www.lenouvelliste.ch/fr/societe/multimedia/les-entreprises-suisses-satisfaites-des-prestations-internet-des-administrations-476-1239889. Accessed Oct 2014
32. Hofman, S., Räckers. M, Becker, J.: Identifying factors of e-government acceptance – a literature review. In: Thirty Third International Conference on Information Systems, Orlando (2012)
33. Fromm, J. Hoepner, P., Pattberg, J., Welzel, C.: 3 Jahre Onlineausweisfunktion - Lessons Learned. Fraunhofer Fokus (2013). www.fokus.fraunhofer.de
34. Harbach, M., Fahl, S., Rieger, M., Smith, M.: On the acceptance of privacy-preserving authentication technology: the curious case of national identity cards. In: De Cristofaro, E., Wright, M. (eds.) PETS 2013. LNCS, vol. 7981, pp. 245–264. Springer, Heidelberg (2013)
35. Brandimarte, L., Acquisti, A., Loewenstein, G.: Misplaced confidences: privacy and the control paradox. In: Ninth Annual Workshop on the Economics of Information Security (WEIS). Harvard University, Cambridge, MA (2010), 7–8 June 2010
36. Miltgen, C., Peyrat-Guillard, D.: Cultural and generational influences on privacy concerns: a qualitative study in seven European countries. Eur. J. Inf. Syst. **23**, 103–125 (2014)
37. Lusoli, W., and Miltgen, C.: Young people and emerging digital services. An exploratory survey on motivations, perceptions and acceptance of risks. EC JRC-IPTS report (2009)
38. Proposal for Regulation of The European Parliament and of The Council on the protection of individuals with regard to the processing of personal data and on the free movement of such data (General Data Protection Regulation)/COM/2012/011 final -2012/0011 (COD). Accessed May 2015

Comparing Local e-Government Websites in Canada and the UK

Laurence Brooks[(⊠)] and Alexander Persaud

Department of Computer Science, Brunel University London, London, UK
laurence.brooks@brunel.ac.uk, 1227294@my.brunel.ac.uk

Abstract. This paper provides an evaluation of eight local e-Government websites in Canada and the United Kingdom, utilizing web diagnostic tools. The results of the diagnostic evaluation are synthesized for a comparative case analysis between the various local e-Government websites, providing recommendations for areas of improvement in terms of accessibility. Furthermore, the study will offer insight into the varied approaches to e-Government website conceptualization and design among local officials. While eight local websites are evaluated, only the city of Calgary and Hillingdon are explored in-depth through interviews with local officials. The exploration of the use of web diagnostic tools as an evaluative method for local e-Government websites will supply local officials and webmasters with a valuable and feasible option for internal evaluation. The study is unique in that it evaluates multiple e-Government websites at a local level rather than a federal level between two countries.

Keywords: Local e-government · Web diagnostics · UK · Canada

1 Introduction

Over the last decade, increased expectations of online services can be attributed to the growth of e-Government services [3]. The dramatic growth in academic investigation of e-Government, as a field, provides significant opportunities to build upon existing research. Indeed, web developers' understanding of the conceptualization, delivery, management, and evaluation of e-Government is in a constant state of change as governments and their affiliates adopt new technologies, standards, and practices.

The internet has become an invaluable resource in the daily lives of citizens across the world, in both private and increasingly public sector services [4]. In acknowledging this appreciation, it is easily recognizable that e-Government practices are an important option for public access and engagement. Jati and Dominic [5, p. 85] state, 'The immediacy of the Web creates an immediate expectation of quality and rapid application delivery, but the technical complexities of a website and variances in the browser make testing and quality control more difficult, and in some ways, more subtle.' Whether it is at a local or federal level, governments have increasingly acknowledged the need for providing services through the Internet – commonly known as e-services [6]. With e-Government services offered through web interfaces, evaluation has become a:

© IFIP International Federation for Information Processing 2015
E. Tambouris et al. (Eds.): EGOV 2015, LNCS 9248, pp. 291–304, 2015.
DOI: 10.1007/978-3-319-22479-4_22

...necessary activity for ensuring returns from investments over time. Financial investment includes spending on equipment and technology necessary for delivering Web-based e-government services. Organizational investment, on the other hand tends to be unobservable, and includes the time and energy that government agencies need to rethinking, reorganizing and streamlining the service delivery system for the Web-based e-government initiatives [7, p. 2].

While the scale of e-Government investment may not match initiatives at a federal level, local e-Government investment still must, '...be able to justify some form of return on investment, which typically requires evaluation of the Web-based e-government services' [7, p. 2]. Early iterations of local city websites in the 1990s adopted a bureaucratic paradigm, where the website was administratively oriented. This has changed more recently as cities that have adopted, '...the e-government paradigm, design their Web sites differently' [8, p. 434]. These new websites tend to use '...portal designs' [8, p. 437].

Wang et al. [7, p. 2] state that, '...despite the importance of the evaluation of Web-based e-government services, especially the performance of government Web sites in facilitating public-government interaction, little research has been generated', with most web-based service evaluation focusing on the private sector. Web diagnostic tools have become a method of evaluation for general websites and e-Government websites. Evaluative methodologies have been developed for e-Government websites (see [1, 9] and [7]). Other research studies have all specifically explored e-Government evaluations using web diagnostics at a federal level for multiple web portals [5, 6, 10]. Web diagnostic tools for local e-Government evaluation has significant room for further research and exploration as few studies investigate e-Government evaluation with web diagnostics, specifically at a local level.

This paper aims to provide a comparative case study analysis of local e-Government websites in Canada and the United Kingdom in terms of accessibility. In this context accessibility is defined in general terms as well as at a technical level. A comparative case study analysis will not only indicate the strengths and weaknesses of each respective website but will also suggest the varied or similar approaches local officials take in the conceptualization of e-Government websites in Canada and the United Kingdom. Eight local e-Government websites in Canada and the United Kingdom were evaluated using selected web diagnostic tools. The two localities selected for interviews were Calgary, Canada (http://www.calgary.ca/SitePages/cocis/default.aspx) and Hillingdon, UK (http://www.hillingdon.gov.uk/residents). The interviews conducted with local officials from Calgary and Hillingdon were relatively general, as a way to obtain unforeseen information.

2 Literature Review

2.1 Conceptualizing e-Government Services

In simple terms, e-Government services can, '...deliver information and services online through the Internet or other digital means', [11, p. 64]. Venkatesh et al. elaborate, stating that: e-Government services can be broadly categorized into informational and transactional services. Informational services refer to the delivery of government information via web pages and transactional services involve two-way transactions between government and citizens (e.g. submission of electronic forms) that may require horizontal or vertical integration of multiple government agencies [12].

E-services are often centralized within a government portal where citizens can access a particular service. Kumar et al. state that the challenge of e-Government is not technical. It is '…to use technologies to improve the capacities of government institutions, while improving the quality of life of citizens by redefining the relationship between citizens and their government' [11, p. 64]. While e-Government has grown from being another option or choice for communication with citizens, global trends have made e-Government a necessity for any country wishing to enter the 21st century as a competitive nation. Beyond the functional benefits of citizen interaction, increased adoption of e-Government services have the potential for enormous savings and cost reduction (Kumar et al. [11]). Important considerations of web navigation, accessibility, aesthetics, and content fit within website design. An exemplary website design increases perceived usefulness and perceived ease of use among citizens, directly impacting e-Government adoption.

Certain user characteristics such as perceived risk and control may depend on perceptions of financial risk, psychological risk, social risk, convenience risk, and overall risk. The use of services may be discouraged due to perceptions of risk related to online security. In the case of the Canadian Government, trust via user identity is verified through an authentication code via the ePass government system, as well as the implementation of the Privacy Impact Assessment (PIA) Policy which outlines assessments for any new or redesigned service that may raise privacy issues [11]. Kumar et al. present a conceptualization framework for e-Government adoption in a Canadian context, though it can apply to other nations as well. Furthermore, while the conceptual framework may focus at a federal level, it can be applied at a local level due to the identification of important considerations in high-quality service delivery, engagement, and growth for e-Government in general.

The provided information and services via e-Government carry a vital purpose within the public sector, enabling citizens and businesses the completion of important and necessary tasks. It is therefore important that the conceptual design of e-Government services carry thoughtful consideration so that user satisfaction is maintained at a high standard. As more services are brought online, governments' ability to maintain accessible and usable services is important for user acceptance, satisfaction, and trust. The preference towards self-service can be partly attributed to the significant saving in time and effort, ease of use, and increased personal control [13]. With self-service in mind, e-Government websites require thoughtful design considerations to positively communicate usefulness, as they often act as an entry point towards available e-services. Wang et al. [7, p. 2] acknowledge the financial benefits of e-Government service implementation in stating that in order to make investments worthwhile, '…government agencies must be able to justify some form of return on investment, which typically requires evaluation of the Web-based e-government services.' It is further noted that the performance of government websites in facilitating exchanges between the public and government agencies are directly related to the return on government's investment in its development of websites and delivered online services [7]. Wang et al. [7, p. 2], state that, 'At a minimum, assuming the unit cost for a delivered service is less on a website than through alternative traditional means, each web interaction represents a cost savings.'

In recognizing the benefits of e-Government, its inevitable growth and ubiquity, and its importance in developing a meaningful relationship between government and citizens, government must ensure that its e-service websites are accessible and usable for adoption as well as overall customer satisfaction among citizens. However, even if the website provides the information necessary to complete the intended task and a consumer struggles when searching or retrieving desired information, the website will be abandoned [14]. The website must compensate for lack of physical contact experienced by online shoppers and at the same time make the shopping experience easy and enjoyable. In this context, online shoppers are citizens exploring e-services options. Great importance is placed on the perceived usefulness of a service.

2.2   Methods of Evaluation for e-Government Service Websites

Public authority web evaluation has seen few attempts to propose and use specific metrics for assessment [1]. Of the various criteria and metrics utilized, Wood et al. [2] describe 4 major classes of web evaluation methods, including usability testing, user feedback, usage data, and web and Internet performance data (Fig. 1). These methods relate to practical evaluation solutions that can work within an existing methodology. The authors identify the utilization of these four classes in creating a robust, multidimensional strategy to web-based evaluation of e-Government [2]. This multidimensional approach focuses particularly on web evaluation of e-Government websites rather than the conceptual assessment of web services [15]. The evaluation of e-Government websites can be attributed to both the Technical Performance and Site Quality layers.

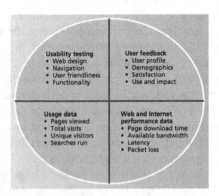

Fig. 1. A multidimensional approach to web evaluation [2].

Usability testing primarily involves feedback on website design, functionality, and navigation, wherein information can be obtained through methods of heuristic or expert review, informal usability testing, and usability lab testing [2]. Using a heuristic review encourages an independent, outside perspective towards website development, which provides web developers a larger context towards their considerations in web design. This can benefit the site layout and structure, navigation tools, search function, fonts and colors, among others. This type of usability testing allows a Web usability expert to review the website, compare it against generally accepted web design and functionality principles, and suggest design improvements.

Usage data is included among the variety of web evaluation classes with multiple methods including web log data analysis (in which web log software is installed on the website server to collect usage data such as page views, total visits, and unique visitors), and internet audience measurement (in which private companies collect usage data from large panels of web users who agree to have their web surfing monitored). Usage data can provide a range of quantitative data at relatively low cost and provide useful evidence of web trends in relation to the offered e-services.

Pearson et al. [16] identify 6 key criteria in evaluating web usability: Ease of use; Navigation; Accessibility; Download Speed; Gender; Customization and personalization. They state that navigation, download speed, personalization, ease of use, gender, and accessibility are integral to web usability evaluation. Navigation is an important consideration relative to consumer preference. Websites aim to achieve customization and personalization as a way of establishing an ongoing relationship with the customer. The findings recognize ease of use as the most important in assessing web usability while personalization and customization as less important. A clear emphasis is placed on the various criteria's impact on user satisfaction, with the most notable being download speed/technical performance. These criteria have commonalities with similar evaluative methodologies [1].

Panapoulou et al. [1] propose an evaluation framework that synthesizes five other authors' approaches to e-Government website evaluation (see Fig. 2).

	Garcia et al (2005)	Smith (2001)	Holzer and Kim (2005)	Henriksson et al (2006)	West (2007)
Content	✓	✓	✓	✓	✓
Navigation	✓	✓	✓	✓	✓
Public outreach	✓	✓	✓	✓	✓
Accessibility	✓	✓	✓	✓	✓
Privacy and security	✓	✓	✓	✓	✓
Online services	✓		✓	✓	✓
Citizen participation			✓	✓	

Fig. 2. Concept matrix of e-government website evaluation methods [1].

The framework consists of three different levels of detail. The first (higher) level '...consists of four axes that measure four different aspects of e-Government websites...' while the second '...consists of factor that measure each distinct axis' [1], p. 520).' The third level consists of the particular metrics used to carry out the evaluation. The highest level is titled the *General characteristics* axis, which include five factors with particular metrics of evaluation: accessibility (with metrics evaluating technical accessibility, accessibility for disabled and non-Internet savvy users), navigation (metrics evaluating searching capabilities, functionality and ease of use features, web page design consistency), multilingualism (metrics evaluating number of foreign languages and content completeness in them), privacy (metrics evaluating privacy statement, secure connections, information on data usage), and finally, public outreach (metrics evaluating contact information, response agility) [1]. This proposed framework provides a comprehensive overview of public authority/e-Government websites.

This synthesis of e-Government website evaluation literature includes public outreach, citizen participation, content, navigation, accessibility, privacy and security, and online services. Though these evaluative criteria provide a strong basis for e-Government website evaluation, the framework lacks an emphasis on technical performance aspects that heavily influence user satisfaction. The evaluation framework can add this seventh metric to provide a holistic overview and better gauge of e-Government website evaluation. In the context of local government websites, an updated Panapoulou et al. framework incorporating the technical performance criteria described by Pearson et al. [16] constructs a suitable and well-rounded framework for evaluation. Perhaps the most important area of consideration for web developers is accessibility and usability, ensuring that navigation and content is clear and disability access, as well as technical aspects, are in compliance with popular web standards.

3   Methodology

A version of the iterative accessibility evaluation methodology from Al-Radaideh et al. [10], is used here, including selected websites from two countries. It also incorporates aspects from Fan, using interviews to provide further insight. This hybrid of quantitative and qualitative data provided a holistic perspective of local e-Government accessibility considerations. In this case, web diagnostic tools are utilized to investigate local government website compliance with Web Content Accessibility Guidelines 2.0 (WCAG) and W3C Guidelines, browser compatibility, acceptable markup language, and download times. Accessibility, in the context of the study, refers broadly to access to information and services as well as technically with consideration of disability access (e.g. visual impairment, etc.). The results of the diagnostics offered comparative insight between local e-Government websites in Canada and the UK. As is the case with many previous e-Government evaluations, web diagnostic tools were used to gauge accessibility and usability. The selected web diagnostic tools comprised of AChecker (http://achecker.ca), W3C Markup Validator (http://validator.w3.org), and Netmechanic (http://www.netmechanic.com) (Fig. 3).

3.1   Selection of Local Government Websites for Evaluation

The study investigated accessibility of local e-Government websites in Canada and the UK using web diagnostic tools. A total of ten e-Government websites (five in each nation) were carefully selected to provide a comprehensible and effective comparison between the two countries. The attributes of the cities that were considered had to be

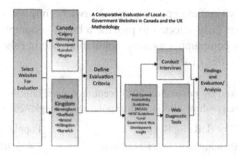

Fig. 3. The evaluative methodology used in the study.

comparable, namely in size (in terms of population) as well as be representative of the country (in terms of geographical location), in order to account for inherent regional disparities. Furthermore, all local government websites had to offer e-services in order to be considered. With the decreasing significance of homepages (due to search engine queries and redirection), web diagnostic tools are utilized on e-service specified pages where less than two clicks are required to access an online service. The presence of e-services in the context of accessibility is important as it provides the study with insight into whether local government websites give all citizens the best chance of engaging with online services. An assumption was made that local government websites that have similar populations within their jurisdiction will have baseline similarities in budget, technical infrastructure, and resources in order to serve citizens effectively. In using population similarity, the scale of e-Government in terms of potential citizens served was balanced and fair. This process aided in the selection of websites for evaluation. Therefore, the results of the study better served comparisons between Canada and the UK. The local websites selected in Canada were, Calgary (http://www.calgary.ca), Vancouver (http://www.vancouver.ca), London (http://www.london.ca), Winnipeg (http://www.winnipeg.ca), and Regina (http://www.regina.ca). These Canadian cities were chosen to provide a broad geographic overview of the country and, for the most part, have comparable municipalities by measurement of population (www12.statcan.gc.ca, 2015) (Table 1).

Table 1. Canadian cities ranked by population (statcan.gc.ca, 2015).

1	Vancouver	British Columbia	2,470,300
2	Calgary	Alberta	1,406,700
3	Winnipeg	Manitoba	782,600
4	London	Ontario	502,400
5	Regina	Saskatchewan	237,800

The population mean of the selected Canadian cities is about 1,079,960 citizens. 50 % of Canadian provinces are represented. The local websites selected in the United Kingdom were the London borough of Hillingdon (http://www.hillingdon.gov.uk), Birmingham (http://www.birmingham.gov.uk), Bristol (http://www.bristol.gov.uk),

Sheffield (https://www.sheffield.gov.uk), and Norwich (http://www.norwich.gov.uk). The UK cities were similarly selected to provide a broad geographical overview of the country and provide a comparable average population size in relation to each other as well as the Canadian cities (Table 2).

Table 2. UK cities ranked by population 2013 (centreforcities, http://www.centreforcities.org/data-tool/#graph=table&city=show-all&indicator=population\single\2013)

#	City (UK)	Region	Population
1	Birmingham	West Midlands	2,453,700
2	Sheffield	Yorkshire and the Humber	818,800
3	Bristol	Southwest England	706,600
4	Hillingdon	London	292,000
5	Norwich	East of England	261,400

The population mean of the selected English cities is 906,500 citizens. 55 % of English regions are represented.

With a comparable total population for citizens served across Canadian and United Kingdom regions, the selection of local government websites for evaluation provided a good foundation for a valid and meaningful study.

3.2   WCAG Evaluative Criteria Background

According to the W3C, the Web Content Accessibility Guidelines (WCAG) state:
...explain how to make Web content accessible to people with disabilities. The guidelines are intended for all Web content developers (page authors and site designers) and for developers of authoring tools. The primary goal of these guidelines is to promote accessibility. However, following them will also make Web content more available to all users, whatever user agent they are using (e.g., desktop browser, voice browser, mobile phone, automobile-based personal computer, etc.) or constraints they may be operating under (e.g., noisy surroundings, under- or over-illuminated rooms, in a hands-free environment, etc.). Following these guidelines will also help people find information on the Web more quickly. These guidelines do not discourage content developers from using images, video, etc., but rather explain how to make multimedia content more accessible to a wide audience (W3.org).

The WCAG 1.0 May 1999 guidelines were updated in December 2008 to 2.0 and further say it: covers a wide range of recommendations for making Web content more accessible. Following these guidelines will make content accessible to a wider range of people with disabilities, including blindness and low vision, deafness and hearing loss, learning disabilities, cognitive limitations, limited movement, speech disabilities, photosensitivity and combinations of these. Following these guidelines will also often make your Web content more usable to users in general (W3.org).

Though it is possible to conform either to WCAG 1.0 or to WCAG 2.0 (or both), the W3C recommends that new and updated content use the latter. The W3C also recommends that Web accessibility policies reference WCAG 2.0.

Web accessibility compliance is prioritized into three categories, as seen in Table 3. W3C symbols are used to certify web pages that meet Priority 1 'A', Priority 2 'Double-A', and Priority 3 'Triple-A' standards.

Table 3. WCAG criteria accessibility descriptions with WCAG 1.0 symbols (W3.org)

Priority	Description	Symbols
Priority 1	A Web content developer must satisfy this checkpoint. Satisfying this checkpoint is a basic requirement for some groups to be able to use Web documents	W3C WAI-A WCAG 1.0
Priority 2	A Web content developer should satisfy this checkpoint. Satisfying this checkpoint will remove significant barriers to accessing Web documents	W3C WAI-AA WCAG 1.0
Priority 3	A Web content developer may address this checkpoint. Satisfying this checkpoint will improve access to Web documents	W3C WAI-AAA WCAG 1.0

3.3   Selection of Web Diagnostic Tools and Background

The AChecker tool was chosen from the W3C recommended list of web accessibility evaluation tools (W3.org). AChecker was primarily chosen because of its free use and open source license. It provides evaluator diagnostic reports according to WCAG guidelines which can be exported in multiple formats. The AChecker can utilize WCAG 1.0 and 2.0 guidelines as well as Priority 1, 2, and 3 standards also known as 'A', 'Double-A', and 'Triple-A' (W3.org). While for each priority issues are categorized as 'Known Problems', 'Likely Problems', and 'Potential Problems' (achecker.ca), only 'Known Problems' were considered for this study.

The W3 Validator tool, also known as the W3C Markup Validation Service, checks the '...markup validity of Web documents in HTML, XHTML, SMIL, MathML...' and so on (validator.w3.org). The W3 Validator verifies websites in accordance with specified markup language rules. Markup validity implies a 'quality criteria for a Web page' among others (validator.w3.org). The important distinction is made that '...a valid Web page is not necessarily a good web page, but an invalid Web page has little chance of being a good web page (validator.w3.org).' For the purposes of the study, markup validity is one of the defined evaluation criteria when assessing local e-Government websites for accessibility and usability.

The third diagnostic tool, Netmechanic, conducts a free website speed test in which download time and browser compatibility are calculated (netmechanic.com). For this study, only download times for the selected e-Government websites were assessed at a standard 56 K connection speed.

The three selected web diagnostic tools offered a comprehensive overview of accessibility considerations. A clear insight into local e-Government websites' compliance to WCAG 2.0 standards as well as performance considerations (as described in previous studies) was gained through the utilization of these tools. As customer satisfaction is heavily dependent on web performance, usability, and accessibility, these tools play a critical role in ensuring proper implementation of local e-Government websites and access to e-services.

3.4   Interviewees Selection and Approach

To obtain added insight into the collected data via web diagnostic tools, interviews were conducted with web development officials in Canada and the United Kingdom, specifically in the localities of Calgary and Hillingdon. An interview was conducted with the team lead for web and digital services in Calgary. A joint interview between the project manager on the access channel migration team and team lead for web development in Hillingdon was also carried out. Interviews were recorded and performed in a semi-structured approach with prepared general, open-ended questions. The purpose of the interviews was to gain insight into the strategies regarding local e-Government website conceptualization, as well as, to learn of the special considerations that are made with regards to usability and accessibility towards services. For the interviews, qualitative data analysis took place through thematic analysis and data coding. The thematic analysis process begins with a collection of data, an identification of data that relate to classified patterns, sub-themes combination and cataloguing, and the construction of a valid argument for chosen themes based on related literature [17]. The identified themes in the study build upon those discussed in the literature review. The transcribed interviews categorized information into common themes of preset categories, although room was left to identify emergent categories. By codifying persistent themes, an identification of connections between categories and their relative importance was conducted with some visible overlap.

3.5   Interview Analysis: Thematic Analysis

Utilizing a thematic analysis method, interview transcripts were studied for common themes. Initially, preset data categories were used via Fan's local government study [18]. Fan's themes include 'top leadership support and management capacity', 'organizational and technical challenges', 'user-centred e-government approach', and 'bridging the digital divide' [18]. While these preconceived themes aided in categorization, new themes became apparent through further analysis. Through data coding and identification of subcategories, five major themes were identified from interview transcripts. These themes were, (1) a user-oriented approach, (2) organizational challenges, (3) integration expectations and challenges, (4) adaptation and growth of access channels, and (5) evaluative methods/tools. The fifth theme can be considered a subcategory of organizational challenges. The interviewees identified evaluative tools utilized for e-Government website improvement with statistic and analytic tools playing a major role in identifying web trends. Based on interview data, the Hillingdon web development team takes more into consideration with regards to accessibility at a technical level than the Calgary team. This is consistent with acquired web diagnostic data, indicating greater accessibility compliance in the UK.

4 Findings

4.1 Diagnostic Results

The following graphs show the results of the diagnostics on the Canadian and UK local e-Government websites, using AChecker, Netmechanic and W3 Validator. Both the UK and Canadian websites were both compared internally within country, as well as between countries. The results will also be discussed in light of their interpretation.

Graphs in Figs. 4 and 5 clearly show that Canada clearly leads known accessibility problems in terms of the WCAG metric.

Graphs in Figs. 6 and 7 clearly show that the UK clearly leads in browser compatibility issues. The reverse is seen for an equivalent analysis of download times, with the UK having generally shorter download times.

Graphs in Figs. 8 and 9 clearly show that overall Canada clearly leads in markup language issues.

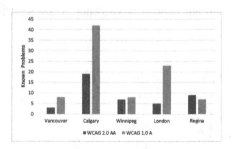

Fig. 4. AChecker results identifying known accessibility problems for Canadian local e-Government websites, according to WCAG Priority 1 - 'A' and WCAG Priority 2 – 'AA'

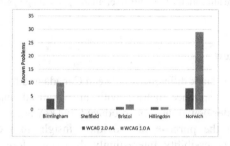

Fig. 5. AChecker results identifying known accessibility problems for UK local e-Government websites, according to WCAG Priority 1 - 'A' and WCAG Priority 2 – 'AA'

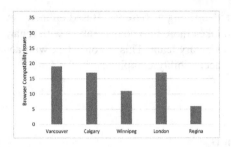

Fig. 6. Netmechanic results for browser compatibility issues for Canadian local e-Government websites

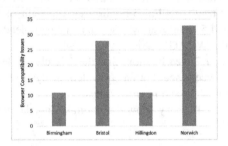

Fig. 7. Netmechanic results for browser compatibility issues for UK local e-Government websites

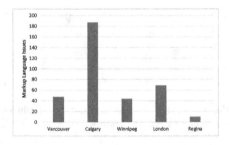

Fig. 8. W3 Validator results identifying browser markup language issues for Canadian local e-Government websites

4.2   Results Overview

The graphs illustrate the stark differences between Canada and the UK in the context of WCAG accessibility compliance metrics, with an overall advantage to the UK. The thematic analysis of interview transcripts produced five key areas of insight. Interviews were conducted with the purpose of providing insight into conceptualization of e-service delivery and accessibility. Interestingly, three out of four metrics of evaluation identified greater accessibility compliance in the UK. While diagnostic data identified an advantage in technical compliance, interview data suggested that the Canadian city

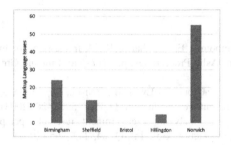

Fig. 9. W3 Validator results identifying browser markup language issues for UK local e-Government websites

of Calgary web and digital services team have a better integrated organizational structure, allowing for quick and responsive changes to e-service delivery. In short, while Calgary's technical presentation of e-services is relatively poor in terms of accessibility, its organizational structure allows for greater flexibility. Conversely, in the London borough of Hillingdon, there are more organizational challenges in managing third parties and integrating services. Third party services are presented and organized on Hillingdon's homepage, acting much more as a web portal in relation to Tat-Kei Ho's description of the user-oriented approach than Calgary's post-homepage user-oriented approach.

5 Discussion and Conclusion

The research builds upon evaluative e-Government studies using previous web diagnostic tools by [5, 6, 9, 10]. Further, the study provided insight into local web development teams perspectives on user-oriented approaches, organizational and integration challenges, adaptation and growth of access channels, and evaluative methods and tools used. This interview approach emulated a previous investigation into local official insight regarding e-services conceptualization [18].

Future research opportunities include conducting interviews with other local officials to compare e-service conceptualization sentiment across regions. As interview data suggests, the homepage is no longer a major area of consideration in the delivery of e-services. Therefore, one can examine the implication of this shift in website presentation and what it means for accessibility at a technical and conceptual level.

This paper offered an exploration of the use of web diagnostic tools as an evaluative method for local e-Government websites, which provides local officials and webmasters a valuable and feasible option for internal evaluation. The results revealed greater accessibility compliance for local e-Government websites in the UK. For individual cities, interview data suggests the organizational structuring in Calgary better served effective, efficient, and responsive online service delivery as opposed to Hillingdon, which faces added organizational and integration challenges. For both parties, exploration of new access channel strategies and platforms provide encouraging prospects for the future of local e-Government development.

References

1. Panopoulou, E., Tambouris, E., Tarabanis, K.: A framework for evaluating web sites of public authorities. In: Aslib Proceedings, pp. 517–546. Emerald Group Publishing Limited (2008)
2. Wood, F., Siegel, E., LaCroix, E., Lyon, B., Benson, D., Cid, V., Fariss, S.: A practical approach to e-government web evaluation. IT Prof. **5**, 22–28 (2003)
3. Heeks, R., Bailur, S.: Analyzing e-government research: perspectives, philosophies, theories, methods, and practice. Gov. Inf. Q. **24**, 243–265 (2007)
4. Henriksson, A., Yi, Y., Frost, B., Middleton, M.: Evaluation instrument for e-government websites. Electron. Gov. Int. J. **4**, 204–226 (2007)
5. Jati, H., Dominic, D.D.: Quality evaluation of e-government website using web diagnostic tools: Asian case. In: International Conference on Information Management and Engineering, (ICIME 2009), pp. 85–89. IEEE (2009)
6. Choudrie, J., Ghinea, G., Weerakkody, V.: Evaluating global e-government sites: a view using web diagnostics tools. e-J. e-Gov. **2**, 105–114 (2004)
7. Wang, L., Bretschneider, S., Gant, J.: Evaluating web-based e-government services with a citizen-centric approach. In: Proceedings of the 38th Annual Hawaii International Conference on System Sciences. IEEE (2005)
8. Tat-Kei Ho, A.: Reinventing local governments and the e-government initiative. Publ. Adm. Rev. **62**, 434–444 (2002)
9. Ma, H.-Y.T., Zaphiris, P.: The usability and content accessibility of the e-government in the UK. Universal access in HCI, pp. 760–764 (2003)
10. Al-Radaideh, M., Nuser, M., Wahbeh, A.: Evaluating accessibility of jordanian e-government websites for people with disabilities. In: Proceedings of International Conference on Information and Communication Systems (ICICS), pp. 127–131. Citeseer (2011)
11. Kumar, V., Mukerji, B., Butt, I., Persaud, A.: Factors for successful e-government adoption: a conceptual framework. Electron. J. e-Gov. **5**, 63–76 (2007)
12. Venkatesh, V., Chan, F.K., Thong, J.Y.: Designing e-government services: key service attributes and citizens' preference structures. J. Oper. Manag. **30**, 116–133 (2012)
13. Meuter, M.L., Ostrom, A.L., Roundtree, R.I., Bitner, M.J.: Self-service technologies: understanding customer satisfaction with technology-based service encounters. J. Mark. **64**, 50–64 (2000)
14. McKinney, V., Yoon, K., Zahedi, F.M.: The measurement of web-customer satisfaction: an expectation and disconfirmation approach. Inf. Syst. Res. **13**, 296–315 (2002)
15. Halaris, C., Magoutas, B., Papdomichelaki, X., Mentzas, G.: Classification and synthesis of quality approaches in e- government services. Internet Res. **17**, 378–401 (2007)
16. Pearson, J., Pearson, A., Green, D.: Determining the importance of key criteria in web usability. Manag. Res. News **30**, 816–828 (2007)
17. Taylor-Powell, E., Renner, M.: Analyzing Qualitative Data. University of Wisconsin–Extension, Cooperative Extension (2003)
18. Fan, Q.: An evaluation analysis of e-government development by local authorities in Australia. Int. J. Public Adm. **34**, 926–934 (2011)

Evaluating a Passive Social Media Citizensourcing Innovation

Euripidis Loukis, Yannis Charalabidis,
and Aggeliki Androutsopoulou[(⊠)]

Department of Information and Communication Systems Engineering,
University of the Aegean, Mytilene, Greece
{eloukis,yannisx,ag.andr}@aegean.gr

Abstract. Governments initially used social media mainly in order to disseminate information to the public about their activities, services, policies and plans. Then they started using social media also in order to collect from citizens useful information, knowledge, opinions and ideas concerning the problems and needs of modern societies and more recently in order to apply crowdsourcing ideas in the public sector context and promote 'citizensourcing'. In this direction governments first used their own accounts in various social media, in which they provide information about specific problems and policies, and solicit citizens' feedback on them (active citizensourcing). Recently, they attempt to take advantage of the extensive public policy related content developed beyond their own social media accounts, in various political forums, blogs, news websites, and SM accounts, by the citizens, without any stimulation (passive citizensourcing). These constitute significant innovations in policy formulation– citizens communication processes and practices of government. Therefore it is important to evaluate them from various perspectives, in order to learn from them as much as possible, identify and address their weaknesses, make the required improvements, and in general achieve higher levels of effectiveness and maturity of these highly innovative practices. This paper makes a two-fold contribution in this direction: initially it develops a framework for evaluating such citizensourcing innovations based on the passive social media monitoring; and then it uses this framework for the evaluation of three pilot applications of a novel method of government passive citizensourcing through social media monitoring, which has been developed as part of an international research project.

Keywords: Social media · Government · Crowdsourcing · Citizensourcing · Innovation · Evaluation

1 Introduction

Governments initially used the Web 2.0 social media mainly in order to disseminate information to the public about their activities, services, policies and plans, influenced strongly by the one-way communication patterns of the Web 1.0 era. Then they started exploiting the extensive two-ways communication capabilities provided by the social media, in order to collect from citizens useful information, knowledge, opinions and

© IFIP International Federation for Information Processing 2015
E. Tambouris et al. (Eds.): EGOV 2015, LNCS 9248, pp. 305–320, 2015.
DOI: 10.1007/978-3-319-22479-4_23

ideas concerning the problems and needs of modern societies, and the public policies they were designing and implementing for addressing them, and more recently in order to apply crowdsourcing ideas in the public sector context and promote 'citizensourcing' [12–14, 23, 33]. In this direction governments first used their own accounts in various social media, in which they provide information about specific social problems and public policies, and solicit citizens' feedback on them, aiming to conduct 'active' forms of citizensourcing [10, 17, 32, 33]. Recently, they attempt to extend these practices beyond their own social media accounts, in order to exploit the extensive public policy related content developed by the citizens in various political forums, blogs, news websites, and also in various Twitter, Facebook, etc. accounts, without any stimulation from government, aiming to combine the above active forms of citizensourcing with more 'passive' ones [3, 11, 25]. This has been driven by the social media monitoring (SMM) practices developed in the private sector, in order to collect opinions, complaints and questions that have been posted in various social media (e.g. forums, blogs, Twitter, Facebook, news feeds, etc.) about their products and services, which are processed and used for improving products and services, and also for designing communication strategies [15, 22, 37]. Government agencies, which have been traditionally monitoring citizens' opinions and attitudes towards their policies and plans (e.g. through surveys based on representative citizens' samples), and also relevant articles in the 'traditional' media (e.g. newspapers), show an increasing interest in SMM for collecting useful information, knowledge, opinions and ideas from the citizens concerning their problems and needs, and also existing and planned public policies.

However, the above constitute big innovations in the government – citizens communication and the policy formulation processes and practices of government. Therefore it is important to evaluate them from various perspectives, in order to learn from them as much as possible, identify their strengths and weaknesses, and also address the latter and strengthen the former, and finally achieve higher levels of effectiveness and maturity of these highly innovative practices. This paper makes a two-fold contribution in this direction:

(i) It develops a framework for evaluating such passive social media citizensourcing innovations, which is based on theoretical foundations drawn from previous research on crowdsourcing (see Sect. 2.3) and innovation diffusion (see Sect. 2.4).

(ii) It uses this framework for the evaluation of three pilot applications of a novel method of government passive citizensourcing based on SMM (described in more detail in [11, 25], which has been developed as part of the European research project NOMAD ("Policy Formulation and Validation through Non-moderated Crowdsourcing" – for more details see www.nomad-project.eu/), partially funded by the "ICT for governance and policy modeling" research initiative of the European Commission.

The paper is structured in seven sections. In the following Sect. 2, the background of our research is presented. The abovementioned novel method of government passive citizensourcing is outlined in Sect. 3. Then in Sect. 4 the proposed evaluation framework is presented. Our research method is described in the subsequent Sect. 5, followed by the evaluation results, which can be found in Sect. 6. Finally, the conclusions are summarized in Sect. 7.

2 Background

2.1 Social Media in Government

Social media have been initially used by private sector firms, mainly in their marketing and customer service activities, and then adopted and utilised by government agencies as well, in order to take advantage of the large numbers of users that social media attract, and the unprecedented capabilities they provide to simple non-professional users for developing, distributing, accessing and rating/commenting various types of digital content, and also for the creation of on-line communities [4, 5, 11, 13, 14, 30].

There has been considerable research analysing the potential of social media for supporting, enhancing and transforming critical government functions, which has identified significant opportunities they provide to government agencies: (i) to increase citizens' participation and engagement, providing to more groups of modern societies a voice in debates on public policies development and implementation; (ii) to promote transparency and accountability, and reduce corruption, by enabling governments to open up large quantities of data concerning their activity and spending; (iii) to drive important innovations in both the internal operations of government agencies and the ways they communicate and interact with the public outside their boundaries; (iv) to collect useful information and knowledge from the citizens' concerning the complex problems and needs of modern societies; (v) to exploit citizens' creativity in order to develop innovative solutions to the serious and complex problems that modern societies face, and in general to apply crowd-sourcing ideas in the public sector (citizensourcing); (vi) to proceed to public services co-production with citizens, enabling government agencies and the public to design jointly government services [4, 5, 10, 17, 27, 30, 32, 33].

The first generation of social media exploitation by government agencies included the creation and operation of their own accounts in several social media, the publication of policy-related content to them (concerning specific social problems and public policies, in order to stimulate relevant discussions with citizens), and the analysis of citizens' interactions with this content, such as views, likes, retransmissions, textual comments, etc. (active citizensourcing); this is usually performed manually, however there is a trend towards higher levels of automation, based on applications accessing various social media platforms through their application programming interfaces (APIs) [10, 17, 32, 33]. As mentioned in the Introduction, recently a second generation of more passive social media exploitation by government agencies has emerged, which is based on adaptations of private sector SMM practices. In particular, it includes collection and processing of policy-related content created by citizens beyond government social media accounts, in various political forums, blogs, news websites, and also in various Twitter, Facebook, etc. accounts, and sophisticated analysis of them, through a central system (passive citizensourcing) [3, 11, 25].

2.2 Social Media Monitoring

SMM, defined as 'the continuous systematic observation and analysis of social media networks and social communities' [16], has been initially developed for and used by private sector firms, in order to address their fundamental need for listening to their existing and potential customers, in a better and more efficient way than the traditional methods used for this purpose, such as surveys, by exploiting the wealth of user-generated content available online [15, 16, 22, 37, 39]. SMM is based on ICT platforms, which enable listening to the social media users, accessing real customers' opinions, complaints and questions, at real time in a highly scalable way, analysing and measuring their activities concerning a specific brand, or an enterprise, or specific products and services, and processing of this information; this leads to valuable insights for firms, regarding how customers view them, their services and solutions, and also their competitors.

However, there is a lack of frameworks for the evaluation of SMM platforms, practices and approaches in general, which is quite important for achieving higher levels of effectiveness, maturity and diffusion. There is only a framework for evaluating SMM tools proposed by Stavrakantonakis [39], which is oriented towards their private sector use. It comprises a set of evaluation criteria that can be used to analyze and assess the functionality of SMM tools from three perspectives: the concepts they implement (data capture and analysis, workflow, engagement – reaction to posts, and identification of influencers), the technologies used (listening grid adjustment, near real-time processing, integration with third party applications, sentiment analysis, historical data) and the user interface (dashboard, results' export) they provide.

Quite limited is the previous literature concerning the use of SMM by government agencies. Bekkers et al. [3] investigate SMM practices of four Dutch public organizations, examining the goals of SMM, its operation and effects. They discriminate between four types of monitored citizens' electronic discussion media based on two criteria: the level of perceived privacy (low or high), and the type of issues discussed (personal or societal); they recommend that more ethical questions arise, so government agencies should be more careful and also transparent, if the citizens' electronic discussion media monitored are characterised by higher perceived privacy and host discussions on more personal issues. There is a lack of frameworks for evaluating the use of SMM by government agencies from various perspectives, which would be quite important for the development of knowledge and effectiveness in this area. Such an evaluation framework should include government SMM assessment from various perspectives. Since this SMM aims to support a citizensourcing innovation, it is necessary to assess it both from the crowdsourcing perspective (see following Sect. 2.3), and also from the innovation diffusion perspective (see Sect. 2.4).

2.3 Crowdsourcing

The great potential of the 'collective intelligence', defined as a 'form of universally distributed intelligence, constantly enhanced, coordinated in real time, and resulting in the effective mobilization of skills' [24], to contribute to difficult problem solving and design activities has lead to the emergence of crowdsourcing and its adoption, initially in the private sector, and subsequently (still experimentally) in the public sector as well. Crowdsourcing is defined as 'the act of a company or institution taking a function once performed by employees and outsourcing it to an undefined (and generally large) network of people in the form of an open call' [19] or as 'a new web-based business model that harnesses the creative solutions of a distributed network of individuals', in order to exploit 'collective wisdom' and mine fresh ideas from large numbers of individuals [9]. While the use of the collective intelligence of a large group of people as a help for solving difficult problems is an approach that has been used for long time [8, 9, 19, 20, 40], it is only recently that crowdsourcing started being widely adopted by firms as a means of obtaining external expertise, accessing the collective wisdom and creativity resident in the virtual crowd.

Crowdsourcing started being applied initially in the creative and design industries, and then it expanded into other private sector industries, for solving both mundane and highly complex tasks. Recently it has started being applied by government agencies as well, usually exploiting the capabilities offered by social media for this purpose, as they enable the wide and low cost application of the 'crowdsourcing' ideas by government agencies, termed as 'citizensourcing' [7, 18, 27, 28, 33, 34], which can be highly useful for public policy making. Social media platforms enable government agencies to mine useful fresh insights into social needs and problems, and ideas concerning possible solutions to them, new public services or improvements of existing ones, or other types of innovations, from large numbers of citizens. Initially it had the form of 'active crowdsourcing', in which government agencies have active role, posing particular social problems, questions or public policy directions, usually in their own social media accounts, and soliciting relevant information, knowledge, opinions and ideas from citizens. Recently a second form of 'passive crowdsourcing' is emerging, in which government has more passive role, collecting through SMM content on a specific topic or public policy, which has been freely generated by citizens in various sources, and performing sophisticated processing of it [11, 25].

However, previous literature notes that the outcomes of crowdsourcing are uncertain, and identifies some important critical success factors, such as the existence of sufficient active crowd, and their quality from a human capital viewpoint, and also some inherent risks, such as digital divide related problems and participation inequalities (i.e. under-representation of some stakeholder groups, and over-representation of some others), and possible manipulation of the crowd [1, 6, 21, 38]. Therefore it is important to evaluate the passive citizensourcing through SMM from a crowdsourcing perspective, assessing the existence of the above critical success factors and risks.

2.4 Diffusion of Innovation

As mentioned above the passive citizensourcing through SMM constitutes a big innovation in the government – citizens communication and in the policy formulation processes and practices of government agencies, so it is important to examine it from this perspective as well, and assess to what extent it has the fundamental preconditions for a wide diffusion. Extensive research has been conducted concerning diffusion of innovations, in order to understand it better and identify factors that favour it [29]. One of the most widely recognised and used theories of innovation diffusion is the one of Rogers [36], which has been extensively employed for analyzing ICT-related innovations in both the public and the private sector [2, 26, 35]. According to this theory, there are five critical characteristics of an innovation that determine the degree of its adoption:

(i)   Relative Advantage (=the degree to which an innovation is perceived as better than the idea, work practice or object it supersedes);

(ii) Compatibility (=the degree to which an innovation is perceived as being consistent with the existing values, past experiences, and needs of potential adopters);

(iii) Complexity (=the degree to which an innovation is perceived as difficult to understand, implement and use);

(iv) Trialability (=the degree to which an innovation may be experimented with on a limited scale basis);

(v)   Observability (=the degree to which the results of an innovation are visible by the external environment).

Therefore it is important to assess to what extent the passive citizensourcing through SMM, viewed as an innovation, has the above characteristics that determine the degree of its adoption and diffusion.

3   A Method of Government Passive Citizensourcing Using SMM

A method of government passive citizensourcing based on SMM has been developed as part of the abovementioned European research project NOMAD [11, 25], aiming to support the formulation of public policies taking into account relevant citizens' knowledge, opinions and ideas. A brief description of it is provided in this section. It consists of four steps:

(i)   The first step is to build the 'domain model', which is an ontology-based representation of the objects of the "world" (domain) we intend to intervene in through a policy (e.g. energy domain, education domain, health domain). The main entities-terms of this are inserted, as well as relations among them, in a tree structure, using a graphical modelling tool.

(ii) Then the second step is to build the 'policy model', which is a representation of the public policy we want to collect relevant content about from the social media; it consists of a number of 'policy statements' associated with one or more nodes of the policy model, and for each of them some positive or negative 'arguments'. A policy model is inserted on a policy model (used as a basis for it) using the above graphical modelling tool.

(iii) Upon the completion of the models, the user provides a list of social media sources (e.g. blogs, news websites, and also Twitter, Facebook, etc. accounts) which are going to be crawled, in order to find relevant content about the topic or public policy of interest (=places on the web that according to our previous knowledge might contain relevant user-generated content, i.e. where citizens are likely to have expressed relevant opinions and suggestions).

(iv) The defined sources (in step iii) are searched against the above domain and policy models (defined in steps i and ii respectively), and the collected content undergoes sophisticated processing using opinion mining techniques: initially opinions and arguments are extracted, and then sentiment analysis of them is performed (the processing is described in more detail in [11]. The results are presented to the user in visualised form; a typical results' visualisation screen (see Fig. 1) includes:

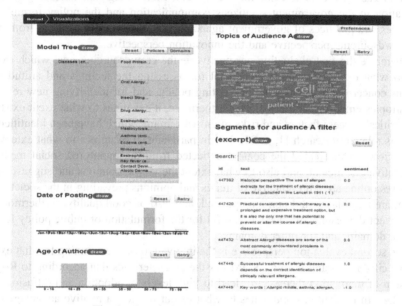

Fig. 1. A typical results' visualisation screen

– In the upper left part of the screen is shown an estimation of the volume of discussion and the cumulative sentiment for all the elements of the domain or policy model (according to the selections made just above it), the former being visualised through the height of the corresponding rectangle, and the latter through its colour (with the green colour denoting positive sentiment, and the orange denoting negative sentiment).

– For the above model, or for a selected element of it, below (in the lower left part of the screen) is shown the distribution of the volume of discussion over time and also across age groups,

– while in the upper right part is shown a word cloud depicting the most frequent terms-topics discussed online (coloured according to the corresponding sentiment),

– and in the lower left part we can see a list of text excerpts from the sources with relevant content (concerning the selected model or element of it).

Also an 'audience comparative view' can be provided, which shows differences among selected different age, gender or education groups, or differences over time, in the discussed topics (concerning volumes of discussion and sentiment, terms-topics frequencies).

4   An Evaluation Framework

Having as theoretical foundation the background presented in the Sect. 2, a framework has been developed for evaluating passive citizensourcing through SMM, which is shown in Table 1 (in the first column). As this constitutes a big citizensourcing oriented innovation in the government – citizens communication and the policy formulation processes and practices of government agencies, it is necessary to assess it from both the crowdsourcing perspective and the innovation perspective.

Therefore the first evaluation perspective is the crowdsourcing one, which examines to what extent it is useful/beneficial for assessing the feelings and attitudes of citizens concerning a prospective or existing policy, and for identifying new relevant issues/topics emerging in the society. Furthermore, it examines to what exent exist the main critical success factors and risks of crowdsourcing which have been identified by previous relevant research [1, 6, 21, 38]. In particular, it examines to what extent the active crowd who created the content collected from the monitored social media is quantitatively sufficient, and also to what extent the views, opinions and suggestions it expresses online are representative of trends and opinions prevailing in the society as a whole, are non-biased and non-manipulated, and also of good quality; furthermore, to what extent the results produced are useful for the formulation of public policy for the specific domain, and for other domains.

The second evaluation perspective is the innovation one, examining to what extent passive citizencourcing through SMM has the characteristics that according to Rogers diffusion of innovation theory [36], lead to high levels of adoption and diffusion (see Sect. 2.4). In particular, it examines to what extent it offers a relative advantage over the existing alternatives for the same purpose, it is easy to use, it is compliant with the policy formulation processes as they are applied in Europe, and also with the needs, the mentalities and the values of the people designing and applying public policies, and it has trialability (i.e. can be tried and experimented on a limited scale basis). We have not included the observability, as such SMM methods due to their nature are not meant to be visible by the external environment.

5   Research Method

Three pilot applications of the above method of passive citizensourcing through SMM have been conducted as part of the NOMAD project, and evaluated using the evaluation framework presented in the previous section. Since this method is intended to be used not only by government agencies in their policy formulation processes, but also by other public policy stakeholders (who want to know citizens' opinions, sentiments/attitudes and suggestions concerning various policy relates topics before submitting relevant policy proposals to government) as well, two of these pilots were carried out by government organizations: the Greek and the Austrian Parliament; while the third one was carried out by an important non-government policy stakeholder in the health domain: the European Academy of Allergy and Clinical Immunology. A detailed scenario has been designed for each pilot, which describes how this method can be used for supporting the specific policy formulation objectives. The topics of these pilot applications were selected so that on one hand they reflect current debates and interests of their owners, and on the other hand cover quite different and diverse domains.

The first pilot application was conducted by the Greek Parliament, and concerns the legal framework for energy management, i.e. the "Greek strategy for energy planning". The objective of the pilot application was to assess public opinion and attitude/sentiment against this prospective legislation, and based on the collected information to propose amendments to the existing legislation. The second pilot application was conducted by the Austrian Parliament, and aimed to monitor the on-going public debate on a 'freedom of information act', i.e. a coherent legal basis for "open government information in Austria" and the open government data policies at large. The third pilot application was oriented towards a more scientific policy topic: it was conducted in collaboration with the European Academy of Allergy and Clinical Immunology (EAACI) in order to assist it in discovering the public stance against "allergy diseases and immunotherapy", and based on this information to design policies for raising awareness in this area, and also to formulate relevant policy proposals to be submitted to the government.

In particular, for each pilot the following process was followed:

- Initially the detailed SMM use scenarios in the selected thematic domain have been defined in cooperation with the 'owners' of the pilot, and then the domain and policy models required for data crawling were created by them, and finally a list of targeted social media sources (which, according to previous knowledge of the pilot owners might contain relevant user-generated content) has been specified.
- After the above preparation, the owners initiated the crawling the specified sources against the corresponding domain and policy models, and the processing of the collected content.
- Then the personnel of the owner organization who participated in this pilot inspected the results, understood them in detail, assisted by members of our research team, and used them in order to draw conclusions about citizens' opinions, sentiments/attitudes and suggestions concerning the topic of each pilot.
- Finally, for each pilot an evaluation focus group discussion was organised, which attended by personnel of the owner organization who were involved in this pilot, and also other invited persons who had relevant knowledge and experience (e.g. for the pilots of the Greek and Austrian Parliament were invited advisors and assistants of Members of the Parliament and journalists specialised in the corresponding domain; for the EACCI pilot were invited doctors, experts and journalists specialised in allergy and clinical immunology). During this focus group discussion the proposed method was introduced to the audience, and particular applications of it with the corresponding results were showcased. Then the attendees had the

opportunity to interact with the ICT application, performing some predefined tasks, under the observation of organizers' staff, who supported them in completing these tasks, and recorded any comments or difficulties.

In order to collect evaluation data from the attendees of these focus group discussions we used a combination of both qualitative and quantitative techniques. According to research methodology literature (e.g. [31, 34, 42], the qualitative techniques allow a more in-depth examination of a phenomenon of interest, and therefore the generation of a deep knowledge about it, which is not limited to a predefined number of variables, enabling a better and richer understanding of 'why' and 'how' things happened; on the contrary, the quantitative techniques focus on a predefined number of variables and enable condensing/summarizing a large quantity of evidence in a few numbers, which makes it easier to draw conclusions. For these reasons in each of these focus groups we conducted initially qualitative discussions focused mainly on the questions of the two perspectives of our evaluation framework shown in Table 1, in order to identify positive and negative elements along each of them, and gain a deeper and richer understanding of why the attendees perceive a low or high level of it. Then we asked the attendees to fill an evaluation questionnaire, which included the questions of the two perspectives of our evaluation framework: these questions were converted to positive statements, and the respondents were asked to provide the degree of their agreement/disagreement with each of them in a five-levels scale (1 = totally disagree, 2 = disagree, 3 = neutral, 4 = agree, 5 = totally agree), which condenses/summarizes all positives and negatives identified with respect to this dimension. The above qualitative discussions were recorded with the consent of the participants, and then transcribed and coded manually using an open coding approach [31]; the data collected through the questionnaire were processed using Excel.

6 Results

In Table 1 (in the second column) are shown the results from the processing of the quantitative data collected through the questionnaire (average ratings for all questions - evaluation metrics).

With respect to the <u>crowdsouring perspective</u> from Table 1 we can see that the respondents perceive as high to very high (closer to the former) the usefulness of this method of passive citizensourcing through SMM for evaluating citizens' feelings and attitudes against a prospective or existing policy (average rating 4.17), and also moderate to high (closer to the latter) its usefulness for identifying emerging new relevant issues/topics in the society (3.74). In the focus group discussions there was an overall agreement that this method provided a time and cost efficient channel to assess citizens' attitudes and feelings on a policy related topic of interest, both from a quantity (e.g. the volume of discussion about it) and a quality (e.g. the sentiments, the most popular topics within relevant discussions) viewpoint, which is better and less expensive than the traditional citizens' surveys conducted by government agencies. However, they mentioned the risk of misusing such SMM results for promoting individual interests, by focusing selectively on some of the results that support their

Table 1. Average ratings for all questions - evaluation metrics

Crowdsourcing perspective	Avg. rating
To what extent passive citizensourcing through SMM is useful/beneficial for assessing citizens' feelings/attitudes against a prospective or existing policy?	4.17
identifying new relevant issues/topics in the society?	3.74
To what extent the active crowd who create the content collected from the monitored social media is quantitatively sufficient?	3.26
the views, opinions and suggestions it expresses online are representative of trends and opinions prevailing in the society as a whole?	3.40
and also are non-biased and non-manipulated?	2.63
are of good quality?	2.89
The results produced are useful... for the formulation of public policy for the specific domain?	3.86
and also for other domains?	3.69
Innovation perspective	
To what extent passive citizensourcing through SMM viewed as an innovation... offers a relative advantage over the existing alternatives for the same purpose?	3.94
is easy to use?	3.02
is compatible with the policy formulation processes, as they are applied in Europe?	3.54
is compatible with the needs, the mentalities and the values of the people designing and applying public policies?	3.57
has trialability (i.e. can be tried and experimented on a limited scale basis)?	3.89

own positions, and hiding some others. Furthermore, they also mentioned the risk of monitoring citizens' postings that are perceived by them as private, which would seem to them as an intrusion into their private sphere. In general, it was concluded that the benefits for society from the use of any web monitoring tool by government depend critically on how this technology is utilised and how its results are exploited. Furthermore, the participants in the focus group discussions mentioned that this method enables to some extent the identification of emerging new relevant issues/topics concerning a particular domain or public policy of interest, however not to the extent they would expect. The word cloud does not seem appropriate for the early identification of new issues, topics or tendencies, as it is dominated by the well established topics-terms (shown with big character sizes, as they are more frequently mentioned by citizens), while the new ones are hardly visible (only some of them are shown with much smaller character sizes, as they are much less frequently mentioned by citizens); new issues, topics or tendencies can be identified mainly by reading the list of text excerpts from the sources with relevant content (lower left part of the typical results' visualisation screen – see Fig. 1). In order to have improvement in this direction two suggestions were made: (a) to add the functionality of temporarily removal out of the word cloud the most frequent topics-terms it includes (shown with big size), so that other less frequently mentioned topics-terms become more visible; (b) to process further the above text excerpts using various opinion mining techniques, in order to automatically identify new topics-terms.

Also, the respondents find the quantity of the active crowd who create the content collected from the monitored social media as moderately sufficient (3.26). Also, they believe that the views, opinions and suggestions it expresses online are to a moderate to large extent representative of the trends and opinions prevailing in the society as a whole (3.40); however, they perceive their quality as low to moderate (2.89), and also that only to a small to moderate extent (but for both closer to the latter) free of bias and manipulation (2.63). Despite these drawbacks, the respondents perceive as moderate to high (being closer to the latter) the usefulness of the results provided by this SMM method for the formulation of public policy for the specific domain, or other domains (3.86 and 3.69 respectively). In the focus group discussions there was skepticism about the representativeness of the citizens' groups who produce the content collected from the monitored social media, and also its reliability (i.e. whether it is non-biased, non-manipulated and of good quality). There was wide agreement that the selection of the social media sources to be monitored is of critical importance in this respect; it was emphasized that it is necessary to select a representative set of high reliability and quality social medial sources to be monitored. Furthermore, a suggestion that emerged was to provide the capability to isolate the results from specific sources (e.g. from sources of a specific political orientation, or corresponding to a particular professional group), or even access the individual source from which a term-topic from the word cloud or a relevant text excerpt originates. It was stressed that it is of particular importance in order to be able understand an opinion, argument or suggestion, or to assess a sentiment, to know the context in which it has been expressed.

Finally, with respect to the innovation perspective from Table 1 we can see that the respondents perceive that this method offers high relative advantage over the existing alternatives for the same purpose (3.94), and has high degree of trialability in a small scale (3.89); also, it has moderate to high compatibility with the policy formulation processes as applied in Europe, and with the needs, the mentalities and the values of the people designing and applying public policies (3.54 and 3,57 respectively). It has been confirmed in the focus group discussions that the potential impact from the integration of the proposed methods and tools in the policy formulation process is positively perceived, as it offers significant relative advantages over the citizens' surveys, which is the main alternative for the same purpose currently in use by governments. It has been mentioned that surveys can neither capture public sentiment nor provide detailed information (e.g. like the frequently mentioned terms-topics, relevant text excerpts provided by this method) about a domain or public policy of interest. However, the ease of use of the whole method is perceived as moderate (3.02). In the focus group discussions it was mentioned that the application of this method does not seem to be easy. The main reason for this is the need to build complex models of the specific domain and also the particular policy we are interested in, which requires much time and effort. As a possible solution for this was suggested the highest possible re-use of existing domain ontologies or vocabularies as a basis for this (and probably add or subtract entities-terms), so the functionality of the ICT application should be enriched in order to provide such import capabilities.

7 Conclusions

Government agencies initially adopted simpler forms of social media exploitation, however latter they started experimenting with more sophisticated ones. Furthermore, while initially they used social media mainly in order to disseminate information to the public about their activities, services, policies and plans, then they started using these highly popular platforms in order to collect from citizens useful information, knowledge, opinions and ideas concerning the problems and needs of modern societies, and the public policies they were designing and implementing for addressing them. Recently they attempt to use the social media in order to apply crowdsourcing ideas in the public sector context, and make 'citizensourcing' oriented innovations in their government – citizens communication and the policy formulation processes and practices. It is therefore important to conduct systematic research in order to create effective methods of using the social media in various 'active' or 'passive' manners for conducting citizensourcing, and then to evaluate them from multiple perspectives based on 'real-life' pilot applications, in order to identify their strengths and weaknesses, design improvements of them, and finally achieve higher levels of effectiveness and maturity of them.

This paper makes a two-fold contribution in this direction. Initially it develops a framework for evaluating passive citizensourcing innovations through SMM, which is based on theoretical foundations drawn from previous research on crowdsourcing and innovation diffusion. Then this framework is used for the evaluation of three pilot applications of a novel method of government passive citizensourcing based on SMM, which has been developed as part of the European research project NOMAD.

These evaluations have provided some first evidence that this method of passive citizensourcing using SMM can provide considerable support for public policy making, enabling the low cost and fast assessment of citizens' feelings/attitudes concerning a prospective or existing policy, and also the identification of emerging new relevant issues/topics in the society, contributing to the improvement of the 'dynamic capabilities' [41] of government agencies (with respect to their 'sensing' component). However, this method poses some risks, associated with the misuse of it for promoting individual interests (by reporting selectively only some of its results which are in desired directions, and hiding some others), and also with the possible intrusion into citizens' private sphere (so in the SMM it is necessary to avoid sources in which contributors perceive their postings and discussions as private). It has been concluded that the quantity and the representativeness of the 'crowd' who created the collected content, on which the results have been based, was satisfactory, but there was some scepticism about the quality and reliability of this content (e.g. due to possible bias of its creators and manipulation). Therefore critical success factor of this method is the selection of an extensive and representative set of high reliability and quality social medial sources to be monitored. However, despite the above drawbacks the overall assessment seems to be positive: this method can provide considerable support for the design of public policies.

Furthermore, this first evaluation provides evidence that this method of passive citizensourcing through SMM viewed as an innovation has most of the preconditions proposed by the theory of innovation diffusion of Rogers [36] for a wide adoption and diffusion. In particular, it has been concluded that it offers strong relative advantage over the existing alternatives for the same purpose, and has high levels of trialability (i.e. can be tried and experimented on a limited scale basis); also, it has a good level of compatibility with the policy formulation processes, and with the needs, the mentalities and the values of the people designing and applying public policies. However, this method does not seem to be easy to use, as it requires building complex models of the specific domain and also the particular policy we are interested in.

The research presented in this paper has interesting implications for research and practice. With respect to research it has developed an evaluation framework that can be used as a basis for the analysis of the emerging new methods and practices of 'citizensourcing' (both active and passive ones) based on social media (possibly enriched with new perspectives, and adapted to the specificities of each particular method and practice), and the identification of their strengths and weaknesses. Furthermore, it has revealed specific weaknesses of the passive citizensourcing through SMM, so it provides guidance on future directions of research for addressing them. With respect to practice, our results indicate that government agencies should not limit themselves to simpler forms of social media use, but also make use of more sophisticated ones as well, and exploiting for citizensourcing purposes not only their own social media accounts, but also the extensive public policy related content developed by the citizens in various Web 2.0 sites, without any stimulation from government. Further research is required for evaluating from different perspectives the emerging methods of passive and active citizensourcing by government agencies in various contexts (e.g. various types of government agencies and other public policy stakeholders, and various types of policies), in order to understand better the benefits they can provide, and also the risks and challenges they pose and their limitations; also research needs to be conducted concerning their combination, and also their integration in the government – citizens communication and the public policy formulation processes, and their impacts.

References

1. Agafonovas, A., Alonderiene, R.: Value creation in innovations crowdsourcing - example of creative agencies. Organ. Markets Emerg. Economies 4(1), 72–103 (2013)
2. Al-Jabri, I.M., Sohail, M.S.: Mobile banking adoption: application of diffusion of innovation theory. J. Electron. Commer. Res. 13(4), 379–391 (2013)
3. Bekkers, V., Edwards, A., de Kool, D.: Social media monitoring: responsive governance in the shadow of surveillance? Gov. Inf. Q. 30(4), 335–342 (2013)
4. Bertot, J.C., Jaeger, P.T., Hansen, D.: The impact of policies on government social media usage: issues, challenges and recommendations. Gov. Inf. Q. 29, 30–40 (2012)
5. Bonsón, E., Torres, L., Royo, S., Flores, F.: Local e-government 2.0: social media and corporate transparency in municipalities. Gov. Inf. Q. 29, 123–132 (2012)
6. Bott, M., Young, G.: The role of crowdsourcing for better governance in international development. PRAXIS - Fletcher J. Hum. Secur. XXVII, 47–70 (2012)
7. Bovaird, T.: Beyond engagement and participation: user and community coproduction of public services. Public Adm. Rev. 67(5), 846–860 (2007)

8. Brabham, D.C.: Crowdsourcing as a model for problem solving: an introduction and cases. Convergence: Int. J. Res. New Media Technol. **14**(1), 75–90 (2008)
9. Brabham, D.C.: Crowdsourcing: a model for leveraging online communities. In: Delwiche, A., Henderson, J. (eds.) The Routledge Handbook of Participative Cultures. Routledge, London (2012)
10. Charalabidis, Y., Loukis, E.: Participative public policy making through multiple social media platforms utilization. Int. J. Electron. Gov. Res. **8**(3), 78–97 (2012)
11. Charalabidis, Y., Loukis, E., Androutsopoulou, A., Karkaletsis, V., Triantafillou, A.: Passive crowdsourcing in government using social media. Transforming Gov. People Process Policy **8**(2), 283–308 (2014)
12. Chun, S.A., Shulman, S., Sandoval, R., Hovy, E.: Government 2.0: making connections between citizens, data and government. Inf. Polity **15**(1/2), 1–9 (2010)
13. Chun, S.A., Luna Reyes, L.F.: Editorial - social media in government. Gov. Inf. Q. **29**, 441–445 (2012)
14. Criado, J.I., Sandoval-Almazan, R., Gil-Garcia, J.R.: Government innovation through social media. Gov. Inf. Q. **30**(4), 222–230 (2013)
15. Croll, A., Power, S.: Complete Web Monitoring. O'Reilly, Sebastopol (2009)
16. Fensel, D., Leiter, B., Stavrakantonakis, I.: Social Media Monitoring. Semantic Technology Institute, Innsbruck
17. Ferro, E., Loukis, E., Charalabidis, Y., Osella, M.: Policy making 2.0: from theory to practice. Gov. Inf. Q. **30**(4), 359–368 (2013)
18. Hilgers, D., Ihl, C.: Citizensourcing: applying the concept of open innovation to the public sector. Int. J. Public Participation **4**(1), 67–88 (2010)
19. Howe, J.: The rise of crowdsourcing. Wired **14**(6), 1–4 (2006)
20. Howe, J.: Crowdsourcing, Why the Power of the Crowd is Driving the Future of Business. Crown Business, New York (2008)
21. Jain, R.: Investigation of governance mechanisms for crowdsourcing initiatives. In: Proceedings of American Conference on Information Systems (AMCIS) (2010)
22. Kasper, H., Kett, H.: Social media monitoring-tools. In: Schwarz, T. (ed.) Leitfaden Online-Marketing. Das Wissen der Branche, pp. 662–669. Marketing-Borse, Waghausel (2011)
23. Linders, D.: From e-government to we-government: defining a typology for citizen coproduction in the age of social media. Gov. Inf. Q. **29**, 446–454 (2012)
24. Levy, P.: Collective intelligence: mankind's emerging world in cyberspace. Plenum, New York (1997)
25. Loukis, E., Charalabidis, Y.: Active and passive crowdsourcing in government. In: Janssen, M., Wimmer, M., Deljoo, A. (eds.) Policy Practice and Digital Science: Integrating Complex Systems. Social Simulation and Public Administration in Policy Research. Public Administration and Information Technology Series. Springer, Berlin (2014)
26. Loukis, E., Spinellis, D., Katsigiannis, A.: Barriers to the adoption of B2B e-marketplaces by large enterprises: lessons learnt from the Hellenic Aerospace Industry. Inf. Syst. Manag. **28**(2), 130–146
27. Linders, D.: From e-government to we-government: defining a typology for citizen coproduction in the age of social media. Gov. Inf. Q. **29**, 446–454 (2011)
28. Lukensmeyer, C.J., Torres, L.H.: Citizensourcing: citizen participation in a networked nation. In: Yang, K., Bergrud, E. (eds.) Civic Engagement in a Network Society, pp. 207–233. Information Age Publishing, Charlotte (2008)
29. MacVaugh, J., Schiavone, F.: Limits to the diffusion of innovation - a literature review and integrative model. Eur. J. Innov. Manag. **13**(2), 197–221 (2010)

30. Margo, M.J.: A review of social media use in e-government. Adm. Sci. **2**(2), 148–161 (2012)
31. Maylor, H., Blackmon, K.: Researching Business and Management. Palgrave-Macmillan, New York (2005)
32. Mergel, I.: Social media adoption and resulting tactics in the U.S. federal government. Gov. Inf. Q. **30**, 123–130 (2013)
33. Nam, T.: Suggesting frameworks of citizensourcing via Government 2.0. Gov. Inf. Q. **29**, 12–20 (2012)
34. Ragin, C., Amoroso, L.: Constructing Social Research: the Unity and Diversity of Method, 2nd edn. Pine Forge Press – Sage Publications, California (2011)
35. Raus, M., Flügge, B., Boutellier, R.: Electronic customs innovation: An improvement of governmental infrastructures. Gov. Inf. Q. **26**, 246–256 (2009)
36. Rogers, E.: Diffusion of Innovations, 5th edn. The Free Press, New York (2003)
37. Sen, E.: Social Media Monitoring für Unternehmen. Social Media Verlag, Cologne (2011)
38. Sharma, A.: Crowdsourcing Critical Success Factor Model Strategies to Harness the Collective Intelligence of the Crowd. London School of Economics (LSE), London (2010)
39. Stavrakantonakis, I., Gagiu, A.E., Kasper, H., Toma, I., Thalhammer, A.: An approach for evaluation of social media monitoring tools. In: Proceedings of the Common Value Management Workshop CVM, Co-located with the 9th Extended Semantic Web Conference ESWC 2012, Heraklion, Crete, Greece (2012)
40. Surowiecki, J.: The Wisdom of Crowds: Why the Many are Smarter than the Few and How Collective Wisdom Shapes Business, Economies, Societies, and Nations. Doubleday, New York (2004)
41. Teece, D.: Explicating dynamic capabilities: the nature and microfoundations of (sustainable) enterprise performance. Strateg. Manag. J. **28**, 1319–1350 (2007)
42. Yin, R.: Case Study Research: Design and Methods, 5th edn. Sage Publications, California (2013)

Three Positives Make One Negative: Public Sector IS Procurement

Aki Alanne, Pasi Hellsten[✉], Samuli Pekkola, and Iiris Saarenpää

Department of Information Management and Logistics,
Tampere University of Technology, P.O. Box 541, 33101 Tampere, Finland
{aki.alanne,pasi.hellsten,samuli.pekkola,
iiris.saarenpaa}@tut.fi

Abstract. The requirement specifications are centric in the IS acquisition process, also in public sector. In addition to the regulatory factors multiple stakeholders are often involved in the procurement process. Yet their expertise varies and is often limited to a narrow sector or a specific field. For this paper, we conducted a single case study on an IS acquisition in a middle-sized city. The function nominated a project manager for the project, with little if any prior experience of IS or of their acquisition. The counterpart in the CIO's office had that knowledge but had little domain knowledge about the requirements. The third party involved was the Procurement and Tendering office. Having specialized in serving the variety of functions in that particular field, the specific areas become inevitably omitted. All three parties argued that their requirements specifications were good, if not great. We observed how such a trident, having reported successful completion of their duties, still missed the point. The tendering resulted in little short of a disaster; two projects were contested, and lost in the market court.

Keywords: Public sector procurement · Information systems procurement · Case study

1 Introduction

Public procurement refers to the acquisition of goods and services to the public sector organizations [1]. In IS context, public sector organizations differ fundamentally from private organizations [2]: they have to simultaneously acquire the best possible IS and comply with public procurement regulations (Moe et al. [6]). This is not, however, easily accomplished [3].

In the public sector, a major hindrance in the way to successful IS acquisition is the lack of know-how in the acquisition process [4]. It can cause severe consequences. For example, the vendor might not be knowledgeable what the customer really wants and/or needs, while the customer might assume the vendor is offering a strange solution, creating ungrounded mistrust towards the vendor. Incompetent, inexperienced, or careless preparation and construction of the requirements result, most likely, foreboding tendering and procurement [5]. Even though the acquisition process is successfully completed, there might be repercussions and unexpected consequences.

© IFIP International Federation for Information Processing 2015
E. Tambouris et al. (Eds.): EGOV 2015, LNCS 9248, pp. 321–333, 2015.
DOI: 10.1007/978-3-319-22479-4_24

For example, it is not uncommon that the party having lost in the competition may use these obscurities to complain about the proceedings to the market justice. This may halt the entire procurement process, so that no organization is able to reach its goals or gain desired advantages.

These simple examples highlight that IS procurement is a complicated process. Studies focusing especially on public sector procurement have also pinpointed the challenges. In addition to "typical" challenges of exceeding schedules and budgets or failing the objectives, public sector specific challenges such as specifying the requirements early on for tendering [4, 6], and coping with the conflicting needs and objectives of different stakeholders [7–10] are common. Even though these problems are well known, IS literature on public procurement seems to be lacking theoretical foundation and empirical evidence [3, 5]. In the literature, the process of public sector IS procurement is often described in rather simplified fashion, or the focus is on one particular task, not on the process on general level [4]. Similarly, with few exceptions, the stakeholders involved are considered often on organizational level – even though there may be several distinct parties within each organization, or the focus has been one specific stakeholder group [11]. As Moe and Päivärinta [3] put it: *"more research is needed on issues such as stakeholder management and on balancing different goals without asking for more than is needed. The interplay between procurers and vendors in public procurement has not previously been much researched."* (p. 318).

To answer this call, we conducted a qualitative, in-depth case study [12, 13] of a public procurement process where multiple stakeholders are participating in the procurement process in its different phases. The project personnel were very confident that they had one of the best requests for tenders they have ever made, yet the case resulted in a disaster. We will thus answer to following question: "How stakeholders participating in the public procurement influence the tendering?" In this paper, we will thus reveal the complex process behind public procurement and identify the stakeholders and their roles. This allows us to better understand the challenges, analyze the issues leading to the problems and potential success, and explain how those emerge in practice.

The paper is organized as follows. First, related research on public procurement, its challenges, and stakeholders is shortly illustrated. Second, research settings, methods, and findings are presented. Finally the findings are discussed and conclusion drawn.

2   Related Research

Public procurement refers to a process of acquiring goods or services for government or public organization through buying or purchasing [1]. It differs from the private sector procurement, even though the differences may not always be radical [2, 7]. For example, the ownership of the private business lies within a limited number of entrepreneurs and/or shareholders while the public organizations are collectively owned by members of political communities, individuals in the society [7]. Furthermore, public organizations are typically funded mainly by taxation. They are thus less likely to be affected by the changing market forces than, for example, stock listed private organizations [14]. Similarly control mechanisms vary between public and private sector. While the economic system defines the constraints for private organization, public organizations are affected by rules imposed by political means. In addition, public organizations seldom have direct competitors offering similar services [7].

Information systems as the subject of procurement is different than more standardized goods or services [3]. The organization acquiring the system must often consider alternatives that may not be simply comparable or their differences easily evaluated. Also a standard system seldom fits with the public organization's needs so customization is almost surely needed. Outsourced development obviously stresses this issue, and calls for intensive cooperation and communication as the external stakeholders may not be familiar with the context. This nevertheless applies to internal parties as well. For example CIO's office may not be able to understand the use context. Consequently systems requirements may neither be clear at the beginning or in early phases of the procurement, e.g. in tendering, yet the scope and requirement related decisions must already been made [15].

The procurement process itself, payment model and standard government contracts holds several pitfalls and limitations. If those are too rigid, they will limit the vendors' interests to make tenders, and further to engage in the projects. This would, in turn, reduce competition, and provide less viable options for the customer organization. In other words, this will not allow the procurer to get the optimal price or quality [6, 16].

Procurement process itself and tendering are highly regulated. For example, in EU and EEA countries the call for tenders must be publicly, either nationally or EU wide, announced when certain threshold values at the acquisition are exceeded. Particularly public sector related problems are the lack of in-house experience and competence about the acquisition in general, poor understanding about the IS or technology, or the lack of resources to create high-quality and valid specifications [6]. Especially in IS procurement, the requirement specification is a crucial element, which is nevertheless very challenging to compose. Due to the regulations and pre-determined procurement process, the requirements need to be specified before announcing the request for tenders. Under the circumstance they are often done without a clear idea about what are the possibilities of different alternatives [3]. This makes it possible that the acquisition or its' scope are incorrect. The result may even prove to be that a wrong system is acquired [6]. This proactive determination of the requirements and scope causes difficulties in finding a suitable assessment and evaluation criteria [3]. In the words of Moe and Päivärinta [3], *"transparency for ensuring fair competition between vendors is clearly a public-sector-specific challenge; private firms can be more pragmatic on these issues"* (p. 316).

In the public sector, multiple different stakeholders with divergent and conflicting objectives are often involved [17, p. 4]. This makes the procurement inherently complex. Abovementioned characteristics frame this; numerous stakeholders have a variety of wishes, needs and objectives, all waiting to be satisfied [7]. Stakeholders participating in the public projects are, however, case-specific and unique, or only partly the same to each situation. This makes the application of general frameworks for analysis difficult. This has been a motivation for different stakeholder studies [9, 17]. Still it should be noted that public organizations often have other identical entities to cooperate with, e.g. other municipalities [3].

The number and variety of stakeholders within and across the organizations make public procurement challenging. Their demands and objectives may be in conflict with each other. Satisfying all of them may not be possible, or at least requires much additional effort. In addition, public organizations themselves tend have more ambiguous goals, practices and responsibilities [7, 9]. Consequently different IS features may be treated differently, as the parties may understand their work tasks, divisions of labor, and responsibilities dissimilarly, or even the objectives or focus points may differ between the supplier and the buyer. For example, the parties may not have a unified view on organizational boundaries and related responsibilities. In addition, there are at least three types of organizational goals to consider, namely regulatory, commercial, and socio-economic. Pursuing all these may lead to conflicts, while overemphasizing one at the cost of others may have adverse effects [8, 18].

The accuracy and level of detail of the requirement specification is also linked to the stakeholders' conflicting interests. For example, the procurer side prefers and strives for a complete and clear specification, while the vendors would like to have more freedom in order to present their qualities and possibilities not mentioned in the request [3, 19]. Technically speaking, the procurement gets difficult and complicated when the target system needs to fit with the customer's current IT portfolio. The integration and compatibility of different systems has been identified as a challenge as public organizations have multiple systems bridging a wide range of sectors and services [3] and little knowledge how to articulate this [20].

Defining project success is challenging. There is no universal definition for success, but the evaluation of different features varies between the viewpoints [21]. For example, the features denoting success include the project's timely delivery or staying within the budget frames. However, these features judge whether the project is successful only in a simplified manner by observing the procedure and effects of procurement [22–24]. The success may also be defined by using other measures. For example, improved organizational information integration, better decision making, and improved inter-organizational communications and/or decreased operational bottlenecks (ibid.). The question remains whether the absence of any one of these factors is enough to declare the project a failure. There may be distinguished different levels of success [25] or, according to a more pessimistic view, an inevitable failure [26].

Despite previously mentioned studies on stakeholders, much work is still to be done. Moe [4] suggests that there is a need for research on how different stakeholders manage and cope with potentially conflicting interests. Flak et al. [17] conclude that the dominant approach of putting the focal organization, i.e. the service procurer, in the nexus of stakeholders is insufficient when the conflicts are addressed. Future work should thus incorporate the relationships between all stakeholders involved in the project. On the other hand, due to lack of research, more focus should also be put on the vendor in the procurement process, for example in its tendering phase [4].

3   The Research Method and Settings

The single case study [13] behind this paper focuses on a social welfare sector of a city of over 200 000 inhabitants. The sector of social services, Home care unit, lists over 830 000 visits and treatment cases a year with over 2000 clients. The clients have various needs; some need attention only in delivering the medication whereas others need more concrete assistance such as heavy lifting, cooking, and handing out medication. Some clients need multiple daily visits while others require less attention. The clients are scattered around the city (surface area 689,6 km^2 divided into four care areas). Similarly to clients, the employees, i.e. the nursing staff, have different limitations. Some are entitled to hand out medication while others may not be permitted to do heavy lifting. The employees are divided into mutually supplementing teams. The complexity of the settings presents the management with challenges. It became suggested that modern ICT might offer a solution to these.

Before the procurement process started, at the beginning of every work shift, the nurses had to visit the central office to receive the latest information about the route of the day, the clients to be visited, keys to their houses, etc. During the home care process, the nurses may receive urgent calls, so they adjust the route accordingly. The shift ends by visiting the office to leave the keys and to report the day. Until recently, a person has been employed to monitor the daily situation and to plan the route and activities. As IT was perceived to ease the planning and execution of these tasks, the CIO's office decided to act. The procurement project begun.

The city uses a so-called purchaser/provider –model in its acquisitions. This model means effectively that the actual provider of the services, i.e. Home care unit, does not concern so much whether and how much care is needed for their individual clients as there is an organization to define the needs. This consists of health care, welfare and social service specialists. They visit the possible client in his/her house to study and to define the circumstances and the specifics of the need for care. When they have drawn a plan, they place an order for the care, and leave it with the Home care unit, which then takes the matter as a part of their routine.

The qualitative data was collected by semi-structured interviews. First the key persons for the IS procurement project were suggested by our contact person. Further interviewees were invited by their suggestions, i.e. snowball sample was used [27]. In total eleven interviews, listed in Table 1, were conducted face-to-face at the case organization premises. All the interviews were recorded and transcribed. The interview themes covered issues related to initiation of the project, available resources and stakeholders, contracting and legal agreements, procurement process and communication, and the evaluation of the success.

The data analysis followed interpretive research approach [28]. Two researchers went through the material several times to gain an overview of the procurement process, stakeholders involved, and different challenges, and to gather all relevant details. Process diagrams and stakeholder maps were drawn to visually aid the interpretations. These visual maps were further iterated. Due to the size of these visualizations and space limitations, they are omitted from this paper. Finally the findings were compared to the literature.

4   Findings

As a public sector organization in European Union, the case organization has to obey the Act on Public Contracts declaring that all acquisitions exceeding the sum of 30 000 Euros, a call for bids is to be placed in a public forum. Then all interested parties are

Table 1. The interviewees and their organizational positions.

Interviewees organization	Interviewees position
CIO's office	Agreement specialist
CIO's office	Coordinator
Home care unit	Project manager
Home care unit	Care person
Home care unit	Supervisor
Home care unit	Supervisor
Home care unit	Work organizer/care person
Procurement and tendering office	Procurement specialist
Social welfare sector	Process manager
Supplier/vendor	Project manager
Supplier/vendor	Supplier project manager

able to inspect the bids, and a place a tender if found appropriate. The process how the procurement is initiated and how the proceedings happened is described next.

The procurement project roughly follows the generic public procurement process [4]. The project was initiated by a business unit (see Table 2). An initial project idea was proposed to the city's CIO's office. The initiative was stored in a centralized repository for initial projects and project ideas to be evaluated later. Each year, after the city's annual budget is released, the repository is reviewed. The projects were assessed and graded according to several criteria, such as criticality and cost-benefit analysis, and the number of citizens affected when the system would be in use. The evaluation was done by the development and steering group for the welfare services. The group constituted members from CIO's office and stakeholders from different functions related to welfare services.

CIO's office decided that a pre-study is needed before final proposal acceptance. A third party consultant was hired to conduct it. CIO's office reviewed their report, and development and steering group officially sanctioned the actual project. A coordinator from the CIO's office, and a steering group were thus appointed. The steering group consisted of the coordinator from the CIO's office, and decision makers from both the purchaser and the provider functions. A project team was also set. In addition to the project coordinator, a person from the Home Care Unit was appointed as a project manager.

> ".. they set off to find a project manager, while the CIO's office's project coordinator was already working on the project plan.." [Project manager, Home care unit]

The project manager from the Home Care Unit was a civil servant with no prior experience of IS outside the actual use or their acquisition, who, in her own words, "hopped onto a moving train". With some support from the CIO's office, the project manager started to write a detailed requirements specification document for the call for bids.

> "..as the pre-study was there.. with some preliminary requirements.. We started the actual project hastily with the requirements matrix.." [Project manager, Home Care Unit]

Table 2. The actions in the project

Actions	Participants
1. Original idea of the solution	Home care unit
2. Proposition of the idea	Home care unit supervisor
3. Filing the proposition	Coordinator, CIO's office
4. Preliminary evaluation of the solutions	Outside consultant appointed by the CIO's office
5. Initial assessment of the ideas	CIO's office
6. Assessment of the various propositions	Development and steering group, Welfare sector
7. Go-decision for individual projects	Development and steering group, Welfare sector
8. Coordinator appointed for project	CIO's office
9. Requirements matrix created	Coordinator at CIO's office
10. Project manager appointed from Home care	Development and steering group, Welfare sector
11. Requirement specifications written	Project manager from Home care (with coordinator and agreement specialist (CIO's office))
12. Redefining the requirements	Project manager, coordinator (CIO's office), specialist, (procurement and tendering office)
13. Opening the call for bids	Specialist, (procurement and tendering office)
14. Tenders	Vendors
15. Initial, formal assessment of bids	Specialist, Procurement and tendering office
16. Assessing the bids	CIO's office, Home care unit
17. Making the decision	Development and steering group, Welfare sector
18. Receiving the complaint	Procurement and tendering office
19. Formulating the rejoinder	Procurement and tendering office, agreement specialist (CIO's office), Project mgr. from Home care unit

The requirement specification work proceeded. The project was first divided into two sub-projects; a system for workflow optimization and tasks related to division of labor, and secondly an electronic door opening system to grant the nursing staff entrance into the buildings without bunch of physical keys. Even though the projects were treated separately, they were tightly connected as the systems were supposed to be integrated. An agreement specialist with a good grasp of tendering from the CIO's office was then consulted if his/her expertise was needed. The tendering specialist argued that sometimes, in some projects, the process and the outcome of the tendering competition is clear from the beginning:

> "..sometimes it is possible to know already at the beginning that a complaint will be filed as qualitative measures are not easy to define in a manner that they leave no room for argumentation or objection" [Agreement specialist, CIO's office]

In this case, no such possibility was deemed likely, although there were signs that should the decision not favor a certain party, there might be repercussions.

"..plaintiff's contract in another area was discontinued. We knew that if this vendor does not get chosen now, they will file a complaint no matter what. And so they did." [Agreement specialist, CIO's office]

The call for bids was published in a public forum. In due course, the bids were received, and an acquisition decision was made. A small company (50 employees, in September 2013), claiming to be able to provide the features in the needed scope for the best price, was selected as an enterprise system provider. However, a complaint was filed in market court due ambiguity in requirement specifications. Similarly an electronic door system provider was chosen. However, the timing was unfortunate as there was a shift in the dominant design [29, 30] of the handheld appliances and the technologies used for this type of operation. It turned out that the technology (Symbian) upon which the applications were designed for, was becoming obsolete.

"Providers had not developed software for any other system but Symbian and both of the providers announced how long it will take to develop them.." [Project manager, Home Care Unit]

Both sub-projects were consequently put on a hold, one for the complaint and the other for technology change, until new directions were identified and assessed. The providers evaluated the significance of the technological change to their products (the optimization and electronic door system), and expressed their will to develop their product further as alternative technologies were recognized.

The negotiations continued. The door opening system provider announced that they could not be able to deliver the systems for the agreed price nor with required features.

"..we didn't have a glue that then the providers don't actually know how to count all their expenses for a fixed price, and then compete so brutally that they, on a way, give underpriced tenders so that they are not committed to the win tendering.." [Agreement specialist, CIO's office]

The original winner declined to sign the contract. After lengthy negotiations with the winning party no solution was found. The city thus signed a contract with the second runner-up. However, then the original winner filed a complaint. For the door opening system, the city appealed to higher legal assistance about the decision. However, due to time pressures, a solution was needed immediately. Again the door opening systems was promoted with the second runner-up on a provisional agreement. Later also this received sentence in favor of the plaintiff declining the city the possibility to continue with the provisional actions.

The enterprise system tendering would have needed to be re-opened. However, as the city owned shares of National Centralized Purchasing organization (NCP), this gave the city a chance to evade public procurement process as the NCP had done the competitive bidding in forehand on behalf of the municipalities. They were thus able to acquire the system through the NCP from the original winner, the one they preferred, without tendering and violating the procurement ruling.

However, its optimization solution did not meet the city's needs and requirements. NCP is an integrator of various services offered to all public sector organizations.

NCP's expertise and experience is on procurement in general with offerings based on general level specifications, not on any particular field of operations. Even inside in a municipality, there are dissimilar processes, practices, needs, and requirements. For example even though the work of Home care unit is controlled by the law and is basically the same in every municipality, the cities have different process models and needs for route optimization. Obviously also the size of the municipality and the number of the users and customers of the future system varies. In our city, the system was expected to optimize the routes, users, and customer incidents well beyond the number of cases which it was tested and found suitable. The optimization algorithms were not entirely on a level that was needed and advertised by the producing company. In other words, the complexity of the optimization and the systems requirements differ significantly between the cities.

> "Depending on the geographical features of the city, route optimization and logistically reasonable route is, for some cities, more important issue in planning a care person's day than for others. For some cases, the most important feature is the person's primary care person. Between the boundaries, there are various whishes depending on the city's operations ideology and how efficiently they want to use their resources" [Project Manager, Supplier/Vendor]

The process in public bidding turned out to have unexpected outcomes; market court interpreted the law and declared both cases for unjustified and unlawful for the city. The interpretation is not always unambiguous, but leaves room for individual reading of the situation. This skill of preparing for the tendering is to be trained, but seldom can it be fully obtained without having paid the dues.

5 Discussion

There were several challenges in the project. The most significant ones are: lack of individual skills and knowledge about the acquisition, the complexity of the acquisition network and the number of participating stakeholders, difficulties in allocating the most suitable resources for the project, and the ambiguity of the overall tendering process and legislation.

The *number of stakeholders* in the city alone was large. Three main entities were Home care unit and the project manager, CIO's office and the coordinator, and the Procurement and tendering office. The project manager knew the work of home care unit and their needs by heart. Yet she was not knowledgeable about IS in general or its acquisition. Meanwhile the coordinator knew IS, technologies, technical terms, and something about the procurement, but he was not the domain specialist. Procurement and tendering office knew how to run through procurement projects, but knew nothing about home care or dedicated IS. This means that although the participants had all vital knowledge, it *was scattered across the network of actors*. The *lack of individuals' skills* on different areas was expected to be compensated by the group work. But, the *lack of skills in cooperating* in this manner prevented knowledge sharing.

The problems in knowledge sharing and group work were multiplied by the *lack of resources*. All but one of the stakeholders were working in other projects, and even this person had duties from the 'real job', so they were running the acquisition project as part-time. Hence, reviewing the documents, requirements, bids, and tenders was most likely done in hurry, with an extensive trust on others that they are able to spot possible mistakes and traps. Yet, as the comprehensive understanding about the acquisition process and its objectives was missing and fragmented across three parties, it was impossible to do this. The *lack of knowledge about the acquisition* was severe.

The *ambiguity of the tendering process and legislation* was also evident. Before the call for bids was out, even before the first call for market court, all the city's interviewees claimed that this would be a success case without any problems. Yet there were not only one, but two plaintiffs, one for both areas of acquisition. Why such surprises? Retrospectively speaking, as no one had a holistic understanding about the case or how it will proceed, all the city's participants believed, from their individual viewpoints, that this is a clear, easy assignment. External incidents, such as technological change or a cancellation of earlier contract, resulted in urgent and unexpected pressures to readjust and change the acquisition process one way or the other. Due to time pressures and lacks of knowledge and skills, the parties were not able to prepare and react appropriately and accordingly.

These findings are not novel in general level. Earlier literature review points out that all of these have been identified earlier [3, 4, 6–9]. Yet, as the case illustrates, there are finer level of details here. Instead of generalizing the customer as one organization, there are several smaller sub-organizations within the customer-organization. Similarly to customer-vendor relationship, also these sub-organizations have their own skills and resources, perhaps even objectives, which evidently have an impact on their collective work. In this case, although the coordinator, the project manager, and the Procurement and tendering office, among other stakeholders, were all working together towards a common goal, their inadequate cooperation and knowledge sharing led to fragmented views on the acquisition project. Three positives became one negative.

Some lessons can be drawn:

- The project manager's role is crucial to the success of the outcome. The zest and energy the person makes or breaks the case.
- Acquiring appropriate knowledge and skills is not an evident or easy task. It is not enough just to gather the expertise together, but to utilize it in a manner that different areas complement each other comprehensively, without forgetting the overall picture.
- The stakeholders form a complex network. Understanding and exploiting this network and its skills and expertise requires special attention. Very easily some essential party is forgotten or ignored, making it difficult to gain the essential understanding or resources.
- The acquisition project has to be prepared for external incidents. This means change management, in all possible forms, and risk management practices have to be in place. Change management is particularly problematic in public sector procurement where legislation steers the process.
- Benchmarking the technology needs to be done in identical situation. Although this is easier to say than do, the use of optimization algorithms in smaller scale situations did not reveal the scalability problems.

There are some limitations there. First, this is a single case study. This means that our findings are context specific. In different cases these issues may emerge differently. More research is thus needed. Second, the study was conducted in Finland which is known for its strict attitude for following the rules. Hence, in some other countries, pending the Act on Public Contracts and making the corners straight may ease the situation. However, this would most likely create new challenges. Nevertheless, cultural and country specific issues cannot be ignored.

6 Conclusion

We have presented a case where it is believed that nothing could go wrong, and all goes wrong. Our point is not to tell yet another failure story, but to show that good intentions could result in bad outcomes if the intentions are not properly executed. This execution is not an easy task. In public sector procurement the number of stakeholders and the network they form complicate knowledge sharing, communication, and collaboration. Without purposeful activities, it becomes impossible to gain a holistic view from different fragments. Very easily three positive opinions become one negative outcome. The complexity of the situation is thus emphasized. Even though all the actions when writing the call for bids were done by-the-book, latter external incidents and their unexpected outcomes were not in that book. No one was prepared for them.

The paper makes a theoretical contribution by focusing a little studied situation: public sector IS procurement and groups of stakeholders. By illustrating how they cooperate, or actually lack the cooperation, results in unsatisfying outcomes. This has not been studied before. Practitioners benefit the paper by learning these mistakes and issues.

Future work could benefit from adopting a stakeholder approach as it has been proven useful both in private sector and in e-government studies [14, 31].

Acknowledgements. Special thanks to our interviewees at the municipality and friends and colleagues for their constructive comments. The study was partly funded by Tekes - Finnish Funding Agency for Innovations and participating organizations, partly by Academy of Finland, grant #259831.

References

1. Hommen, L., Rolfstam, M.: Public procurement and innovation: towards a taxonomy. J. Public Procure. **9**(1), 17 (2009)
2. Caudle, S.L., Gorr, W.L., Newcomer, K.E.: Key information systems management issues for the public sector. MIS Q. 171–188 (1991)
3. Moe, C.E., Päivärinta, T.: Challenges in information systems procurement in the public sector. Electron. J. E-Gov. **11**(1) (2013)
4. Moe, C.E.: Research on public procurement of information systems: the need for a process approach. Commun. Assoc. Inf. Syst. **34**(1), 78 (2014)

5. Johansson, B., Lahtinen, M.: Requirement specification in government IT procurement. Procedia Technol. **5**, 369–377 (2012)
6. Moe, C.E., Risvand, A.C., Sein, M.K.: Limits of public procurement: information systems acquisition. In: Wimmer, M.A., Scholl, H.J., Grönlund, Å., Andersen, K.V. (eds.) EGOV 2006. LNCS, vol. 4084, pp. 281–292. Springer, Heidelberg (2006)
7. Boyne, G.: Public and private management: what's the difference? J. Manag. Stud. **39**, 97–122 (2002)
8. Erridge, A.: Public procurement, public value and the Northern Ireland unemployment pilot project. Public Adm. **85**(4), 1023–1043 (2007)
9. Pan, G.S.: Information systems project abandonment: a stakeholder analysis. Int. J. Inf. Manag. **25**(2), 173–184 (2005)
10. Virtanen, P.P.: Team leaders' perceptions in the renewing of software production process. In: Proceedings of the 2013 Annual Conference on Computers and People Research, pp. 159–166 (2013)
11. Rowley, J.: e-government stakeholders—who are they and what do they want? Int. J. Inf. Manag. **31**(1), 53–62 (2011)
12. Klein, H.K., Myers, M.D.: A set of principles for conducting and evaluating interpretive field studies in information systems. MIS Q. 67–93 (1999)
13. Yin, R.K.: Case Study Research: Design and Methods, vol. 5. Sage Publications, Incorporated (2008)
14. Flak, L.S., Rose, J.: Stakeholder governance: adapting stakeholder theory to e-government. Commun. Assoc. Inf. Syst. **16**(1), 31 (2005)
15. Saarinen, T., Vepsäläinen, A.P.: Procurement strategies for information systems. J. Manag. Inf. Syst. 187–208 (1994)
16. Doshi, B.: The new OGC guidance: the future roadmap for government IT procurement. Comput. Law Secur. Rev. **21**(4), 344–348 (2005)
17. Flak, L.S., Nordheim, S., Munkvold, B.E.: Analyzing stakeholder diversity in G2G efforts: combining descriptive stakeholder theory and dialectic process theory. E-Serv. J. **6**(2), 3–23 (2008)
18. Thai, K.V.: Public procurement re-examined. J. Public Procure. **1**(1), 9–50 (2001)
19. Alanne, A., Pekkola, S., Kähkönen, T.: Centralized and distributed ERP development models: operations and challenges. http://www.pacis-net.org/file/2014/1861.pdf (2014)
20. Lemmetti, J., Pekkola, S.: Understanding enterprise architecture: perceptions by the finnish public sector. In: EGOV, pp. 162–173 (2012)
21. Al-Turki, U.M.: An exploratory study of ERP implementation in Saudi Arabia. Prod. Plan. Control **22**(4), 403–413 (2011)
22. Hsu, L.-L., Chen, M.: Impacts of ERP systems on the integrated-interaction performance of manufacturing and marketing. Ind. Manag. Data Syst. **104**(1), 42–55 (2004)
23. Olhager, J., Selldin, E.: Enterprise resource planning survey of Swedish manufacturing firms. Eur. J. Oper. Res. **146**(2), 365–373 (2003)
24. Spathis, C., Ananiadis, J.: Assessing the benefits of using an enterprise system in accounting information and management. J. Enterp. Inf. Manag. **18**(2), 195–210 (2005)
25. Heeks, R.: Information systems and developing countries: failure, success, and local improvisations. Inf. Soc. **18**(2), 101–112 (2002)
26. Gargeya, V.B., Brady, C.: Success and failure factors of adopting SAP in ERP system implementation. Bus. Process Manag. J. **11**(5), 501–516 (2005)
27. Atkinson, R., Flint, J.: Accessing hidden and hard-to-reach populations: snowball research strategies. Soc. Res. Update **33**(1), 1–4 (2001)
28. Walsham, G.: Doing interpretive research. Eur. J. Inf. Syst. **15**(3), 320–330 (2006)

29. Suarez, F.F.: Battles for technological dominance: an integrative framework. Res. Policy **33**(2), 271–286 (2004)
30. Utterback, J.M., Abernathy, W.J.: A dynamic model of process and product innovation. Omega **3**(6), 639–656 (1975)
31. Poon, P.-L., Yu, Y.T.: Investigating ERP systems procurement practice: Hong Kong and Australian experiences. Inf. Softw. Technol. **52**(10), 1011–1022 (2010)

Proactivity Postponed? 'Capturing' Records Created in the Context of E-government – A Literary Warrant Analysis of the Plans for a National e-archive Service in Sweden

Ann-Sofie Klareld[✉]

Department of Archives and Computer Science, Mid Sweden University,
Härnösand, Sweden
ann-sofie.klareld@miun.se

Abstract. Proactive records management is often described as a prerequisite for a well-functioning public administration that is efficient, legally secure and democratic. In the context of e-government, official information is seen as a valuable asset, which is why technical solutions are developed to improve accessibility and reusability. Yet how to 'capture' and preserve the information is still unclear, and adaptations of routines which have originated in a paper based administration to practices suitable for managing digital records are often lacking. This risks impeding on the work of public agencies, their services toward citizens, and the goals of e-government. This paper uses current plans for developing a national e-archive service in Sweden as a case, applying literary warrant and the records continuum model to discuss how archives management can support the goals of e-government and facilitate proactivity. A special focus is placed on 'capture' as a vital part of holistic recordkeeping. The result shows that despite regulations and ambitions supporting proactivity, 'capture' is not emphasized as a necessity for using, sharing and preserving official information. This could create archives that are incomplete, and risk contributing to a decline in governmental transparency and openness.

Keywords: Archives · E-government · Literary warrant · Records continuum model · Records management

1 Introduction

Managing official records correctly is crucial from a democratic perspective. To 'capture' and preserve public records facilitates access, traceability, and reuse – today as well as in the long term. Yet measures for proactive records management are often perceived as being outside core business [1] and too resource demanding [2], which can be the reasons why these measures are often postponed to the future. Existing routines developed to ensure appropriate official archives management are largely based on a paper administration, where records are 'captured' using manual strategies such as stamps with the date of arrival, registration in a records management system, and preservation in filing cabinets. In recent years scanning has been used to facilitate access,

© IFIP International Federation for Information Processing 2015
E. Tambouris et al. (Eds.): EGOV 2015, LNCS 9248, pp. 334–347, 2015.
DOI: 10.1007/978-3-319-22479-4_25

usability and preservation. However, e-government introduces unique possibilities and challenges: it is not enough to 'digitize' documents and present information in formats which resemble A4 sheets.

E-government is defined by the EU as "the use of information and communication technologies in public administrations combined with organizational change and new skills in order to improve public services and democratic processes and strengthen support to public policies" [3]. The goals of e-government are generally thought to be of concern for the state administration as a whole, to be realized through collaboration and coordination, rather than addressed by single agencies and departments on their own [4]. This requires a holistic approach to information management. 'Capturing' records created in e-services needs to be developed, where registration ideally should be performed automatically, and archives management needs to be adapted to suit the current conditions. Digital information has the potential to become a valuable asset for citizens as well as other actors and agencies external to the public administration.

This paper aims to contribute to international research on archives in the context of e-government by highlighting the importance of proactivity. The aim is also to inspire others to conduct research in the area of electronic records management within e-government by showing that this is a highly relevant and interesting topic. The case studied is the current plan to develop a national e-archive service in Sweden. This context is used as an example to discuss how archives management can support the goals of e-government and facilitate proactivity. A special focus is 'capture', since according to the records continuum model this is a vital part of holistic recordkeeping. A literary warrant [5] study of national regulations is used, and therefore relevant legal, adminis-trative, and archival conditions are explained briefly to make the paper comprehensible to readers unfamiliar with Sweden. Similar studies could be made in other contexts to gain insight on the relationships between existing legal frameworks and planned tech-nical and administrative solutions.

The holistic concept of the archive, as used in this paper, implies that rather than being seen as going through different linear phases ('active', 'semi active' and 'archival'), records are viewed as existing in a continuous flow, which may 'begin' with the archives creation at the public agency and 'continue' to the long term preservation at an archival authority [6], yet may also 'start' at the archival authority and 'continue' on through use and re-use to administrative, cultural or personal uses [7].

2   Research Problem

American archivist David Bearman described 'capture' as one of two major problems in relation to records management: "(...) two of the greatest moments of risk, at capture and access, are outside the scope of many "archival preservation" models" [8]. E-government poses new challenges and possibilities for managing and preserving offi-cial records, thus increased knowledge is needed about how current technical and organ-izational developments affect recordkeeping, archives management and e-government.

This paper uses Sweden as a case study to discuss the universal problem of 'capturing' records created in the context of e-government. 'Capture' is to some extent regulated in Sweden through demands on registration, and cannot be described as entirely left out of the archival preservation model, but despite its recognized importance there is no designated government authority with mandates and responsibilities for registration issues. In 2006 the report *To preserve digital documents: Proposal for future orientation* emphasized that it was fundamental to develop models, methods and routines for preparing digital information for long term preservation already at the point of creation [9], yet nine years later there is still a long way to go before official records are regularly created in formats suitable for long term preservation. Similar situations can also be found in other countries around the globe. According to Mnjama and Wamukoya many public sector organizations in Africa lack procedures for managing electronic records, which may lead to the loss of valuable information resources [10]. Jaeger and Bertot have studied the information dissemination of the Obama administration and concluded that long-term access to information is an important part of transparency, but that the use of internet-enabled technologies, such as social media, can make preservation difficult [11]. In a study based on the Canadian government, Park et al. found that with the current e-government development comes a need to further systematize the capture of information using metadata architectures and standards [12].

The solutions which governments develop and employ to address the problems of capturing and preserving records created in the context of e-government will affect future transparency and access to information. The research question addressed in the paper is:

Do the current plans for developing a national e-archive service support the goals of e-government and facilitate existing legal demands on proactivity?

3   Material and Method

Managing material used in the study is primarily (1) the government's decision on how to implement a national e-archive [13], and (2) an interim report authored by the responsible agencies [14]. Press releases and information from the website of the State Service Center are used as complement. The material was chosen as a suitable base for the study because it represents recent plans and discussions relevant for understanding how current developments may affect official recordkeeping and archives management. The material was analyzed using literary warrant found in existing legal framework, mainly the Freedom of the Press Act [15]; the Archives Act [16]; the Archival Ordinance [17]; and the Public Access to Information and Secrecy Act [18]. Literary warrant means to use authoritative sources such as laws, standards, codes of ethics, and professional best practices as theoretical frameworks of reference [5, 19]. This method has previously been used by the University of Pittsburgh Electronic Recordkeeping Project to study the professional and societal endorsement of the concept of the recordkeeping functional requirements. An important result of the project was Wendy Duff's compendium of statements describing the requirements for records or recordkeeping systems [20]. Literary warrant defines the requirements for capturing, maintaining, and using records over time [21].

This paper followed the literary warrant method with a specific focus on Swedish laws as the framework of reference, in particular the Archives Act, the Freedom of the Press Act, the Public Access to Information and Secrecy Act and the Archive Ordinance because these include instructions about 'capture' and proactive management of public records. These laws are also an expression of the holistic concept of the archive as it is implemented in Sweden.

While the legal principles, for example regarding transparency, preservation, and privacy protection, remain the same in the context of e-government, the practical implementations may need to change to achieve the wanted results. It is therefore important to study current changes in relation to their legal and administrative context. The paper focuses especially on 'capturing' official records, which is why the second dimension of the records continuum model is used as a theoretical lens. According to the records continuum model, 'capture' is a crucial dimension of holistic recordkeeping [7], thus this dimension is useful for understanding current developments in the light of a holistic concept of the archive.

4   Related Research

Researchers in the field of e-government have argued: "Records constitute an important corner stone of governance. As more governments are introducing e-government solutions, digital preservation turns into an important challenge" [22]. However, as recently as 2013 a survey by Scholl, said electronic records management is an area "of special interest and only appeal to a small sub-group of the EGR [Electronic Government Research] community" [23]. This paper argues that the area of recordkeeping is an important part of EGR since e-government is based on the access to trustworthy information. Sound recordkeeping and archives management are prerequisites for open government and transparency, which are two of the areas of interest that Scholl's study shows to be popular EGR topics [23].

Archiving and recordkeeping have been described as bothersome, unnecessary and bureaucratic, despite their actual importance for business [24]. Researchers in the field of archival science and information systems have even said that archiving can be seen as a 'necessary evil' [1]. According to Canadian archivist Terry Eastwood who has studied the significance of archives in society, there is often little political will to invest resources in archives and records management. Eastwood also argues that it often is a challenge to explain the role of archives and archivists to political and administrative decision makers [2] and Maria Kallberg's recent doctoral thesis indicated that there is currently a lack of awareness as regards the need of proactive recordkeeping [25]. Transactions registered with the help of e-services can be seen as records created in a 'grey zone', since it is unclear who is responsible for archiving records created in an integrated e-service, therefore a proactive approach and regulation of responsibilities by clear agreements before an e-service is designed has been recommended [1]. Informatics researchers have argued that more research is needed about systems development in the context of e-government [26].

The discipline of Archives and Information Science has much knowledge to offer on issues related to electronic records management. According to American archivist and scholar Richard Pearce-Moses there is no clear-cut boundary separating the "paper era" from the "digital era", and therefore there is a point in seeking knowledge in traditional theories: "Much of archival knowledge transfers directly to the digital era, and established principles give us insight into solutions" [27]. This study is based on the assumption that traditional theories and principles of official archives management are transferrable to the context of e-government, but that practical management needs a clear proactive stance to meet the requirements of use, preservation, and access. As Canadian archivist Terry Cook has argued, archivists need to shift their focus from the physical objects to the originating context where records are created, since the archival paradigms of the 'custodial age' are obsolete in the electronic environment [28].

5   Holistic Recordkeeping and the Importance of Proactivity

There are two major established methodologies in the archival world: *the life cycle approach*, which assumes that recordkeeping is the result of objective business activities and follows a predictable timeline, and *the records continuum approach*, which views it as "(...) a continually interacting and evolving set of contingent activities with individual, institutional, and societal aspects" [19]. The holistic approach as represented in the records continuum model corresponds to the goals of e-government: information should be (re)usable also to actors outside the context in which it was originally created. This poses new demands on proactivity: "In today's administration agencies are expected to streamline their information management with the support of automated case processes and e-services. For the agencies, it is important to have tools for information governance that contribute to both efficiency and legally secure handling. Issues of management, preservation and disposal should be addressed already at the stage of planning and defining requirements. A proactive approach should permeate the authorities' information- and records management" [29, my translation].

Bearman has described the dimensions of the records continuum model with the words *event, documentation, risk* and *societal*. In the first dimension a record is created as the trace of an event. In the second dimension the event is "witnessed" by a system and the transaction becomes evidence. In the third dimension the record is appraised using risk assessment criteria by the organization that created it and is destroyed or preserved. In the fourth dimension society gives meaning to the record by institutionalizing it [30]. The first three dimensions focus on the organizational management of records while the fourth focuses on reproduction and access. The fourth dimension can be seen as a way of describing the discourse that surrounds the whole process of archiving. Records are always *created* in the first dimension but *exist* in all dimensions simultaneously. Considerations of the different characteristics of the model affect choices of rules, software, and work processes.

A core component of the holistic approach is that records are given a context. This can be ensured through registration, which is a way of 'capturing' the information by connecting it to the setting in which it is used. 'Capture' implies that a record, by being communicated or connected to other records, becomes part of a chain of events (for example case administration). Through 'capture', records can be shared, accessed and understood: "(...) metadata elements needed to make the context of the document known are added and the record is able to be referenced or drawn upon by others" [31]. In other words, the crucial *evidential value* of an official record is obtained in the second dimension. Public agencies are often required to ensure that their transactions are documented, or as Bearman says: "witnessed". Being able to guarantee the accuracy of official information is crucial for the trustworthiness of the public administration and not least becomes important if a dispute should arise. Ensuring that records belonging to the same case are registered, searchable, and accessible makes it possible to understand how the case has been handled and upon what grounds a certain decision was based. In a digital environment this demands proactive measures. When the Swedish Tax Authority developed their e-archive solution they demanded that it should meet the requirement to first archive cases, and then administer them, thereby emphasizing the importance of proactive recordkeeping. Archiving at the point of creation was seen as a prerequisite to fulfill the legal requirements [32]. This approach is, however, far from usual, and though public agencies' business systems, e-mail systems and web servers currently hold substantial amounts of official information [58, 59], it doesn't automatically mean that the information is 'captured' as part of an archive.

6   Research Context

The Swedish concept of the archive is often described as holistic. It is constructed after the principle of transparency in government businesses: citizens have a constitutional right to access official records from the point of creation or arrival at a public agency, unless the information is confidential due to official secrecy, personal integrity, or other specified reasons [15]. This requires *searchability*, which is why official records should be registered as soon as they arrive or are created [18] and *accessibility*, hence registration should take into account its importance for effective archiving, using materials and methods appropriate to the needs of archival permanence [16]. There is no equivalent to 'record' and 'archive' in the Swedish language, both are referred to as 'allmän handling', a term that can be translated to 'official record'. The Archives Act stipulates that "the *archives* of an authority are composed of the *official records* created through its activities [16]. Consequently an archive can consist of both 'active' records still used by the organization, and 'inactive' records that are preserved.

Records created or received by Swedish public agencies are to be preserved, kept in order and handled in ways that ensure: "(1) The right of free access to public records; (2) The information requirements of the public jurisdiction and administrations; and (3) Research requirements" [SFS, 1990:782 as translated by 33]. Official records should be assigned metadata explaining : (1) when the record was created or received, (2) registration number or other designation, (3) sender or receiver, and (4) in brief what the record concerns [18]. The traditional way to do this is through a 'diarium' or registry, and by manually adding metadata to the records. 'Diarium' is not a juridical term in the manner of 'registry' or 'registering', but is indirectly explained in the Public Access to

Information and Secrecy Act [18] as a continuing register of the records which have arrived or are created at a public agency. The basic meaning of 'e-diarium' is 'electronic registry', yet the term increasingly tends to imply integrated solutions for case- and document management where registration is only part of the functionality [34]. There are currently no binding regulations saying that public agencies should incorporate this functionality into their business systems, yet contextualization is required since citizens not only have the right to know *which* information public agencies preserve, but also *how* it has been used [35].

National recommendations for how e-services should be developed do not include considerations of the legal requirements to preserve and provide access to official records. Yet adherence to the close connection between records management and archiving becomes increasingly important in the context of e-government, and it has been discussed several times by different authors that the mandates of archival authorities (for example the National Archives) could include supervising the registration of official documents [36–38]. This is however not the case today.

The Swedish National Archives has a double role, being a cultural heritage institution and at the same time an administrative actor with powers to supervise and advise state public agencies on matters concerning archives management. According to its mandate the National Archives is required to "promote the development of methods for the production, preservation and availability of documents as part of government development" [39, my translation]. It has, however, proved difficult for the archival authority to keep up with technological development. A survey made in 1998 by two Dutch experts showed that existing policies and strategies related to digital preservation were conducted at an operational level, based on issuing constitutions and lacked a coherent vision, leading to confusion and uncertainty of public agencies concerning delivery of digital material [37]. A report written in 2006 said the National Archives strove to cater for archival requirements by assisting public agencies already at the beginning of their system development processes [9]. However, four years later a survey showed that only 5 % of the public agencies had a strategy for taking care of their e-records and although 21 % of the authorities had some form of system for preservation, none of these had an export function that enabled transfer to another system or e-archive [38]. At the time of writing, digital archives management, as in many other countries, is still a notable practical problem for public agencies.

When Swedish public agencies started to deliver information from IT systems to the National Archives at the beginning of the 1970s, digital preservation was seen as primarily the concern of archival institutions. The Archives Act of 1991 however emphasized the responsibility of public agencies as part of their statutory archival activities. The Archives Act is a framework law and consequently it is up to each public agency to implement it in practice in such a way that it suits their respective business. However, while the legal framework assumes that each agency keeps and controls their own records, current political goals point to a future where information is shared and used by more than one actor [40].

7 Plans for a National e-archive Service

A recent government decision has made the State Service Center (SSC) and the National Archives responsible for developing a national e-archive solution for state public agencies. The State Service Center is a public agency under the Ministry of Finance, established in 2012. It offers services related to payroll administration, financial management and e-commerce to other agencies [41]. A pre study report concluded that implementing a common e-archive would result in considerable cost savings compared to each public agency creating their own [42]. A number of public agencies are nominated to pilot the e-archive service once it is in place.

Archives management is formed in relation to ideals regarding how society should be organized, what good governance means and how official records should be used. This currently includes the goals of e-government. The Swedish national e-archive service is meant to make it easier and cheaper for public agencies to preserve and provide access to information about the state administration. It is described as: "(...) a necessary component of the technical infrastructure of e-government, and a prerequisite for a digitally collaborative administration", which will become part of the state's long-term information management [43, my translation]. An interim report states that "A joint management service for e-archives is part of the necessary infrastructure for a sustainable e-government and a long-term information supply for the state as a whole" [14]. It also aims to facilitate openness. A press release from the Industry Ministry has stated: "Transparency is a cornerstone of our democracy. e-archives can mean greater transparency and better access to information for the general public, journalists and researchers" [13, my translation]. The e-archive service will be the first service developed within the government's *Digital step*, an investment intended to facilitate citizens' and companies' contacts with the public administration through public e-services, which will provide digital meetings as a complement to personal meetings, the main principle being: "digitally wherever possible, and personal where needed" [44]. The e-archive is planned to function as a 'middle archive', which means a repository where official records are to be preserved in a standardized way before transfer to the final long term preservation at the National Archives [45], in other words it will hold 'semi active' records.

An interim report from the State Service Center on the implementation of the e-archive service stated that public agencies have a tendency to postpone the demanded measures to facilitate long term preservation and instead prioritize their daily business. This is described as a problem which each agency needs to address. But despite stating that "waiting to take care of information means more rather than less expenses" [14, my translation], notwithstanding the risk of losing information, the authors argue against developing a national e-registry simultaneously as the national e-archive. Paradoxically it is however concluded that: "In the long run, it would be a great advantage for the civil service as a whole if the SSC was able to offer a comprehensive concept for the authorities' case and document management where information with the status archived can be directly transferred to the e-archive service" [14, my translation]. Such a comprehensive concept would require the inclusion of an e-registry system.

8 Analysis and Discussion

Common services such as the national e-archive studied in this paper are often intended to contribute to the goals of e-government and make the public administration more efficient. The Director General of the State Service Center has said in an interview: "Today it is a costly and time-consuming process to deliver records from each agency to the National Archives for final archiving. Economies of scale with an intermediate repository become very large" [46, my translation]. Using the service however demands preparatory work to ensure that records that are not worthy of long-term preservation and should have been destroyed are not delivered into the e-archive [43]. Failing to take control of the entire archives management process risks counteracting the interoperable, collaborative administration which is the goal of e-government. The government's decision on a national e-archive service says legal obstacles, economic considerations and reuse of information must be taken into account before implementation [47], yet nothing is mentioned about the actions needed before records are transferred to the e-archive, though this will require considerable time and effort on behalf of the consumer agencies [14].

According to the new process-based archival description standard, issued by the National Archives in 2008, and meant to be implemented by 2013, all public agencies should represent their information in a classification scheme, aimed to give an overview of the records and to facilitate management and searchability [48]. A holistic, proactive approach is advocated: "Information management and archives should not be seen as two separate areas. There are advantages with creating common structures for registering, archival representation and, not the least, security classification. Archival representation should be used as a control instrument in the information management of public agencies" [49, my translation]. However, although e-services are often said to facilitate open government it is far from usual that registration or archiving are included as functions. A case can be administered using several different e-services. The functionality of business systems and the interdependencies between records will not follow into the e-archive [50], thus these must be documented before transfer. Citizens are to be able both to follow a case in real time, and subsequently go back and review a chain of events [17]. In cases where information is continually and automatically updated it becomes even more important to capture the information upon which decisions are based. If not, it can prove impossible to recreate a chain of events.

The records continuum model recognizes the social and political role of archives management, showing how a record can be read and interpreted differently depending on the context [51]. Paper records are often described as physical objects while digital records are seen as intangible and primarily logical, but though there might seem to be profound differences between the 'real' and the 'virtual' world, the two are intertwined. Australian scholar Frank Upward, who created the records continuum model, has said: "Even when they are captured in a medium that can be felt and touched, records as conceptual constructs do not coincide with records as physical objects" [52]. An example is the driver's license which functions as a record and proof of identity because the information it holds can be verified in relation to the archives of the issuing agency and of the national population registers. In the context of e-government such interrelations become increasingly complex.

Official archives management is affected by business organization and formal relations between creating agencies and archival authorities, both currently undergoing changes. In 2002 the Publicity and Confidentiality Committee suggested a new law on the management of official records, and argued that the National Archives should be given the mandate and responsibility to supervise the whole information management process at public agencies [35]. A later report commented: "(…) the formulations can be considered to give an indication that the archival authority should get a say in the very beginning of the administration process" [36]. Despite similar formulations since then, and clear regulations stating that official records should be registered [18] and connected to case management where applicable, the challenge of preserving context is notably absent from the discussions concerning the national e-archive service. More emphasis is put on issues regarding efficiency and information sharing. The interim report analyzed in this paper refers to the 'life cycle' of e-records which is noteworthy given that the legal framework presumes a holistic concept of the archive.

Archive services have traditionally been seen as more of a support function than as a regulatory function. Digital records require another approach. Caspar Almalander, the project leader of eARD (e-archive and e-diarium), a nationwide project focusing on transfer of information between any and all information systems though developing a set of Common Specifications for Government Agencies (FGS) [53], has stated that archives and e-government are closely connected and requires changes in the way records are managed: "Archives are the engine of e-government. Therefore, we must move from ownership to leadership" [54, my translation]. However, previous research and government reports show that although it is the responsibility of public agencies to manage their official information, many lack knowledge regarding archives management and require advice and guidance. These problems could be tackled with a clear proactive stance from archival authorities and development projects. The current plans for developing and implementing a national e-archive service however seem to lack loyalty to the holistic concept of the archive, according to which 'capture' is a prerequisite for successful archives management. Resources have been allocated to nationwide projects focusing transfer and preservation of official information, but issues regarding registration attract less attention.

The *Pre study report on the future of electronic archives* from the State Treasury said that it should technically be fully possible to complete most existing systems to fulfill reasonable demands on electronic archiving: "The key is to identify early the electronic archives evolving needs, both short and long term, and to take them into account at the design of new procedures and the specification and procurement of additional IT support" [36, my translation]. Ten years later a similar remark was made in a report from a National Archives-related project: "A consistent registration, with similar structure and metadata, provides conditions for reliable information management, searchability and an easier transmission to the e-archive" [55, my translation]. The same report however also said changes should be implemented as operational systems are developed or replaced with new systems or services: "The harmonization of e-diaria may be seen as a long-term process, as it may cause considerable work with the adaptation of operational systems. But as systems evolve or are replaced there will be opportunities to make demands to get it right from the beginning" [55, my translation].

Official information is often described as a social common resource. Public agencies are requested to increase their publication of open data to the benefit of citizens, companies and organizations. As a consequence, archival management needs to be developed accordingly: "Archives reflect not just technologies (...) but also the changes in culture that accompany changing technology" [56]. Technical solutions and administrative routines should be developed in the light of the existing legal framework and considerations related to costs, legality and efficiency [57], issues which e-government development aims to support.

9 Concluding Remarks

The research question addressed in this paper was: Do the current plans for developing a national e-archive service support the goals of e-government and facilitate existing legal demands on proactivity?

Despite the literary warrant supporting 'capture' as a crucial part of holistic records management, the national e-archive project has chosen to exclude a national e-diarium (e-registry) from their work. Developing a national e-archive service without simultaneously discussing these issues could be a step away from the holistic concept of the archive toward procedures which are less suitable in the context of e-government and that risks contributing to a decline in adherence to existing legal and theoretical frameworks.

Suggested solutions for implementing a national e-archive service would likely be different if 'capture' of records was emphasized as a prerequisite for using, sharing and preserving official information. If implemented according to the existing plans and suggestions, 'capture' risks taking place at the end of a 'lifecycle' rather than at an early stage as part of holistic recordkeeping. Preparations for e-archiving risk becoming costly without a proactive approach and resulting in archives that fail to contribute to the goals of e-government. Transparency and openness are also at risk if proactive records management continues to be postponed to the future.

References

1. Asproth, V., et al.: Förvaltning och medborgarskap i förändring: etablerad praxis och kritiska perspektiv [Governance and citizenship in transition: the established practice and critical perspectives]. In: Lindblad-Gidlund, K. (ed.). Studentlitteratur: Lund (2010)
2. Eastwood, T.: Reflections on the goal of archival appraisal in democratic societies. Archivaria 54(1), 59–71 (2002)
3. Commission of the European Communities: The role of eGovernment for Europe's future (2003)
4. IT-standardiseringsutredningen: Den osynliga infrastrukturen – om förbättrad samordning av offentlig IT-standardisering [The invisible infrastructure - on improved coordination of official IT-standardization], Näringsdepartementet, Editor (2007)
5. Duff, W.M.: Harnessing the power of warrant. Am. Archivist 61(1), 88–105 (1998)

6. Jörwall, L., Lönnroth, L., Nordström, G.: Det globala minnet: nedslag i den internationella arkivhistorien [The global memory: examples from the international history of archives]. Jörwall, L., Lönnroth, L., Nordström, G. (eds.). Riksarkive, Stockholm (2012)

7. McKemmish, S. (ed.): Archives: recordkeeping in society. Centre for Information Studies, Charles Sturt University, Wagga Wagga (2005)

8. Bearman, D.: Moments of risk: identifying threats to electronic records. Archivaria **62**(1), 15–46 (2006)

9. Riksarkivet: Att bevara digitala handlingar Förslag till framtida inriktning [To preserve digital documents Proposal for future orientation]. In: Kristiansson, G. (ed.) Kulturdepartementet (2006)

10. Nathan, M., Justus, W.: E-government and records management: an assessment tool for e-records readiness in government. Electron. Libr. **25**(3), 274–284 (2007)

11. Jaeger, P., Bertot, J.: Transparency and technological change: ensuring equal and sustained public access to government information. Gov. Inf. Q. **27**(4), 371–376 (2010)

12. Park, E., et al.: Running ahead toward interoperable e-government: the government of Canada metadata framework. Int. J. Inf. Manage. **29**(2), 145–150 (2009)

13. Näringsdepartementet, Uppdrag att utveckla gemensamt e-arkiv [Mandate to develop common e-archive] (2014)

14. Statens Servicecenter: En förvaltningsgemensam tjänst för e-arkiv - delrapport [A common management services for e-archives - interim report]. Gävle (2015)

15. SFS: Sweden. Tryckfrihetsförordning [The Freedom of the Press Act]. 105, Stockholm (1949)

16. SFS, Sweden. Arkivlag [Archives Act]. 1990:782: Stockholm

17. SFS: Sweden. Arkivförordning [Archive ordinance]. 446, Stockholm (1991)

18. SFS: Sweden. Offentlighets- och sekretesslag [Public Access to Information and Secrecy Act]. 400 (2009)

19. McKemmish, S., Gilliland, A.: Archival and recordkeeping research: past, present and future. In: Williamson, K., Johanson, G. (eds.) Research Methods: Information. Systems and Contexts. Tilde University Press, Prahan (2013)

20. University of Pittsburgh School of Information: Functional Requirements for Evidence in Recordkeeping: The Pittsburgh Project 2004. http://www.archimuse.com/papers/nhprc/. Accessed 8 June 2015

21. Pearce-Moses, R., Baty, L.A.: A Glossary of Archival and Records Terminology. Society of American Archivists, Chicago (2005)

22. Kulovits, H., et al.: Archives and digital repositories in an eGovernment context: when the subsequent bird catches the worm. In: 13th IFIP WG 8.5 International Conference, EGOV 2014, Dublin, Ireland, 1–3 Sept 2014. Proceedings Springer, Berlin (2014)

23. Scholl, H.J.: Electronic government research: topical directions and preferences. In: Wimmer, M.A., Janssen, M., Scholl, H.J. (eds.) EGOV 2013. LNCS, vol. 8074, pp. 1–13. Springer, Heidelberg (2013)

24. Myndigheten för samhällsskydd och beredskap (MSB) och Riksarkivet, Vägledning för processorienterad informationskartläggning [Guidance for process-oriented information mapping]. Stockholm (2012)

25. Kallberg, M.: 'The Emperor's New Clothes' recordkeeping in a new context. Dissertation, Mittuniversitetet: Sundsvall (2013)

26. Karlsson, F., Hedström, K.: Förvaltning och medborgarskap i förändring: etablerad praxis och kritiska perspektiv [Governance and citizenship in transition: the established practice and critical perspectives]. In: Lindblad-Gidlund, K. (ed.) Studentlitteratur: Lund (2010)

27. Pearce-Moses, R.: Janus in cyberspace: archives on the threshold of the digital era. Am. Archivist **70**(1), 13–22 (2007)

28. Cook, T.: Electronic records, paper minds: the revolution in information management and archives in the post-custodial and post-modernist era. Arch. Soc. Stud.: J. Interdiscip. Res. 1(0) (2007)
29. Riksarkivet: Panera och styra [Plan and govern] (2013). http://riksarkivet.se/planera-och-styra. Accessed 20 Feb 2015
30. Bearman, D.: Item level control and electronic recordkeeping. Cult. Heritage Inf. Q. 10(3), 195–245 (1996)
31. Reed, B.: Reading the records continuum. Arch. Manuscripts 1(33), 41 (2005)
32. Standéus, R.: e-Arkivprojektet vid Skatteverket [The e-Archive project at the Tax Authority], Malmö (2007)
33. Hörnfeldt, T.: The concept of record - on being digital. In: Abukhanfusa, K. (ed). The Concept of Record: Report from the Second Stockholm Conference on Archival Science and the Concept of Record, 30–31 May 1996, Riksarkivet, Stockholm (1998)
34. Riksarkivet eARD: Delprojekt 1 (DP1) inom e-arkiv och e-diarium (Begreppsdefinitioner) Ordlista [Subproject 1 within e-archive and e-diarium (Concept definitions) Glossary] Version 1:1, 14 January 2013, Stockholm (2013)
35. Offentlighets- och sekretesskommittén: SOU 2002:97 Ordning och reda bland allmänna handlingar [Orderliness among official records], Stockholm (2002)
36. Wessbrandt, K.: Förstudierapport om framtidens elektroniska arkiv [Pre study report on the future of electronic archives], Statskontoret, Editor (2003)
37. Hofman, H., Buckens, K.: Willing to Change: The Swedish National Archives at the Threshold of the Digital Age (1998)
38. Riksarkivet: Förstudie om e-arkiv och e-diarium Rapport [Pre study of e-archive and e-diarium Report] (2011)
39. Sweden. Kulturdepartementet, Förordning med instruktion för Riksarkivet [Statute for the National Archives], Kulturdepartementet, Editor. SFS 2009:1593, Västerås
40. Näringsdepartementet, Med medborgaren i centrum. Regeringens strategi för en digitalt samverkande statsförvaltning [With the citizen in the center. The Government's strategy for a digital collaborative public administration], N.M.o. Industry], Editor. Stockholm (2013)
41. Statens servicecenter. Om oss [About us] (2014). http://www.statenssc.se/OmOss/Sidor/default.aspx. Accessed 27 Mar 2015
42. Aspenfjäll, J.: Förstudie Statens servicecenter e-arkiv och e-diarium [Pre study State Service Center e-archive and e-diarium] (2013)
43. Statens servicecenter: Uppdrag e-arkiv (2014). http://www.statenssc.se/OmOss/Sidor/Ingen%20menyrubrik/Uppdrag-e-arkiv.aspx. Accessed 11 Nov 2014
44. Näringsdepartementet, Anna-Karin Hatt presenterade regeringens nya utvecklingsprogram, Det digitala steget [Anna-Karin Hatt presented the government's new development, the digital step] (2014)
45. Statens Servicecenter: Gemensamt e-arkiv ger samhället miljonvinster [Common e-archive saves society millions] (2014)
46. Statens Servicecenter: Ny e-arkivtjänst bidrar till en effektiv e-förvaltning [New e-archive service contributes to effective e-government] (2014). http://www.statenssc.se/VaraTjanster/Sidor/Ingen%20menyrubrik/E-arkivintervju-med-Thomas-P%C3%A5lsson.aspx. Accessed 20 Jan 2015
47. Sweden. Näringsdepartementet, Uppdrag att utveckla och använda en förvaltningsgemensam tjänst för e-arkiv [Assignment to develop and use an administration common service for e-archive], Näringsdepartementet, Editor, Stockholm (2014)

48. Riksarkivet, Föreskrifter om ändring i Riksarkivets föreskrifter och allmänna råd (RA-FS 1991:1) om arkiv hos statliga myndigheter [Regulations amending the National Archives regulations and general advice (RA-FS 1991: 1) if the archives of state authorities], vol. 4, (2008)

49. The National Archives: Arkivet som resurs [The archive as resource] (2013). http:// riksarkivet.se/arkiv-som-resurs. Accessed 17 Feb 2015

50. Sambruk, eSamhället och arkivet Elektroniskt Bevarande etapp 2 Slutrapport [eSociety and the archive. electronic preservation phase 2 final report], Sandviken (2011)

51. Reed, B.: Beyond perceived boundaries: imagining the potential of pluralised recordkeeping. Arch. Manuscripts 33(1), 176–198 (2005)

52. Upward, F.: Structuring the records continuum - part one: postcustodial principles and properties. Arch. Manuscripts 24(2), 268–285 (1996)

53. Riksarkivet: The e-Archive and e-Diarium Project, eARD (2014). http://riksarkivet.se/Media/ pdf-filer/Projekt/eARD_informationstext_eng.pdf. Accessed 7 Mar 2014

54. Almalander, C.: E-arkiv en personlig reflektion [E-archive a personal reflection]. Arkiv 3, 10–11 (2014)

55. Riksarkivet eARD, Vägledning och funktionella krav [Guidelines and functional requirements] by Engvall, Tove, Stockholm (2013)

56. Lubar, S.: Information culture and the archival record. Am. Archivist 62(1), 10–22 (1999)

57. SFS, Sweden: Förvaltningslag [Administrative Procedure Act], 1986:223

58. Larsson, E.: Måste jag diarieföra det här? : En handbok om regler och rutiner för ärenderegistrering [Do I have to register this?: A handbook about rules and routines for registering cases]. 2nd rev. ed. SKL Kommentus media, Stockholm (2012)

59. Riksarkivet, Hanteringen av arkiv från myndigheter som avvecklas (The management of archives from discontinued public authorities), Stockholm (2010)

Author Index

Abu-El Seoud, Mai 118
Alanne, Aki 321
Alcaide Muñoz, Laura 59
Androutsopoulou, Aggeliki 305
Axelsson, Karin 183

Balta, Dian 233
Bowen, Frances 19
Brooks, Laurence 291
Brous, Paul 156

Charalabidis, Yannis 305
Christiansson, Marie-Therese 183
Crompvoets, Joep 209

De Marco, Marco 31
Depaoli, Paolo 31

Gidlund, Katarina L. 222
Greger, Vanessa 233

Hellsten, Pasi 321
Henriksen, Helle Zinner 144

Ingrams, Alex 105

Jansen, Arild 197
Janssen, Marijn 79, 156

Kalampokis, Evangelos 130
Khatchatourov, Armen 273
Klareld, Ann-Sofie 334
Klievink, Bram 170
Klischewski, Ralf 118
Kræmmergaard, Pernille 3
Krcmar, Helmut 233

Laurent, Maryline 273
Levallois-Barth, Claire 273

Lindgren, Ida 91
Loukis, Euripidis 305
Lourenço, Rui Pedro 105

Madsen, Christian Ø. 3
Matheus, Ricardo 79
Melin, Ulf 91, 183
Mkude, Catherine G. 44

Ølnes, Svein 197

Panagiotopoulos, Panos 19
Pekkola, Samuli 321
Persaud, Alexander 291
Pfister, Joachim 246
Piotrowski, Suzanne 105

Ramaprasad, Arkalgud 258
Rodríguez Bolívar, Manuel Pedro 59

Saarenpää, Iiris 321
Sánchez-Ortiz, Aurora 258
Schwabe, Gerhard 246
Snoeck, Monique 209
Sorrentino, Maddalena 31
Syn, Thant 258

Tambouris, Efthimios 130
Tarabanis, Konstantinos 130

Van Cauter, Lies 209

Wassrin, Siri 91
Wimmer, Maria A. 44
Wolf, Petra 233

Zuiderwijk, Anneke 79

Printed in the United States
By Bookmasters, Inc.

Printed in the United States
By Bookmasters